OXFORD ETHICS SERIES

Series Editor: Derek Parfit, All Souls College, Oxford

THE LIMITS OF MORALITY

The Limits of Morality

SHELLY KAGAN

CLARENDON PRESS · OXFORD

*This book has been printed digitally and produced in a standard specification
in order to ensure its continuing availability*

OXFORD
UNIVERSITY PRESS

Great Clarendon Street, Oxford OX2 6DP

Oxford University Press is a department of the University of Oxford.
It furthers the University's objective of excellence in research, scholarship,
and education by publishing worldwide in

Oxford New York

Auckland Bangkok Buenos Aires Cape Town Chennai
Dar es Salaam Delhi Hong Kong Istanbul Karachi Kolkata
Kuala Lumpur Madrid Melbourne Mexico City Mumbai Nairobi
São Paulo Shanghai Singapore Taipei Tokyo Toronto

with an associated company in Berlin

Oxford is a registered trade mark of Oxford University Press
in the UK and in certain other countries

Published in the United States
by Oxford University Press Inc., New York

© Shelly Kagan 1989

The moral rights of the author have been asserted
Database right Oxford University Press (maker)

Reprinted 2002

ISBN 0-19-823916-5

For Peter Harvey

Everything has been said before, but since nobody listens we have to keep going back and beginning all over again.

André Gide

CONTENTS

PREFACE

MORALITY can be thought of as involving two different kinds of limits. Or rather, morality as it is commonly conceived—ordinary, commonsense morality—can be usefully thought of in this way. On the one hand (or so it is thought) morality imposes certain limits on our actions, ruling out various kinds of acts—e.g., harming the innocent—even if greater good might be brought about by an act of the kind in question. Limits of this first kind are imposed *by* morality. But there are also what we might think of as limits imposed *on* morality—for it is typically believed that there are limits to what morality can demand of us. Thus, it is generally held that although morality does sometimes require us to make sacrifices for the sake of others, we are not morally required to make our greatest possible contributions to the overall good. There is a limit to moral requirement.

This book is concerned with the limits of morality in both of these senses. Or perhaps I should say that it is concerned with the *purported* limits of morality—for one of the central aims of my argument will be to call into question the widespread belief that morality genuinely has limits of either of these kinds. Of course, it is undeniable that both sorts of limits have a significant place in our ordinary, commonsense moral views; they constitute basic features of (what I will call) *ordinary morality*. But I will argue that these two fundamental features of ordinary morality cannot be adequately defended.

In criticizing ordinary morality on this score I will be, in effect, indirectly defending consequentialism, the view which holds (roughly) that agents are morally required to perform the act that will lead to the best results overall. For consequentialism incorporates neither of the two kinds of limits I have described, and critics of this view have often objected to it on precisely these grounds. If consequentialism is correct there are no limits of the first kind for, in principle, any sort of act at all might be permissible in the right circumstances, provided only that it leads to the best consequences overall. And there are no limits of the second kind, for there is simply no limit to the sacrifices that an agent might be required to make in the pursuit of the greater good. Advocates of ordinary morality have, accordingly, complained that consequentialism permits too much (permitting acts that should not be permitted) and they have complained that it demands too much (requiring sacrifices that are not in fact morally required). These are, I believe, the two most intuitively forceful objections to consequentialism.

Most discussion of consequentialism has focused on the first objection—i.e., that it permits too much. This is somewhat surprising, for in practical terms consequentialism may not differ in this area all that much from ordinary morality. Killing the innocent, e.g., will generally not have the best results overall, and so consequentialism and ordinary morality will typically be alike in forbidding it. And in many complex cases it is often unclear what act will lead to the best results, and so unclear whether consequentialism actually diverges in that case from ordinary morality. In contrast, the second objection—which turns on whether there is a limit to the sacrifices that morality can demand of an agent— indicates an area in which consequentialism and ordinary morality diverge sharply and undeniably. For consequentialism is *far* more demanding than ordinary morality in terms of the sacrifices that must be made for the greater good. In practical terms it matters enormously which view is correct. Yet this issue has received almost no careful discussion.

My driving concern in undertaking this work is with this second issue—the question of whether there are limits to the sacrifices that morality can demand of us. But as we shall see, the discussion of the second quickly necessitates discussion of the first—the question of whether certain kinds of acts are morally off-limits, even when they are necessary for promoting the overall good. As I have already indicated, I will be arguing that neither sort of limit can be successfully defended.

This work, then, constitutes a sustained attack on two of the most fundamental features of ordinary morality. This provides, in turn, indirect support for consequentialism. However, except for a few relevant comments at the end, the book does not in itself offer anything like a *positive* defense of consequentialism (something I hope to provide in a later work). My aim here is only to gain consequentialism a more sympathetic hearing by driving home the inadequacies of the common view—inadequacies that we generally overlook.

ACKNOWLEDGMENTS

THIS book began as a conversation in the hallway of Russell House, at Wesleyan University, when Peter Harvey suggested to me that the really troubling question about utilitarianism was whether or not it was too demanding. That was about a dozen years ago, and since then the question that Peter first raised has never stopped bothering me for very long.

Eventually, at Princeton, I wrote a dissertation about it. This book is a revision of that dissertation, which I was fortunate enough to write under the supervision of Thomas Nagel. My debt to him will be obvious to all those who know his work, and even more obvious to those who know him personally. If I have any sense at all of philosophical depth, it is thanks to Tom; if I do not, it is not for lack of his trying to teach me.

After finishing the dissertation, several years were pleasurably consumed while I tried to find answers to objections and criticisms gleefully thrown my way by friends and colleagues; looking back, it seems to me that Kurt Baier, David Gauthier, Tim Scanlon, and Michael Slote were among the most gleeful. I think the book got better as a result of this process; at any rate, it certainly got longer.

It got longer still thanks to the extraordinary and painstaking attention showered on it by Derek Parfit. Derek commented on the whole, not once, but three times, and I have incorporated his suggestions in well over a hundred passages. My thanks go beyond this, however, for his general encouragement and enthusiasm have themselves been equally important to me.

Years ago, in graduate school, my friends and I would console ourselves (for not having published anything) by reciting the motto 'Good times and high standards'. That my standards have not been high enough will soon, I fear, be all too apparent to the reader; but that the times have indeed been good I can readily attest, and to all those who helped make them so, I am grateful.

1

Against Ordinary Morality

Morality requires that you perform—of those acts not otherwise forbidden—that act which can be reasonably expected to lead to the best consequences overall.

Few of us believe this claim; none of us act in accordance with it. Consider just how radically demanding it is. It bids us to act not with an eye to merely furthering our own projects and interests, or those of some individuals we may favor—but with regard for the interests of all individuals, the world as a whole, overall good. It demands that I ask how I can make my greatest possible contribution, all things considered—even though this may impose considerable hardship on me—and it forbids me to do anything less. If the claim is correct, most of my actions are *immoral*, for almost *nothing* that I do makes optimal use of my time and resources; if I am honest with myself I will recognize that I constantly fail to do as much good as I am able.

When I go to the movies I may spend a few dollars and enjoy myself for an hour or two. The pleasure I get is genuine, and it seems absurd to say that I have done anything *wrong*. Yet this is exactly what the claim entails, for both my time and my money could be better spent: the pleasure one could bring in an evening visiting the elderly or the sick quite outweighs the mild entertainment I find in the movies; and the money itself would have done much more good were it sent to famine relief—for even a few dollars is sufficient to enable another human being to survive a temporary food shortage brought on by drought. If the claim is right, then in going to the movies I do what is morally *forbidden*. This strikes us as wildly implausible; we agree that it would be *meritorious* to visit the elderly and donate the money to charity— but no more than that. If the claim is right, however, it is not merely that it would be nice of me to forgo my slight pleasure: it is morally *required*.[1]

To live in accordance with such demands would drastically alter my life. In a sense, neither my time, nor my goods, nor my plans would be my own. On this view, the demands of morality pervade every aspect and moment of our lives—and we all fail to meet its standards. This is why I suggested that few of us believe the claim, and that none of us live in accordance with it. It strikes us as outrageously extreme in its demands—so much so that I shall call its defender the *extremist*. The claim is deeply counterintuitive. But it is true.

This book is part of a defense of the extremist's position. Yet little will be said supporting it directly. For the most part, I want to critically examine the alternative position which is almost universally believed. If the difficulties with this alternative can be shown, then perhaps the extremist will be taken more seriously.

The alternative position is so widespread (in our culture, at the very least) that we can refer to it as *ordinary morality*. Although there is disagreement over the details of this position, certain broad features are shared by the different versions. I have already pointed to one of these features—the claim that there is a limit to what morality requires of us. Many acts which would lead to the best results overall[2] nonetheless are *not* required of us by ordinary morality, typically because the sacrifice would be too great to demand it of us. I am not required to devote my free time to fighting political oppression, nor must I give up my luxuries to support cancer research.

---

[1] I use the term 'required' as the positive counterpart of 'forbidden'—i.e., a given act or (act-type) is required if and only if not performing that act (or act-type) is forbidden. I use this somewhat unusual term in the hope of avoiding fruitless disputes over the proper scope of more traditional terms such as 'duty' or 'obligation'; for on some accounts of these terms, even though performing an act is neither obligatory nor a duty, it might still be forbidden to fail to perform that act. Similarly, on some accounts, 'ought' is too weak a term for my purposes: it may be that one ought to perform some act even though not performing the act is not forbidden. I should also note that I reserve the terms 'forbidden' and 'required' for moral judgments all things considered; that is, as I understand these terms it is improper to say, e.g., 'Fritz is required to do X, but all things considered he ought to do Y'; and so on. Finally, as I intend to use the term 'wrong' (departing from some accounts), if an act is wrong it is forbidden.

[2] The extremist's position presupposes the availability of an agent-neutral ranking of possible outcomes according to overall value. Although the notion of such a ranking is controversial in other contexts, it won't be examined here—for the

On this view morality permits me to favor those things I most care about—whether my own welfare, the welfare of others, or any projects to which I am committed. It will be convenient to have a single term covering all of those things in which I take a special interest and which, as a result, I may want to favor. Let us call all of these things my *interests*, recognizing that this use of the term goes somewhat beyond its ordinary scope. In particular, it should be noted that my interests, as I will use the term, need not be limited to what is in my self-interest as that is normally understood. Rather, my interests include all of the objects of my concern, and so may include the well-being of family or friends, as well as various impersonal goals that I support, which may have little or no connection to my own individual welfare.[3]

On the view of ordinary morality, then, I am permitted to favor my interests, even if by doing so I fail to perform the act which leads to the best consequences overall. Since the agent is given the option of performing (or not performing) acts which from a neutral perspective are less than optimal, we may call such permissions *agent-centered options*, or more briefly, *options*. The first feature of ordinary morality, then, is the belief in the existence of options.

This is not to say that no sacrifices at all are required by ordinary morality, but they *tend* to be rather modest and limited. If a child is drowning in front of me, and I can save her by throwing a life preserver, ordinary morality certainly requires me to do so—even though it takes some slight physical effort, and my clothes may

dispute between the defender of ordinary morality and the extremist is not over whether we can *rank* possible outcomes, but rather over whether we are required to *pursue* that outcome we judge to be best from a neutral perspective. I will also leave unexamined the question of whether there is a uniquely correct ranking of worlds, and such familiar problems as decision-making under uncertainty and whether this requires a cardinal (and not merely ordinal) ranking, whether the extremist should require maximization of expected value of outcomes, what sorts of ignorance and miscalculation on the part of the agent will be excused, and so on. These problems are important; but not for the issues which concern us in this work.

[3] In many contexts, it is a controversial philosophical question to what extent an individual's interests (in my broad, inclusive sense) rather than her *self*-interest (more narrowly understood) is the appropriate object of concern (whether on the part of the individual herself, or on the part of others). Given the inclusive meaning I have just adopted, my regular use of the term 'interests' will abandon neutrality on several aspects of this issue. I will, at a few relevant points, have something to say in defense of this practice, but these remarks will hardly be decisive. Accordingly, some readers may find certain portions of the discussion more plausible if (when appropriate) they interpret my talk of 'interests' as referring only to 'self-interest'.

become soaked. Generally, however, I am not required to significantly sacrifice my interests in order to provide aid to others—even
though objectively greater good would result from my doing so. Of
course I am *free* to make such sacrifices if I choose to—and
morality encourages me to do so—but these acts are not *required* of
me: there are agent-centered options.

The second broad feature of ordinary morality is that it lays
down certain strict limits on our actions—forbidding various types
of acts *even* if the best consequences overall could be achieved only
by performing such an act. I may not murder my rich uncle Albert
in order to inherit his wealth. Nor may I murder him even if this is
the only way to guarantee that his millions get spent on famine
relief—my act thus saving many more lives than it takes.
Restrictions arising from rights, prohibitions against intending
harm, and the like, are all examples of this second feature. A second
class of examples of this second feature can be found in the special
obligations to others that can arise due to past promises, or through
institutionally defined roles, such as family or professional duties,
and so on. Here too, ordinary morality forbids violating such
special obligations, even if this is the only way to achieve the best
consequences overall. Advocates of ordinary morality may differ as
to whether these various restrictions and special obligations are
absolute, or may be violated in pressing enough circumstances—
but all are agreed that the limitations they impose cannot normally
be transgressed. Since both the restrictions and the special
obligations forbid agents to perform acts which from a neutral
perspective might be optimal, let us call such limits *agent-centered
constraints*, or more briefly, *constraints*. The second feature of
ordinary morality, then, is the belief in the existence of constraints.

Both features of ordinary morality temper the relentless pursuit
of the best consequences. Options give the agent permission to
pursue his own interests rather than the overall good; constraints
forbid certain courses of action—even when they are necessary
means to achieving the overall good. Within the limits of the
constraints, there *are* occasional demands, but typically only rather
modest ones are made.

It is clear that ordinary morality stakes out a more moderate
position than the one espoused by the extremist. It imposes certain
limits, and requires certain sacrifices—but it does not come near, as
does the extremist's morality, to pervading and dictating every

aspect of our life. For this reason, I shall call the defender of ordinary morality the *moderate*.

As I have noted, on some views of ordinary morality behavior which is normally forbidden by a constraint may be permissible under pressing enough circumstances (e.g., when the number of lives at stake is sufficiently great). If there is such a cutoff point, beyond which the constraint is 'relaxed', we may say that the constraint has a (finite) *threshold*. Along a similar vein, it is also worth remarking that options need not be unlimited either—but may instead have thresholds beyond which the agent is not permitted to react in the normally permissible manner. Now in principle, such thresholds (whether for constraints or options) could be extremely low. If this were the case, the corresponding constraints and options would temper the pursuit of the good in only a very limited way: whenever much of anything was at stake (in terms of the overall good) the thresholds would be crossed, and the agent would be required to promote the greater good. Thus the mere presence of constraints and options does not in itself logically guarantee that the resulting position is significantly less extreme than that of the extremist.

In fact, however, if a view is to capture anything close to our ordinary moral beliefs, thresholds will generally have to be quite high (if not infinite). And if this is the case, the presence of constraints and options will indeed significantly temper the relentless pursuit of the overall good, yielding a much more moderate position. As the defender of ordinary morality, then, the moderate deserves his name.

Our list of *dramatis personae* will be complete with the introduction of the *minimalist*. His position will be less sharply defined, for in this essay he will act largely as a foil to the moderate. His purpose is to remind us that the moderate is trying to maintain a middle position, and as such can perhaps be criticized for having gone too *far* in his demands. Minimalists, of course, may differ with one another as to which of the moderate's demands are to be rejected; but for our purposes there will be no need to offer a more fine-grained classification.[4] Provided that one can coherently

---

[4] Note that a variety of sharply diverging positions will fall within the minimalist camp, including egoists (who believe that one is never required to sacrifice overall self-interest), nihilists (who believe that everything is morally permitted), and extreme libertarians (who recognize the validity of constraints, but deny that there is a moral requirement to provide aid).

imagine *some* position rejecting the given demand on the grounds that far less is actually required than the moderate claims, I will offer such a rejection as the view of the minimalist. For it is important to bear in mind that ordinary morality can indeed be challenged as too demanding, despite its being a more moderate position than that of the extremist. Thus, as we have noted, the moderate does require some minor sacrifices—e.g., to save the drowning child. The minimalist, however, argues that this is already to ask too much: one is never required to aid another. Similarly, the moderate rules out certain courses of action—e.g., murdering my uncle for personal profit—but some minimalists deny that such acts are prohibited.

It should be clear that all of the positions we have marked out encompass broad ranges of more specific views which have important features in common. Reducing the multitude of possibilities to three broad types,[5] however, allows us to focus on a central philosophical problem: the moderate is under simultaneous attack from both sides. He must defend his position from both the extremist *and* the minimalist—or admit defeat. The tension inherent in his position is apparent. By abandoning the ideological purity of the two ends, the moderate risks internal incoherence. This is not to say, of course, that the mere fact that the moderate lies in the middle is in itself reason to assume that his position is implausible. But if, as I believe, the moderate's view cannot be given a coherent justification, its vulnerability to attack from both sides may make this easier to see. Forcing the moderate to defend his position against the extremist's demands without collapsing into the arms of the minimalist may expose that lack of coherence.

As we have seen, the moderate denies that we are morally required to do all that we can to promote the overall good. In contrast, the extremist claims that in fact there is such a requirement. It should be pointed out, however, that in making this claim, the extremist is not committing himself to any particular *account* of the good. That is, the extremist asserts that we must each make our greatest possible contribution to the overall good, but this claim does not in itself specify which factor or factors make one outcome better than another—i.e., what it is by virtue of which

---

[5] Even these three do not exhaust the field, but there is no room here to consider all the possibilities. In Chapter 5, however, we shall examine the position of the neo-moderate, who embraces options while rejecting constraints.

one outcome is better than another. Individual extremists may well differ on this question, as may moderates. Presumably, on all plausible accounts of the good, human well-being will be a central component. (For this reason, my examples will involve this crucial factor.) But it should be noted that nothing prevents the extremist from adopting a *pluralist* theory of the good—i.e., one that gives independent weight to several factors. For example, it might be claimed that various distributional factors are relevant to the goodness of outcomes:[6] all things being equal, one outcome may be better than another if well-being (or, more broadly, the satisfaction of interests) is distributed according to effort, or desert, or in an egalitarian manner. And other factors might be brought in as well.

Articulating and defending an adequate theory of the good is an important task for moral philosophy, but not one that will be addressed in this work. The point to bear in mind is simply this: whatever the most plausible theory of the overall good, it can be incorporated into an extremist framework. Thus the extremist and the moderate need not be conceived as disagreeing over the correct account of the good. Rather, the point of disagreement is simply whether or not we are morally required to do all that we can to *promote* the overall good.

The moderate might be tempted to object that an agent can go overboard on sacrifices—exhausting and impoverishing herself—ultimately destroying her ability to make continual contributions to the overall good (however this is ultimately understood). In this way the extremist's position might be thought to be self-defeating: were it only more moderate in its demands, agents would—in the long run—be able to do the world more good.

Such an objection, however, would rest on a misunderstanding of the extremist, who does not demand sacrifices for their own sake—but only insofar as they are the cost of producing the greatest possible good. The extremist would be the first to urge that mindlessly driving oneself to exhaustion or recklessly dispensing one's goods can be counterproductive. Far from being required, such behavior is forbidden. What each agent is required to do is to

---

[6] Since, on a pluralist theory of the good, the very performance of a given type of act may itself be a factor in how well the history of the world goes, talk in the text of the goodness of the 'outcome' of a particular act should not be understood in a narrow sense, i.e., limited to what causally follows from the act, or what happens after the act. (Similarly for talk of 'consequences', 'results', and the like.)

act in such a way that she can make her greatest possible contribution to the overall good (given her own particular talents). Very likely this involves taking a hard look at her life plans, and reshaping them accordingly; at the very least it involves taking into account the long term effects of her action and not only the more immediate ones—and this is quite enough to explain the need for relaxation and a judicious apportionment of resources.

There *is*, however, an important qualification in the extremist's claim which we have not yet considered. According to the extremist, morality does not straightforwardly require you to choose that act, *whatever* it is, which can be reasonably expected to lead to the best consequences. Rather, it restricts your choice to those acts not otherwise morally forbidden. However, the extremist's claim itself is neutral on the issue of whether morality ever *does* forbid an act which would lead to the best consequences. Let us consider both possibilities.

One of the central concerns of this book will be to examine whether agent-centered constraints—which create barriers to promoting the good—can be justified. For the moment, suppose that they cannot be. In this case, the qualification drops out as vacuous, and the extremist requires that you perform the optimal act, *simpliciter*. This is consequentialism.

Perhaps, however, constraints *can* be justified. Such a result is still compatible with the extremist's claim, and the extremist will continue to demand far more of an agent than the moderate. I may be forbidden to murder uncle Albert to free his vast fortune for famine relief, but nonetheless I am permitted to donate my own more modest fortune, and if the extremist is right I am required to do so. If there are constraints, then you are required to perform the optimal act among those acts which do not violate them.

It might be thought, however, that the extremist will not provide a significant alternative to ordinary morality if he recognizes the existence of special obligations. But this is a mistake. Consider, for example, an obligation to provide my children with a decent education. Admittedly, meeting this obligation may require the expenditure of a portion of my resources which could do even *more* good were it devoted instead to famine relief. Such obligations are, after all, constraints, providing potential barriers to the performance of optimal acts. But it would not be plausible to claim—and certainly the defender of ordinary morality would not want to claim—that *all* of my resources are tied up in this way through special obligations. Typically, the most significant portion remains unconstrained. Of course there may be exceptions—rare cases where an individual's special obligations are *quite* demanding, and make an exhaustive claim on his resources. But such cases are, indeed, exceptions. For most individuals the special obligations recognized by ordinary morality are modest enough to leave the individual with a considerable portion of his resources. It is here that the moderate believes that options come into play: provided that I have met my obligations to my family (and any other special obligations I may have), I am permitted to spend my remaining time and money as I choose. But if the extremist is correct, then once my special obligations are met I am required to devote myself to making my greatest possible contribution to the overall good. Presumably this rules out doing many things that the moderate believes to be permitted—favoring my family even more, say, with expensive gifts. Therefore, even if the extremist recognizes the existence of constraints, including special obligations, by denying the existence of options he provides a significantly more demanding position than ordinary morality.

I will often express this fundamental difference between the extremist and the moderate by saying that the extremist accepts, and the moderate rejects, a *general* requirement to promote the good. A few words of explanation about this expression may be helpful. After all, even the moderate believes in *occasional* requirements to promote the good, since in the right situations (e.g., the drowning child) the agent may well be required to act in a way that will lead to the greatest good overall. What the moderate denies, however, is the claim that the agent must—in *general*—do all he (permissibly) can to promote the good. The moderate believes in the existence of options, and these will often permit the agent to act in a way that fails to make his greatest possible contribution to the overall good. It is, then, to the moderate's embrace of options that I am pointing when I say that the moderate rejects a general requirement to promote the good. Second, as we have just seen, if there are indeed constraints, then even the extremist will not accept an *unqualified* requirement to promote the good. What the extremist is committed to, rather, is a requirement to promote the good—*within* the limits of constraints (if there are any). When I say that the extremist accepts a general requirement to promote the good, this (often implicit) qualification should be borne in mind.

Properly understood, then, the extremist's claim is itself neutral on the issue of whether or not there are any constraints. Either way, the extremist goes beyond ordinary morality by insisting on a general requirement to promote the good. The extremist is perfectly capable of recognizing the existence of constraints—if such there be—while still denying the existence of options.

As we shall see, however, the most straightforward extremist position recognizes neither options *nor* constraints, while the moderate's *defense* of options *requires* him to establish the existence of constraints. For this reason I shall portray the extremist as dubious of the claim that there are constraints, and shall place the burden of establishing their existence squarely upon the shoulders of the moderate. But, as we have just noted, even if there are constraints the extremist offers a significant alternative to the moderate—a far more demanding alternative.[7] In opposition to it, the moderate insists upon the existence of options: admirable as it may be to sacrifice one's career, time, possessions, or life for the greater good, such behavior—he assures us—is surely not *required* by morality. As long as one stays within the bounds set by moral constraints, and makes the typically *minor* sacrifices occasionally required, one does all that morality demands of us. To the minimalist, however, even the demands of the moderate are unreasonable: a minor sacrifice is a sacrifice for all that, and there is no justification for requiring that an individual forsake his interests for the greater good.

The moderate stands squeezed in between the extremist and the minimalist—and I intend to increase the pressure. We are going to ask the moderate to try to justify ordinary morality. Yet the moderate may feel secure; after all, ordinary morality seems to be supported by our intuitions. Isn't this an adequate justification? I believe, however, that intuitive support is *not* adequate for justifying a moral theory, and it is important to see that this is so. Let us take a brief look at one aspect of the method of moral philosophy.

---

[7] Interestingly enough, it seems that few extremists have actually embraced this position. I believe that Godwin can be interpreted as such an extremist—one who denies options, but recognizes constraints—but he is the only prominent defender of this view of which I am aware.

MORAL METHODOLOGY

Let me start with a model of moral theorizing which is, I believe, inadequate. On this account we begin moral philosophy with a set of pretheoretical moral intuitions—beliefs about the moral character of a variety of specific situations (both actual and hypothetical). Our goal—on this model—is to discover a set of moral principles which will yield judgments about the range of possible cases, striving to discover those principles which give the closest possible 'fit' to our original intuitions—which act as our data.

But not just any principles will do on this account—for principles of *one* sort could *always* be cooked up to fit our intuitions exactly. If this were sufficient, we would need to do no more than translate those intuitions directly into *ad hoc* lists: in situations of type 1 do A; of type 2 do B; of type 3 do C. . . Such *ad hoc* principles are unsatisfactory, for we want our moral principles to amount to more than shopping lists. In moral philosophy we want to apply the same sort of criteria that we use for theory building quite generally: we want our moral theory to have simplicity, power, and coherence.

There is no room here to give these matters the attention they deserve, but *roughly*, a moral theory has *simplicity* if it yields a body of judgments out of a relatively sparse amount of theory, deriving the numerous complex variations of the phenomena from a smaller number of basic principles. The shopping lists fail on this criterion, requiring a principle for each case. A moral theory has *power* when it yields judgments not included in the original data base. The shopping lists fail here, too, being no help in those cases where our original intuitions offer us no guidance. *Coherence* on this account can be taken as consistency, and if we find ourselves of two minds for some cases—with incompatible stances both having some intuitive plausibility—then the shopping list approach will fail once more. Rejecting the shopping lists, then, the model is only satisfied with principles which have simplicity, power and coherence.

Finding principles to fit our intuitions which are acceptable by these criteria is not a trivial matter: generally we can expect that the fit will not be perfect—and the principles we arrive at will differ from our initial intuitions for some cases. Hopefully, however, the principles themselves will have some intuitive plausibility—and at the very least their ability to yield judgments with which we are substantially in accord gives them some credibility. Thus, the principles themselves may give us grounds for rejecting some of our initial intuitions, and the altered set of intuitions may in turn give us grounds for altering the principles. In this manner, we work back and forth between intuitions and principles until a stable point is reached. The remaining intuitions represent our considered judgments, and the moral principles at which we have arrived can guide us in difficult cases. The entire process forms a justification of the end products: the underlying principles justify our intuitions, and the intuitions in turn support our claims for the underlying principles.[8]

Now in several ways this model is misleading. It is doubtful that we have any *pretheoretical* intuitions, and so our actual intuitions cannot provide a special foundation for theorizing. It would be more correct to say that we begin moral philosophy already possessing some moral theory—albeit theory which is only half-formed, and largely unarticulated. We have a variety of beliefs—about specific cases, and about general moral principles. We are more wed to some of these than to others; there are those we are more immediately disposed to assent to while others require reflection; and so on. As we critically reflect, and face new experiences, our theory evolves, striving for greater simplicity, power, and coherence. We abandon beliefs, adopt new principles, and our intuitions may change—conditioned by our altered judgments. If we ever reach a stable point, it may be far removed from the point where we began.

The original account is even more misleading in what it does *not* say, for it fails to bring out adequately the importance of *coherence*. It is not sufficient justification for a set of moral principles—even when they have simplicity, power, and are mutually consistent—that they yield (the bulk of) our intuitions about specific cases. All that this guarantees is that we will have succeeded in axiomatizing the moral view, so to speak. But we want more from a moral *theory*. The original model would in effect be satisfied with a set of maxims, guiding our behavior. For it, coherence is only a matter of consistency: the maxims must not give contradictory advice. But surely there is more to coherence than this. We want the principles to hang together, to be mutually supportive, to be jointly illuminated by the moral concepts to which we appeal. If the

---

[8] Readers will doubtless recognize some semblance of Rawls' notion of reflective equilibrium in the hasty sketch I've given here. Cf. Rawls, pp. 19–21, 46–51.

principles are only maxims, albeit consistent maxims, then they are not enough. Rather, they must form, or be part of, a coherent moral theory.

Seeing that the criterion of coherence is richer than that of mere consistency should also lead us to recognize the importance of a fourth criterion for moral theories—one that seems altogether neglected by the original model: a theory must be *explanatory*. As noted, it seems that the original model would be satisfied with a mere set of maxims. But even if the maxims form a mutually consistent set, we *still* want our theory to provide an *account* of the distinctions, goals, restrictions, and the like, which they embody as well. An adequate justification for a set of principles requires an *explanation* of those principles—an explanation of why exactly these goals, restrictions, and so on, should be given weight, and not others. Short of this, the principles will not be free of the taint of arbitrariness which led us to move beyond our original *ad hoc* shopping lists. To reduce the many to the few is not yet to *support* the few. Unless we can offer a coherent explanation of our principles (or show that they need no further justification), we cannot consider them justified, and we may have reason to reject them.

This need for explanation in moral theory cannot be over-emphasized. We want our moral theory to help us to understand the moral realm. (Indeed, one of the things we want our moral theory to help us to understand is how there can even be a moral realm, and what sort of objective status it has.) A large part of the motivation for the criteria of simplicity and power is the drive to understand: by reducing the complex to the simple, we can hope to understand the complex; by having a powerful theory we can hope to move from a base which is understood to an understanding of new areas. Power, simplicity, and consistency are valuable in themselves, but it is the need to understand the moral realm which is, I believe, paramount. Ultimately, unless we have a coherent explanation of our moral principles, we don't have satisfactory ground for believing them to be true.

Suppose that in analyzing our intuitions, we find a distinction which if appealed to yields our intuitive judgments. Morally, we still need to know whether the difference *ought* to make a difference. Perhaps a slaveholder might find that a principle which distinguished according to skin color yielded intuitively correct judgments about when a gentleman is morally required to aid someone being whipped, and when he is not. Merely having *found* the distinction underlying his intuitions is not sufficient to *justify* it. We want to know *why* difference in skin color should support differential treatment. If the slaveholder cannot offer an explanation, then the distinction hangs free of the rest of his moral theory, and considerations of coherence give him reason to reject the distinction as morally irrelevant, as well as repudiating the intuitions which turn on it. We might call such cases where there is a critical lack of support *dangling distinctions*. An adequate defense of a moral theory must not leave its distinctions dangling.[9]

Most commonly, of course, a distinction will not be left *totally* unsupported. Generally, *something* can be mustered in its defense. The key issue is really whether the support offered will withstand critical examination; and the criticism may well be internal. Our slaveholder may find that other principles to which he is committed militate against the moral relevance of the black/white distinction. And presumably, at the very least, he is opposed to *others* drawing lines they cannot support—and he may turn this standard back upon himself. In such cases, there is an internal tension in the moral theory, pushing it toward revision. We cannot say in advance how the tension will be best resolved—two or more directions may suggest themselves—but it is especially this drive to explanatory coherence which may produce a moral theory quite unlike the original.

It may be objected that explanations have to come to an end *somewhere*. Perhaps this is so, but it would still be no license to cut off explanation at a superficial level. If a distinction stands isolated, or is at odds with more firmly supported beliefs, we have grounds for rejecting it, despite its intuitive appeal. What I want to suggest is that the distinctions which underlie the moderate's position dangle, and appeal to their intuitive support is no more adequate than such an appeal would be for the slaveholder.

Given the nature of the internal tension in ordinary morality, there are two directions moral theory can go: toward the extremist,

---

[9] It may be that Rawls intends reflective equilibrium to encompass the elimination of dangling distinctions. Or maybe not. I won't argue the point of exegesis here. (It may also be worth noting that the methodology of some so-called 'intuitionists' may not differ substantially from the one I am endorsing here. Arguably, Sidgwick is among this group; but once again, I'll not pursue the point of exegesis.)

or toward the minimalist. My sympathies—as I've indicated—lie with the extremist, but I'll not attempt criticism of the minimalist here. To attack ordinary morality is ambitious enough.

We should be clear about just what such an approach can accomplish. Even if the internal incoherence of the moderate's position can be shown, it will not necessarily make the intuitions which support it disappear. Even if the slaveholder is persuaded to abandon his racist theory, he may continue to intuitively *feel* that there is a difference. But he will reject such intuitions as unjustified—a sort of ineliminable moral illusion, similar to certain optical illusions which do not lose their intuitive hold on us even when our theory tells us better.[10]

This freedom of moral philosophy to reject many of our intuitions is of a piece with its ability to justify moral theories radically different from our original beliefs. In criticizing the moderate, I am *not* merely arguing that although ordinary morality must be given a different foundation than we generally believe, the moderate is, nonetheless, basically correct about moral practice.[11] Nothing so comforting. Rather, I claim that our moral beliefs and practices need to be drastically revised.

PROMOTING THE GOOD

The moderate may believe that there is a quick path to justifying ordinary morality. He may be tempted to argue that ultimately one only has reason to do what one is motivated to do. (This needs to be made a bit more sophisticated, but it will do for now.) It is then a simple psychological fact that most of us are disposed to help those suffering in front of us when it is not difficult to do so, and not otherwise; and that most of us are disposed to refrain from hurting others so long as they refrain from hurting us. The moderate may suggest that this is all the justification that ordinary morality needs.

---

[10] A complete explanation, of course, will also have to *account* for the rejected intuitions.

[11] This seems to be the opinion of many consequentialists. Mill, e.g., claims that generally one need only make sure that one's act violates no one's rights, for 'the occasions on which any person (except one in a thousand) has it in his power . . . to be a public benefactor . . . are but exceptional; and on these occasions alone is he called upon to consider public utility; in every other case, private utility, the interest or happiness of some few persons is all that he has to attend to' (Chapter 2, paragraph 19).

Such an approach, however, would leave it too contingent a matter whether an agent has reason to refrain from killing others: if the slaveholder has no feelings of sympathy for his slaves, he may have no moral reason not to kill one who displeases him. And so on. This is an unacceptably minimalist conclusion for most moderates. Therefore, they must forgo the shortcut, and attempt a more substantial justification.[12]

The need to provide such a justification for ordinary morality will be felt even more acutely when we realize that the moderate himself recognizes a reason, all things being equal, to promote the greater good. It will therefore be all the more pressing for him to justify his belief in constraints and options which temper the pursuit of the good.

Suppose a building is on fire. Upon entering, I find a child and a bird trapped within. Needing one hand free to clear a path back outside, I can only save one of the two, and I hastily pick up—and escape with—the caged bird.

Clearly I have done something wrong. Even if the moderate believes that I was not morally required to risk my safety by entering the building in the first place, he nonetheless believes that once I have decided to undertake the risk, I should have promoted the greater good, by saving the child. If my interests are equally affected by either of two courses of action, I have reason to pick that act with the objectively better outcome.

The moderate even believes that there are cases where I am morally required to act so as to promote the good even though there is some cost to myself which I am not inclined to take on: e.g., I am required to throw the drowning child the life preserver, even though my clothes will get soaked, and I risk catching a cold.

If the moderate is asked to account for his judgments here, the best explanation seems to involve the quite general thesis that one

---

[12] It may be objected that my reply presupposes that moral principles are universal—binding on all agents. But this is not so. It only assumes that advocates of ordinary morality would be unwilling to let typical agents escape so easily from, e.g., a requirement not to kill. At any rate, even those moderates who see themselves as doing no more than describing their personal (or societal) moral code should, I believe, want that code to have the sort of internal coherence I described in the previous section. We want to be able to offer a satisfying explanation of the various aspects of our moral code; it should be coherent—at least by our own lights. The problem of dangling distinctions should be felt even by those who make no claim to universal (or nearly universal) moral principles; and so the shortcut is not sufficient. (We'll return to the issue of universality in Chapter 8.)

always has a (morally acceptable) reason to promote the good. Now this thesis should not be misunderstood as being more bold than it is. It does not claim that one always has an *overriding* reason to promote the good; there may well be morally acceptable countervailing reasons at times, whose net effect is to outweigh the standing reason to promote the good. Presumably the moderate believes that there frequently *are* such countervailing reasons: some merely make it *permissible* to refrain from promoting the good; others may *require* it. But, although the reason to promote the good may be overridden, it does not disappear: it is a *pro tanto* reason.

The term 'pro tanto' may be somewhat unfamiliar (partially, perhaps, because my use of it is also slightly ungrammatical), so a word of explanation may be in order. A *pro tanto* reason has genuine weight, but nonetheless may be outweighed by other considerations. Thus, calling a reason a pro tanto reason is to be distinguished from calling it a *prima facie* reason, which I take to involve an epistemological qualification: a prima facie reason *appears* to be a reason, but may actually not be a reason at all, or may not have weight in all cases it appears to. In contrast, a pro tanto reason is a genuine reason—with actual weight—but it may not be a *decisive* one in various cases.[13] The claim, then, is that the best explanation of the various judgments that the moderate wants to make involves the acceptance of a standing, pro tanto reason to promote the good.

The belief in this pro tanto reason is common ground for the moderate *and* the extremist. The moderate proceeds to argue for the existence of other, potentially overriding, reasons as well. But in the most straightforward case, the extremist simply *stops* with this common belief. He shares with the moderate the belief that promoting the good is a reason for performing an act; and he simply recognizes no other morally acceptable reasons at all. This makes more urgent the moderate's need to find a justification for his belief in constraints and options. For he himself recognizes the grounds for the extremist's position; he cannot deny the pro tanto reason to promote the good without retreating into the minimalist's

---

[13] It may be helpful to note explicitly that in distinguishing between pro tanto reasons and prima facie reasons I depart from the unfortunate terminology proposed by Ross, which has invited confusion and misunderstanding. I take it that—despite his misleading label—it is actually pro tanto reasons that Ross has in mind in his discussion of what he calls prima facie duties. See, e.g., Ross, pp. 19–20, 28–29.

camp (although there would still, of course, be some disagreements between the moderate and the minimalist, e.g., over the existence of constraints). Indeed, to the extent that options and constraints are at ideological odds with the drive to promote the good, we may well wonder whether the moderate will be able to provide a philosophical house capable of holding all three.

Of course, it should go without saying that the belief in the existence of a pro tanto reason to promote the good is itself in need of defense. After all, the claim that there is a standing reason to promote the overall good is one that will be rejected by the minimalist—who will not be satisfied with the observation that acceptance of such a reason is compatible with the belief that it is frequently overridden. For the minimalist sees no reason to accept the pro tanto reason to promote the good in the first place. Obviously enough, the mere fact that belief in such a reason is common to both the moderate and the extremist hardly constitutes an adequate justification for that belief.

Examining whether there is indeed any kind of reason at all to perform an act simply by virtue of the fact that it will lead to a greater amount of good overall is, then, yet another essential task for moral philosophy. A defense of the pro tanto reason to promote the good would be an important element in a complete justification of ordinary morality, and, as I have just suggested, it would be the crucial step in a defense of the most straightforward extremist position. Nonetheless, in this work I will not be considering whether the pro tanto reason to promote the good can, in fact, be successfully defended. As I have indicated, my primary, driving interest in this work is to see whether the moderate can defend ordinary morality against the greater demands of the extremist (without, of course, retreating into what the moderate takes to be the inadequate moral demands of the minimalist). Since the belief in the pro tanto reason to promote the good is common to the moderate and the extremist, it is not an element of ordinary morality that the extremist will want to challenge. Indeed, as we have seen, by emphasizing the moderate's acceptance of that reason, the need for an adequate defense of options and constraints is made all the more pressing.

There may, however, be moderates who will resist my suggestion that they are committed to the existence of a pro tanto reason to promote the good. I certainly do not mean to claim that this is an explicit component of all versions of ordinary morality. Rather, my claim is that the existence of such a reason provides the best explanation of various judgments that the moderate wants to make; and so, wittingly or not, the moderate is implicitly committed to such a reason. I will defend this claim in greater detail in Chapter 2. My purpose here is simply to bring out how the recognition or acceptance of such a reason sharpens the bite of the general demand that the moderate provide an adequate justification for ordinary morality. But it is worth stressing that the need for such a justification was already established in the previous discussion of moral methodology. Even if, for the time being, some moderates resist the pro tanto reason to promote the good, I have argued that they must recognize the need to provide a more adequate defense of constraints and options than the mere appeal to intuitions.

RESISTING OPTIONS TO DO HARM

How then is the moderate to justify his belief in constraints and options? Let us start by observing the logical independence of these two features of ordinary morality: a moral theory needn't have both (nor either, of course). A system might have options without constraints; an extreme case of this would be the minimalist system in which the agent is permitted to do absolutely everything—there being no requirements at all. Similarly, a system might have constraints without options; we mentioned such a possibility when noting that the extremist could concede the existence of constraints and still insist that the agent is required to do the optimal act within the limits of those constraints. Thus, a defense of one feature might be able to proceed without defending the other. Since the dispute between the extremist and the moderate turns on the existence of *options*, let us consider how the moderate might go about defending them.

For the extremist, the requirement to pursue the good pervades an agent's entire life—all its aspects, every moment. The moderate wants to carve out a sphere in which the agent can find relief from the demands of morality which would otherwise be constantly pressing upon him. Options provide such a protected sphere, and within it agents are free to pursue their own interests, at the possible expense of the good.

The problem facing the moderate is this: a moral system might include not only options to *allow* harm, but also options to *do* harm.[14] For example, a system with no requirements at all includes an option to bring about harm no matter how bad the outcome. I am not saying that such an option is particularly *plausible*—but its theoretical possibility must not be neglected. The moderate might respond that what was desired was that the demands of morality should be limited—not eliminated. But this reply won't really help, for we can always make the option to harm more modest, without yet making it acceptable. If the option to harm is given a finite threshold, or is restricted to particular forms of harm—say, harpooning newborn males—then we will have succeeded in giving the agent a protected sphere, without giving him complete license. This point is worth stressing: moral systems can provide options of a sort which are unacceptable to the moderate.

Strictly speaking, of course, it must be admitted that not all options to do harm are unacceptable to the moderate. He may well believe, for example, in an option to kill in self-defense, even when it is not optimal to do so.[15] Such options are rare, however, and for simplicity of exposition, I will write as though the moderate *does* reject all options to do harm. (On certain broad, encompassing conceptions of 'harm', acceptable options to do harm will be somewhat more common; but this doesn't really affect the main point being made.) It is clear, at any rate, that many or most imaginable options to do harm would not be acceptable to the moderate. For example, we are not in general permitted to kill another for mere personal profit; the moderate would obviously find an option to do harm of this sort unacceptable. Yet if the motivation behind options is to provide the agent with a protected sphere, free from the demands of morality, it seems that such unacceptable options are just as likely to fit the bill as options of a kind that the moderate may find more palatable.

Thus we can see how, in fending off the attack of the extremist, the moderate is in danger of retreating into an overly minimalist position. Against the extremist's claim that agents are required to

---

[14] In Chapter 3 I shall differentiate between the do/allow distinction and the intend/foresee distinction—but for the present, talk of doing harm and allowing harm is meant to be neutral between the two.

[15] Permitting self-defense at all—even when it is optimal—may be problematic for some moderates; this point is discussed in Chapter 4.

do all they can to promote the greater good, the moderate asserts the existence of options. But the general motivation for options seems more powerful than the moderate may have realized: it runs the risk of leading to the construction of a minimalist system—a system that the moderate cannot embrace.

The moderate, of course, will have to support his case for options with more than a general plea that the agent should have some protected sphere. Perhaps the *specific* considerations which he offers in favor of options will support *only* options to allow harm, and *not* options to do harm. If this were so, then the problem would be avoided. But in fact the problem *cannot* be avoided in this way, for the most plausible and straightforward defense of options appears to support both options to allow harm *and* options to do harm. Let's see why.

If the extremist is right, there is no limit to what you might be called upon to sacrifice in the pursuit of the good. Your material possessions, time, effort, bodily parts, or life itself—all of these might be commandeered by morality, and put to purposes quite unlike those to which you would dedicate them were morality's demands less severe. Taking a stand against this view, the moderate seems to be the voice of reason itself when he claims that there surely must be a limit to the costs that morality can inflict upon an agent.

The most straightforward defense of options will be grounded in such an appeal to considerations of the cost to the agent which would be imposed by various moral demands. The greater the sacrifice which morality requires, obviously enough, the more significantly it will decrease the agent's ability to mold his life as he chooses and to promote his interests. The moderate may want to argue that more than a certain loss of such autonomy is morally intolerable. Hence, morality can only exact so much, and no more.

Obviously, a great deal more needs to be said about such an appeal to cost. (Hereafter, 'cost' means 'cost to the agent'.) This is only a sketch of an argument. Rather than pursuing these matters now, however, I want to put aside for the time being the question of whether an appeal to cost would in fact be sufficient to ground options,[16] and ask instead: regardless of whether it is adequate to *justify* them, what *sorts* of options would an appeal to cost support? Now it seems intuitively clear that an appeal to cost will

[16] We will return to this question in Chapter 7.

support an option to *allow* harm—for preventing harm can be quite costly. (It would be a limited option, of course, for I would still be required to act in those cases—e.g., the drowning child—where the cost of providing aid would be minimal.) The point I want to press here, however, is that an appeal to cost supports options to *do* harm as well as options to allow harm, and the moderate, therefore, may have to *abandon* his appeal to cost. For it is not only *preventing* harm which can be costly—*refraining* from harming can be costly too. And, if this is right, then an appeal to cost would support an option to do harm in such cases.

The claim that refraining from harming can be costly may not seem correct. After all, it takes no time, resources, or physical effort to keep from kicking a passing stranger whose face I happen to dislike. In general, it seems, refraining from performing some act requires no significant sacrifice. Thus prima facie requirements not to do certain sorts of acts seem immune to appeals to cost.

But not all requirements to refrain from harming exact only an insignificant sacrifice. Recall my wealthy uncle: suppose that by murdering dear old uncle Albert I stand to inherit one million dollars. The cost of complying with the requirement that I not kill is enormously high. It is not an out-of-pocket expense, to be sure—but we might speak of a *prospect* cost: I stand to gain one million dollars by killing my uncle, and if morality is going to close off that act to me, then it exacts a tremendous cost. If high cost is indeed ground for denying the existence of a requirement, then we seem to have such a case here—and it is permissible to kill uncle Albert. But this is quite unacceptable to the moderate.

The moderate might be tempted to argue that it is illegitimate to weigh the cost of not killing my uncle in at one million dollars. I have already noted that there is no out-of-pocket expense. Perhaps *prospect* costs are not sufficient to undermine the claim of a prima facie moral requirement.

On reflection, however, it is clear that the moderate can't make this move—for he does want to count prospect costs when it comes to prima facie requirements not to *allow* harm. Suppose a second rich uncle, Bruno, plans to leave me his million—unless I tell him to donate it instead to famine relief. Am I required to tell him to donate it? The moderate thinks not. Yet this is a case where I could prevent an immense amount of suffering, with little effort and no out-of-pocket expenses. Nonetheless the moderate wants to grant me an option to allow the suffering and further my own interests instead. The reason, clearly enough, is the prospect cost: asking me to forgo the prospect of gaining one million dollars is asking too much.

So prospect costs *do* count, and if they tend to support options to allow harm in the Bruno case, they must also support options to do harm in the Albert case. But options to do harm are unacceptable to the moderate. Indeed, it is precisely those cases where the moderate most wants to insist upon the requirement not to kill—i.e., where the agent stands to gain the most by killing—that the appeal to cost tends to undermine ordinary morality.

Since the appeal to cost supports *both* sorts of options, if the moderate is going to maintain his defense of options to *allow* harm without being forced into accepting options to *do* harm, then he must argue that there are overriding *independent* reasons why an agent must not do harm. That is, he must offer an explanation of why doing harm is *forbidden*—an explanation backed by considerations forceful enough to override the pro tanto support *for* an option to do harm. He must defend the existence of a constraint against doing harm.[17]

If the moderate can first defend the existence of the appropriate sorts of constraints, then he may be able to argue as follows: 'Considerations of cost tend to support the existence of options— both options to allow and options to do. I have already given strong reasons for thinking there is a constraint against doing harm—and these reasons override the considerations of cost insofar as the latter support some sort of option to *do* harm. But with regard to an option to *allow* harm, the considerations are not overridden. Consequently, I have provided a justification for an option to allow harm, to supplement my earlier justification for a constraint against doing harm.'

Despite the logical independence of constraints and options, then, the moderate's defense of the latter will require him to also establish the existence of the former as well. Only if the moderate can provide such an independent overriding defense of the constraint against doing harm, can he put forward the appeal to

---

[17] Theoretically, the moderate *might* be able to provide reasons for not doing harm which were *not* strong enough to establish constraints against doing harm, but which *were* strong enough to override considerations of cost. This possibility will be examined in Chapter 5.

cost in opposition to the extremist, without fear that in doing so he will be backed into too minimalist a position. If he *cannot* provide a defense of constraints, then his defense of options will have to be abandoned.[18]

CONSTRAINTS

Although we could discuss in a perfectly general fashion the difficulties of arguing for any sort of constraint, our primary interest in the question is motivated by the moderate's need to block various unacceptable options that would otherwise be supported by the appeal to cost. For example, the moderate needs to provide an overriding reason why I must not kill uncle Albert. Now cases involving the doing of harm may not be the only ones where the moderate would find an option unacceptable, but they are probably the most important such cases. In any event, if the moderate is to retain his use of the appeal to cost, then blocking or overriding that appeal in cases involving the doing of harm will certainly be essential to the moderate's defense of ordinary morality. So let us focus the discussion by examining the constraint against doing harm—and more specifically, the constraint against killing. (A discussion of constraints other than the constraint against harming would, of course, require corresponding alterations in the arguments about to be considered; in the case of certain special obligations, these alterations might be rather extensive. Still, the arguments given below are typical of those moderates offer in defense of constraints.)

In principle, our investigation could proceed by considering an example of what is doubtless the most common kind of case, i.e., one in which the best outcome will *not* be brought about by violating the constraint against killing. In such cases, of course, the

[18] It may sound peculiar to speak of the moderate's *choosing* to abandon the appeal to cost should he find that he cannot resist options to do harm through the establishment of constraints. After all, considerations of cost either support options or they don't—independently of whether or not the moderate is pleased with the outcome. Ultimately, however, the moderate has to make a judgment about the relative weight of countervailing reasons—and the moderate may come to acknowledge that the weight of the pro tanto reason to promote the good is greater than he had originally been inclined to judge. Abandoning the appeal to cost would be abandoning the judgment that considerations arising from cost are powerful enough to outweigh the pro tanto reason to promote the good.

moderate and the extremist are in agreement that the constraint must not be violated. But such agreement masks the deeper disagreement between the two as to the *reason* why the given act of killing should not be performed. The extremist believes the act in question to be forbidden because, by hypothesis, it would not lead to the best outcome overall. The moderate, however, believes that this answer fails to bring out the distinct and far more important reason why the given act of killing is forbidden, a reason so compelling that it grounds a *constraint* against such acts. In principle, it should be possible for the moderate to isolate that reason even in the typical cases in which the moderate and the extremist have no dispute over whether the killing is permitted.

Nonetheless, there is a clear danger of confusion if we focus on a case in which violating the constraint will not bring about the best outcome. We run the risk of misdiagnosing the source of the moral prohibition against killing in such cases. In the attempt to isolate a reason capable of grounding a constraint against killing, we may mistakenly produce instead variants on the already-noted fact that the given act of killing will not lead to the best outcome available. (And *this* consideration, obviously, cannot justify a constraint against killing, which would prohibit such acts even when they *would* lead to the best outcome.) At the very least, by focusing instead on cases in which the extremist and the moderate disagree about the permissibility of killing, we may hope to bring the grounds for constraints more sharply into relief, better enabling the moderate to articulate and defend his belief.

Let us, therefore, imagine a case in which it *would* promote the good to kill. Imagine that by killing one innocent person I can prevent the murders of two other innocent persons. That is, by violating the constraint against killing, I prevent two other violations of the same constraint, and this is the only way to promote this desirable outcome. In short, if I kill the one, I save the two.[19]

Several features of this case deserve comment. Most importantly, the description is obviously schematic; I have deliberately neglected

[19] Since the present discussion is meant to be neutral between a constraint against doing harm and a constraint against intending harm (see n. 14), it may be best to assume explicitly that, in the case being described, my killing the one is an essential means to (and not a mere side-effect of) my saving the two. (For a related discussion of a similar schematic example, see Scheffler, pp. 80–114, especially pp. 84–90, 98–101.)

filling in most of the details of the case. This is not because such details cannot have any moral significance. On the contrary, it is quite possible that filling in a concrete example would introduce a variety of *additional* morally relevant considerations. That is the very reason why I have left the case schematic. If the moderate is going to justify a constraint against killing, it will not help to have our attention distracted by accidental features that may muddy the moral waters. This is true regardless of whether the additional factors would happen to make the given act of killing even worse, or serve to make it somewhat more acceptable in the given case. It may, therefore, help us to focus on the constraint against killing, if we simply stipulate that in the case we are considering there are no other morally relevant factors (no mitigating side-effects, no more desirable course of action open to me, and so on).

What the case does involve, of course, is a situation in which, by hypothesis, a greater amount of good will be done by killing than by refraining from killing. This description assumes, obviously, that it is worse—all other things being equal—if two innocent people die than if only one innocent person dies. But it would be hard to deny this claim. (Matters might be different if one or more of the three people were morally culpable, or somehow responsible for being in the situation; that is the reason for imagining all three to be innocent. Of course, many other differences in the individuals might be relevant as well; but let us assume that the three are, in the relevant respects, similar.) However, since we are leaving open the possibility that a pluralist account of the good should be accepted, we cannot assume that the loss of innocent life is the only factor relevant to the goodness of the two possible outcomes.

On some accounts, for example, it might be suggested that the existence of an act of murder makes the world bad above and beyond the badness of the resulting loss of innocent life. On such a view, even if killing the one were the only way to save the two from dying of natural causes, we could not automatically assume that killing the one would result in the greater amount of good overall. For the choice would be between, on the one hand, the badness of two innocent deaths and, on the other hand, the badness of one innocent death *plus* the additional badness of an act of murder. It would be possible that the contribution that an act of murder makes to the badness of outcomes is so great that murdering the one so as to save the two from dying of natural causes would not actually promote the greater good.

I do not propose to examine the plausibility of such views. In fact, I have deliberately described our case in such a way as to sidestep the difficulty. We are not imagining that, by killing the one, I am merely saving the two from death by natural causes. Rather, I prevent the two from being murdered themselves, let us say, by two other potential murderers. Even if the existence of an act of murder makes outcomes bad in its own right, since my act of murder prevents two other acts of murder, it will remain true that by killing the one I bring about the better outcome overall. (Similar remarks, or minor variations in the case, could handle other versions of the objection.)

We are imagining, then, a situation in which it is genuinely the case that killing the one so as to save two others promotes the best available outcome. I do not mean to suggest that such cases are especially common. On the other hand, I also do not mean to concede that such cases never arise. (In point of fact, I believe that they do sometimes arise.) For our purposes it should not matter whether such cases actually occur or not. The moderate needs to defend a constraint against killing. Such a constraint would rule out killing even in cases where it would lead to the best consequences overall, so it should rule out killing the one to save the two. And this is just as the moderate would have it. He believes that it *is* morally forbidden for me to kill the one, even though this is the only way to save the two. But the moderate needs to defend this belief.

If I kill the one, I save the two. What reason can the moderate give for prohibiting me from doing this?[20]

1. Moderates typically try to defend the constraint against killing by stressing what a horrible thing I am doing to the victim if I kill

---

[20] If the arguments criticized in this section appear to be straw men, the blame should fall upon the moderates themselves, for they have made quite a poor showing at defending their views. Most moderates are unusually vague or sloppy about the basis of constraints (even by the standards of moral philosophy); even when they are not, there is rarely much offered by way of *justification* of their views. Often they merely present their particular moderate position, at best appealing to intuition for support. Thus, e.g., Nagel in 'War' seems to describe a particular constraint without *arguing* for it (except perhaps for an implied appeal to intuition). Similarly, one looks in vain in Dworkin's *Taking Rights Seriously* or Melden's *Rights and Persons* for something like an explicit defense of constraints. There are occasional comments which seem germane, but it is hard to tell if such authors take themselves to be offering arguments or not, and if so what these might be. In this section I have attempted to construct arguments based on comments made by moderates—making the assumption (which may not always be fair) that the comments are *meant* to be/ contain arguments.

him. And it is indeed a horrible thing to be killed. But it does not seem that emphasizing this point brings the moderate any closer to justifying the constraint. The death of my victim is a horrible thing to happen to him; but the deaths of the two other potential victims are obviously horrible things to happen to *them*. My victim is uncompensated—but the two others would be uncompensated too. If my victim's death is a bad thing, then the deaths of the two would, together, be worse. Why should I be forbidden to minimize the badness?

As long as the moderate sticks to what happens to a person when the constraint is violated he gets no closer to justifying the constraint. Talk of the value of an individual's being able to shape his own life, the disvalue of a life being violated, and the like—none of this helps explain why a constraint against killing should be erected; it only supports the extremist's view that it is permissible to inflict one such harm in order that a greater number of such harms—a greater overall amount of badness—may be avoided. The barrier to promoting the best outcome created by a constraint is inexplicable in terms of the badness of what happens to the victims.[21]

2. The inadequacy of stressing the badness of what *happens* to the person when the constraint is violated may suggest shifting the focus of the moderate's argument to the *relationship* which obtains between the agent and his victim.[22] Moderates have often emphasized the quality or character of the acts they wish to constrain—as distinct from merely noting their outcomes. If I kill my victim, I stand in a particular relationship to him—and moderates have stressed how horrible it is for that relationship to obtain. In killing my victim, even for a good end, I am degrading him, violating his integrity as a person, treating him as a means, breaching our common humanity, and the like. Presumably I do not stand in these horrible relationships with all those whom I merely allow harm to befall.

Once again, however, the moderate's argument fails to bring him any closer to justifying the constraint. For however horrible the

---

[21] Moderates who seem to offer arguments of the sort criticized here include Nozick, pp. 48–51, and perhaps 33–4; Mackie, p. 355; Fried, p. 34; and Dworkin, pp. 272–3.

[22] The criticisms in the previous paragraph are also made by Nagel in 'Libertarianism', pp. 143–4, as is the suggestion that the defense of constraints must turn on the relationship between agent and victim. But he does not go on to *offer* such a defense.

interpersonal relationship in which I stand to my victim, the relationships between the two would-be murderers and their victims would be equally horrible. Violating the constraint may put me in a horrible relationship with my victim, but if it prevents a greater number of violations then the moderate has as yet no reason to forbid it.[23]

So far the moderate has concentrated on badness—the badness of what happens, and the badness of relations—but it seems clear that such an approach cannot justify a constraint against killing. For *badness* relates to the objective value of the outcomes.[24] The extremist wants to promote the most valuable outcome open to him. Considerations of the disvalue of this or that can only affect judgments about what *is* the best outcome—but it can't possibly justify creating a barrier to promoting the best outcome once we determine what that is. Constraints cannot be erected on considerations of badness.

Perhaps when the moderate says how horrible it is to kill, we misunderstand him if we take him to be arguing for a constraint on the basis of the objective disvalue of killings. It may be so clear that considerations of disvalue are not sufficient justification for constraints, that it is unfair to read the moderate in this way. Perhaps his saying that it is bad to kill is simply a way of saying that it is *wrong* to kill—that killing is forbidden. But this, of course, is simply to state the claim, not to justify it; and surely, the moderate thought he was offering *reasons* for his view. So let us ask again: why is there a constraint against doing harm even when this is necessary to prevent greater harm?

3. We soon come to a fundamental intuition for the moderate. He feels there is something deeply wrong about the extremist's willingness to do evil in order to prevent it. Somehow it seems utterly against the spirit of morality to be flirting with evil in the name of the good. The extremist, of course, may bemoan the fact that he was forced to do evil at all; but the moderate's intuition is that we have *misconceived* our relation to evil, if we will enter into

---

[23] The moderates cited in n. 21 may have the horribleness of the *relationship* in mind as well. A more explicit attempt at this sort of argument may be DiIanni, Section 4.

[24] Recall the point of n. 6: 'outcome' must not be construed too narrowly; on a pluralist theory of the good, an act's 'outcome' may include the act itself. Indeed, assessing the value of an act's outcome may potentially require taking into account complete world histories.

partnership with it for whatever purpose. It is the nature of evil that we should *avoid* it. It is the nature of evil that we should simply never turn our mind to bringing any about.[25]

No doubt all of us have felt the force of this view. Indeed it is embedded in our language, making it all the harder to recognize it as an assumption which needs to be questioned. We may find ourselves being reassured by the thought that if it is *evil* to perform some act, then clearly one cannot perform that act. One cannot do an act which is itself evil—a fortiori one cannot do the evil act for some desirable end. Hence one cannot do evil—even that good may come of it. But such thoughts conceal a non sequitur: we cannot move without argument from 'one cannot do what is forbidden' to 'one cannot do harm'. The non sequitur is covered by the fact that both claims can be expressed as 'one cannot do evil'—and the ambiguity is doubtless due to the belief of ordinary morality that doing harm *is* forbidden, even for good ends. But the moderate must *show* that it is evil (forbidden) to do evil (harm).[26] The extremist believes that although we cannot eliminate suffering from the world, we should at least do what we can to minimize it. To the moderate, this attitude is fundamentally misguided. But whatever the force of his intuition, the moderate still needs to justify it.

4. The moderate may return to the nature of the relation between me and my victim. He may suggest that to deliberately harm another degrades not only the victim of the harm, but the *agent* of the harm. It is hard to escape metaphor here: when I kill another, I become *polluted*. (Even those who believe in thresholds for constraints will feel soiled and profaned if forced to do harm in order to prevent some catastrophe.) The constraint against killing—the moderate argues—respects the agent's need to preserve his moral integrity.[27]

[25] See, e.g., Nagel, *Nowhere*, pp. 181–2.

[26] I think Donagan falls prey to such a non sequitur, although it is not clearly committed in any one passage; but cf. pp. 86 and 154–5. (I critically examine these passages in 'Donagan'.) Also, Fried may be beguiled by his using 'wrong' indiscriminately in the sense of 'harm', 'forbidden' and 'prohibited by a constraint'. See, e.g., pp. 2–3.

[27] Fried, p. 2: 'If deontology, the theory of right and wrong, is solicitous of the individual, it is primarily solicitous of his claim to preserve his moral integrity, to refrain from being the agent of wrong, even if such fastidiousness means forgoing the opportunity to promote great good or to prevent great harm.' A discussion of integrity is also provided by Williams (see 'Critique', especially pp. 108–18); although it is obscure just what his comments are supposed to show, I think they at least *evoke* this argument.

It seems, however, that a concern with the moral integrity of the agent cannot provide a justification for having a *constraint* against doing harm. At the very best it could only help ground an option to refrain from harming others in pursuit of the good; but if an agent were willing to sacrifice his moral integrity in order to promote the greater good, the moderate has given no reason to prohibit his doing so. If I am *willing* to kill the one out of my concern for the two, then the moderate still needs to provide a reason to forbid the killing.

The moderate might reply that even if this objection is sound—and a concern with the moral integrity of the agent cannot justify a constraint—the extremist has been defeated nonetheless. Granted, some other argument will be needed to establish constraints; and granted, the moderate ultimately hopes to establish a far broader range of options than the mere option to refrain from doing harm; but still: if the appeal to moral integrity is indeed sufficient to ground even this limited option, then the extremist has been refuted, since he denies the existence of any options at all.

The extremist, however, has a compelling response. It is clear that no argument based on the loss of moral integrity can succeed—regardless of whether it is meant to establish a constraint or an option—unless killing the one does actually involve a sacrifice of the agent's integrity. But if killing the one to save the two is justified—as the extremist believes—then it is no sacrifice of moral integrity for the agent to do so. What this means is that the moderate's appeal to moral integrity simply begs the question against the extremist. The moderate believes that killing the one is morally forbidden, but he has still given no reason to accept this claim.

5. The moderate may return to the relation between agent and victim once again, and suggest that if I kill the one to save the two, I am failing to respect the one as a person. As a member of the moral community, each person deserves to be treated in accordance with his standing *as* a person; that is, I must treat other individuals as the persons that they are. But to deliberately harm an individual, even for a desirable end, is to reduce that individual to a mere means in my treatment of him, and to fail to accord to him the respect due him as a person. A person must be treated as an end, not a means—and so I am forbidden to kill the one.

The general tenor of this argument is, of course, a familiar one.

The concept of treating an individual as a person (or an end) is often used to try to bridge the gaps which have bothered the extremist. But the concept won't do the job. The extremist will certainly want to agree that each person deserves to be given the sort of treatment befitting the valuable type of being that he is. But the moderate is too hasty in assuming that the appropriate sort of treatment rules out harming one person to prevent harm to others—for this is the very claim that he needs to establish. The moderate hasn't shown that treating a person with the respect that is due him requires something *different* from taking his well-being equally into account in weighing the objective value of an outcome and promoting the best outcome overall. To kill without justification is undoubtedly to fail to treat the person with respect, and the moderate *claims* that to kill one in order to save two is *not* adequate justification; but he has given no reason to think so.[28]

The cataloguing of attempts by the moderate to establish the existence of a constraint against killing could go on; but I know of none that succeed.[29] What is striking about all of these arguments is that they suffer not from failures of detail, but from failure to get off the ground altogether. The moderate's belief in constraints may well be backed by intuition, but I have argued that this is not sufficient to justify the belief if it cannot be supported by a coherent explanation. Not only has the moderate failed to give an adequate explanation; he has failed to give even the beginnings of one.

THE TWO-LEVEL CONCEPTION OF MORALITY

Actually there is a possible explanation of constraints which at least seems to move in the right direction. I want to sketch it briefly and indicate why it may not serve the moderate's purpose.

[28] Fried is typical in assuming without argument that to harm intentionally is a denial of the victim's status as a person. See, e.g., pp. 29, 43–4. Donagan may beg the question on p. 86. Dworkin, p. 198, suggests 'there are ways of treating a man that are inconsistent with recognizing him as a full member of the human community'. Cf. pp. 272–3. Melden seems to simply conflate granting an individual status as a full member of the moral community and granting that person rights—not even seeing the potential gap. See, e.g., pp. 62, 175–6, 194–7.

[29] Obviously I make no claim to having here canvassed all of the arguments which have been offered for constraints—not even all of the most common ones. Many of these arguments are vitiated by the simple neglect of the question whether harm to one might be justified by its preventing harm to others; those arguments aware of the question often unblinkingly beg it against the extremist.

The moderate might appeal to a two-level conception of morality, in which particular acts are judged in terms of their conformity to a system of moral rules, and those rules themselves are judged in terms of their overall promotion of the good. In judging a system of rules, one would have to take into account various positive and negative effects of their promulgation in a society, and it might well be that the optimal moral code from this perspective is one which forbids (requires) acts in certain particular cases which would (would not) in themselves be optimal. That is, it might well be that a society in which agents directly appeal to considerations of consequences would be worse than a society in which some other moral rules were current.

The extremist is in ready sympathy with part of the motivation for such a two-level view. He too will want to stress the importance of taking into account not only the direct effects of a given act, but also the various side-effects which his act might have. Since it is easy to miscalculate, to overlook relevant long term effects of one's action, or to be biased in one's assessment of the outcomes due to the pressures of the situation, the extremist may advocate appeal to general rules which have been tested in cooler moments of reflection by consideration of their overall promotion of the good.

But there is still a theoretical dispute between this approach to general rules and the two-level approach: for in the rare case where the agent *knows* that it would promote the best outcome to violate a general rule (and the possibility of error is outweighed by the potential gain), the extremist would say that it is permitted to violate the rule, while the two-level approach would say that it is forbidden. Although it is unclear how the moderate would defend this aspect of the two-level view, let us leave this problem aside for a moment, and see what such an approach yields.[30]

Given the two-level view, the moderate may be able to suggest several factors which support adopting constraints against harming.

[30] This is, of course, the question of defending rule-utilitarianism's, as opposed to act-utilitarianism's, notion of rules. Related, familiar problems may also arise for rule-utilitarianism when the optimal moral code is not *in fact* promulgated. It should also be noted that there are other versions of the two-level approach that I do not discuss: on some versions, the rules are to be selected not in terms of the optimality of their social promulgation, but rather in terms of the optimality of their acceptance or adoption by the individual whose act is being evaluated; on other versions, it is not the optimal set of rules that is selected, but rather the optimal set of dispositions, or motives; and so on. I believe, however, that all of these are subject to comments similar to the ones I offer in the text.

Human nature being what it is, when their interests are at stake, people are apt to be biased in their assessment of the objective value of outcomes or the probable effectiveness of courses of action. Their judgment that a harm to one is justified by the likely prevention of harm to others, e.g., is frequently distorted as a result of emotional ties to those in need of aid. A system which allows direct appeal to consequences in justifying harm will probably result in numerous cases where harming someone actually pro- motes a worse outcome. A constraint against harming provides a safeguard against such miscalculations and abuse.

Obviously, the details of this argument would need to be filled in, and the overall benefits of a system with constraints would have to be weighed against those of other possible systems. But we understand how the argument might proceed, and it is not implausible to think that constraints might be defended in this way. Has the moderate, then, finally provided a basis for a defense of constraints, enabling him to return to the appeal to cost and thus establish the existence of options? I think not. For the two-level view, at the same time that it supports constraints, may *undercut* options. That is, I find it plausible to believe that a two-level approach would yield a moral system *with* constraints but *without* options.

Contrast a system of constraints and options with a system of constraints but no options: in the latter, but not the former, the agent is required to perform that act (within the limits of the constraints) which promotes the best outcome. It seems plausible to believe that under such a system there would be people who would make various sacrifices in the pursuit of the good since morality requires it of them—but who would not make such sacrifices if they were *not* required. Thus it seems, at least at first glance, that more good would be produced if the set of moral rules promulgated required such sacrifices; that is, the optimal system of rules will lack options.

It might be suggested, however, that some (many?) people would lose their incentive to produce goods if their possessions could be forcefully appropriated by others under an appeal to the best outcome. On balance, this loss of incentive might lead to an overall decline in the resulting goodness of the outcome. Thus the optimal moral code might actually need to offer people some protection against the forceful appropriation of their possessions, even appropriation for the sake of the greater good.

Although the extent of this factor could be disputed, it should certainly be admitted that the possibility of such an effect must be taken into account. But whatever its extent, such a consideration only supports a *constraint* against sacrifices being forcefully imposed by others. It does not speak against the system of moral rules nonetheless including a *requirement* that agents make the sacrifice themselves (even though, given the imagined constraint, compliance with such a requirement could not necessarily be compelled). Of course, some may fail to make the sacrifices—but this would be true on both sorts of systems, and all the more so in a system which did not include the requirement in the first place. In the system without options, however, i.e., one which did include a requirement to promote the good, some may be prompted to make sacrifices they would not otherwise make. So something is gained, and nothing is lost—and the two-level view supports the system without options.

It might be objected that if morality demands too much—lacks options—then when people fall short of its requirements (as doubtless they will do) they will say to themselves that they might as well obey none of morality's requirements at all. Given this all-or-nothing attitude, it is important that morality's requirements not be too severe—for were they severe morality would fall into wide neglect, and this would clearly be less advantageous than if morality had been less demanding, and had its demands met. Thus, the two-level view supports a system *with* options.[31]

But I think we would be right to be sceptical of the claim that people have this all-or-nothing attitude. Many people disobey the speed limit; few consequently feel free to run down pedestrians. I see no reason why we couldn't teach people to think, 'Well, I'm not doing all that I should—but only a *monster* would fail to do at least . . .' Morality could continue to require the sacrifices while drawing various lines marking out different levels of moral offensiveness. This might well stem most (all?) of the all-or-nothing reaction, and when we recall the extra gain from those people who will make extra sacrifices because it is required of them, I think it is plausible to conclude that the two-level approach yields a moral system in which agents are required to promote the good within the limits of constraints.

If this is correct, then the moderate faces a dilemma, for both constraints *and* the requirement to promote the good within the

[31] Urmson argues this way, I believe, pp. 211–12.

limits of those constraints would be supported by the same *sort* of reasons: consideration of the overall value of the promulgation of a set of rules. Now either this sort of reason is powerful enough to override the appeal to cost, or it is not. If the moderate holds that it *is* sufficiently powerful to override the appeal to cost, then his defense of options collapses and the extremist emerges victorious. If, on the other hand, the moderate holds that this sort of reason is *not* powerful enough to override the appeal to cost, then the appeal to cost can override the support that the two-level view provides for the optimal set of rules. But this means that the appeal to cost can override *both* the requirement to promote the good (within the limits of constraints) *and* the constraint against doing harm, in which case the moderate is forced to recognize an option to do harm and the minimalist emerges victorious. Either way, the moderate's position has to be abandoned.

Alternatively, of course, the moderate can abandon the two-level approach—but then he is back at the start, unable to provide a justification for constraints. And without such a justification, I have argued, he is unable to fend off the simultaneous attacks from the minimalist and the extremist.

My argument that the moderate faces a dilemma if he embraces the two-level view obviously relies on the assumption that the optimal system of moral rules will not include options, even though it may contain constraints. I have given some reasons for accepting this claim, but it must be admitted that the claim is an empirical one, and might be rejected. Rather than continuing the survey of possible considerations for and against the claim,[32] it may be better to consider the extremist's response to a moderate who embraces the two-level view and who believes that the optimal system of rules will indeed include not only constraints, but options as well.

Originally, it will be recalled, the two-level approach was introduced merely as a potential method of defending constraints. If constraints could be defended, it was suggested, the moderate would be able to turn to the appeal to cost in an attempt to justify options (without fear that this might yield an overly minimalist position). However, on the view now being considered there is no

---

[32] Further relevant discussion can be found, although in a different context, in Chapter 8 (which considers, in greater detail, certain aspects of the link between morality and motivation) and in Chapter 9 (where various objections concerning the importance of our loves, commitments, and the like, are examined).

need for the moderate to go beyond the two-level approach in the defense of options. The two-level approach, combined with the empirical claim that the optimal system of rules would contain both options and constraints, would already constitute a defense of options.

What this shows, of course, is that if we grant the empirical claim for the sake of argument, the extremist is forced to criticize the two-level approach itself. But this is a challenge that the extremist is eager to meet, for the view does seem questionable in its own right. Intuitively, the extremist's basic objection is this: the moderate who advocates the two-level approach seems to be conflating, without justification, social norms and individual morality. More precisely, he simply assumes that the question of what moral considerations appropriately impinge upon a given individual in a given situation is exhaustively answered by a description of the considerations that would be recognized by the social code whose promulgation would be optimal. That is, the two-level approach assumes that once we know what set of norms it would be best to have taught in a society we also know the complete set of moral considerations relevant to an individual agent's actions; morality is exhaustively captured by the optimal set of social norms. But this is a substantive, controversial thesis, and it is hard to see what reason there could be to accept it.

The optimal set of moral rules consists of those rules whose promulgation in society leads to the greatest amount of good overall. In effect, the question here is what set of moral norms it is best to teach and have accepted across society, given the various limitations and shortcomings common among the members of that society. It seems plausible to suspect that suitable sets of rules will need to be fairly simple, easily learned, and will sacrifice subtlety for the sake of generality. Whether or not this is so, such a possibility immediately raises the objection that there might be morally relevant considerations that would not be fully and precisely captured by the set of moral rules whose promulgation would be optimal. Yet such a possibility seems neglected by the two-level view, which simply assumes without justification that the moral status of an act is determined solely in terms of its conformity to the optimal set of rules.

This general objection to the two-level view is directly relevant to the moderate's attempt to use that view to defend options. Even if it is granted, for the sake of argument, that the optimal system of social norms would lack a general requirement to promote the good, the extremist will note that promoting the good may still be *morally* required nonetheless. Unless the moderate can show that there are no moral considerations relevant to an individual's action beyond those taught in the optimal system of social norms, there is no reason to assume that there are no moral requirements beyond those listed in that system. Not only has the moderate given no reason to accept this claim, it is hard to see how he can, especially given the motivation behind the two-level view. After all, the promulgation of the given system of rules is itself justified by its promotion of the greater good. An agent in the position to make a significant sacrifice may well see that even though it would not have served the greater good to teach a requirement to make such a sacrifice, since the sacrifice itself *would* promote the greater good, it may be morally required nonetheless.

Thus the moderate's defense of options through the two-level approach seems inadequate. The moderate cannot assume that the moral considerations stated in the optimal system of social norms exhausts the list of genuinely relevant considerations. In particular, he has no reason to assume that the moral importance of the promotion of the good is limited to its impact on the selection of social norms. The two-level approach, therefore, does not provide a sufficient justification for the moderate's belief in options.

The moderate might hope that even though the defense of options is inadequate, the two-level view might nonetheless provide a defense of constraints. As we have seen, this would allow the moderate to turn to the appeal to cost in an attempt to defend options. But the extremist's general objection to the two-level approach undermines the adequacy of that approach for defending constraints as well. Once more, for the sake of argument, the extremist may grant that the optimal set of social norms will include rules against the performance of certain acts, e.g., harming an innocent person. Nonetheless, once we have recognized that the optimal set of social norms need not capture morality exhaustively nor completely accurately, we can see that the moderate has not yet given us an adequate defense of constraints. As was noted earlier, the extremist readily recognizes the value of general rules as guides to correct for various biases, easily overlooked side-effects, and other possible sources of miscalculation. It seems plausible to suggest, therefore, that an extremist will generally hesitate to harm an innocent person, even when it appears that greater good may be done in this way. But in those exceptional cases in which the agent *knows* that greater good would be promoted by violating the general rule, the moderate has given no reason why the harmful act should not be done. Morality may well permit killing the one to save the two, for example, even though the optimal set of social norms would rule out such an act.

Unless the moderate can give us reason to believe that the morally relevant considerations are presented with complete accuracy by the optimal set of social norms, he cannot show why the optimal rules should not be violated in the exceptional cases in which it would promote the best outcome to do so. And as before, given that the very justification for the promulgation of the social norms is that this promotes the good, it is extremely hard to see how an advocate of the two-level view can justify his insistence that those rules be obeyed, even when their violation would lead to a better result.

In the absence of a plausible defense for the key claim that morality is accurately and exhaustively captured by the optimal set of social norms, the two-level approach does not provide the moderate with an adequate defense of constraints. And as we have already seen, it does not succeed as a defense of options either. But what this means, of course (at least, as things stand), is that the moderate is still no closer to a defense of ordinary morality.

CONTRACTS

For the two-level view, the ultimate basis of morality lies in the promotion of the overall good; yet individual acts are not assessed directly in terms of their contribution to the best outcome. Rather, particular acts are judged in terms of their conformity to a favored set of moral *rules*, and it is only the rules which are themselves directly evaluated on the basis of whether their promulgation would best promote the overall good. Such a view is an example of an *indirect* moral theory: one which selects a set of rules on some favored basis, and then judges acts in the light of those rules, rather than assessing the moral status of individual acts directly in terms of that ultimate moral basis. Other indirect theories would differ from the two-level view in offering some alternative basis for the selection of the favored set of rules. Despite the shortcomings of the two-level view itself, the moderate may be hopeful that such an alternative indirect theory would be more successful in establishing the existence of both constraints and options, or, at the very least, constraints.

There is, of course, no room to consider all the possible ways an indirect theory could be filled in, i.e., all the various ways that the favored set of rules might be selected. But there is a second kind of indirect theory that especially warrants our attention, for it has been extremely popular among moderates. On this approach, the favored set of rules (in the light of which individual acts are to be judged) are those that would be selected as the result of a hypothetical agreement. We imagine the members of society trying to reach a mutually acceptable conclusion as to the rules by which they shall all be bound. An individual act is morally acceptable if it conforms to the rules that would result from this hypothetical bargain. In effect, the rules of morality are conceived of as the content of an imaginary social contract.[33]

Different contract theorists will disagree as to the precise specification of the conditions under which the agreement is to be imagined as taking place. But the general idea is this: We imagine the parties to the bargaining session to be rational, and each is concerned only to further his own interests. Each is in principle willing to accept rules that would place restrictions on his own behavior, since this may be the only way to reach agreement on a set of rules that he expects overall to be to his advantage. Thus, recognizing the potential gains to be had through social coordination and cooperation, each favors reaching some form of agreement in the expectation that such an agreement can prove to be mutually advantageous.

Since the agreement is conceived of as strictly a hypothetical one, it might be wondered why the rules that would be selected by such an imaginary bargain should be thought morally binding. After all,

---

[33] Rawls is, of course, the most prominent contemporary advocate of a contract approach. And although he self-avowedly does little to draw conclusions concerning individual morality from his theory, restricting his discussion for the most part to the basic institutions of society, Rawls does believe that his approach would indeed yield a defense of ordinary morality. See, e.g., pp. 108–9, 114–17. Many others, similarly, have argued (or assumed) that a defense of ordinary morality could be provided by the Rawlsian approach. The fullest such discussion can be found in Richards.

we do not normally take ourselves to be bound by mere consideration of agreements that we did not actually make. The most plausible answer to this objection is that the hypothetical agreement is to be imagined in such a way that the conditions under which discussion, bargaining, and agreement take place are *fair*; morally unjustifiable or arbitrary differences between the parties to the agreement are imagined removed, or their impact on the agreement is blocked. The contract theorist claims that if we then refuse to be bound by the rules that would be selected by such a fair agreement, it can only be because we are bent upon taking advantage of special opportunities or powers we possess, even though acting in this way is unfair.

In order to make the conditions under which the agreement is reached fair, the parties to the agreement are imagined stripped of their knowledge of their actual position in society. This prevents a given individual from advocating or holding out for rules that would especially favor the group of which he happens to be a member. Now it might be questioned whether making the parties ignorant of their actual status is indeed the best way to guarantee that the agreement is a fair one. But it seems that the moderate, at any rate, will favor the imposition of this condition, for otherwise the contract approach is in danger of yielding overly minimalist results. After all, if the agreement took place in the knowledge of one's actual status, the rich and powerful might well hold out for rules which gave them considerable moral privileges against the weak, the poor, and the powerless, as well as children, the aged, and the infirm.

Obviously, a great deal more would need to be said to describe and defend the contract approach, but let us leave these problems aside, and ask what such an approach might yield. Can it help the moderate defend ordinary morality? What would be the results of the hypothetical agreement?

As just noted, the moderate imposes upon the parties to the agreement ignorance of their actual position in society, in part so as to fend off the minimalist. But once this condition is imposed, the following line of argument seems open to the extremist: Each member of the agreement is rationally concerned to support those rules which have the greatest likelihood of promoting his interests. Given his ignorance of his actual position in society, however, he is unable to single out those rules that would most favor his actual position. The best he can do, then, is to support a system according to which the average person in society is to be made as well off as possible. More precisely, he will favor a system according to which the level to which each person has his interests satisfied is to be made, on average, as high as possible. His expectations for such a system (as to the degree that he is likely to find his interests promoted) are higher than for any rival system, which does not seek to make the average as high as possible. Since this is true for everyone, all will agree to the rule that the average is to be made as high as possible.

But what this means—the extremist continues—is that the contract approach seems to yield a defense of an extremist system in which agents are required to promote the overall good. The particular conception of the overall good favored would apparently be one according to which an outcome is better if it consists of a higher average level of satisfaction of interests. In effect, all members of society are given the common moral goal of promoting the greater good so conceived. Furthermore, since an act is morally permissible exactly when it conforms to the rule that the average is to be made as high as possible, there are no constraints forbidding acts that would lead to a greater amount of good (i.e., a higher average). Similarly, there are no options permitting agents to pursue their own interests at the expense of the greater good overall.[34]

The extremist will readily admit that this argument could only succeed given the assumption that the parties to the agreement do not know their actual position in society. Were they to possess this knowledge, e.g., those who would later be called upon to make sacrifices for the sake of others would have reason to reject the rule that the average is to be made as high as possible. But without the imposition of ignorance, it seems plausible that an unacceptably minimalist system would emerge from the hypothetical agreement. Either way, then, the contract approach seems unavailable to the moderate.

The moderate may question the extremist argument just sketched. He may suggest that individuals ignorant of their own actual position will not so readily agree to a rule requiring that the *average* level be made as high as possible. For a high average is logically

---

[34] A similar argument is discussed at length by Rawls, who offers the response to be given in the second paragraph below. See, especially, pp. 150–83.

compatible with extremely low levels for people at the bottom. Fearful that he might turn out to be a member of the bottom group, each party to the agreement will favor instead a rule according to which the level of the *worst* off is to be made as high as possible. Secure in the knowledge that, should they end up one of the worst off, their position will be made as comfortable as possible, each is willing to forgo the incremental benefits that might have come his way under alternative rules—had he been one of the lucky ones.

There is no need to settle here the question of whether the members would indeed select a rule favoring the worst off. The extremist will note that even if this is so, it is still of no help to the moderate. At best, all that the moderate's argument succeeds in showing is that the hypothetical agreement will yield a conception of the good differing from the one originally suggested. If the new argument is correct, the favored conception of the good will actually be one according to which an outcome is better if the level of the worst off is higher. Such an account is sensitive to the distribution of well-being and the satisfaction of interests (unlike the account based on the average). But as was noted earlier, the extremist is perfectly capable of adopting such a pluralist account of the good. Thus this change in the favored account of the good does not alter the fact that it is an *extremist's* system that is selected by the hypothetical agreement. All members are still required to promote the greater good; it is simply that a different account has been offered concerning what makes one outcome better than another. An act is still permissible exactly when it promotes the greater good, and there are still neither constraints nor options.

Nor is the moderate's situation improved if he tries to argue that the members will also agree to accept certain constraints. Rather than rehearsing the arguments for this view, it should suffice to note that a system in which agents are required to promote the good within the limits of various constraints is still an extremist one.[35] Even if the contract approach yields constraints, if it rules out options at the same time, it cannot be embraced by the moderate. But this seems to be exactly where the contract approach leads. It may be open to dispute as to what conception of the good would be

[35] Depending on the constraints selected by the contract, it may be impermissible (in certain cases) to *force* others to promote the good. But, as noted previously, it would be a non sequitur to conclude from this alone that individuals are not themselves morally required to *make* the given sacrifice. Richards seems to fall prey to this confusion (e.g., p. 103).

favored by the hypothetical agreement; but we have seen so far no reason to hold that agents would not be required to promote the good properly conceived (possibly within the limits of constraints).

If the moderate is to remain open to the contract approach, he must argue for the conclusion that the hypothetical agreement would include options. On the face of it, this does not seem especially plausible. Options would be purchased at the cost of a reduction in the expected level of good to be attained. Members anxious to see that the level of the worst off is as high as possible will reject proposals that would reduce that level. (The corresponding point can be made if it is the original suggestion that is correct, and it is the average level that members are eager to have as high as possible.)

The moderate may be tempted to suggest that members will indeed favor the inclusion of options in the contract, since each will realize that his having an option in a given situation will typically increase his ability to favor his interests, freeing him from a requirement to make some sacrifice for the greater good. Options may be viewed as a sort of insurance, guaranteeing the individual at least *some* opportunity to promote his interests, should it turn out that his interests are not well served otherwise. Since each member is concerned to further his interests, the moderate may argue, all will agree upon a system that includes options.

In response, the extremist will obviously grant that having an option can free one to pursue one's interests. Ideally, each party to the agreement would like to adopt a contract which granted *him* options while denying them to others. However, since each member is ignorant of his actual position and identity in society, he does not know how to identify the rules that would in fact favor him in this way (even if he could get the other members to agree to grant him such unique privileges). The choice is thus between all having options, and none having them, and the question facing the individual member is which of *these* better meets his concern to further his interests.

It is true, of course, that for any given individual *his* having an option makes it more likely that his interests will be promoted. But it is equally true that for that same individual, the fact that *others* have options makes it *less* likely that his concern will be met. On balance, it will not be a reasonable trade. If the members—ignorant of their actual position—are anxious to have the level of the worst off be as high as possible, then each must recognize that granting options to others to pursue their own interests will interfere with the promotion of that goal. (Similarly, if the members would rather have the average level be as high as possible—since this gives each the greatest likelihood of finding his interests promoted—each will recognize that granting options to others is likely to result in the average level being lower.) It is true that options are *one* form of insurance, but they do not appear to be the most *effective* form of insurance available to the parties to the hypothetical agreement: better to require all to contribute to the overall good.

Of course, once they discover their actual position in society, various well-off individuals may find that they themselves would have had their interests better satisfied under a system in which all had options. But this does not alter the argument. From the position of ignorance in which the rules must be selected, each will find it more reasonable to favor a system in which all are required to promote the greater good.[36]

The contract approach rules out options. This means that the moderate cannot appeal to it, even if such an approach could have yielded a defense of constraints.

Once again, it must be noted that the extremist's argument only works given the assumption that the parties to the agreement are to be made ignorant of their actual position in society. But as we have seen, the moderate requires this assumption in order to avoid the minimalist. It seems, then, that the moderate is unable to simultaneously fend off both the minimalist and the extremist from within the framework of the contract approach. If he is not to abandon ordinary morality, the moderate must apparently abandon that approach.[37] But then, once more, the moderate finds

[36] Mightn't the parties to the agreement adopt a contract that includes options out of concern for the fact that otherwise—once the actual positions in society are revealed—certain well-off individuals will be unable or unwilling to keep the agreement? (Cf. Rawls, pp. 145, 176–8, on 'the strains of commitment'.) Once again, such an argument depends on assumptions which I find implausible (for reasons similar to those given in the previous section) concerning the effects of imperfect compliance with a demanding moral code upon the more general motivation to obey that code.

[37] It must be admitted, however, that many different versions of the contract approach have been offered, and I have not here tried to review or to rebut them all. In particular, it should be noted that certain moderates have attempted to defend ordinary morality through the contract approach *without* assuming that the parties to the agreement are to be made ignorant of their actual position in society. See, e.g., Gauthier, and Scanlon. (Brandt might also be mentioned in this regard, although I

himself without a defense of constraints. And as I have argued, without an adequate justification of constraints, the moderate cannot long survive the combined attacks of the minimalist and the extremist.

PROMISSORY NOTES

Old intuitions die hard. Despite the moderate's repeated failure to defend his belief in constraints (at least without simultaneously undermining his defense of options) that belief is apt to persist. The intuitions which support it do not vanish, and the moderate is likely to take refuge in the hope that an adequate defense might eventually be forthcoming. We are, therefore, going to take an extended look at the difficulties which surround the two most popular accounts of the constraint against harming. Despite the variety of problems, however, the moderate may retain his belief in constraints. For this reason we must examine whether the appeal to cost is indeed adequate to justify agent-centered options. But I want to emphasize the importance of the barrenness of the moderate's attempt to defend constraints. I have argued that intuitive support is not sufficient; it is only a promissory note suggesting that a more adequate justification can be provided—but not all promises can be fulfilled. Despite his intuitions, the slaveholder must face the realization that his distinctions dangle, and revise his views. So should the moderate.

think it a mistake to interpret Brandt as adopting the contract approach. See, especially, p. 243. At any rate, Brandt's dismissal of a general requirement to promote the good seems insufficiently motivated in terms of his own system. Cf. pp. 276–7, and 295.) Much more would have to be said to demonstrate (what I take to be the case) that *no* plausible version of the contract approach would be adequate for a defense of ordinary morality.

2

The Structure of Ordinary Morality

Ordinary morality rejects any unqualified requirement to promote the overall good, and it does this in two ways. First of all, agent-centered constraints rule out certain reactions,[1] even though such reactions might lead to the greatest amount of good overall. But secondly, even within the limits of those constraints, agents are not generally required to promote the good. On the contrary, agent-centered options permit the agent to react in various ways, even though those reactions may not constitute the agent's greatest possible (permissible) contribution to the overall good. In both of these ways, then, ordinary morality tempers the pursuit of the good. Of course, this is not to say that the promotion of the good has no role in ordinary morality. As I have noted, there are particular cases—e.g., saving the drowning child—in which the promotion of the good is indeed required of the agent. And what is more, as I argued in the previous chapter, I believe that the moderate is in fact committed to the existence of a pro tanto reason to promote the good.

This last claim may well be a controversial one. I do not mean to suggest that the existence of such a reason is an explicit element of all formulations of ordinary morality, nor do I mean to claim that all moderates will readily recognize themselves as being committed to such a reason. Rather, my claim is that the existence of a pro tanto reason to promote the good provides the best explanation of a number of judgments that the moderate wants to make. In a moment I will go on to argue this point in somewhat greater detail.

---

[1] My use of the term 'reaction' is a little idiosyncratic: I use it to refer to the agent's response in a situation, even if that response amounts to doing 'nothing at all'. Thus, although it might be improper (on some accounts) to speak of an agent's allowing harm through inactivity as an *action*, I will happily classify allowing harm in such a case as the agent's *reaction*.

Yet even after the argument is presented, the conclusion may still be resisted, until I also go on to offer a fuller explanation of how it is that ordinary morality combines a belief in the existence of the pro tanto reason to promote the good with its embrace of constraints and options. A discussion of this latter issue will serve to clarify the structure of ordinary morality, as well as making clearer the framework that I will be using in the following chapters in my investigation of the moderate's ability to defend constraints and options. But before turning to these other issues, we must first consider the plausibility—from the moderate's perspective—of the initial claim that there is a pro tanto reason to promote the good.

A word of warning to the reader may be in order, however. The discussion in this chapter is rather abstract, especially in the second half. Accordingly, those already prepared to accept the claim that the moderate is committed to the existence of a pro tanto reason to promote the good may prefer to skip over the first half of this chapter (i.e., the first two sections). And those uninterested in the technical details of how the belief in this reason can be combined with the belief in constraints and options may prefer to skip over the second half (i.e., the last three sections). In short, those who are not especially troubled by the fairly abstract issues with which this chapter shall be concerned should feel free to proceed directly to the start of Chapter 3. Later chapters should, I believe, be fully intelligible even to readers who choose to pass over the remainder of this chapter.

With this warning—and the corresponding invitation—to the reader in place, we can turn to the first issue before us: examining the claim that the moderate is committed to the existence of a pro tanto reason to promote the good.

A moderate sceptical of the pro tanto reason to promote the good might hold that although there is *sometimes* reason to promote the good, there is no *standing* reason to this effect. Such a moderate might argue as follows: In the case where the child can be saved from drowning by throwing the life preserver it is clear that this is morally required; here, and in similar cases, there is indeed reason to promote the greater good (i.e., reason to save the child's life, and so on). But to claim that there is a pro tanto reason to promote the good is to claim that there is *always* a reason to promote the good, and this is implausible, for in many cases the promotion of the good is not required. For example, I am not required to give away half of my savings to pay for life-saving surgery for some innocent stranger, even though doing so might clearly promote the good. And so—the moderate might conclude—we can see that there is no *pro tanto* reason to promote the good.

Against this argument, however, it must be remembered that the mere fact that some action is supported by *a* reason does not entail that it is supported by the *balance* of reasons. A pro tanto reason is one that always has force, but this force can be countered, and overridden, in various ways; a given act can be supported by a pro tanto reason even though that act is not morally required. The question then, roughly, is whether there is always *some* reason to promote the good—even in those cases where this is not required. And surely the moderate should claim that this is so. The moderate certainly does not believe that I am required to sacrifice half of my savings to pay for surgery to save the life of a stranger. But surely the moderate would not want to claim that there is no reason *at all* to save the stranger (only the minimalist would say that). I take it that the moderate would, rather, want to say that there is indeed some reason to promote the good in this case (i.e., make the sacrifice and save the life), even though that reason is not here sufficient to ground a requirement.

Furthermore, consider the case of the drowning child again: here the moderate certainly recognizes the existence of a reason to promote the good. Now imagine that the cost of saving the child somehow becomes so significant that ordinary morality would no longer require the necessary sacrifice. Surely the moderate does not want to hold that suddenly there is no longer any reason to save the child. Rather, I take it that the moderate believes that the difference in cost affects the issue of whether or not there is a *requirement* to save the child, but it does not affect the fact that there is a reason— the same reason—to save the child in both cases. The reason to promote the good does not pop into and out of existence as the cost of promoting the good varies: rather there is a standing reason to promote the good, which may or may not be overridden.

The sceptical moderate might admit that in those cases where the promotion of the good is morally permitted but not required, there is indeed always a reason to promote the good (albeit not one sufficient to ground a requirement in the given case). But he might still resist the claim that there is a pro tanto reason to promote the good, holding that in those cases where the act necessary for the promotion of the good would violate a constraint, and hence is *forbidden*, there is no reason generated at all in favor of promoting the good.

But once more, such a view would fail to make sense of the judgments that the moderate wants to make. Consider the case where killing one innocent person is the only way to save two others from being killed. The moderate believes that it is forbidden to kill the one; but I take it that he does not want to say that there is no reason at all to save the two—i.e., that there is no consideration at all that speaks in favor of killing the one. Rather, he recognizes that there is *a* reason to kill the one (i.e., that it would save the two), but holds that this reason is overridden by the considerations that ground the constraint (i.e., that it would involve sacrificing an innocent person). Again: the moderate wants to claim that were it possible to save the two through some morally permissible means, there would be a very strong reason to save the two. I take it that the moderate does not want to deny that that strong reason to save the two still exists in the case where doing so requires killing the one. On the contrary, there is the very same reason to save the two in both cases; it is simply that when the violation of a constraint is involved, this overrides that reason, without eliminating it. So here, too, the best explanation of the moderate's various judgments appears to involve acceptance of the existence of a pro tanto reason to promote the good.

For those moderates who believe that constraints have (finite) thresholds, a further argument to the same effect can be offered. Imagine that although a given constraint would normally rule out a particular kind of act even though greater good might come of performing that act, nonetheless the constraint has a threshold, so that the act in question is permitted if *enough* is at stake. For example, although it is forbidden to kill the one to save the lives of two others, let us suppose that it is permitted to kill the one if this is the only way to save the lives of *one hundred* others. (Different moderates might want to consider examples involving other thresholds, or a different constraint.) In a case where the threshold is passed, and it is permissible to kill the one, presumably the moderate wants to claim that the possibility of saving the lives of one hundred people generates a reason powerful enough to override the constraint. But what is the moderate to say of a case in which the number of lives at stake falls just short of the threshold—

say, ninety—and so killing the one would still be forbidden? If a sceptical moderate were to deny the existence of the pro tanto reason to promote the good, he would have to hold that there is no reason at all to save the ninety people, although there *would* (suddenly?) be a very powerful reason if the number were one hundred (imagine the number of endangered lives slowly increasing).[2] In contrast, if the moderate accepts the existence of the pro tanto reason to promote the good, he can plausibly explain that although there is indeed significant reason to save the ninety people, it is not quite powerful enough to outweigh the constraint, and will only become powerful enough if the number of lives at stake reaches the critical threshold number. I take it, once again, that the existence of the pro tanto reason to promote the good provides the best explanation of the various judgments that the moderate wants to make.

Such considerations—and they could easily be multiplied—support the view that the moderate is committed to the existence of a pro tanto reason to promote the good. Once more, it should be borne in mind that the acceptance of such a reason does not commit the moderate to any sort of general requirement to promote the overall good. That a given reaction would promote the greater good provides some reason for reacting in that way; but various countervailing reasons may well make the given reaction merely optional or even forbidden.

Up to this point, the discussion has focused on the question of whether, from the moderate's perspective, the promotion of the good is supported by a *pro tanto* reason—i.e., one that is always generated, even if it is often outweighed or overridden. It might be claimed, however, that although the forgoing considerations establish the moderate's embrace of a particular reason with pro tanto status, they do not show that the moderate is committed to a pro tanto reason to *promote the good*. It might be observed that the

---

[2] Of course the moderate might deny that there is a *precise* threshold, holding instead that for a certain range in the number of lives at stake, it is indeterminate whether or not the constraint is overridden. But we can assume that one hundred lives and ninety lives clearly fall, respectively, above and below this imprecise threshold. It still seems unlikely that the moderate will want to hold that although there *would* be a powerful reason to save one hundred, there is *no* reason at all to save ninety. (This possibility of imprecise, or rough boundaries, it should be noted, is one that could be raised at several points in the chapters that follow; generally, however, I will not pause to consider this issue, or to add the relevant qualifications to the discussion.)

examples I have just given all involve saving lives, or preventing harms, in various ways. But it is, after all, one thing to save a life, and quite another to help someone, say, gain the pleasures of reading science fiction. Yet a pro tanto reason to promote the good would have to cover the latter as well as the former. Thus a sceptical moderate might concede that ordinary morality recognizes the existence of a pro tanto reason to *prevent harm* and yet nonetheless deny that ordinary morality goes beyond this by recognizing the existence of any pro tanto reason to promote the overall good.

This objection is a complex one. It presupposes an ability to distinguish between harms—or, more generally, bads, or evils—and goods, and concedes that both may enter into our assessment of the overall value of an outcome (it is, after all, better if the various goods obtain); but it holds that although ordinary morality includes a standing reason to prevent the harms, it does not include a standing reason to promote the goods. In effect, the objection claims that in ordinary morality there is a pro tanto reason to reduce suffering, but no pro tanto reason to create pleasures. And so on.

Once again, however, such a claim fails to account for various judgments that the moderate wants to make. Consider more carefully the example of the pleasures of reading science fiction. Imagine that I am considering giving my copy of Kilgore Trout's short stories to someone who I believe might enjoy them. Now it may well be that I am not *required* to give the book to some such worthy individual, but I take it that the moderate does not want to claim that morally there is *no* reason at all for me to give it. The fact that I can bring some good into the world provides me with some reason for reacting in that way, albeit a reason that may be often overridden.

What does seem to be supported by reflection on the example of science fiction is the thought that some goods may well be far less important than some evils. But this realization does nothing to show that ordinary morality does not include a pro tanto reason to promote the good. It merely underscores the fact that some things have a greater impact on the overall value of a state of affairs than other things. Those things with the greater impact on overall value will generate a stronger reason. Consequently, the pro tanto reason to promote the good will provide a more forceful reason when it comes to minimizing the significant evils than when it comes to promoting the less pressing goods. But again, this does not show that there is no reason to promote the goods, but only that in certain cases this reason may be relatively weak. (It is also worth bearing in mind that the creation of some significant goods may well be more pressing than the elimination of some trivial evils. A complete theory of the good would need to investigate these matters, but for our purposes the issue can be put aside.)

It may be helpful to consider the sceptical moderate's position more carefully. The claim is that although ordinary morality recognizes a pro tanto reason to prevent harm, it does not recognize a pro tanto reason to promote the good. There is a standing reason to prevent suffering, but not to create happiness. Put this way, the objection actually runs together two different distinctions. The first distinction, already noted, is that between goods and evils. The second distinction is the difference between preventing a *deterioration* in the level of well-being of an individual (or, more generally, a deterioration in the value of a state of affairs) and *improving* the level of well-being of an individual (or the value of a state of affairs). These two distinctions together actually yield four possibilities. One can prevent the deterioration of an individual's welfare either by (1) preventing the loss of some good, or by (2) preventing the addition of some evil. Similarly, one can improve an individual's welfare either by (3) removing some evil, or by (4) promoting the addition of some good.

The claim that ordinary morality does indeed recognize a pro tanto reason to 'promote the good' is intended as a convenient way to cover all four of these possibilities:[3] it is the claim that there is a standing reason both to prevent deteriorations and to bring about improvements, and that the relevant deteriorations and improvements can involve either evils or goods. Now when the sceptical moderate suggests, in contrast, that ordinary morality only contains a pro tanto reason to 'prevent harm'—but not a pro tanto reason to promote the good—it is somewhat unclear what he

---

[3] For simplicity of exposition I am allowing a slight inaccuracy in the discussion. If there is a pro tanto reason to promote the good there is reason not only to *cause* improvements and to *prevent* deteriorations, but also to *allow* such improvements and preventions by others. (Similarly, even if there is only a pro tanto reason to prevent harm, presumably it is also a reason to *allow* the prevention of harm.) In the vocabulary to be introduced in the next chapter, it would be more accurate to talk of countenancing improvements and countenancing the preventions of deteriorations.

	Goods	Evils
Prevent deterioration	(1) Prevent loss of a good	(2) Prevent addition of an evil
Cause improvement	(4) Cause addition of a good	(3) Cause elimination of an evil

means to include under this rubric. Presumably, at the very least, he means to exclude (4)—the clearest case of doing good, as opposed to preventing harm. But what of the other cases? It might be suggested that, strictly speaking, only (2) should be classified as preventing harm. But I take it that the sceptical moderate means to include more than this. An individual can be harmed, after all, either by the imposition of some evil—case (2)—or by the loss of some good—case (1). (Often, in fact, it may be somewhat arbitrary how we classify a given example.) Presumably, therefore, the sceptical moderate means to include cases of type (1) as among those covered by the pro tanto reason to 'prevent harm'. (Indeed, it has already been conceded that ordinary morality includes a pro tanto reason to prevent the loss of life, and it certainly appears plausible to claim that this should be classified as a case of type (1)—i.e., as preventing the loss of a good.)

Similarly, it would not be plausible to suggest that ordinary morality recognizes a pro tanto reason with regard to cases of type (2), but not of type (3). It would be, for example, implausible to claim that ordinary morality recognizes the existence of a pro tanto reason to prevent disease—i.e., a case of type (2)—but does not recognize the existence of a reason to *cure* disease—i.e., a case of type (3). Thus if the sceptical moderate's claim is to have any plausibility at all, he must be using the phrase 'prevent harm' rather broadly, so as to include cases of types (1), (2), and (3). The claim, then, is that although ordinary morality recognizes a pro tanto reason with regard to cases (1)–(3), it does not recognize a pro tanto reason with regard to case (4).

Once the sceptical moderate's position is understood in this way, however, I believe that it loses whatever plausibility it may initially have had. Why should ordinary morality recognize the existence of a pro tanto reason with regard to (1)–(3) and yet balk at (4)? Had the sceptical moderate been able to claim that there is only a pro tanto reason with regard to preventing deterioration, but not with regard to bringing about improvement, this might have provided a motivated ground for excluding (4). But the inclusion of case (3)—where an evil is removed, or cured—shows that the distinction between deterioration and improvement does not carry that kind of moral weight. Similarly, had the sceptical moderate been able to claim that there is only a pro tanto reason with regard to evils, but not with regard to goods, this too might have provided a motivated ground for excluding (4). But the inclusion of case (1)—where it is the loss of a good that is prevented—shows that the distinction between evils and goods does not carry that kind of moral weight either. What, then, is the ground for excluding case (4), and only case (4)?

Now I do not mean to be suggesting that there is some sort of inconsistency in the sceptical moderate's claim: it is perfectly consistent to hold that a case must involve either deterioration or evil, in order to be covered by a pro tanto reason, even though neither of these is individually necessary. It is rather that it is difficult to see what grounds there could possibly be for holding such a position. Of course, if it could be maintained that the 'mere' addition of a 'mere' good contributes nothing to an increase in the overall value of a state of affairs, then there might be ground for excluding (4). But such a position is clearly untenable.

It might be suggested, appropriately enough, that the immediately preceding remarks at best demonstrate the implausibility of a view that merely recognizes a pro tanto reason to 'prevent harm' as opposed to the more general pro tanto reason to promote the good. But even if successful, this does not show that ordinary morality in fact recognizes the pro tanto reason to promote the good. It might be that—implausible or not—it is only a pro tanto reason to prevent harm that is endorsed by ordinary morality. But this brings us back to my original response to the sceptical moderate's suggestion: since, as I take it, the moderate does want to admit that there is *some* reason to bring about the addition of goods—even if this reason is often inadequate to ground a requirement—he is, after all, committed to the existence of a pro tanto reason to promote the good. The existence of such a reason provides the best explanation of the judgments that the moderate wants to make.

THE CONCEPT OF THE GOOD

Scepticism on the part of the moderate may remain. He may concede that the various moderate judgments to which I have been appealing help to show that ordinary morality is committed to the existence of a pro tanto reason; and he may concede as well that this pro tanto reason has broad scope—encompassing both deteriorations and improvements, both goods and evils. But the sceptical moderate might argue, nonetheless, that to ascribe to ordinary morality the acceptance of a pro tanto reason to promote the good is to misdiagnose the source of these various moderate judgments. In any given case in which I can aid someone, there is indeed always a reason to provide that aid—even though that reason may not be sufficient to ground a requirement. But it is not the fact that the overall good can be promoted which generates the reason for acting; rather, it is the very fact that, by thus acting, the specific individual in question can be aided. After all, there would still be reason to aid the given individual, even were the facts such that helping that individual would *not* promote the greater good overall.

There are actually two different objections contained in the sceptical moderate's remarks, and they need to be treated separately. One objection can be spelled out as follows: Suppose that there are three individuals in need of my help, but that unfortunately I am unable to save all three: I must choose between saving the life of one, Nahman, or saving the lives of the two others. Assuming that all other things are equal, greater good will be done by saving the two than by saving Nahman alone. And an appeal to a pro tanto reason to promote the good might therefore explain why there is some reason—indeed, perhaps overriding reason—to save the two. But surely the moderate also wants to hold that there is nonetheless *some* reason to save Nahman, even if this reason may be overridden by the need to save the others. Now it would not be plausible to suggest that the reason I have to save Nahman is different *in kind* from the reason I have to save the other two; it is, perhaps, outweighed, but it is not of a different sort. Yet an appeal to a pro tanto reason to promote the good seems inadequate to account for this judgment, and indeed inadequate to account for the existence of any reason to save Nahman at all since, by hypothesis, saving Nahman would *not* lead to the greater good.

Thus it seems as though we must reject the claim that the best explanation of the various judgments that the moderate wants to make involves the existence of a pro tanto reason to promote the good. (Note that for the purposes of this first objection, it does not matter what should, in fact, be used to provide a better account of ordinary morality.)

This first objection establishes the necessity of a certain clarification in the notion of the pro tanto reason to promote the good, but it does not undermine the claim that ordinary morality is committed to the existence of such a reason, properly understood. For as I intend it, the claim that there is a pro tanto reason to promote the good is a convenient way of asserting that there is a pro tanto reason to promote each individual good. When no one reaction will promote all of the individual goods that are at stake in some situation, a reason will be generated corresponding to each individual good. The more important the particular good, the greater the reason that is generated; similarly, when a single act will promote several goods, these may cumulatively generate a stronger (combined) reason. Since, on balance, the strongest reason will be generated in favor of the reaction that will promote the greatest amount of good overall, I have often spoken of the pro tanto reason to promote the overall good. But this does not mean that the pro tanto reason to promote the good *only* generates a reason in favor of the reaction that leads to the greatest good overall. On the contrary, reasons are also generated in favor of reactions that would lead to a smaller amount of good overall, although these reasons are, of course, outweighed.

Thus the fact that Nahman's life is in danger does indeed provide a reason to save him, even if it is a reason that is outweighed in the circumstances. And it is precisely this judgment that is supported by the claim that there is a pro tanto reason to promote the good. For the saving of Nahman's life is itself the promotion of a good; it is not the only good at stake in this case, but it is a good nonetheless, and so it generates a reason. The first objection, therefore, does not succeed in undermining the claim that ordinary morality is committed to the existence of a pro tanto reason to promote the good.

There was, however, a second objection contained in the sceptical moderate's remarks. It might be suggested that to embrace a pro tanto reason to promote the good is to mislocate the ultimate source of moral value. It is to view the well-being of a person as a mere means to obtaining the good, rather than recognizing that the person has a moral claim on us in his own right. If Nahman is in need of my help, then under ordinary morality I certainly have a reason to help him (whether or not this reason grounds a requirement). But to explain this by appeal to a pro tanto reason to promote the good reduces Nahman to a mere instrument through which the good can be realized; he himself is of no direct moral importance. Such an account may yield the same answers, with regard to what we have reason to do, as would be given by ordinary morality. But it irredeemably fails to capture ordinary morality's position on the source of these reasons. The sceptical moderate may urge, then, that Nahman's well-being matters in its own right, and therefore directly generates a reason, as opposed to generating such a reason indirectly, through the mere fact that aiding Nahman happens to promote some good.

This second objection misunderstands the nature of the good. It pictures the good as an abstract and alien goal, distinct from such concrete concerns as Nahman and his well-being. The good is viewed as something separate and potentially opposed to Nahman: forced to choose between the two, the sceptical moderate proclaims that his allegiance is to Nahman himself, rather than to the abstract objective good; to answer otherwise would be to view Nahman as of importance only *because* his well-being potentially helps to realize the good.

But it is a mistake to think of the good in this way—as though it consisted of something *other* than Nahman's well-being, along with the well-being of Clementina, and Phoebe, and so on. Nahman's well-being is no mere instrument to the realization of the good—it is the very *stuff* of which the good consists. The overall good is not some distinct and separable goal, for the sake of which one promotes the welfare of individual persons. On the contrary, the overall good simply *is* the overall well-being of individual persons. (At least this is so in large part; there may well be other components to the good as well, for example, equitable distribution of well-being. But the point remains that the overall good is not something distinct from the presence of the various goods—and the absence of the various evils—of which it consists.)

Thus, if I am unable to save all of three people who need me, and I reluctantly forgo the opportunity to save Nahman, choosing instead to promote the greater good by saving the other two, I have not abandoned Nahman for the sake of something impersonal and abstract: The Good. Rather, I have been forced to choose between three concrete goods—three individual lives—and I have chosen to save two lives rather than simply one: those two lives are not a mere instrument to the realization of the greater good in this case—they *constitute* the greater good.

In short, to speak of the overall good is not to speak of something that can be properly contrasted with the various *goods* that compose it. When the sceptical moderate suggests that one who embraces a pro tanto reason to promote the good will fail to see that Nahman's well-being directly generates a reason—that Nahman himself is a direct object of our concern—he misconstrues the nature of the good. There is no need to choose between ascribing to ordinary morality the acceptance of a pro tanto reason to promote the good, and, say, a pro tanto reason to promote individual well-being. Given a plausible account of the good, the former simply encompasses the latter, under a different level of description.

It is worth discussing this matter further. To say that an object or state of affairs is good is to say that it (adequately) meets the standards appropriate for things of that sort. Similarly, to say that one object or state of affairs is better than another is to say that it more fully meets the appropriate standards. (This is, of course, somewhat rough, but it should do for our purposes.) Now in many familiar cases it is perhaps fairly uncontroversial which standards are appropriate for objects of a specific sort: good watches must keep the time accurately, and so on. On the other hand, in the case of the evaluation of the moral goodness of states of affairs, the question of the appropriate standards is notoriously a matter of considerable disagreement. As I have previously remarked, on any plausible account of the matter, the overall level of individual well-being is presumably *one* factor relevant to the assessment of the goodness of an outcome. But on a pluralist account, there will be other factors as well, and such accounts will need to specify how trade-offs between these factors are to be assessed. Thus, a complete theory of the moral good would need to list the relevant factors, and explain their relative weights. It would, that is, describe the appropriate standards for assessing the goodness of outcomes, and it would have to justify the claim that those standards *are* the appropriate standards. While such a task is a pressing one for moral theory, it is not one that we need to pursue here.

What is important for our purposes, however, is the reminder that to speak of the good is in part to use a placeholder: to say that there is a pro tanto reason to promote the good is to say that there is a standing reason to promote those outcomes that best meet the appropriate standards—whatever those standards might be. A fuller description of our goal cannot be provided until we take a position on the content of the standards themselves. But once we have taken such a stand—holding, e.g., that the level of individual well-being is one central factor in the standards appropriate for outcomes—we are able to see that the good simply *is* (in part) individual well-being. To speak of the good is not to speak of something distinct from well-being; it is rather to speak of well-being itself, but under a certain abstract description: i.e., as that by virtue of which outcomes better meet the appropriate standards.

I conclude, then, that the moderate is indeed committed to the existence of a pro tanto reason to promote the good. Properly understood, the claim that there is such a reason provides the best explanation of various claims that the moderate wants to make. Of course the existence of such a reason does not come close to providing a *complete* account of ordinary morality. As I have repeatedly noted, the moderate believes in the existence of various countervailing reasons as well. But an adequate account of the structure of ordinary morality cannot focus on these other reasons alone; it must take cognizance of the fact that ordinary morality is also committed to the existence of a pro tanto reason to promote the good.

My general remarks on the concept of the good were introduced so as to help answer the sceptical moderate's objection. But these observations allow a second point to be made as well. To describe an object as good is to assert that it meets the appropriate standards. Yet even without knowledge of the content of those standards, there is more that can be said: by virtue of meeting the appropriate standards, the good object is, in typical situations, an appropriate object of choice. That is, when one has to choose among objects of the given kind, typically one has reason to pick the best such object. Once more, however, there is not much more that can be said—concerning who does and who does not have such a reason—without detailed knowledge of the standards.

However, when we are talking of the moral goodness of outcomes, there is still more that can be said. To say that from the moral standpoint one outcome is objectively better than another, is to say that *everyone* has a reason to choose the better outcome. This reason may not be the overriding one in any given case; countervailing considerations may give a particular agent greater reason still to react in a way that will not lead to the best outcome overall. But whether overridden or not, the fact that some outcome is objectively the best available outcome overall generates a reason for promoting that outcome, and it generates a reason for everyone. It is, in this sense, an *agent-neutral* reason: one that is equally generated for all moral agents, regardless of, e.g., their particular concerns or other interests.[4] This agent-neutral reason is, of course, the pro tanto reason to promote the good.

Thus, on one level, to say that there is a pro tanto reason to promote the good is actually to make a trivial claim. Everyone has a standing reason to promote the objectively best outcome, because the existence of such a reason is in part just what it *is* for something to have objective value. It is, in large part, by virtue of the fact that some (possible) state of affairs generates a reason for all agents that that state of affairs warrants the label of having *objective* value. On this level, the substantive question is only whether there is anything at all that *has* objective value.[5]

A given set of descriptive standards for assessing outcomes will fail to be the appropriate standards for assessing the *objective* value of outcomes, unless there is something that makes it the case that everyone has a reason to promote those outcomes that better meet the proposed standards. It might be the case that no set of standards at all can meet this test: nothing would then be any better objectively than anything else. This is the view of some minimalists.

On most views, however—including those of extremists, moderates, and many minimalists—there are some states of affairs that have greater objective value than others. This is, of course, a substantive claim (although not one that will be defended in this work, for it is common ground between the moderate and the

---

[4] For the distinction between agent-neutral and agent-relative reasons, see Nagel, *Nowhere*, pp. 152–4 ff.; cf. Parfit, p. 27 and passim.

[5] It is sometimes suggested that the notion of an objective value is unintelligible. But surely those who make this claim underestimate their powers of comprehension. It is reasonably clear what it means to say that something is objectively valuable. What is obscure is whether there is anything that *has* objective value, and, if so, how.

extremist). It is also a substantive claim to offer specific standards—
$S_1 \ldots S_n$—and to hold that *these* are the appropriate standards for
assessing the objective value of outcomes. For now one is claiming
that there is an agent-neutral reason—i.e., that *everyone* has a
reason—to promote those outcomes that best meet $S_1 \ldots S_n$. And
this, obviously, will not be a trivial claim.

Clearly, an adequate defense of the given set of standards will
need to explain what it is about $S_1 \ldots S_n$ that makes it true that
everyone has a reason to promote those outcomes that meet these
standards. Such a defense obviously cannot be carried on in the
absence of a detailed specification of the standards, although one
might attempt to proceed on a piecemeal basis. I have indicated my
acceptance of the common belief that the level of individual well-
being is a central factor in the objective value of an outcome; but I
do not intend to defend that belief here. To repeat the point:
although it is a substantive claim, one for which the minimalist can
appropriately demand a justification, it can be taken as common
ground between the moderate and the extremist. If the moderate is
to fend off the extremist without retreating into an overly
minimalist position, he must retain his commitment to the pro
tanto reason to promote the overall good, including such objective
goods as individual well-being.

Some additional comments about the objective good may be in
order. I have claimed that it is part of our notion of the objective
good that it generates an agent-neutral reason. It is, therefore,
impartial or impersonal—in one sense of these ambiguous terms.
Those objects that meet the appropriate standards generate a
reason for everyone, and the appropriate standards for assessing
the objective value of outcomes do not vary from individual to
individual:[6] if one outcome is objectively better than another, it is
so for everyone, and everyone has a reason to promote it. Objective
value is, in this sense, insensitive to variations in the person
involved. It is not affected by the question of who is making the
assessment.

It should be noted, however, that this does not entail that the
objective good is impartial in a second sense of this term. It is

---

[6] If the appropriate standards did vary from individual to individual, then the
force of saying that objective values generate reasons for everyone would be lost. (If
the standards are not agent-neutral, then any specific objective good will not
necessarily generate an agent-neutral reason.)

sometimes suggested that the objective value of an outcome cannot depend upon the specific identities of the persons affected by the outcome. For example, assuming that they are otherwise relevantly similar, it cannot be of greater objective value for Daphne to have the pleasure of smelling a rose than for Cordelia to have that pleasure: the brute fact of difference in recipient cannot affect the objective value. Objective value must be insensitive to variations in the mere identity of the recipient. There is, no doubt, a great deal of plausibility to this claim,[7] but I shall not assume its truth. Impartiality in this second sense is not guaranteed by impartiality in the first sense (it could be objectively more valuable for Daphne to smell the rose than for Cordelia to do so, and Cordelia herself might appropriately share this assessment). When I refer to the impartiality of the objective good, it is only the first sense that I intend.

One final point. As I have indicated, I will continue to assume that individual well-being is a central component of the objective good. Although this is a substantive assumption, as a defender of ordinary morality the moderate is unlikely to deny this. However, I will also be assuming something somewhat more controversial, i.e., that the satisfaction of interests is also a component of the objective good. This second assumption goes beyond the first, since an individual's interests (as I am using the term) include all of the objects of her concern, and not merely her own self-interest, or personal well-being. Thus I will assume that (certain complications aside[8]) the pro tanto reason to promote the good not only yields a reason to promote a given individual's well-being, but also yields a reason—albeit one that may frequently be overridden—to promote the various other interests that that given individual may have as well.

The claim that the satisfaction of interests is a factor in the overall good is, of course, a substantive one; which, once more, I'll not attempt to defend here. There is, what's more, some reason for uncertainty as to whether the moderate accepts this claim. After all, an individual's interests may go beyond her concern for her own

[7] Although it is hardly self-evident. If the objective value of someone's possessing a good can depend on various ordinary facts about that person—e.g., whether the recipient has suffered in the past, or has worked to produce that good, or is currently the worst-off person in the society—why can't it depend on the brute fact of who that person *is*?

[8] Some interests may, perhaps, be intrinsically irrational, or morally unacceptable. Arguably, satisfaction of such interests would not contribute to the overall good. But we need not pursue these complications here.

well-being. Thus promoting those interests may not be to that individual's advantage (in terms of her own level of well-being). So the question might be raised: Since promoting an individual's interests may not be good for her—or for anyone—why would it be covered by the pro tanto reason to promote the good?

I suspect, however, that most moderates would accept the claim nonetheless. There is an obvious sense in which satisfying an individual's interests is doing something *for* that individual (even if it does not particularly promote her self-interest). It is providing a certain sort of benefit, of a morally relevant kind. Most moderates, I take it, will want to admit that the fact that a given reaction will help to promote or otherwise satisfy an individual's interests gives me *some* reason to react in that way. Other things being equal, one outcome is better than another if there is a higher level of satisfaction of interests. But this is just to say that the satisfaction of interests is a component of the overall good.

Most moderates, I think, will accept all of this[9] (or, at least, could be persuaded to accept it, through a series of arguments similar to the ones I have been giving in this chapter). And I will write accordingly; I will speak of the satisfaction of interests as being of objective value, and the sacrifice of interests as being of objective disvalue—typically without pausing to distinguish between interests and self-interest. (To avoid unnecessary controversy, however, I will continue to draw on examples involving human well-being.) But even if I am wrong, this should not affect the main point for which I have been arguing—namely, that the moderate is committed to the existence of a pro tanto reason to promote the good. Disagreement over the *contents* of the overall good does not in itself call into question the existence of a pro tanto reason to *promote* the good.

MORAL REQUIREMENT

In the two preceding sections, I have attempted to argue for the claim that ordinary morality is committed to the existence of a pro tanto reason to promote the good. It has been necessary to clarify that claim, but I have seen no serious reason to reject it. However, as I noted at the start of this chapter, some doubts may persist until

---

[9] Those who do not should see Chapter 1, n. 3.

it is more fully explained how the moderate can accept the pro tanto reason to promote the good while at the same time embracing options and constraints. After all, if the moderate does indeed accept a standing reason to promote the overall good, why *doesn't* this commit him to the existence of a general requirement to promote the best available outcome overall?

The answer—or, at least, a rough answer—is one that I have indicated several times: despite the existence of a pro tanto reason to promote the good, there will be no general *requirement* to this effect, if the pro tanto reason is in turn often outweighed by various countervailing reasons. This answer calls upon a familiar picture of how moral requirements are generated: a given reaction will be morally required if and only if the balance of (morally acceptable) reasons supports reacting in that way. This model is indeed a familiar one, and so long as the notions of 'balance' or being 'outweighed' are not construed too narrowly, I believe it is largely correct. But the model is only a rough one nonetheless, and I think we can profit by making it somewhat more precise. (However, those uninterested in pursuing the rather abstract details are invited, once again, to turn directly to the start of the next chapter.)

A given reaction is morally required if and only if it is supported by a morally decisive reason. Putting the matter this way leaves open the question of whether a reductionist stance is appropriate. That is, one might accept this account and go on to urge—in a nonreductionist vein—that although being supported by a morally decisive reason is what *grounds* being morally required, the former is nonetheless distinct from the latter. Or—in a reductionist vein— one might accept the account and go on to urge that in fact being supported by a morally decisive reason simply *is* what it is for a reaction to be morally required. In what follows, I will often help myself to reductionist or nonreductionist formulations; but none of the arguments turn on this. The discussion could be recast in somewhat more awkward but neutral language.

For a given reaction to be morally required is for it to be supported by a morally decisive reason. Along similar lines, we can say that a given reaction is morally forbidden if and only if there is a morally decisive reason for *not* reacting in that way. Furthermore, if we make the plausible assumption that an action is permitted provided that it is not forbidden, we can say that a given reaction is morally permitted if and only if there is *no* morally decisive reason for not reacting in the given way. Note that on this account what makes a reaction permitted is the *absence* of a certain kind of reason—i.e., the absence of a morally decisive reason for *not* reacting in that way. Thus a reaction's being permitted does not entail that there is any sort of reason at all which *supports* reacting in that way. It is not the presence of a 'morally adequate' reason which grounds permission; rather, it is the absence of a reason sufficient to ground a prohibition.

Given the notion of a morally decisive reason, then, we can offer an account of what it is to be morally required, forbidden, or permitted.[10] Obviously, however, this account will not be very helpful until something is said about what it is for a reason to be morally decisive. Let us start with two preliminary points. First, since we are concerned with what is required by *morality*, the relevant reasons—whether decisive or not—must be moral ones. That is, the reasons must be morally acceptable. It is logically possible that there are some reasons for action which, although genuine, have no weight from the moral standpoint; if so, these are simply irrelevant to our discussion. For a reaction to be morally required it must be backed by a morally decisive reason. Such a reason must itself be morally acceptable, and it needs to be decisive only in comparison to the other morally acceptable reasons.[11]

Second, it should not be thought that the morally decisive reason has to be, in some sense, a *single* reason. In any particular case, there may be several reasons that support reacting in a given way, and it might be that although no one of them would be decisive by itself, together they do provide a decisive reason for reacting in that

[10] Note that, on this account, talk of what morality requires does not presuppose the existence of a moral law-giver (whether divine or human). The suggestion that such a law-giver is presupposed by talk of moral requirements is no more plausible than the comparable claim that talk of what reason requires presupposes a giver of the laws of thought.

[11] Thus it is logically possible that a reaction is *morally* required, and yet the agent is nonetheless *rationally* required (or perhaps, required all things considered) not to react in that way. On some moral theories this possibility can be ruled out (either there are no genuine reasons for action that are not morally acceptable, or there are such reasons but moral reasons always outweigh them); but I will not pursue the issue here. The possibility should also be noted that there may be reasons which have weight from the moral standpoint but which are not genuine reasons for action for some individuals. Once again, this possibility is ruled out by some moral theories, but the issue will not be pursued here: those sympathetic to the possibility should make the assumption that we are merely examining the question of what is required from the moral standpoint.

way. In such cases, it is typically a matter of convenience whether we refer to 'the' morally decisive reason, or speak instead of the various reasons that are collectively decisive. (Similarly, of course, even when the various reasons for reacting in a given way are not collectively decisive, it is still often convenient to speak of 'the' reason for reacting in that way.)

These two general points are familiar ones, but they do not take us very far toward understanding what it is to be a morally decisive reason. Assuming that the reason in question is a morally acceptable one, what more is necessary for it to be morally decisive? Now the original model, in effect, assumes that being morally decisive is simply a matter of outweighing the opposing reasons. In a typical case, a given reaction will be supported by various reasons, while other reasons will oppose reacting in that way, and favor reacting in some alternative manner. (In rare cases, of course, all relevant reasons may support the same reaction.) In some cases, however, the weight of the reasons in support of the given reaction may be greater than the weight of the reasons that oppose it. On balance, that is, the reasons that support the given reaction may outweigh the opposing reasons; the latter may be overridden by the former. In such cases, according to the original model, there is a morally decisive reason for reacting in the given way. In short, all that is required for a reason to be morally decisive is that it outweigh the opposing reasons.

Now the suggestion that a morally decisive reason must outweigh the opposing reasons is an extremely plausible one. It is certainly hard to see how a reason for reacting in a given way could be decisive if it was itself outweighed by more powerful reasons that supported reacting in some other way. And even if those countervailing reasons were only *as* weighty as the original reason, it still seems inappropriate to claim that the original reason provides a *decisive* reason for reacting in the given manner. So let us assume that a necessary condition for being a morally decisive reason is that the reason override the opposing reasons.[12]

What is less clear is whether we should take this condition to be

[12] Assuming that outweighing is an asymmetrical relation (if A outweighs B, B cannot outweigh A), introducing this condition may rule out the possibility of some or all types of moral dilemmas (situations in which no matter how the agent reacts, to react in that way is immoral). I will not explore the question of how those who wish to leave open the possibility of such dilemmas should alter the account I am offering.

not only necessary but also sufficient. It is not obvious that the mere fact that a morally acceptable reason outweighs the opposing reasons guarantees that the reason is morally decisive. Could there be cases in which a reaction is backed by a morally acceptable reason which is, in fact, stronger than the opposing reasons—and yet, nonetheless, the reaction is not morally required? On the original model, this question could not easily be entertained: being required just *is* a matter of being backed by the balance of reasons. But one advantage of speaking in terms of morally decisive reasons is that it allows us to raise the possibility that other conditions must be met as well before an overriding reason grounds a moral requirement. We can ask: What else, if anything, is necessary for a reason to be morally decisive?

Not surprisingly, this is a point on which competing moral theories may differ. For any given proposal, it is obvious that an adequate defense would need to explain why the given candidate should be taken as a necessary condition on being a morally decisive reason. But here I only want to mention several possibilities. First, it might be suggested that a morally decisive reason must be of a certain minimum strength. Otherwise, even if the reason outweighs the opposing reasons, the whole matter may be too trivial to ground a moral requirement. Second, for reasons related to the first point, it might be suggested that a morally decisive reason must outweigh the opposing reasons by more than a certain minimum. Third, it might be suggested that a morally decisive reason must meet certain specifications as to its content (e.g., that the supported reaction involves the welfare of *others*). We have already assumed that a morally decisive reason must be a morally acceptable one, but this suggestion would go beyond that restriction: there may be some morally acceptable reasons whose content nonetheless makes them incapable of grounding moral requirements. Fourth, it might be suggested that a morally decisive reason must meet certain motivational conditions, conditions that are not necessarily met by all morally acceptable reasons (not even overriding ones). For example, it might be suggested that a morally decisive reason must be capable of providing motivation for action, in some specified way.

Conditions of the sort I have been describing might be called *direct* conditions on moral decisiveness: in a given choice situation, whether a reason is morally decisive or not will depend only upon the nature of the reason itself and the nature of the various opposing reasons. Intuitively, moral decisiveness is here determined directly by the reasons at play in the choice situation itself. But one might propose *indirect* conditions on moral decisiveness as well: for such conditions, intuitively, moral decisiveness is determined in part by global considerations concerning the system of reasons as a whole.[13] Thus it might be suggested, fifth, that a morally decisive reason must be a member of a set of reasons, the general acceptance of which *as* morally decisive would be optimal. Or, sixth, it might be suggested that a morally decisive reason must be a member of a set of reasons which rational contractors could agree to accept as morally decisive. Finally, it might be suggested that a morally decisive reason must be one such that if an agent fails to act on it, there is a morally acceptable reason for the agent to be punished, or otherwise blamed.

Obviously, the list of possible conditions—whether direct or indirect—could be expanded considerably. Without taking the time to evaluate the various proposals, it would be inappropriate to assume that none could be adequately defended. Therefore, I propose to leave open the possibility that more will be required for moral decisiveness than the mere fact that the reason in question outweighs the various opposing reasons. Furthermore, for the time being at least, when entertaining the possibility that extra conditions are indeed necessary for moral decisiveness, I will try to be neutral on what those conditions might be.

To be morally required, then, is to be backed by a morally decisive reason. And, at the very least, for a reason to be morally decisive it must outweigh the various opposing reasons. But it is possible that this is not sufficient; there may be extra conditions necessary for moral decisiveness.

Suppose, then, that we have a factor which normally generates a reason to react in a given way. It does not automatically follow that in any particular case there will be a moral requirement to react in that way, since the reaction may not be backed by a morally decisive reason. For our purposes it will be helpful to distinguish three basic ways this might occur.

[13] Recall the distinction between direct and indirect moral theories introduced in Chapter 1.

First, we must not overlook the possibility that, although a reason is normally generated to react in the given way, in the particular case at hand that reason may not be generated at all. Other factors present in the specific case may interact with the original factor in such a way as to prevent it from generating a reason of the kind that it normally generates. In effect, the reason to react in the given way will have been *undermined*—it won't actually arise at all in the particular case in question. Obviously, if the given reason is not even generated in the particular situation, it can hardly be morally decisive.

Second, assuming that the reason is indeed generated in the specific case, opposing reasons may be sufficiently strong so that the given reason fails to outweigh them. The clearest case, of course, will be one where the countervailing reasons actually manage to override the given reason; but so long as the reason in question fails to outweigh the countervailing reasons, it will not be morally decisive.

Third, even if the given reason outweighs the opposing reasons, it may fail to meet some extra condition necessary for moral decisiveness. It may fail to meet this condition through some intrinsic shortcoming (e.g., it is not the right kind of reason to be morally decisive), or the failure may be the result of various other factors (e.g., factors at work in the particular case).

There are, then, three basic ways that a reason which is normally generated can nonetheless fail to ground a requirement in any particular case. The reason can be undermined, overridden (or, more generally, fail to outweigh), or fail to meet some extra condition necessary for moral decisiveness. Depending on the details of the specific case, different factors may be responsible for the reason's failure to ground a requirement: the failure may be due to the existence and nature of other reasons, the intrinsic character of the given reason itself, the presence of various factors which undermine the generation of the reason, and so on. It will be helpful, however, to have a single term to cover all of these possibilities, so let us say that—regardless of the details—*countervailing considerations* prevent the reason from generating the requirement.[14]

---

[14] I can now confess that I was somewhat imprecise in several earlier passages where I spoke of a reason's being outweighed as though this were the only mechanism that could explain why the given reason does not ground a requirement; as we have seen, it is actually only one of the ways in which countervailing considerations can prevent the generation of a requirement.

ORDINARY MORALITY

Armed with this account, we can return to the explanation of how the moderate can be committed to the existence of a pro tanto reason to promote the good and yet nonetheless also embrace constraints and options. The moderate must hold that despite the existence of the pro tanto reason to promote the good, countervailing considerations in particular cases frequently prevent the pro tanto reason from grounding a requirement. And depending on the specifics of the case, these countervailing considerations may generate a constraint or an option. Let us consider these points more carefully.

When the moderate denies the existence of a general requirement to promote the overall good, he does not of course hold that one is never required to promote the good. Rather, the claim is that specific cases in which one is required to promote the good are sufficiently rare so that it is misleading—or worse—to speak of any such general requirement. In more typical cases, options may permit one to react in a nonoptimal manner, and, in at least some cases, the optimal reaction may even be ruled out by a constraint. Thus the moderate must hold that, despite the existence of the pro tanto reason to promote the good, in typical cases the promotion of the overall good is not backed by a morally decisive reason.

Now although there are, in principle, three basic ways in which countervailing considerations can prevent a reason from generating a requirement, only two of these are available with regard to the pro tanto reason to promote the good. For the moderate cannot claim that the pro tanto reason to promote the good is sometimes undermined. That is, the moderate cannot hold that although a reason to promote the good is often generated, in many specific cases such a reason is not generated. For as I have already argued, the moderate is committed to the existence of a *pro tanto* reason to promote the good: even if the reason often cannot ground a requirement, the fact that a given reaction will promote the good always provides *some* reason for reacting in that way.

If, then, the moderate is to hold that in particular cases the pro tanto reason to promote the good fails to be morally decisive, he must avail himself of one (or both) of the two remaining approaches. He can argue that in the given case the pro tanto reason to promote the good is overridden by various opposing reasons (or, at least, that it fails to outweigh the opposing reasons). Or he can argue that in the given case the pro tanto reason to promote the good fails to meet some other condition necessary for being morally decisive. Much of this book can be understood as an investigation of alternative attempts to pursue one or another of these strategies.

The first approach is reasonably straightforward. For example, we intuitively take constraints to be backed by extremely forceful reasons, presumably reasons powerful enough to outweigh the pro tanto reason to promote the good. If the moderate can defend the existence of such reasons, we have a clear account of why an agent is not required to promote the good when doing so involves violating a constraint. Similarly, if the appeal to cost can be shown to generate reasons powerful enough to outweigh the pro tanto reason to promote the good, the moderate will have an account of why an agent is not required to promote the good when doing so involves a considerable sacrifice.

The second approach is somewhat less familiar. Whether the moderate can show that in typical cases the pro tanto reason to promote the good fails to meet some further condition necessary for moral decisiveness (other than that of being overriding) will obviously depend, in part, on which specific conditions are endorsed. It is clear that some such arguments are doomed to failure. For example, since the moderate holds that in some cases the agent is in fact required to promote the overall good, the moderate cannot very well go on to claim that the pro tanto reason to promote the good is by its very nature incapable of being morally decisive. But other arguments may be available to show that the pro tanto reason will often—although not always—fail to meet some necessary further condition. As we shall see, e.g., there is a way to understand the appeal to cost so that it involves the claim that when the cost to the agent is significant, the pro tanto reason to promote the good fails to meet a specific motivational condition necessary for morally decisive reasons. If this view can be defended, the moderate will have, once again, an account of why promotion of the good is not required in those cases where it involves significant sacrifice.

If the moderate can successfully pursue either or both of these approaches he will have an explanation of why there is no unqualified requirement to promote the good; if either approach can be adequately defended specifically with regard to the appeal to cost, the moderate will in fact have an explanation of why there is not even a general requirement to promote the good—that is, not even within the limits of constraints. And, obviously enough, this explanation will be compatible with the moderate's commitment to the existence of a pro tanto reason to promote the good. But regardless of his actual success in defending this view, recognizing the possibility of such countervailing considerations helps to clarify the structure of ordinary morality. Indeed, analyzing the features of ordinary morality in the terms suggested here better enables us to see what it is that the moderate must show if ordinary morality is to be successfully defended. Let us reconsider constraints and options in this light.

An agent-centered constraint forbids the agent to react in certain ways, even though such a reaction might best promote the overall good. Now if there is to be such a general prohibition against the agent reacting in the way in question, this must be due to the typical existence of a morally decisive reason not to react in the given way. Therefore, the heart of the defense of any given constraint will be the justification of the claim that in the relevant cases the agent has a reason not to react in the given way. The moderate must point to some feature of the type of reaction in question and explain what it is about this feature that typically generates a reason for the agent not to react in that way. (Of course, this reason need not be generated in every case; most obviously, it need not be generated if none of the reactions available to the agent is of the given type.) Furthermore, obviously enough, the reason pointed to must be sufficiently powerful so that in a broad range of cases it will be morally decisive.

In particular, since a constraint forbids a given reaction even when it would promote the overall good, the reasons backing the constraint must be powerful enough to outweigh the pro tanto reason to promote the good. For example, the moderate holds that I am forbidden to kill the one to save the two, and he supports this claim by appealing to a constraint against harming. A defense of this constraint, therefore, would need to identify some feature of harming and explain how this feature generates reasons distinct from, and able to outweigh, the pro tanto reason to promote the good.

Given a defense of this sort, the moderate may go on to claim that the reasons backing the constraint *always* outweigh the pro tanto reason to promote the good. That is, the moderate might hold that no matter how much good is at stake (e.g., whether it is two lives, one hundred lives, or one million lives that can be saved by killing the one), the pro tanto reason to promote the good cannot possibly provide a reason sufficiently powerful to balance the reasons backing the constraint. If so, then the constraint will be absolute; it will lack a (finite) threshold. It should be noted, however, that the moderate could defend the constraint along the lines suggested, but go on to deny that the constraint is absolute. Such a moderate could plausibly maintain that although the reasons backing the constraint are normally powerful enough to outweigh the pro tanto reason to promote the good, in extremely unusual cases—where a great deal of good is at stake—they are not. In such unusual cases, the given reasons will not be morally decisive, and it will be permissible to promote the good even though this involves reacting in a way that the constraint would normally forbid. In short, the reasons backing the constraint may be quite powerful without being infinitely so; the constraint may have a (finite) threshold.

It is worth noting that the reasons backing a constraint will be, in an important sense, agent-relative. A defense of a constraint against a given reaction locates some morally offensive feature in that reaction, and explains how that feature generates reasons. Now if the constraint is to hold for all, the feature must generate reasons regardless of the agent: anyone who entertains reacting in the given way must face the existence of a reason *not* to react in that way. But this does not mean that *everyone* has equal reason to be concerned with *every* reaction of the given type—regardless of whose reaction it is. The reason is not agent-neutral in this way.

If the reason backing the constraint were agent-neutral, then an agent would have as much reason to be concerned with the violations of the constraint performed by others as he would have to be concerned with his own violations: the reasons backing the constraint would support violating the constraint when this was the only way to minimize other violations. It would be, e.g., permissible to kill the one in order to save the two from being killed. But obviously this was just the sort of reaction that was supposed to be forbidden by a constraint against harming. In short, if the moderate is to defend a genuine constraint against a given reaction, the reasons backing the constraint cannot be agent-neutral; they must, instead, be agent-relative. In any particular case, the reason is only generated for the individual agent who might react in the way in question. It is the *agent* who has a particular reason to see to it that that specific instance of the given reaction does not occur. If, then, the moderate can establish the existence of such an agent-relative reason, and demonstrate that it is typically morally decisive, he will have established the existence of an agent-centered constraint.

In contrast to agent-centered constraints, agent-centered options do not require or forbid any particular reactions. Rather, options permit the agent to react in various ways that are nonoptimal, if the agent so chooses; but they do not require that the agent react in the nonoptimal manner. Still, if the moderate is to defend an option, a central part of what he must show is that in a range of cases the agent is permitted to react in a nonoptimal manner. Now as I have discussed, a given reaction will be permissible provided that nothing forbids it—i.e., in the absence of a morally decisive reason for *not* reacting in that way. The moderate, therefore, must show that in the given range of cases, the promotion of the good is not typically supported by a morally decisive reason.

Of course, if there are constraints, it will trivially follow that there is at least one range of cases in which promotion of the good is not backed by a morally decisive reason—those cases where the optimal reaction would violate the constraint. But such cases obviously do not involve *options*, for with an option the agent is *permitted* to react in the optimal way if he so chooses. To defend an option in a given case, therefore, the moderate must show not only that the promotion of the good is not supported by a morally decisive reason, but also that the promotion of the good is not *opposed* by a morally decisive reason.

It may be worth remarking on a second point that arises in connection with constraints. The extremist holds that even if there are constraints, agents are required to promote the good within the limits of those constraints. The moderate, of course, denies this. Imagine, then, a case in which the reaction that would *best* promote the overall good is forbidden since it would violate a constraint. Assuming that the second best reaction in terms of the promotion of the good would not violate any constraint, the extremist would claim that *this* reaction is required. The extremist would argue that although the pro tanto reason to promote the good provides somewhat greater support for the initial reaction than it does for this second best reaction, when the force of the reasons supporting the constraint are added in as well, the balance of reasons supports reacting in the second best way—and these reasons are morally decisive.

Now if the moderate is to deny this claim—i.e., if he is to maintain the existence of an option to refrain from reacting in this second best way—it obviously will not suffice to have argued that the reaction that *best* promotes the good will not be backed by a morally decisive reason. Thus, in order to defend options, the moderate must show that the pro tanto reason to promote the good typically fails to be morally decisive, even in its support for the reaction that best promotes the good *within* the limits of constraints. Presumably, however, if the moderate can demonstrate how countervailing considerations can prevent the pro tanto reason to promote the good from generating a requirement in those cases where constraints are not involved at all, these same considerations will prevent the generation of a requirement to promote the good even within the limits of constraints.

Clearly, then, if he is to defend an option, the moderate must point to countervailing considerations that prevent the pro tanto reason to promote the good from grounding a requirement, but— as we have also noted—these countervailing considerations must not themselves be sufficient to ground a constraint. As we have seen, there are two basic approaches available to the moderate. First, the moderate might argue for the existence of reasons which—in the relevant range of cases—counter the force of the pro tanto reason to promote the good. If, in a given case, the pro tanto reason to promote the good is unable to outweigh these opposing reasons, it will not be a morally decisive reason, and so the agent will not be required to promote the good. Provided that the moderate can also show that the opposing reasons are not themselves morally decisive, he will have established the existence of an option.[15] Second, the moderate might argue instead that—

[15] Must the opposing reasons be agent-relative ones? Since, by hypothesis, these reasons can oppose and outweigh the pro tanto reason to promote the good, the answer depends on whether or not one can coherently maintain that a given goal lacks objective value, even though it is backed by agent-neutral reasons. If one can maintain such a position, then the opposing reasons need not be agent-relative ones (although they may be); if such a position cannot be maintained, however, the opposing reasons must be agent-relative.

although it typically outweighs the opposing reasons—the pro tanto reason to promote the good frequently fails to meet some extra condition necessary for moral decisiveness. In such a case, the agent will not be required to promote the good. Yet, at the same time, since the opposing reasons will themselves be outweighed by the pro tanto reason to promote the good, they too will fail to be morally decisive—and so the agent will not be forbidden to promote the good either. In short, the moderate would again have established the existence of an option.

Neither approach commits the moderate on the question of whether the option has a threshold. Suppose, for example, that he takes the first approach, and defends the claim that in a certain range of cases reasons will be generated that oppose the reaction that will promote the good. The moderate can claim, plausibly, that in extremely unusual cases in which a great deal of good is at stake, the pro tanto reason to promote the good can indeed outweigh the opposing reasons, even though it cannot do so normally. The option will then have a threshold. Or the moderate can maintain instead that in the relevant range of cases the opposing reasons can never be outweighed by the pro tanto reason to promote the good. The option will then lack a threshold: the agent will be permitted to react in the relevant nonoptimal way no matter how much good is at stake. Similarly, if the moderate adopts the second approach, he can hold that although the pro tanto reason to promote the good normally fails to meet some extra condition necessary for moral decisiveness, it does meet the condition in extreme cases, so the option will have a threshold. Or he can maintain that for the relevant range of cases the pro tanto reason to promote the good never meets the extra condition, and so the option lacks a threshold.

Understanding options and constraints in the way I have been discussing allows us to redescribe a central argument of the first chapter. I suggested there that the most plausible defense of options will be based on an appeal to the cost to the agent of promoting the good. The difficulty for the moderate was that the appeal to cost seemed to support not only options to allow harm, but also unacceptable options to do harm. I argued that if he is to avoid options to do harm, while retaining the appeal to cost, the moderate must establish the existence of constraints. We can now state this argument more precisely.

To defend options the moderate must identify countervailing considerations that prevent the pro tanto reason to promote the good from grounding a requirement. The appeal to cost is the most plausible candidate for such an argument, and, in principle, the moderate could try to develop it in two ways. He could claim that the potential cost to the agent generates reasons that oppose making a sacrifice, and when the cost of promoting the good is significant enough these reasons outweigh (or at least balance) the pro tanto reason to promote the good. Or he could claim that when the cost is significant this will somehow guarantee that the pro tanto reason to promote the good will fail to meet some further condition necessary for moral decisiveness. Regardless of which approach the moderate takes, the appeal to cost, if successful, helps to demonstrate the absence of a morally decisive reason for promoting the good.

Consider, then, the permissibility of doing harm. In typical cases, no doubt, the pro tanto reason to promote the good will provide some reason why an agent must not react in this way. But if the appeal to cost is successful, then this reason cannot be a morally decisive one when the cost to the agent is significant. Therefore, if the moderate is to resist options to do harm, he must point to the existence of some *other* reason not to do harm—a reason that will normally be morally decisive. And, obviously enough, the sort of reasons that would ground a constraint against doing harm will be of just the right kind. Thus, if the moderate can establish the existence of the relevant constraint, he can retain the appeal to cost while resisting options to do harm.

However, one difficulty remains. It seems logically possible that although certain features of doing harm normally generate reasons adequate to ground a constraint, the appeal to cost might prevent those reasons from grounding a constraint when the cost to the agent would be significant. After all, if considerations of cost generate reasons that oppose making significant sacrifices, then it is logically possible that these same reasons will outweigh (or balance) the reasons that normally generate the constraint. And on the other hand, if considerations of cost can prevent the pro tanto reason to promote the good from meeting some further condition necessary for moral decisiveness, perhaps they can do the same for the reasons supporting the constraint. The possibility remains, therefore, that it will be permissible for the agent to do harm when the cost to the agent of not doing so would be significant. Even an appeal to a constraint may not be adequate to resist options to do harm.

The logical point must be conceded. Appeal to the sort of reasons that would normally support a constraint does not automatically guarantee that the moderate can avoid options to do harm. Yet despite the logical possibility of inadequacy, the constraint may nonetheless be quite sufficient—in fact—for the moderate's purposes. On the one hand, the reasons backing the constraint may very well be sufficiently powerful to override the reasons generated by the appeal to cost; and on the other hand, despite the fact that considerations of cost may prevent the pro tanto reason to promote the good from meeting some extra condition necessary for moral decisiveness, the reasons backing the *constraint* may well be immune to such an attack. Whether the constraint can actually overcome the appeal to cost in this way will, of course, depend on the details of the appeal to cost and the constraint. But the moderate can take comfort in the fact that there is no reason to assume that a constraint against harming will be inadequate for resisting options to do harm.[16]

Given the general account that I have been suggesting, then, the moderate's success at defending ordinary morality will turn on his ability to establish the presence or absence of various morally decisive reasons. Now it should be noted that the reasons in question are reasons for action: that is, they are reasons for a given agent, in a given situation, to react in a given way. Thus a constraint turns on the *agent* having (from the moral standpoint) a reason—indeed a morally decisive reason—not to react in certain ways. And an option turns on the agent lacking (from the moral standpoint) a morally decisive reason to react in various ways. But

---

[16] It may be worth remarking that it is open to the moderate to claim that although the reasons backing the constraint are typically able to overcome the appeal to cost, this is not *always* so. The moderate might suggest that in very rare cases (perhaps where the harm to be done is slight, and the cost to the agent of refraining is extremely great) the appeal to cost does prevent the reasons that support the constraint from being morally decisive. In such a case it would be permissible to do harm. In effect, the constraint would have a second kind of threshold—one based on the cost to the agent, rather than on the objective good that could be promoted—although presumably this threshold must be an extremely high one if the position is not to be unacceptably minimalist. In adopting this position, the moderate would thereby also be embracing a severely restricted option to do harm. I will not consider this possibility further.

it might be suggested, however, that it is a mistake for us to focus on what reasons the *agent* has to react or not react. Rather, we should focus on what reasons there are for *morality* to require, forbid, or permit, various reactions.

I believe, however, that there is less to this objection than meets the eye. Nothing would be lost if we restricted ourselves to analyzing questions of moral requirement and permissibility in terms of the agent's reasons for action.[17] For example, if one holds that there is sufficient reason for morality to *require* a given reaction, then presumably one would also want to claim that—from the moral standpoint at least—the agent does indeed have a morally decisive reason to react in that way. Similarly, if one holds that there is sufficient reason for morality to *permit* a given reaction, then presumably one would also want to claim that, even if the agent happens to have *some* reason not to react in the given way, his reason is not a *morally decisive* one. (Suitable additions to the account of what is necessary for moral decisiveness should be able to guarantee this.) I see no reason, therefore, to modify the approach I have been suggesting. But having noted this point, it must also be admitted that there is no pressing need to regiment all ensuing discussion into the terms I have been suggesting here. Although it will often be helpful to keep them in mind, in what follows I will not tediously limit myself to presenting the moderate's arguments in terms of the presence or absence of morally decisive reasons.

THE NEUTRALITY OF THE FRAMEWORK

The discussion in this chapter, particularly in the second half, has been rather abstract. I have been concerned to articulate a framework in which the structure of ordinary morality can be examined. And I have used this framework to try to clarify what it is that the moderate must demonstrate if he is to defend the basic features of ordinary morality. But I have largely tried to do this

[17] And something might be gained: we would reduce the temptation to assume that morality is something that has been (or could be) designed. Such a view sometimes seems to be implicitly suggested by talk of what reasons there are for morality to have or lack certain features. The view may or may not be correct; but our official language of analysis should not bias the question.

without committing the moderate in advance to any particular arguments; we have considered structural possibilities and necessities compatible with a variety of specific positions, and this has given the discussion its fairly abstract character. In the following chapter, however, I will return to the detailed investigation of the moderate's attempts to put flesh on these structural bones. We will examine the moderate's specific attempts to defend options and constraints.

But before returning to this subject, one last issue must be examined. We must be sure that the framework I have been developing is a neutral one. That is, we must be sure that my way of setting out the problem does not beg any questions against the moderate. For it might be suggested that by beginning with the pro tanto reason to promote the good, I have unfairly prejudiced the issue in the extremist's favor. After all, the key ingredient in a defense of the extremist's position is simply being assumed without argument, while the moderate is being required to defend all the pieces essential to ordinary morality.

As this chapter should have made clear, however, the moderate has no real ground for making such an objection. The pro tanto reason to promote the good is indeed one element in ordinary morality, and the moderate cannot deny this without retreating into a minimalist position. So the moderate can hardly complain about the fact that he is not being asked to defend some feature of ordinary morality—that the feature will be taken as given. The moderate would, of course, have an objection if I presupposed that the pro tanto reason to promote the good has a strength or importance which it does not possess in ordinary morality. But I have made no such assumption.

Now it must be admitted that an objection similar to the one given might be legitimately raised by a minimalist. For the minimalist denies the existence of the pro tanto reason to promote the good, and consequently the existence of such a reason cannot be assumed without begging the question against the minimalist and in favor of the moderate and the extremist. In a full investigation of the positions of the extremist and the moderate, it would indeed be appropriate to insist that a defense of the pro tanto reason to promote the good must be provided. But in this work we are only asking whether the moderate can successfully fend off the simultaneous attacks of the minimalist and the extremist. It would be a hollow victory indeed if the moderate could only avoid the extremist by accepting an overly minimalist position.

If ordinary morality is to be defended, the moderate must establish the existence of both constraints and options. It is to the attempt to do this that we now return.

3

Doing Harm

Moderates specify some range of reactions and erect constraints against them. In the first chapter we considered some general attempts to justify a constraint against harming—more specifically, against killing. But we did not attempt to demarcate the line between 'killing' and 'not killing' at all precisely, relying instead on the intuitive consensus that even if killing one individual is the only way to save two others from being murdered, if I refrain from killing the one, I have not *killed* the two. However the boundaries of 'killing' are marked off, the constraint against killing is not meant to be so broad as to encompass my relation to the two if I fail to save them. To evaluate the arguments of the first chapter it wasn't necessary to draw the line more precisely.

In this chapter and the next, I want to consider two of the most plausible ways of drawing the line. These two approaches are not extensionally equivalent (although there is a great deal of overlap); consequently, the corresponding constraints are not identical. Equally importantly, the most plausible motivations for the two approaches differ, thus suggesting distinct ways that the corresponding constraints might be defended, and distinct problems. Defenders of each approach have tended to downplay the importance of the distinction championed by defenders of the alternative approach, but I think that both distinctions have at least some intuitive support. The first distinction is that between doing (or bringing about) and (merely) allowing. The second distinction is that between intending (as an end or as a means) and (merely) foreseeing.

Intuitively, we distinguish between cases where I bring about some event by my actions, and cases where I (merely) fail to prevent some event although it was within my power to do so. If I hold Basil's head under water until he is dead, that death is something I have brought about; his drowning is something that I have *done*. In contrast, if I stand back idly and watch Maude drown rather than pull her out, I have not drowned her—have not brought about her drowning by my actions—but I have *allowed* her death. It is not as though when I allow her death I must be doing nothing at all, of course: I may be skipping stones or admonishing her for going out so soon after eating, etc. But the salient moral feature of my reaction is not any of these acts which I *am* doing, but rather the fact that there is an act which I am *not* doing—but which I could do, and which would prevent the death if I did it.

If I watch Friedrich shoot Immanuel when I could have stopped him by tripping him, then I not only allow Friedrich's shooting of Immanuel, I allow Immanuel's death. (In appropriating the term 'allow' to cover all those cases in which an agent fails to prevent some event although it was within her power to do so, I may depart somewhat from ordinary usage.) But Friedrich's shooting and Immanuel's death are not things I bring about, not things I *do*, only things I *allow*. Had I tripped Friedrich, however, we would have a case of doing—his bloody nose is something I would have brought about.[1]

Having suggested the distinction, let me immediately introduce a term to straddle it, for it will be useful to have an expression covering the entire range of possible reactions: regardless of whether I bring about an outcome or merely allow it, let us say that I *countenance* that outcome. When I *allow* harm (or good), there is some alternative reaction—other than my actual one—under which the countenanced outcome would not have occurred. But when I *do* harm (or good), my reaction itself brings about the countenanced outcome.[2]

The distinction between doing and allowing is one to which we frequently appeal—and (at least at first glance) one which intuitively carries moral weight. If I kill the one to save the two, the death of the one is something I bring about; while if I refrain from

---

[1] Although one can comfortably speak of 'doing harm' (or good), it is, of course, improper to talk of 'doing an outcome'. One needs to shift terms, and speak instead of 'bringing about' a given outcome. No similar shift is necessary for 'allowing'. I do not think, however, that these various incomplete grammatical parallels, and other infelicities of expression, indicate any serious problems for our discussion.

[2] It is worth noting that sometimes we (correctly) speak of ourselves as allowing social evils to continue—thereby hiding from ourselves the more disturbing fact that we may actually be involved in sustaining those evils.

killing the one, and the two die, their deaths are harms which I merely allow. This has suggested to many moderates that the difference between doing and allowing is the distinction we seek—that is, that the constraint against harming should be construed as a constraint against *doing* harm.

The second commonly suggested distinction is that between harm which is intended (whether as an end or as a means) and harm which is merely foreseen. When I fail to send a check to famine relief, after reading an appeal for funds, I can foresee that some individuals will die who might have been saved, but I do not intend their harm as a means to accomplishing some end. In contrast, if I kill uncle Albert in order to inherit his wealth, his death is a *means* to my accomplishing my end: the harm to him is something I intend. Puzzling cases can be constructed where it is difficult to decide whether some event is a means or not, but for the most part the distinction seems clear. When I set out to accomplish some end, some events I countenance are means to my end—whether because they will cause the end, or because they are necessary to ensure the end is not prevented, and so on. Other events I bring about or allow, however, are merely foreseen, but are not means to my end—are not themselves part of my plan to achieve my goal: they are unintended (even though foreseen) side-effects of my reaction. It should be noted, in particular, that it does not follow from the mere fact that a harm is brought about or allowed intentionally—i.e., deliberately, not accidentally—that it is *intended* (in the sense being distinguished here): rather, harm is intended only when it is countenanced as a means or as an end. (This restriction of the term 'intend' to those cases where the harm is countenanced as a means or as an end is a common one in moral philosophy, although it may be another departure from ordinary usage.)

If I kill the one to save the two, then the harming of the one is a *means* to accomplishing the end of saving the two: here the harm *is* intended. If, however, I refrain from killing the one, I foresee that the two will die—as a side-effect of my reaction—but I do not *intend* their deaths as means to some end. This has suggested to many moderates that the constraint against harming should be construed as a constraint against *intending* harm.

These two interpretations of the constraint against harming agree on the the impermissibility of killing the one to save the two. For this reason, it was not necessary to distinguish the two interpretations

in considering the arguments of the first chapter.[3] However, the
two distinctions are not coextensive, but rather cut across each
other, yielding four possibilities.

	Do	Allow
Intend	(1) Doing harm that is intended as a means or an end	(4) Allowing harm that is intended as a means or an end
Foresee	(3) Doing harm that is merely foreseen as an unintended side-effect	(2) Allowing harm that is merely foreseen as an unintended side-effect

The two cases we have concentrated on are: (1) doing harm
where this is intended as a means—such as killing uncle Albert to
inherit his wealth, or killing the one in order to save the two; and
(2) allowing harm where this is merely foreseen—such as (presumably) allowing the two to be killed, rather than killing the one. But
there are two other possibilities: (3) doing harm where this is
merely foreseen as an unintended effect of achieving one's end—
such as killing people downstream with chemical wastes introduced
into the sewage by new processes intended to increase production;
and (4) allowing harm where this is intended as a means—such as
deliberately allowing a patient to die so that his body can be used
for medical research.

A constraint based on the distinction between doing and
allowing would prohibit countenancing harm in cases (1) and (3),
but not in cases (2) and (4)—although, of course, *other* moral
considerations might speak against specific cases of (2) or (4). A
constraint based on the distinction between intending harm and
merely foreseeing it would prohibit countenancing harm in cases
(1) and (4), but not in cases (2) and (3)—although, again, other
moral considerations might speak against specific cases of (2) or

[3] Talk of doing harm and allowing harm in the first chapter was meant to be
neutral between these two distinctions, although for obvious reasons it may have—
unfortunately—suggested the first. Since the sort of killings we considered were
cases of intending as well as doing, while the allowings to die were cases of
unintended (merely foreseen) allowings of harm—I believe that no questions were
begged against either interpretation.

(3). Thus the two interpretations agree about (1) and (2), but differ over the status of cases (3) and (4).

Advocates of the one distinction have generally denied any moral weight at all to the other distinction. Initially, at least, this seems misguided—for *both* distinctions appear to carry intuitive weight. It would be surprising if advocates of the doing/allowing distinction didn't themselves feel any pull toward the claim that cases of type (4), e.g., are worse than cases of type (2)—thus giving *some* moral weight to the distinction between what is intended and what is foreseen. Similarly, advocates of the intend/foresee distinction presumably often feel some pull toward the claim that, e.g., cases of type (3) are worse than cases of type (2)—thus giving *some* moral weight to the distinction between doing and allowing. This suggests that a defense of ordinary morality, if it wants to do full justice to our intuitions, should recognize the importance of *both* distinctions—even if one is considered less central. (I am, however, unaware of any moderate who has attempted to defend such a system.)

Be that as it may, most discussion has been by way of championing one distinction over the other. A great deal of energy has been devoted to constructing hypothetical cases in an attempt to determine whether intuition actually supports a constraint against doing harm, or a constraint against intending harm. Such discussions certainly have value, but I do not intend to enter that contest here. For intuitive support may still leave the distinctions dangling. Instead, I want to consider some of the problems that face erecting constraints on the two distinctions. In this chapter we will examine the distinction between doing and allowing, and the suggestion that there is a constraint against doing harm. In Chapter 4 we shall turn to the constraint against intending harm.

PARALYSIS

It seems plausible to locate the moral offensiveness of doing harm in its causal character. (Indeed, this is the obvious suggestion.) Now a moment's reflection reveals that this will have to be modified slightly: for it cannot only be *actually* causing harm to another which is forbidden; some forms of merely *risking* harm to another must be prohibited as well. But this in turn suggests an important objection—and our discussion must begin with it. If sound, it would reduce the constraint to absurdity—for it claims that a constraint against doing harm would prohibit my doing anything at all.[4]

Suppose that in order to save the two from death I need not actually *kill* the one, but need only point an electric harpoon at his heart and squeeze the trigger. Undoubtedly he will die, of course, but let us imagine that it is simply the pulling of the trigger (when the gun is loaded and aimed) which saves the two others. The constraint against doing harm forbids me to shoot—for I will be bringing about the death of the one, and this is prohibited. So far so good. But what if I were to object that it is not certain that my victim will be killed, indeed it is not even certain that he will be harmed? There is, after all, *some* probability that he will escape unharmed, through some fluke of electronic malfunction. If the constraint only prohibits *certain* harm, then in our contingent world it will prohibit next to nothing. The response to such an objection, of course, is that the constraint against doing harm rules out more than those cases (if such cases there be) where it is 100 percent certain that harm will result. But this is where the problem arises: how *much* more?

Imagine that there is a gizmo attached to my electric harpoon, with a dial marked off in gradations from 0 percent to 100 percent. As I move the dial down from 100 toward 0, I effectively decrease the likelihood that the harpoon will actually fire when I squeeze the trigger. Does the constraint permit me to pull the trigger when there is only a 90 percent chance of killing my given victim? What about 89 percent? It seems that the defender of the constraint against doing harm can only offer two sorts of answers. The first possibility is this. He can pick some general cutoff point, and claim that, say, the constraint only forbids a 73 percent or greater chance of doing harm; below that risk a simple balancing of moral considerations is permissible. But this first response, obviously, is hopelessly arbitrary. How could 73 percent be so important? How could 72 percent be different in kind?

It might be suggested that 50 percent makes the most plausible choice. After all, when the risk is greater than 50 percent, it is more likely than not that harm will actually be done; and for any risk lower than this, it is most likely that harm will not be done. Thus

---

[4] The objection derives from Fried, pp. 18–20.

the 50 percent mark does not seem to be an arbitrary cutoff point. Yet it seems inadequate nonetheless. For if the constraint only forbids a 50 percent or greater chance of doing harm then, clearly, it permits a 49 percent chance of doing harm. That is, the constraint does not forbid my squeezing the trigger so long as the dial is set at 49 percent instead of 50 percent. But despite the fact that it is now more probable than not that no harm will actually be done, it remains true that the decrease in the risk (in moving from 50 to 49) is all but negligible. It is hard to see how this minimal decrease in risk can morally introduce an utter difference in kind. The risk, after all, is still quite significant: it is only *slightly* more likely than not that no harm will be done. It seems implausible to suggest that suddenly, at 49 percent, the constraint against doing harm simply no longer applies; and it seems unlikely, at any rate, that the defender of the constraint would be willing to accept this claim.

If we rule out this sort of cutoff response, however, then it seems that the defender of the constraint must answer instead that *any* chance of doing harm (i.e., anything greater than 0) would be forbidden by the constraint. I cannot aim the harpoon and squeeze. Indeed, I cannot even aim without squeezing, for surely there is some chance that it will fire accidentally.

But this second response would simply lead to general paralysis. For there is absolutely *nothing* that I can do which does not carry *some* risk of harming others. Driving a car risks maiming a pedestrian, cooking supper risks harming my housemates, and turning on a light risks electrocuting my neighbors. As long as a constraint against doing harm rules out any action which has some probability (no matter how small) of bringing about harm—then no actions at all will be permitted. I will have to stay huddled in the corner, not daring to move, trying not to breathe too loudly.

The result is clearly unacceptable, and if the objection cannot be met we have an uncommonly good argument against any proposed constraint against doing harm. Can the objection be met? I believe it can be, but not in a manner which will be acceptable to all defenders of the constraint.

What I suggest is that the constraint against doing harm must be construed as having a sliding threshold, a threshold which diminishes with the decrease in probability of harm. The threshold for risking taking the life of another with 90 percent probability may be quite high—high enough, e.g., so that I cannot shoot a gun at one even in order to save two. But the threshold is not infinite: I may be able to risk a 90 percent chance of killing another in order to save, say, 100 others. At 60 percent the threshold is lower, perhaps making it permissible to impose such a risk in order to save 70 others. At 10 percent the threshold is lower still; and at 1 percent, even lower. As the risk of death approaches 0 percent, the threshold itself approaches zero—the constraint offering next to no barrier to the promotion of the good. (Matters, of course, are more complicated, since one would have to weigh the 60 percent likelihood of killing one against the probability distribution of saving a number of others, e.g., the 85 percent chance that at least 80 others will be saved, the 95 percent chance that at least 60 will be saved, etc. But it is easier to get the idea across if we keep things simple.)

According to this suggestion, cooking supper—despite its risk of poisoning others—does not fall under the constraint because the risk is so slight that the threshold is easily passed when trying to achieve some good. Driving the car runs a somewhat greater risk, but presumably here too the threshold is low enough so that the constraint is relaxed in the face of the good which can be accomplished. Similarly for the various other low risk actions which were in danger of being prohibited by the constraint. This is not to say, of course, that other considerations may not prohibit some of these acts in various cases—but this will not *trivially* (and unacceptably) follow from the constraint against doing harm.

This meets the objection, I believe, but will not be acceptable to all who are inclined to defend the constraint. First of all, this reply is not available to those who believe that the constraint is absolute—having an infinite threshold—for the reply requires a sliding threshold.[5] More importantly, the reply may unacceptably remove various acts from the jurisdiction of the constraint. Thus, the threshold when my harpoon is set at 90 percent may be high

---

[5] This is slightly inaccurate. The sliding threshold approach actually is compatible with the view that the constraint has an infinite threshold—provided that the threshold is only infinite when the risk is great enough. There may be a particular level, say N percent, such that the threshold asymptotically approaches infinity at that level (and the constraint will thus be absolute when the chance of doing harm is greater than N percent); provided that the threshold is finite and decreases as the risk decreases from N percent to 0 percent, this will solve the problem of paralysis.

enough so that the constraint forbids my squeezing the trigger in order to save the two; and the threshold—though lower—may still be high enough at 30 percent to forbid my squeezing to save the two. But at *some* probability the threshold is going to have to be low enough so that the constraint is relaxed in the face of the opportunity to save the two.[6] So the constraint will not forbid pulling the trigger with the dial set at that (low?) probability. Yet many will find this unacceptable, thinking that to deliberately aim and pull the trigger of a harpoon—even if there is only a slight chance that the harpoon will actually fire—is just the sort of act which the constraint against doing harm was supposed to forbid.

For such people, then, my suggestion meets the objection—but at too great a cost. I do not, however, know of any other way around the objection. This may give some moderates reason to abandon their advocacy of the constraint against *doing* harm, and switch instead to the constraint against *intending* harm. (It should be noted that one cannot offer a parallel objection to the constraint against intending harm. On the one hand, squeezing the trigger with the dial set at 2 percent can be prohibited by such a constraint on the grounds that it is intentionally risking harm as a means. And on the other hand, although driving a car may similarly risk harm to pedestrians, their facing the chance of harm is only an unintended side-effect, and so driving is *not* prohibited by the constraint. Consequently there is no general paralysis: not all risks are prohibited by a constraint against *intending* risk.) Other moderates, however, may be comfortable with this sort of sliding threshold, and what it implies.[7] So let's consider other problems the constraint faces.

[6] Thus in any given situation there will be a cutoff point of sorts; but it will not be the same point for all situations, and so it will not be arbitrary in the same way that the general cutoff point of the original proposal would have been: although on the sliding threshold proposal a slight increase in the probability of the harm may be prohibited when the expected benefit remains constant, the increased risk *will* be permitted if there is a slight corresponding *increase* in expected benefit; the original proposal, however, would have selected some probability point and made it different *in kind* from its neighbors. Of course it might be objected that any sliding threshold will *still* be arbitrary in that it could have been made higher or lower, and it is hard to see what could justify a particular curve. This may be so. If it *is* so, then the only suggestions which would escape arbitrariness altogether would be an infinite threshold for any risk of harm—which leads to paralysis—or a zero threshold—which would fail to rule out killing the one to save the two. (For more on zero threshold constraints, see Chapter 5.)

[7] The sliding threshold approach discussed in the text is, in effect, the suggestion that the level of the threshold is a function of the probability of inflicting harm. This

INTERFERING

I have suggested that it is plausible for the moderate to locate the moral offensiveness of doing harm in the causal character of doing. (I also noted the need to include the mere risk of causing harm, and not only actually causing harm—but let us hereafter leave this problem to one side.) Although the suggestion is obvious enough, it may lead to difficulties for the moderate—for on some views, agents cause far more harm than we might have realized. Some extremists have argued that if I fail to prevent some harm when I am in a position to do so then I am a *cause* of that harm—for had I not failed to react appropriately the harm would not have occurred. They would say that when I stand back and allow Maude to drown, e.g., I am a cause of her death.[8] If this is correct, then we seem to have a powerful objection against the moderate who advocates a constraint against doing harm—for either the constraint must be abandoned, or it must be interpreted more liberally than the moderate desires.

Extremists who hold the view that I am a cause of harms I fail to prevent need not deny that there are differences between the various ways I cause harm. Situations which we have wanted to describe as examples of merely allowing harm might be called examples of *negative* causation; for it is the absence of the appropriate reaction which is a cause of the ensuing harm. Negative causation can be contrasted with the more typical case of *positive*

view should not be confused with the independent suggestion that the level of the threshold is (also) a function of the *size* of the harm that may be inflicted—although it is compatible with this suggestion, which is also quite plausible. Note, furthermore, that neither of these two suggestions entails that the functions in question are linear. For example, an act with twice the risk of inflicting a given harm as a second act need not have exactly twice as high a threshold: it could be lower than twice as high, or much higher. Similarly, an act that will inflict a harm twice as great as a second act need not have twice as high a threshold: it could be lower than that, or much higher. Finally, note that the approach discussed in the text (whether alone, or in combination with the second view) does *not* imply that acts with identical expected harms (size of harm × probability of inflicting that harm) must have identical thresholds. That is, an act with a high risk of inflicting a small harm need not have a low threshold, even though the expected harm is the same as for some other act with a small risk of inflicting a greater harm which *does* have a low threshold.

[8] 'A cause of her death' or 'a cause of her dying'? Why does one sound better than the other?

causation—e.g., when I hold Basil's head under water until he dies—where my reaction directly brings about the result. The extremist can concede that the difference between positive causation and negative causation may be important for the purposes of action theory, or metaphysics. But he will deny that the distinction has moral importance, and he can bring out the problem that this creates for the moderate by posing a question: Shall we consider all cases of causing harm—whether positively or negatively—cases of doing harm? Or shall we consider only the positive causation of harm to be doing harm?

If all cases of causing harm are to be considered cases of doing harm, then in the case where I can save the two by killing the one, the constraint against doing harm apparently forbids not only my killing the one (positive causation of harm) but also allowing the two to die (negative causation of harm). But I cannot avoid doing one or the other. So either the constraint must be abandoned, or it must be interpreted more liberally, permitting me to *minimize* the harm I do when I cannot altogether avoid doing harm. And this would mean killing the one so as to save the two. Thus the constraint against doing harm would be retained (at least in name), but given our decision that allowing harm is a form of doing harm, the constraint would be barely recognizable by the defenders of ordinary morality.

If, on the other hand, only cases of positive causation are to be considered doing harm, then the extremist might object that the only explanation of the moral offensiveness of doing harm which has been suggested, is that it is the *causing* of harm. But once we realize that allowing harm is negatively causing harm, there is no justification for having a constraint singling out *doing* harm. We would either have to erect a second 'constraint', against *allowing* harm—interpreting both liberally so as to permit the minimization of my causing harm—or more straightforwardly, do away with both constraints. Once again, this would mean permitting killing the one to save the two.

How might the moderate respond to this objection? The most obvious way, of course, is to deny the extremist's initial claim that to fail to prevent some harm is to be a cause of that harm. (I myself am unsure about the issue of negative causation, and find the arguments of both sides uncompelling.[9]) Instead of pursuing this

[9] Cf. the papers by Harris, Kleinig, and Mack.

line, however, I want to suggest a second response. The moderate might argue that we have inadequately diagnosed the source of the moral offensiveness of doing harm. When we locate it more precisely, we find sufficient reason for singling out positive causation for special treatment—regardless of whether there is such a thing as negative causation. For what is wrong with doing harm is not causing harm per se, but interfering with the welfare of another.

Intuitively, the idea is this: often agents step into the causal flow in such a manner as to alter the outcome of processes which were already under way. This is in contrast to cases where the agent simply lets the on-going process continue. In the former case, but not the latter, the agent can be said to *interfere*: he makes a difference in a way that he does not when he merely refrains from altering the causal flow.

Obscure as the notion of on-going processes may be, the concept of interfering certainly seems to point to *something* of importance. When I bring about harm to another he is worse off because of me; I interact with the causal nexus in such a way that it would have been better for him had I not interacted at all. The relevant processes which were under way would have sustained his well-being. But I step in, alter them, and interfere: and he is the worse for it. Had I simply left him alone—indeed, had I never even existed— he would have been better off. When I merely allow harm, however, I do *not* interfere with the well-being of another: I simply permit the processes which were already under way to take their course. That I do not alter the processes is brought out by the fact that had I never even existed he would have been no worse off. This suggests a rough intuitive test of whether an agent has interfered with another, thus falling foul of the constraint against doing harm. It is a counterfactual test: we ask whether the victim would have been better off had the agent not existed: if the answer is 'yes', then the agent has interfered; if the answer is 'no', then he has not.

Our intuitions about interfering seem to discriminate correctly between my holding Basil's head under water until he drowns, and my mere failure to save Maude when she is struggling with the waves. Basil is worse off for my being in the world: had I never existed, the harm would not have befallen him. I have interfered with his life. But Maude can make no such complaint. She is none the worse for my existence; had I never existed, she would still be drowning. I have not interfered with *her* life.

Therefore, even if the extremist is correct to say that my failure to provide aid is a negative cause of Maude's death, by locating the moral offensiveness of doing harm in interference rather than causation per se, the moderate can defuse the extremist's objection. And if there is *no* negative causation, the moderate will still have gained by having more carefully focused the explanation of what is *wrong* with doing harm. Thus the moderate can sidestep the issue of negative causation altogether. Even if positive causation is the only sort of causation there is, the notion of interfering may help us to adjudicate difficult cases, articulating what it is to do harm. And if there *is* negative causation, the notion of interfering will also enable the moderate to protect the constraint against doing harm from the extremist's criticism.

We will still need, of course, an explanation of why a *constraint* against interfering should be erected; but the focus on interfering seems to fit well with other of the moderate's beliefs, such as the intuition that the special compellingness of constraints must arise from the appropriate sort of facts about the particular agent herself. If the endangered individual would have been harmed even had the agent *never existed*, it might plausibly be maintained that the appropriate sort of facts about the agent's relation to the world— necessary to ground a constraint on her action—do not obtain.

The rough counterfactual test works well with standard cases: if I fail to send famine relief, and some individual dies of starvation, I have not interfered, for he would have been no better off had I never existed. If I send poison to some unsuspecting stranger, however, I *have* interfered: he would have been better off had I not existed. In the latter case, but not the former, I violate the constraint against doing harm.

Now in fact the counterfactual test as I have described it won't quite do. There are gimmicky cases for which the test gives what is intuitively the wrong answer about whether the agent has interfered. Suppose a King slits the throat of his oldest son, so that the second oldest may inherit the throne. Surely the father has interfered with the welfare of the poor boy, violating the constraint against doing harm. Yet the King might exclaim that had he never existed the *son* would not have existed, and so the victim would have been no better off. Thus the counterfactual test yields the intuitively incorrect result that the King has not interfered. Qualms about whether the dead son might not actually have been better off never having been born at all just don't seem to the point: the test, as I've stated it, excuses too much.

As a second gimmicky case, suppose that after the coronation of the second son, the third son squanders his lesser inheritance and—dying of starvation—comes before his older brother, begging for food. But the second son is as ruthless as his father, and allows his younger brother to starve to death. He is ruthless, yes. But intuitively we feel that the second son has not *interfered* with the welfare of the third. Yet (the ghost of) the third son might exclaim that had the second son never existed the third son himself would have inherited the kingdom and would not have starved; so the victim would have been better off had the agent never existed. Thus the counterfactual test yields the intuitively incorrect result that the ruthless son has interfered with his younger brother. Therefore the test, as I've stated it, condemns too much.

These are, as I say, gimmicky cases. The moderate's response to them is undoubtedly that they show only that the counterfactual test would need to be made a bit more precise in order to capture adequately the notion of interfering. Our intuition is quite clear that the test has gone wrong in these cases; and it may not be worth the trouble to describe the test more accurately.

In fact, however, it is not at all clear whether the counterfactual test can be adequately repaired. To see this, let's ask how we might revise the test so as to handle the first case, where the King cuts the throat of his oldest son. The King truthfully observes that since the son owes his very existence to his father, had the King never existed the son would have been no better off. The problem with the test seems to be this: since we are wondering whether the King interferes when he cuts the throat of his son, our focus is too broad if we imagine the King's never having existed at all. The relevant question seems to be not, would the son have been better off had the King never existed, but rather, would the son have been better off had the King not existed at the time he was cutting his son's throat. To the latter question the answer is obviously yes. This suggests that the proper counterfactual test for interference is to ask whether the victim would have been better off had the agent not existed at the time of the reaction in question.

Intuitively, an agent can interfere with an on-going process even though the existence and nature of that process is not altogether independent of the agent's existence. In particular, an agent can interfere with a process at a given time even though the process would not exist at that time were it not for the *previous* existence of the agent. Since the original, rough counterfactual test asked what would have happened if the agent had never existed *at all*, the change it asked us to imagine was too drastic. The test altered too much. What was needed was a more fine-grained approach, and this is provided by the suggested revision. Furthermore, not only does the revised counterfactual test give us the intuitively correct answer for the gimmicky case of the King, it continues to provide the intuitively appropriate answers in the more standard cases as well. (It must be admitted, however, that the revised test still *condemns* inappropriately in the second gimmicky case, in which the second son allows his younger brother to starve.)

Unfortunately, however, even the suggested revision is still too crude. Imagine that while dining alone with the Queen, the King confesses his ill treatment of their son. Stunned by the news, the Queen begins to choke on her food and is in danger of choking to death. The King rushes to her side, pounds her back with his left hand until the food is dislodged, and the Queen's life is saved; at the same time, however, he deliberately stabs her in the leg with the dagger in his right hand, causing the Queen to limp for the rest of her days. Having saved the Queen's life is, of course, commendable. But surely the King's stabbing the Queen interferes with her welfare, and violates the constraint against doing harm. Yet the King may exclaim anew that had he not existed at the time of the stabbing, the Queen would have died, and so would not have been better off than she is (with her limp). Thus even the revised test excuses too much, yielding the intuitively incorrect result that the King has not interfered.

Apparently we need to focus the counterfactual test even more narrowly. The original test altered too much in asking whether the victim would have been better off had the agent never existed at all. Although the revised test is an improvement, it seems that in asking what would have happened had the agent not existed at the time of the act in question, it still changes too much. We need to focus on the act itself, and see whether *its* existence alters the outcome of the on-going processes. This suggests the following refinement of the counterfactual test: the agent interferes by reacting in a given way if the victim would have been better off had the given reaction not occurred. Since the Queen would have been better off had the King not stabbed her, the King's stabbing the Queen interferes with her well-being. Here, at last, we have a test that does not seem to excuse too much.

But if this latest version of the test does not excuse too much, this is at least in part because it condemns far too much. Not only does the test still fail on the second gimmicky case, involving the death of the youngest son, even in *standard* cases where we want to say that the agent has not interfered, the test no longer gives the intuitively correct answers. If I stand back idly and watch Maude drown, for example, I have not interfered with her. Yet consider my reaction of refusing to jump in and rescue her: had that reaction not occurred, I would have reacted differently; in particular, it seems, I would not have refused to jump in.[10] But had I jumped in, we can suppose, Maude would not have drowned. So in failing to jump in—the test now tells us—I *do* interfere with Maude's life. Similarly, in failing to send money to famine relief I interfere with the life of some stranger who dies of starvation, for had my reaction not occurred— had I sent money—someone's life would have been saved. And so on. Furthermore, if we stick to the suggestion that the moral offensiveness of doing harm should be located in interference, it now turns out that all of the cases we want to classify as cases of merely allowing harm are nonetheless cases of interfering, and so are just as offensive. Thus the justification for the constraint against *doing* harm (as opposed to merely allowing harm) disappears.

Rather than accepting this consequence, it seems more plausible for the moderate to insist that the latest version of the counter-factual test is grossly inadequate as a test of whether an agent has interfered or not. Our intuitive picture of interference is that of an agent stepping into the causal flow and altering it. That notion has not been captured by any test that yields the result that failure to step into the causal flow is itself a way of stepping in.

So the latest version of the test needs to be rejected as well. Indeed, the most vivid way of bringing out the inadequacy of that version is that it accuses the agent of interfering, even in cases where the victim would have been no better off had the agent never existed at all! But this, of course, brings us back to the original

---

[10] The argument could be considerably complicated by considering rival views in action theory on the individuation and identity of events. Some of these views would require modifications in the statement of the test, and corresponding modifications in the argument.

version of the counterfactual test, whose own shortcomings we have already noted.

It does seem that in our successive revisions of the counterfactual test we have ended up with a version that has largely lost contact with the notion of interference it was meant to capture. But this still leaves us with the question of whether the test can be salvaged after all. I can let the point go for now, remarking only that I do not know of any more promising ways to sharpen the test so as to get around gimmicky cases (while at the same time, of course, preserving our judgments in the standard cases);[11] nor do I know of any more promising alternatives to the counterfactual test. As we shall see, this may lead to a genuine problem when we consider more controversial cases.

For the most part, however, it remains true that reliance on the notion of interference seems to help in explicating our judgment about various cases. And the original counterfactual test remains a rough and ready guide. If the doctor withholds medicine and you die, he has not brought about your death—for he has not interfered with your life: you would have been no better off had he never existed. But if I stop the doctor at gun point as he is about to give you the medicine, and keep him tied up until you have died, then I *have* brought about your death—for I have interfered with your life: you would have been better off had I never existed. (Gimmicky case: suppose I was the inventor of the medicine. More difficult case: suppose that in the original example, where the doctor freely withholds your medicine, had the doctor never existed, some other doctor would have been assigned to give you your medicine, and would have done so—so you would have been better off. Is that a gimmicky misapplication of the test?)

Problems about gimmicky cases aside, then, the notion of interfering seems to capture correctly those reactions which the

---

[11] What about this proposal? The agent has interfered when the victim would have been better off had the agent not been *present* at the time in question. Interestingly, this meets the original two gimmicky cases: the oldest son would have been better off had the King not been present at the time he slit his throat; and the youngest son would not have been better off had the second son not been present while he starved. Unfortunately, this test still fails for the gimmicky case involving the King and Queen. Furthermore, since what counts as not being 'present' must be relative to the power of the purported means of interfering, disputes over whether the imagined change of location is sufficient will arise. Ultimately, for example, the youngest son may claim that no change of physical location of the second son successfully eliminates his presence, only nonexistence will do that; and so the second gimmicky case would return.

constraint against doing harm is meant to cover. We can use the concept both to interpret the constraint, and as a beginning of an explanation of the constraint. Indeed, I am unable to think of any other explanation that the moderate might offer of the moral offensiveness of *doing* harm. He must begin with the observation that the agent is *interfering* with the welfare of another. (Recall that for those who are sceptical of negative causation, the notion of interfering may simply be an attempt to explicate our original concept of (positive) causation.)

As I have observed, even if the moderate locates the moral offensiveness of doing harm in the fact that it involves interfering, he will still need to defend the claim that this supports the erection of a *constraint*. But it should be noted that once we assume that the proper response to the moral offensiveness of interfering does involve the erection of a constraint, then it is a constraint against *doing* harm that is supported. For as we have seen, intuitively at least, cases of doing harm involve interference with the welfare of another, while cases of allowing harm do not involve such interference.

In contrast, a constraint against *intending* harm cannot be supported by an appeal to the notion of interfering. For in the two types of cases in which the constraint against intending harm diverges from the constraint against doing harm, an appeal to interfering supports the latter as opposed to the former. On the one hand, a constraint against intending harm forbids countenancing harm as a means (or an end) even when this harm is only allowed. Yet since allowing harm does not involve interfering—even when the harm is deliberately allowed as a means—an appeal to interfering cannot justify the full prohibition against intending harm. And on the other hand, a constraint against intending harm does not automatically prohibit doing harm in those cases where the harm is not a means (or an end). Yet since all cases of doing harm involve interference—even when the harm done is not a means but only a mere side-effect—an appeal to interfering cannot justify the constraint's restriction to cases where harm is intended.

In short, it is only the constraint against doing harm, and not the constraint against intending harm, that is supported by an appeal to the moral offensiveness of interference. This reinforces the point made at the start of this chapter, that it is important to distinguish clearly between these two constraints, for the most plausible motivations for the two constraints differ. And it strongly supports the suggestion that the constraint against doing harm should be interpreted and defended in terms of interference.

But if this is correct, then the moderate faces serious difficulties, for I believe that so construed the constraint against doing harm will in fact yield judgments unpalatable to the moderate. It is not that there are more gimmicky cases than might at first meet the eye, but that the constraint itself (as interpreted with the aid of the concept of interfering) has some unexpected implications.

DIFFICULT CASES

Consider this case: my rival is sure to win the coveted Wise Prize for Living Philosophers, unless he dies before a given date—in which case the lucrative award will go to me. Fortunately for me, he lies comatose in the hospital, and his condition is deteriorating. Unfortunately for me, he is being sustained by a variety of life-support equipment, and he will not die in time for me to win in his stead. Seizing my chance, I sneak into his room late at night, and turn the machinery off. He breathes a last breath—and dies. I have killed him.

Contrast this with the following case: after months of seeing their comatose son kept alive through the use of exotic and resource-consuming medical equipment, the parents decide it would be better to let their son die than to meaninglessly prolong his deteriorating life. The proper legal/medical boards add their consent, the duly authorized doctor disconnects the life-support machines—and the boy dies. After months of prolonging life, the doctor has allowed him to die.

Not everyone, perhaps, will agree with the intuitive judgments I have offered about these two cases. But many, I think will be inclined to accept them. When I maliciously unplug my rival's life-support machines, I kill him; when the doctor—acting out of due concern for all those involved—disconnects the machines preserving the comatose boy, she merely allows him to die. This, at least, is the way that many people would like to describe the cases.

It is rather puzzling, however, how the judgments about both cases can be maintained. For the two cases seem structurally similar. The medical condition (we can suppose) of the two patients is the same. In both cases, the life-preserving machinery is turned off, and death is the outcome; had the machines continued to operate, neither patient would have died. How can the cases differ according to the doing/allowing distinction?

One difference between the two cases, of course, is the fact that the second case involves a doctor, who—it might be suggested—may have special obligations or rights by virtue of her professional role. But even if such differences can help justify different moral evaluations of the two cases, it is not clear how the fact that the agent in the second case is a doctor can affect the question of what it is she *does*. If I have killed my rival, how can it be denied that the doctor—justifiably or not—has killed the comatose boy?

Those who support the claim that the doctor merely allowed the boy to die will argue that the medical staff had been providing aid, and then—after careful consideration—*stopped* providing aid. And to refrain from giving aid is not to kill—it is merely to allow to die. So it might be said. Yet what the doctor did was turn some machines off—and this is just what *I* did when I *killed* my rival. Left plugged in, each set of machines would have continued to aid its patient. The doctor took steps to see that this would not happen; so did I. How can we treat the cases differently?

Similar problems greet many other judgments we are intuitively inclined to make: if parents starve their children to death, many of us want to describe the reaction of the parents as *killing*—a case of doing harm. Yet if the same people were to pass by a starving beggar, knowing that he will soon die unless he eats, their reaction would typically be described as *allowing* to die. Given the structural similarities, it is difficult to see how both judgments can be maintained. For in both cases, the reaction is failure to provide food, knowing that death will be the outcome. Once more, not everyone will agree with these judgments. But for those who share them, there is a problem. How can we treat the cases differently?

The problem remains for the moderate who follows the suggestion of the previous section and construes doing harm in terms of interfering. This certainly seems to settle the question of how the difficult cases are to be described, but it leaves us unable to make the various discriminations that our intuitions support. On the one hand, the doctor and I *both* violate the constraint—for the concept of interfering suggests that both of us are involved in cases of killing: had we not acted, the patients would have remained alive; they are worse off for our having been in the world. (If the moderate tries to excuse the doctor on the grounds that she was part of the group which provided the aid in the first place, isn't this an inappropriate gimmicky response, like that of the King to his oldest son?) And on the other hand, the parents apparently do *not* violate the constraint, no matter whom they leave to starve, for it seems that failing to provide food—even to one's own offspring—will not be a case of *interfering*. (Might the moderate claim that to have brought a child into the world and then to have allowed her to starve is to have made her worse off than if she had never been brought into the world at all—thus suggesting that the parents interfere after all? Or is this merely a gimmicky misuse of the concept of interference?) Thus if we explicate the distinction between doing and allowing in terms of interfering, we will be unable to preserve our intuitive judgment that for each pair of cases, one member of the pair is an example of doing harm, while the other member is an example of merely allowing harm. So let us ask again: how can we treat the cases differently?

One possibility is this: when we make judgments about killing and allowing to die, we make implicit reference to a set of norms. If the reaction violates the norm, then it becomes the salient feature of the explanation of the ensuing death—and we say that the agent brings about that death. If, however, the reaction is in keeping with the norm, then it is not the salient feature of the explanation of the death—and we say that the agent merely allows the death. When parents deliberately fail to provide food for their own children, it violates the appropriate norm—and so they have killed; but if one merely fails to provide food to a stranger, one acts within the norm—and so the death is merely allowed.

Something like this seems capable of explaining the difference between our original two cases. When I disconnect the machines keeping my rival alive, I plainly do what is forbidden; I violate moral norms (whether in acting without authorization, or in having the wrong motive, or what have you)—and so we say I've *brought about* the death of my rival. But the doctor is not in obvious violation of any moral norm—indeed, many would insist that she clearly does what is morally right—and so we say that she has merely *allowed* the death of the boy. The thought that it is the very people who have been providing the aid that now want to stop providing that aid—and that surely this is their right—may add to the intuition that the doctor acts within the appropriate norms. In contrast, *I* stop the aid being provided by *others*—surely something I have no right to do—confirming the intuition that I violate the appropriate norms.

So a theory that turns on the notion of norms might be able to preserve many of our intuitions about doing and allowing. Obviously, to develop the theory one would have to say much more about the concept of norm on which it is based. Two senses seem potentially relevant. First, there is a descriptive sense—the norm may express typical, common, *normal* behavior. Second, there is a *normative* sense, a moral sense—the norm may express the boundaries of what is permitted, required or forbidden. These two senses may be connected: the typical reasonable person may be expected to act within the bounds of morality, or at least the morality promulgated in his society.

Now the theory I have just sketched is too crude to withstand careful examination. We certainly do not seem to judge a harm to be allowed in all and only those cases where the agent acts in keeping with the norms. On the one hand, an agent who fails to save the drowning child by throwing the life preserver only allows her death, even though such behavior presumably violates the appropriate norms. And on the other hand, an agent who kills in self-defense has clearly brought about the death of his attacker, even though his response presumably does not violate the appropriate norms. So at best, such a norm theory would have to be limited to some specified range of cases. I do not know whether an adequate version of such a theory could be developed; but it still seems to be at least a promising possibility, and it is hard to see how else we might preserve our judgments about the difficult cases.

What does seem clear, however, is that if the advocate of a constraint against doing harm were to adopt a theory of this type it would fatally weaken his position. For the moderate wants to justify moral judgments about various cases by reference to a constraint against doing harm. Yet with such a norm theory, he would have to settle which reactions are cases of doing harm—as opposed to merely allowing harm—by referring to the appropriate set of norms. As a result, judgments about which reactions are examples of doing harm will *presuppose* moral judgments rather than being grounds for *making* moral judgments.[12]

---

[12] Cf. Davis, 'Priority'.

This is most obvious if—once the theory is developed—the appropriate sense of norm turns out to be that of moral norms. For in that case, a judgment about whether we had a case of doing or allowing would presuppose a decision about whether or not the given reaction violates moral norms. Thus such a judgment would be no aid in settling moral disputes: it would beg the question.

If the appropriate sense of norm turns out to be the descriptive sense, the moderate is still in trouble. For typical behavior is likely to be largely informed by the morality which is promulgated in the society. If judgments about whether we have cases of doing harm or allowing harm are relative to what behavior is common in the society, then such judgments cannot provide independent moral justification or condemnation of that behavior.

Either way, then, the moderate risks replacing a substantive moral principle with a trivial one. If in certain crucial cases the line between doing and allowing is relative to a set of norms, then—in those cases, at least—the constraint against doing harm is only an illusion of a significant moral guideline.

The moderate, of course, need not adopt this norm theory, and can thus avoid trivializing the constraint against doing harm. But then we are back to our original difficulties arising from our different intuitions about what appear to be structurally similar cases. I do not know of any other promising suggestions for preserving those judgments. The only solution then would seem to be abandoning one or the other of the intuitions for each of the pairs.

Which intuitions the moderate will abandon will, of course, be guided by his account of what it is to bring about an outcome. But I imagine that the most plausible line would be to claim that the doctor kills the boy (just as I kill my rival), and that the parents merely allow their children to starve (just as they allow the beggar to starve). As we have seen, these are the judgments that the moderate must offer if he is to explain doing harm in terms of interfering. And this means that for many, the constraint against doing harm will have unpalatable implications. If starving one's children is merely allowing their deaths, then it seems that the appeal to cost cannot be ruled out for such cases, and the moderate may have to concede the permissibility of a parent starving his offspring when it would (significantly?) interfere with his projects to feed them. Thus, when coupled with the appeal to cost, the constraint against doing harm would *excuse* too much. Similarly, since the constraint against doing harm not only forbids my unplugging my rival, but also forbids the doctor disconnecting the comatose son, many will have to conclude that the constraint also *condemns* too much.

These problems may cause some moderates to rethink their conviction that a constraint against doing harm is the line they actually want to draw. But there may be some who are comfortable with what the constraint implies about the difficult cases we have discussed. Such moderates need to be shown just how deep the difficulties run.

AID

The difficult cases in the previous section suggest (if nothing more) that the constraint against doing harm may both excuse too much and condemn too much. But such cases may seem of limited interest. For if the constraint inappropriately excuses the parents who starve their children, the moderate can still hope that some *additional* constraint might be found to prohibit such reactions. (Perhaps a special obligation to one's children? Belief in such constraints is common, although rarely defended.) And if the constraint is thought to inappropriately condemn the doctor, the moderate can still hope that such cases are fairly rare, arising only under unique conditions.

But this last hope won't withstand reflection. There is a common sort of case which it seems we must describe as one of doing harm—at least given the account of interfering we have sketched—but which the moderate presumably does *not* want to describe as doing harm. This type of case suggests that the constraint against doing harm is far stronger than the moderate has realized. Unacceptably strong.

In all of these cases aid is, so to speak, on the way. Some good will soon be in the possession of some individual—unless the agent interferes. Either it will be delivered to those in need, or the one in need is on his way to claim it. If the agent reacts in such a way as to keep the individual from receiving/taking the aid, then he interferes, and it seems that such cases must be described as examples of doing harm—forbidden by the constraint.

Let's begin with a case of this pattern, which everyone (?) will agree is an example of doing harm. Imagine that food is en route to aid the starving members of some poor village, but that Abdul robs the caravan laden with the provisions, and escapes with the food: the villagers die of starvation, but would *not* have died had the food arrived. Abdul does harm to the poor villagers: he violates the constraint. (Does he *kill* them? That seems too strong. Yet on what grounds do we withhold such a description?) The moral import of the case does not alter if the caravan is not actually carrying food, but is rather carrying gold with which the villagers can purchase food. If Abdul prevents the gold from reaching the village, he still does them harm. And the same must be true if there is no caravan, but only a mailman carrying a certified check. If aid is forthcoming, to react in such a way as to prevent that aid is to violate the constraint against doing harm. For if Abdul had never existed, the villagers would not have been as badly off: he interferes with their welfare. To stop the mailman is to do the villagers harm.

Apparently the same must be true even if the check which the mailman is carrying is a personal check, voluntarily written by Abdul himself in an earlier, more philanthropic mood. For Abdul to try to excuse himself by noting that had he never existed the check would never have been on its way in the first place, is for Abdul to make the same gimmicky excuse that the King made when he slit the throat of his oldest son. We agreed that the counterfactual test would have to be spelled out in such a way as to eliminate such gimmicky loopholes; Abdul's excuse will evidently be eliminated as well. Therefore, if Abdul robs the mailman who carries Abdul's check to the starving villagers, he does harm.

Yet what can turn on the fact that the check is in the hands of the mailman? Suppose that Abdul writes the check, and hands it to a trustworthy friend, asking her to mail it. If he thinks better (worse?) of it a moment later, and asks the friend to return the check—then it seems he is still guilty of doing harm. For if *he* did not ask, the money would eventually reach the villagers—and Abdul thus interferes with that process of aid. Once we rule out the gimmicky excuse that he *started* the process of aid, we find that for him to try to stop that process is to do harm—in violation of the constraint. And if Abdul belongs to a voluntary program at work which regularly deducts from his paycheck a certain amount to send to famine relief, then the constraint forbids his ever quitting that program. And so on.

Presumably the moderate finds these conclusions unacceptable.

The constraint against doing harm condemns a range of cases, which the moderate has no desire to condemn. Nor should the moderate take refuge in the hope that the already recognized problem of gimmicky cases might be settled in such a way as to block the King, while leaving an out for Abdul.[13] For there are problematic cases where the agent has not himself instituted the process of aid.

Suppose that it is not Abdul who has written the check, but his uncle Moshe. Moshe points to the check lying on the desk and says, 'If you wish, you may take this check, and fill in your own name—with my blessing. But I have instructed my valet that if the check is still here in ten minutes, he is to send it to famine relief.' Abdul takes the check. Had he not acted, however, the money would have gone to the starving villagers: so apparently he has done them harm. The hope that adjudication of the gimmicky cases might help the moderate here seems slender indeed.

Obviously the cases can be multiplied endlessly. (If Gertrude does not come to the reading of the will, her younger sister Mopsy will inherit all. Gertrude does come, and Mopsy inherits less: apparently Gertrude has done harm to her sister.) Consider one more example: imagine that some liberal reformer has been elected to Congress, and has proposed a bill which will radically redistribute wealth in order to aid the poor and disadvantaged. The bill will pass unless some individuals vote against it: so anyone who votes against it does harm. (Does anyone who even *speaks* against it *risk* bringing about harm?) Similarly, the constraint earlier prohibited voting against the reformer during her bid for office—for without opposing votes, the reformer was sure to be elected. (Does the reformer do harm in proposing her bill—for without it, the property-owners would not lose their wealth? Apparently, the constraint forbids introducing the bill, or voting for it; but, once it is introduced, the constraint also forbids *opposing* it.)[14]

---

[13] It might be suggested, e.g., that we should distinguish between (1) stopping the very process of aid that the agent has initiated *before* it provides a (further) benefit, and (2) removing or undoing a benefit that has *already* been received (including benefits that the agent previously initiated). Intuitively, (1) can be acceptable, even though (2) is not; and Abdul, in taking back his check, is a case of the former kind, while the King only provides a case of the latter kind. However, whatever the intuitive merits of the distinction, it is far from clear how the moderate can avoid the unwanted conclusion that even cases of type (1) are examples of *doing harm*—given that the process of aid is already underway.

[14] This is a tricky case, so let me mention a similar one: It is wrong for Robin

These have all been cases where aid to some individual is forthcoming, and the agent acts so as to stop the process which will result in aid. There are also cases where the individual himself will take/claim some goods unless the agent acts in such a way as to prevent this. However, I do not know whether anything important turns on this classificatory distinction, so let me simply quickly mention some examples. (1) Responding to a knock, I open the door, and find a starving beggar. Unless I close the door, he will come in of his own accord, and take some food. I close the door. (2) There is medicine enough for one, but two of us need it. If I don't take it first, the other will take it. I take it.[15] (Indeed, I cannot take the unowned medicine even to save my *three* children, if I know that such a reaction will prevent someone from using all of the medicine himself.) (3) I go to the store and buy the last item of some product, knowing that if I don't purchase it, someone else will.

In all of these cases, someone is worse off as a result of the reaction of the agent. Gimmicky problems aside, we can roughly say that had the agents not existed, the various individuals would not have been as badly off.[16] The agents prevent the individuals from receiving the goods. Thus the agents do harm to those individuals, and the constraint against doing harm is far stronger than moderates have realized.[17] In a vast range of cases, it forbids reactions which the moderate clearly wants to permit. The constraint condemns far too much: the moderate must abandon it.

I can think of only two answers which the advocate of the

Hood to take from the rich to give to the poor—for this harms the rich. But given that he is bent on his evil ways, it is wrong for the Sheriff of Nottingham to try to stop him—for this harms the poor.

[15] Compare the case where there is enough medicine for both of us—but I rush ahead, gather it all, and lock the door. Or the case where I fence off the entire water hole.

[16] Suppose I raise the prices of the goods in my store, and some customers can no longer afford them and have to do without. Had I not raised the prices, the customers would have been better off: so I harm them. (Is it gimmicky to reply that if I weren't there at all they would be no better off? What if we assume that someone else would sell the goods? What if we assume that I manufacture the goods myself?) Apparently, successful capitalists harm their competitors as well as their customers: imagine that I open a new store and your business suffers as a result.

[17] Indeed, it may still not be appreciated just how strong it is: Suppose that I save Elias from choking to death. If—had he died—his organs would have been used to save the lives of two others, it appears that in saving Elias I do harm to those two other people; and thus I violate the constraint.

constraint against doing harm might offer. He might suggest that when the notion of interfering is carefully spelled out, the constraint will be seen not to have such unacceptably strong results after all. There is certainly no refuting such a reply, for it is simply holding out a hope. But there is no reason to be sympathetic to it either. Instead, it may well be that when we give substance to the concept of interfering we will find that it is not that the agent is not *actually* interfering with the welfare of others in the problematic cases, but that the moderate simply does not think that it is *wrong* to interfere in such cases.

This suggests a second response, however, which is that our notion of interfering is sensitive to the prior question of whether the agent acts in keeping with an appropriate set of norms (e.g., perhaps, within his rights). Perhaps the process of aid is not considered on-going in a sufficiently independent manner if the agent is able to affect the outcome while acting within the appropriate norms. One way to understand such a suggestion is this: we must not conceive of the on-going processes too narrowly, taking them to be already fixed. Instead, the status quo is rather fluid—for part of the status quo consists of the fact that various individuals have a certain range of actions legitimately open to them. As long as the agents act within that range they merely help determine what the status quo *is*, as opposed to *interfering* with it. But when agents act outside the legitimate range, transgressing the appropriate norms, they do not simply help determine the on-going processes—they interfere with them.

When Abdul robs the caravan, he does not act within his rights; but asking his friend to return the check *is* acting within his rights. Thus the former, but not the latter—according to this suggestion— is interfering. Similarly, to vote against the liberal reformer is to act within the appropriate norms; so is purchasing the last item at the store. Thus it might plausibly be suggested—at least for some important range of cases—that when we consider whether some agent's reaction interferes with some process of aid, if the reaction is within the appropriate norms, then we do not consider it interference. At the very least, such cases are not considered cases of *doing* harm.

This second response is familiar. It is simply a revision of the view we considered briefly in the previous section. And it is plagued by similar problems. For the moderate needs to offer an independent criterion for judging which reactions are cases of doing harm—in order to give the constraint substance. By building in considerations of norms, the moderate replaces his substantial moral constraint with the appearance of one—masking the fact that moral lines still need to be drawn, in a way that the moderate has not specified or defended. On this suggestion, it is not really the line between doing harm and merely allowing harm which is doing the work—for a constraint erected on the former notion, as it is straightforwardly construed, yields unacceptable restrictions. If the moderate is not to trivialize it, he apparently must abandon it.

THE RELEVANCE OF THE DISTINCTION

So far we have not pressed the moderate to justify the constraint against doing harm, but rather have tried to bring out some of the problems and unpalatable implications of adopting such a constraint. The problems raised in the previous sections are serious ones, and cannot be lightly dismissed; alone they might be enough to cause the moderate to abandon the constraint. But I want to go on now to consider the problems that the moderate faces when he actually tries to justify the constraint itself. So let us bracket the previous objections, and pretend that the notion of interfering can be spelled out in a nontrivial manner so that the corresponding constraint neither condemns nor excuses too much.

In Chapter 2 I argued that if the moderate is to defend a constraint against a given type of reaction, he must point to the existence of a morally decisive reason not to react in the way in question. Establishing the existence of such a morally decisive reason can be viewed in terms of a series of tasks. First, the moderate must isolate some feature of the given reaction, and indicate what it is about this feature that generates a reason not to react in that way. Second, since the reason will not be morally decisive in any particular case unless it overrides the countervailing reasons (if any), the moderate must argue that in a typical range of cases the given reason does indeed outweigh any relevant opposing reasons. Finally, it will be recalled that in Chapter 2 I left open the possibility that there may be additional conditions—beyond overriding the opposing reasons—that are also necessary for moral decisiveness. If so, then the moderate will have to argue that the given reason meets these extra conditions as well. Obviously enough, unless the moderate can perform all of these tasks, he will not have established the existence of a constraint.

Thus, to defend a constraint against doing harm, the moderate must demonstrate (for a broad range of cases) the existence of a reason which opposes doing harm—one which does so with sufficient power to override countervailing reasons, and which also meets any additional conditions that may be necessary for moral decisiveness. Now imagine, for the moment, that the moderate could fulfill the first of the tasks just outlined, establishing the existence of a reason which particularly opposes doing harm. The second and third tasks would, of course, still remain. However, I want to put aside discussion of the third. For although I have noted the possibility that there may be extra conditions necessary for moral decisiveness (beyond being overriding), I have not actually examined the plausibility of any particular candidates. Furthermore, even if there are such extra conditions necessary for moral decisiveness, I see no reason to believe, in the abstract, that they will pose any special difficulties for the moderate's defense of his constraint. So I am going to assume in this discussion that the third task could be met. It should go without saying, however, that any individual moderate who embraces a specific extra condition will eventually need to establish that the reason which opposes doing harm does indeed meet that extra condition.

What of the second task? We are imagining that the moderate has demonstrated the existence of a reason which especially opposes doing harm. But if that reason is to be a morally decisive one—grounding a *requirement* not to do harm—it must be able to outweigh any countervailing reasons in typical cases. In particular, since the moderate is interested in defending a constraint which rules out doing harm even when greater good might be brought about by doing harm, the reason not to do harm must be sufficiently powerful to override the pro tanto reason to promote the good.

Now, strictly speaking, the mere existence of a reason not to do harm does not guarantee that that reason will ever be able to outweigh the pro tanto reason to promote the good. It is logically possible that in every single case, the pro tanto reason to promote the good outweighs (or at least balances) the particular reason not to do harm. Thus, even if the moderate were able to isolate something especially morally offensive about doing harm, it would not automatically follow that the particular reason which opposes doing harm would ever be morally decisive in cases where greater good could be done by *doing* harm. Without a further argument about the relative strengths of the two kinds of reasons, the moderate would not have established the existence of a constraint.

Nonetheless, it would not be implausible for the moderate to hold that *if* there is a reason that particularly opposes doing harm, this reason is at least sometimes able to override the pro tanto reason to promote the good. After all, the pro tanto reason to promote the good can be fairly weak in some cases (when not much good is at stake); and there is no particular reason to assume that the reason which opposes doing harm will be *in principle* incapable of outweighing the pro tanto reason, no matter how weak. The question, then, would be just how strong the pro tanto reason to promote the good could be in a given case and yet still be overridden by the reason which opposes doing harm. Answering this question would, in effect, determine how high a threshold was had by the constraint against doing harm.

Most moderates believe that the threshold of the constraint against harming is in fact quite high (if, indeed, there is a finite threshold at all). Establishing this claim, obviously, would require a more detailed argument about the relative strengths of the two kinds of reasons. (Those who believe that the constraint is absolute would have to show that the reason which opposes doing harm always overrides the pro tanto reason to promote the good, no matter *how* strong the latter reason in a given case.) However, I do not intend to examine such arguments here. Let us simply assume, for the sake of argument, that if the moderate can indeed demonstrate the existence of a reason which particularly opposes doing harm, this reason will typically (and perhaps always) be able to override the pro tanto reason to promote the good.

I have been suggesting, in effect, that if he can defend the existence of a special reason not to do harm, it might not be implausible for the moderate to hold that such a reason grounds a *constraint*. This redirects our attention to the issue of whether the moderate can actually fulfill the first task. Note, however, that it clearly will not do for the moderate to point to some morally offensive feature which obtains in *all* cases of countenancing harm, regardless of whether the harm is brought about or merely allowed.

(Such a feature could at best generate a reason which opposes each instance of countenancing harm—grounding, perhaps, a requirement to minimize harm.) Consider, for example, killing the one to save the two. No doubt there are reasons which oppose killing the one, but those reasons will not be morally decisive if there are similar reasons (ones just as strong, or stronger) which oppose allowing the two to die. Obviously, then, if there is to be a constraint against doing harm, the moderate must point to something special about *doing* harm, as opposed to merely allowing harm. In short, the moderate must demonstrate that there is a morally important difference between doing harm and allowing it.

Therefore, the major assumption underlying the constraint against doing harm is that there is a morally relevant distinction between doing and allowing. To allow harm may be a serious enough matter; but doing harm is a more serious matter. That is, the reasons that oppose doing harm are weightier than the reasons that oppose merely allowing harm; there is something especially morally offensive about the doing of harm. Some such view must underlie the moderate's attempt to defend a constraint against doing harm: I cannot do harm even in order to prevent some greater harm, for in such a situation I am presented with a choice between actually *doing* harm, and merely *allowing* harm—and the former is more significant than the latter.

The first problem facing the moderate, then, is to justify the claim that doing is morally more significant than merely allowing. I conceded at the start of this chapter that the moral relevance of the distinction probably has some intuitive support. The question is rather whether the moderate can *justify* this position.

Three possibilities suggest themselves. The first is the typical difference in cost to the agent of avoiding doing harm as compared to the cost of avoiding allowing harm. In the light of the minimal sacrifice that it generally takes to avoid doing harm, the moderate might suggest that it is reasonable for morality to judge an agent who does harm severely; while the significant costs of preventing harm make it reasonable for morality to judge failure in this regard more leniently. Thus, doing harm is morally more significant than merely allowing harm. As I argued in the first chapter, however, some instances of refraining from doing harm exact tremendous costs; and as we know, some cases of providing aid require next to no sacrifice. Thus if the moral significance of countenancing harm depends upon the cost of preventing it, the doing/allowing distinction will supply only a rough guide which frequently needs to be corrected. Therefore, cost cannot provide the moderate with a defense of the moral relevance of the doing/allowing distinction itself.[18] If the moderate is to support the claim that doing is morally more significant than allowing, he needs a different approach.

The second possibility—mentioned in the first chapter—is that doing harm to an individual is more disrespectful of that person than merely allowing harm to befall him. But this is easier to claim than it is is to defend: if I stand back and idly watch Maude drown, when all that need be done to save her is to toss out a life preserver, it would seem that my reaction evidences straightforward lack of respect for her person. No doubt many allowings of harm are motivated more from simple indifference than from positive contempt. But on the one hand, it is hard to see how the moderate can claim that indifference to the fate of some entity as valuable as a person does not amount to disrespect; and on the other hand, if indifference does escape the charge of disrespect, then the moderate will have to face the existence of cases of doing harm which do not possess the offensive lack of respect for persons.

Finally, the moderate might try to develop the view that the appropriate sorts of facts about a particular agent can ground especially compelling moral requirements. Many moderates share the intuition that if a moral requirement is to be able to get its 'hooks' into some given agent, this can only be because of the presence of the right sorts of facts about that agent, which allow the requirement to 'grab hold', as it were, in the particular situation. For a countenanced outcome to be of special moral concern for an agent, the right sort of linkage between agent and outcome must exist, or be in the offing. Given a view of this sort, it might then be suggested that having done a harm may forge the right sort of connection between agent and outcome, while merely having

---

[18] The moderate might support the need for general rules, and observe that refraining from doing harm *typically* is not costly, while providing aid typically *is* costly—concluding that this is reason to consider doing more significant than allowing. But there is little reason to think that such general rules need to be cast in terms of the doing/allowing distinction at all: other systems of rules might be equally practical yet offer a closer approximation of direct regard for cost—permitting the agent to do harm in certain cases where he clearly stands to gain a tremendous amount.

allowed a harm does not. I have already noted the connection between this view and the attempt to construe doing as interfering: when an agent interferes and alters an on-going process, this seems to pick out some salient fact about *him* connecting him to the harm; but when an agent merely allows a harm and has not interfered, nothing about the harm seems to connect to the agent himself (it would have been the same even if he hadn't existed). Nonetheless, it seems to me that this sort of explanation of the moral relevance of the doing/allowing distinction cannot be used to ground a *constraint.* For even if the agent need not take an interest in harms he is merely allowing (a dubious claim, at any rate), there is no explanation of why the agent should not be free to take such an interest if he chooses—thus providing himself with a justification for doing harm when it is necessary to prevent greater harm.

It should be noted that, in one way or another, all three of the suggestions just reviewed focus on the agent: cost to the agent, the attitude of the agent, facts about the agent. Given this focus, it may not be surprising that these approaches are all unsuccessful in defending the moral relevance of the distinction between doing and allowing (at least in such a way that the defense can be used to support a constraint). Perhaps the moderate would do better if he were to consider suggestions that focus on the victim. It is, after all, presumably because of the fact that harm is done to the victim that the moderate feels it appropriate to erect a constraint against the doing of harm.

Now the most straightforward approach along these lines would be for the moderate to argue that the cost to the victim is somehow greater or worse in cases when harm is done than in cases where it is merely allowed. But such a claim is clearly untrue. The cost to the victim is no less grave when he has been merely allowed to die than when he has been killed. At any rate, even if some such claim were true, it is obvious that it could not help to justify a constraint. We would still need an explanation of why harm may not be done even when this would genuinely minimize the overall amount of harm.

A more promising approach is open to the moderate.[19] If we take seriously the suggestion that the moral offensiveness of doing harm should be located in the notion of interference, then we need to ask what is it that is so morally offensive about interfering with the welfare of another? Let's start by considering this question from the

---

[19] It derives from Kamm, pp. 304–5.

initial standpoint of the victim, prior to the agent's harmful act. The victim is in possession of a good—e.g., his life—and the agent's harmful act deprives the victim of that good. In effect, the agent changes the 'distribution' of the good (in this case, destroying it) in a way opposed to the wishes of the victim. This intuitively strikes us as morally offensive. In contrast, when an agent merely allows harm, he has not brought about such an unwanted redistribution.

It would not, however, be any help to the moderate to argue that doing harm is morally more offensive than allowing harm, since it involves bringing about the unwanted redistribution as opposed to merely allowing it. For it is clear that such an argument simply presupposes the relevance of the distinction it is meant to be defending. It has been admitted all along that it is one thing to bring about a harm, and another to merely allow it. Talk of the unwanted redistribution of a good does not make it any clearer why the distinction in question should have any moral weight.

But the analysis has not yet taken any real advantage of the suggestion that doing harm should be understood in terms of the concept of interference. When an agent interferes, he alters an on-going process, i.e., a process that is going on independently of the agent. In the particular case at hand, where an agent deprives his victim of some good, the on-going process in question is the victim's possession of that good. (In some cases, of course, the on-going process may involve the victim's *coming into* possession of some good, rather than his *already* possessing it. For simplicity of exposition, however, I'll leave this qualification aside.) That is, what the concept of interference draws our attention to is the fact that the good that the victim has (prior to the agent's act) is one that he has and can maintain independently of the agent. It is not merely that the agent redistributes a good, but that he redistributes a good that is independent of him. If we add the intuition that a good should be distributed in accordance with the desires of those on whom the good is dependent, this may be thought to provide a key to the offensiveness of doing harm.

Contrast the situation where harm is merely allowed. Here the victim is in need of aid, and the agent refuses to provide it. Once again, the result is the distribution of a good—e.g., the continuation of the victim's life—in a manner unwanted by the victim (he fails to possess that good). But notice that it cannot be said that that good, were it provided to the victim, would be one that he possesses and maintains *independently* of the agent. On the contrary, the very fact that aid from the agent is required by the victim brings out the fact that the good in question is not one that is independent of the agent.

Thus in cases both of doing harm and allowing harm the agent countenances the distribution of a good in a manner that is unwanted by the victim; but in cases of doing harm the unwanted distribution is of a good that is independent of the agent, while in cases of allowing harm the good is not independent of the agent. On the assumption—already noted—that a good should be distributed in accord with the desires of those on whom it is dependent, we find that there is something particularly morally offensive in cases of doing harm. For in such cases, the ultimate distribution of the good reflects the desires of the agent—despite the fact that the victim possessed (and could maintain) the good independently of the agent. But in cases of allowing harm, the good is not one that the victim would possess and maintain independently of the agent, so there is nothing as clearly offensive in the fact that it is still the agent whose desires are reflected by the ultimate distribution of the good.

Notice that an argument of this sort does not simply presuppose the moral relevance of the distinction between doing and allowing. Rather, the relevance of the distinction emerges from the combination of an independent moral view and a structural difference between doing and allowing. The moderate locates an underlying moral offensiveness in an agent's countenancing the distribution of a good in a manner opposed to those on whom the good is dependent. In principle this does not assume that it is worse to cause such a distribution than to merely allow it. But given the structural fact that in cases of allowing harm the good in question is never independent of the agent, the offense cannot here arise. Cases of doing harm, however, will typically display the offensive feature, for the good in question generally is independent of the agent.

A fully developed argument along these lines would need to describe the underlying moral view in greater detail. In particular, the moderate needs a statement of how to handle cases in which the good in question is dependent on more than one person, and they disagree as to how it should be distributed. For it is not always true that in cases of doing harm the victim is deprived of a good that is independent of the agent. Clearly, the mere fact that an agent has made *some* contribution to the victim's possession of a good does not guarantee that it is appropriate that the distribution should reflect only that agent's desires (and perhaps they should not be reflected at all). As the gimmicky case of the King and the oldest son brings out, the moderate had better not hold that the moral offensiveness of doing harm can be removed by the mere fact that the good being redistributed is not totally independent of the agent.

It may, however, be possible for the moderate to defend the view that in certain cases when the good is significantly dependent on more than one person, it is appropriate for the distribution to reflect the desires of someone other than the victim.[20] If so, the moderate might be able to salvage the intuition that in many cases it is permissible for an agent to cut off a process of aid instituted by himself. The moderate would have an explanation of why the constraint against doing harm—properly understood—would nonetheless permit such acts. Such cases would indeed be cases of harming the victim, but the morally offensive element would be missing: the good would be distributed in accordance with the desire of the person on whom it is most significantly dependent. A defense along these lines would need to give guidance on ruling out the gimmicky cases (why doesn't the fact that the King fathered the son make the son's life 'significantly dependent' on the King?); but it is, at least, an intriguing possibility.

We have, then, what appears to be a promising line of argument for the moderate. By appealing to underlying moral intuitions about the inappropriateness of a good's being distributed in a manner opposed to the desires of those on whom it is dependent, it seems that the moderate may be able to provide a defense for the claim that the distinction between doing and allowing is morally relevant.

Nonetheless, I believe that this defense of the distinction is ultimately unsuccessful. Two objections seem particularly worth

---

[20] Some such view may also be necessary for the moderate to defend the claim that allowing harm is not morally offensive. For if we take the good in question to be the continuation of the victim's life, then although this good may be dependent on the agent's contribution, it will typically also be dependent on the victim as well. And so the moderate will need to be able to explain why it is not morally offensive for the good to be distributed in accordance with the agent's rather than the victim's desires. The case is complicated, however, by the fact that if we focus instead on the the *aid* that could be contributed by the agent, it seems that it is only the agent on whom the good is dependent. A more precise specification of the underlying moral view might clarify these matters.

stressing. First of all, it is clearly an oversimplification for the moderate to assert that in cases of doing harm, the good that is redistributed by the agent is altogether independent of him. I am not here simply repeating the point that in special cases the agent may have made a previous positive contribution to the existence of the good. Rather, even in a standard case, such as when an agent shoots and kills a stranger with whom he has had no previous contact (direct or indirect), the redistributed good—the victim's life—is not altogether independent of the agent. There is admittedly an obvious sense in which the victim's possession of the good is indeed independent of the agent (he would have had the good even had the agent never existed!). But there is also an obvious sense in which the good is *not* one that the victim possesses and maintains independently of the agent, for it is only the agent's refusal to do harm that permits the victim to retain possession. If the moderate is to defend his argument, he needs to articulate the underlying moral view in such a way as to make clear why the latter sort of dependence is not morally relevant. In effect, the moderate needs to claim that it is only what we intuitively think of as *positive* contributions that make a good dependent on an agent. But I do not see how this view could possibly be defended without presupposing the moral relevance of the doing/allowing distinction. Yet if this is so, the moderate has simply drawn an elaborate circle, and has failed to provide a defense of the relevance of that distinction.

A second difficulty may arise once we press the moderate to explain what it is that is offensive in countenancing the distribution of a good in a manner opposed to the desires of those on whom the good is dependent. The moderate may suggest that those through whose efforts a good exists *deserve* to have the good distributed as they wish, or perhaps that it is not *fair* if the good is not distributed in accord with the desires of those who worked for it. Such intuitions, however, are easily incorporated into an extremist framework, by adopting a pluralist theory of the overall good that is sensitive to whether individual goods are distributed in accordance with the desires of those on whom they depend. And such an approach seems far more in harmony with the underlying moral view than does the moderate's proposal to erect a constraint against doing harm. For if I kill the one to save the two from being killed, at least I minimize the extent to which goods are distributed in a manner opposed to the desires of those on whom they depend.[21] Of course the moderate might insist that it is worse to bring about such a distribution than it is to allow it, but this would once again simply presuppose the distinction whose relevance the moderate meant to defend.

I conclude, therefore, that despite the initial appeal of this approach, it too fails to serve the moderate's needs. And I know of no more promising approach. Yet if the moderate is going to defend the constraint against doing harm, he needs to establish the moral relevance of the distinction between doing and allowing. Given the failure of the various proposals that we have examined and rejected, it remains a mystery how the moderate is to do this.

THREE MYSTERIES

If the moderate is to defend a constraint against doing harm, he must demonstrate that doing harm is opposed by a morally decisive reason. This, in turn, requires the moderate to claim that there is a morally relevant difference between doing harm and allowing it. But it is exactly this claim which was challenged by the discussion of the last section. I have argued that it is a mystery how the moderate is to defend the moral relevance of the distinction between doing and allowing (at least in such a way that the defense can be used to support a constraint against doing harm). This, of course, seriously calls into question the moderate's ability to establish the existence of a reason which particularly opposes doing harm. And, a fortiori, the defense of the constraint is thereby undermined as well.

It is worth noting, however, that this failure—the failure to establish the relevance of the do/allow distinction—is by no means the only difficulty that faces the moderate's attempt to defend the constraint. A second problem arises when we realize that the distinction between doing and allowing covers not only

---

[21] The moderate might object that since the two need my aid, the good in question is not one that they could possess independently. However, as was already noted, the moderate needs to claim that a victim can possess a good independently, in the relevant sense—despite the fact that the harmful deeds of others may deprive him of it. But then it must be admitted that the two that I save are also able to maintain their goods independently in the relevant sense—i.e., but for the harmful deeds of others.

countenancing harm, but also countenancing good. That is, if we can distinguish between doing harm and merely allowing harm, then we can also distinguish between doing good, and merely allowing good. If I stand back and watch Esmeralda save Quasimodo from drowning, when I could have prevented the rescue by tripping Esmeralda, then I have merely *allowed* the good. But if I myself dash into the water and pull out the drowning man perhaps Esmeralda is nowhere to be seen), then I have brought about the good—it is something I have *done*.

The problem which faces the moderate then is this: even if we were to grant that doing is morally more significant than merely allowing, there is no reason to think that doing *evil* is more significant than doing *good*. It would seem that the two concepts should be on all fours: if doing harm is especially morally offensive, then doing good should be especially morally pleasing. If we locate the moral importance of doing evil in its causal character, for example, then we find that the corresponding concept of doing good—causing good—demands treatment as equally morally important.

The same is true if we follow the suggestion of locating the offensiveness of doing evil in interference, for this notion presumably comes into play for good as well as evil. When I refrain from tripping Esmeralda as she rushes to save Quasimodo, I do not interfere: there is an on-going process which would have had the same result even had I not existed. But when I jump in the water to save Quasimodo myself (with Esmeralda nowhere to be seen), I do interfere: had I not existed, he would have been worse off.

Admittedly, it may sound odd to describe bringing about good as *interfering*; talk of interfering may suggest that it is evil which is being done, not good. If so, perhaps we should use the more neutral sounding word 'intervening' to cover both sorts of cases, and then restate the point: Interfering is simply a matter of intervening for evil. But the importance of intervening for evil should not blind us to the fact that I can also intervene for good. And the notion of intervening cannot explain why the former should take on a moral significance that the latter lacks.

If this is correct, then the argument for a constraint against doing harm cannot even get off the ground. Recall once more the case where two will be killed unless I kill a third. Presumably the moderate hoped to argue that if I kill the one I am *doing* harm, while if I refrain I am merely *allowing* harm; and if we concede that doing harm is more significant than allowing harm it might seem to follow that I should not kill the one. But such an argument would not be sound. If I kill the one I am doing harm, to be sure—but I am also doing good: saving the two. I 'interfere' with the welfare of all three individuals. If intervening for evil takes on a special moral importance for the agent, so must intervening for good. So in considering killing the one to save the two, the magnification due to intervention can simply be factored out: the situation seems to reduce to a matter of two lives or one life—and so the moderate has no reason to forbid killing the one. Focusing the discussion on *doing* harm is therefore actually a red herring. Even if doing is a morally weightier category than allowing, the distinction apparently helps not at all for justifying a *constraint* against doing harm.

If there is to be a constraint, the moderate must establish the existence of a morally decisive reason—one which particularly opposes doing harm. But the attempts to isolate what it is about doing harm that generates such a reason have all focused on the special character of doing (as opposed to allowing). Nothing in such an approach explains why doing good should not generate a reason exactly corresponding to the reason generated by doing harm. Yet unless the moderate can rule out the existence of an equally strong reason which favors doing good, there will be no reason to think that the reason which opposes doing harm is morally decisive.

The only way out of this problem, of course, is for the moderate to argue that doing *harm* is morally more significant than doing *good*. But it seems fairly clear that the concept of *doing* offers no grounds for creating such an asymmetry. Apparently the moderate simply has to make the brute assertion that morality is more concerned with evil than with good. (The notion of doing, or interfering, will then take an explanatory back seat.) But this should strike us as a desperately dangling distinction. Nothing the moderate has said even begins to explain how the distinction might be justified; and this should cause the moderate to suspect that it cannot be.

It is important to avoid confusion here. The moderate will not be aided by an argument to the effect that various evils (for example, pains) are morally more important than various goods (pleasures, perhaps). If this were so, there might be a sense in which bringing about such evils would be morally more significant than bringing about such goods (and, as noted in Chapter 1, this point could easily be accepted by the extremist). But it would not help the moderate establish a constraint against doing harm. For such a constraint rules out doing harm even when this is the only way to bring about a genuinely better outcome overall—for example, even when this is the only way to eliminate or prevent a greater amount of *evil*.

Talk of 'doing good' should not blind us to the fact that the good that is done may involve a significant evil. (Nor should talk of 'doing harm' blind us to the fact that the harm done may involve only the prevention or elimination of a good.) If I kill the one to save the two, the good that I bring about (saving the lives of the two) is no less significant than the harm that I bring about (the death of the one). Indeed, the kind of good/evil involved is identical: life, and its preservation or loss. Thus the moderate is still in need of an explanation of why doing harm should be thought to be more significant than doing good.

The moderate might hope to reduce the dangle of his asymmetrical treatment of doing harm and doing good by noting an asymmetry in the dischargeability of the corresponding moral requirements. An agent can completely fulfill a requirement never to do harm: there need never be a situation in which the agent cannot avoid bringing about evil. But an agent cannot in the same way completely fulfill a requirement to do good: there will frequently be situations in which the agent cannot avoid allowing harm, cannot avoid failing to do some good that needs to be done. Thus it is possible for the agent to do no harm at all; but he cannot do all the good that needs doing. At best, then, a moral system can only incorporate the ideal of doing good into a requirement that the agent do as much good as he can; but a system can go further in its treatment of doing harm: it can require that the agent never do any harm at all. The moderate might point to this difference in dischargeability as reason for his asymmetrical treatment of doing harm and doing good.

Yet even if the difference in dischargeability is genuine, this does not explain why doing harm should be considered morally more significant than doing good. Considerations of dischargeability may indicate that it is *possible* to require an agent never to do harm (and also that it is *impossible* to incorporate the corresponding requirement to do good)—but they give no reason why a moral system should *do* so. The fact that doing good and doing harm *can* be treated differently is not yet a justification for such differential treatment; and it does not suggest where such a justification might be found.

The moderate may hope that when he finally offers an account of why doing harm is morally more significant than allowing harm, he will also find himself provided with an explanation of why doing harm is more significant than doing good. Once more, there is no refuting a hope. But there is no reason to consider the lumping together of two mysteries progress.

One final problem for the moderate should be mentioned. Even if we assume that evil is more significant than good, so that doing harm takes on an importance which doing good does not have, the moderate is still a far cry from justifying a constraint against doing harm. For he still needs to provide an explanation of why a given agent should be peculiarly concerned with the harm that *he* does, as opposed to having a more neutral concern with the harm done by any agent whatsoever. If I fail to kill the one, where this is the only way to prevent two would-be murderers from killing their victims, then I countenance more instances of *doing* harm than I would countenance if I *did* kill the one. If doing harm is so significant, why shouldn't I be permitted to do harm in order to minimize the doing of harm?

What the moderate wants to argue, of course, is that there is (only) an *agent-relative* reason to avoid harm-doing: for any given agent, the harm that *he* does takes on a special moral significance. As I noted in Chapter 2, if the moderate is to establish a constraint against a given type of reaction, it is not enough to identify a reason which particularly opposes reactions of that type; the reason must be an agent-relative one. The moderate does not want to incorporate the importance of harm-doing into an agent-neutral structure, where all agents have reason to be equally concerned about the harm-doing of anyone at all.[22] Rather, the moderate wants to defend the existence of a constraint—an agent-relative

[22] Would such an agent-neutral structure necessarily be consequentialist—where harms brought about by some agent are simply considered more objectively bad than harms which aren't so brought about? It depends on whether we can make sense of a theory which claims that all agents have a reason to promote some end, even though that end is not objectively good (a question already raised in Chapter 2, n. 15). If we can, the agent-neutral system needn't be a consequentialist one, although it will be extensionally equivalent to a consequentialist system. If we cannot, the system *will* be consequentialist.

structure—and so he must argue that harm-doing generates (only) an agent-relative reason. This much is clear. What is not at all clear is what the moderate can say to support incorporating the importance of doing harm into the sort of structure he favors.

The moderate may think it obvious that *my* instances of harm-doing should be of special concern to *me*. But in fact this is not at all obvious. It is (perhaps) trivially true that harm-doing is done by a particular agent; but it is certainly not a trivial consequence of this that that agent's doing of harm takes on a special moral importance for that agent alone, rather than being (what should be) a subject of equal concern for all agents who are in a position to do something about it.

It is, of course, true that I almost inevitably have more control over my own actions than I do over the actions of others. But this is hardly adequate to establish the moderate's position that harm-doing generates (only) an agent-relative reason. For sometimes we *are* in a position to influence the actions of others, or their outcomes, and thus minimize the number of instances of doing harm overall. If—as in the case of killing the one to save the two—I have some control over whether others shall do harm, the moderate still needs to explain why the harm-doing of others should not be of as much concern to me as the harm I may bring about myself.

The moderate may argue that a moral system which gives an agent special concern with the harm that he himself brings about, as opposed to a more general agent-neutral concern with the harm done by anyone at all, is on the way to limiting the moral responsibility of each agent. It may thus appear to fit in well with the moderate's larger motivation of freeing the agent from what would otherwise be the all-encompassing demands of morality. In fact, however, such a motivation would be far better served by giving the agent an option to countenance harm-doing—whether his own or that of others—when the cost to the agent would be too great otherwise. The appeal to cost can hardly explain why morality should impose upon an agent a special concern with the harm that he does. Thus the moderate has still not justified his belief that the importance of harm-doing is best captured in an agent-relative structure.

There are then three mysteries hovering about a constraint against doing harm. For the defense of the constraint is doomed unless the moderate can establish the existence of a reason of exactly the right sort. Yet the moderate is hard pressed to explain why doing is morally more significant than allowing, why doing harm is more significant than doing good, and why harm-doing generates agent-relative reasons rather than agent-neutral ones. In short, from start to finish, the constraint against doing harm is desperately in need of justification—essential support which is never provided. Add to this the realization that the constraint itself probably has unacceptable implications, and the moderate is faced with excellent reasons for abandoning it.

4

Intending Harm

HARM INTENDED AS MEANS

In Chapter 3 we considered a number of problems facing any attempt to erect a constraint against doing harm. As I noted at the start of that chapter, however, many moderates would draw the line against killing not in terms of the distinction between doing and allowing, but rather in terms of the distinction between what is intended and what is merely foreseen. Indeed, advocates of a constraint against intending harm may have been *encouraged* by the difficulties which face the constraint against *doing* harm. In this chapter, therefore, I want to go on to consider some difficulties with the constraint against intending harm, and suggest reasons why it too should be rejected. If these criticisms are successful then the moderate will be in an uncomfortable position, for we have seen that a constraint against harming is necessary to resist the options to do harm[1] which are supported by the moderate's appeal to cost. If the two most promising ways of articulating a constraint against harming can be shown to be untenable, then the moderate must either embrace an unacceptably minimalist position, or abandon his defense of options against the extremist.

A constraint against intending harm forbids the agent to countenance a harm where the agent's reason for doing so is that the harm is either itself an *end* of the agent's or a *means* to some end.[2] Before considering objections to adopting such a constraint, a few preliminary comments may be in order.

---

[1] As I noted in Chapter 1, I will continue to speak in a general way of the moderate's need to resist 'options to do harm', despite the fact that not all such options are unacceptable. Similarly, although moderates who endorse a constraint against *intending* harm will feel that talk of 'options to *do* harm' somewhat miscategorizes the class of unacceptable options, I will retain the evocative expression.

[2] It might be better to say, in the vocabulary to be introduced shortly, that the constraint forbids countenancing harm where the agent's reason for doing so is that the harm is an end or a *vehicle* to some end.

First, the constraint forbids intending harm as a means and not only intending harm as an end. It is this feature, of course, which gives the constraint its bite. Were the constraint only against harm intended as an end, it would be of limited interest, for perhaps only sadists have harm to others among their ends. If I kill uncle Albert to inherit his wealth, for example, his death will not be one of my ends. Indeed, I might wish there were some way to get the money without killing the old man, of whom I am rather fond. But his death is a *means* to my end—gaining the fortune—and so killing him is prohibited by the constraint. Similarly, when I kill the one to save the two, the harm to the one is surely not among my ends— would that there were a better way of saving the two!—but it is a *means* to my end, and so my reaction is prohibited by the constraint.[3] (For simplicity, since the cases that will concern us involve intending harm as a means, and not as an end, I will hereafter write as though the constraint simply prohibited the former.)

Second, the constraint against intending harm is not limited to harms which I *do*, but also covers harms which I merely *allow*. That is, I am forbidden to *countenance* a harmful outcome, where my reason for doing so is that the outcome is a means to some end; and it does not matter whether the outcome is one I have brought about myself, or merely one I have failed to prevent. Thus, even if all that is required to save the two is the *death* of the one, and the one is about to drink cyanide, mistaking it for tea, I must not keep silent if my reason for doing so is that by allowing his death I may save the two. The constraint forbids allowing harm as a means, and not only doing harm as a means.

Third, an adequate explication of the constraint against intending harm would obviously have to give an account of what it is for an event to count as a *means* to some end. Puzzling cases suggest that this may not be a trivial task,[4] but for the most part I won't press the moderate on this score, and am willing to rely on our intuitive feel for the distinction between what is a means, and what is merely a side-effect. For example, if I foresee that in the struggle of an attempt to rescue the two some one innocent bystander may be shot, the death of that one is not a means to the end of saving the two: it is ('merely') a foreseen side-effect of procuring the desired

---

[3] When I kill uncle Albert to inherit his wealth, is it his death, or my killing him, which is the means to my end? Following common practice, I shall speak both ways—but officially I conceive of the harm itself and not the harming as the means.

[4] See, e.g., Davis, 'Double Effect'.

end. But if I must shoot the bystander in order to procure the release of the two, then the death of the one would be a means—and shooting would be forbidden by the constraint.

Fourth, the constraint only forbids countenancing harms which are means to some end if that is the agent's *reason* for countenancing the harm. Before I illustrate this point, however, let me note that putting it this way may actually be improper, for on some accounts of the term 'means', an event is a means only if the agent intends it as such. So we must introduce a new term. Now obviously an event may bring about an end, guarantee that it is not prevented, and so on, independently of whether the agent's reason for countenancing that event is his recognition of the fact that the event has this property. Let us call an event which is causally related to an end in this way a *vehicle* to that end. (This stretches the common use of the term, but perhaps not unrecognizably so.) A vehicle to some end functions as a means to that end if and only if the fact that the event is a vehicle is the agent's *reason* for countenancing it. The fourth point, then, is this: the constraint only forbids countenancing harms which are means to some end; it does not forbid countenancing all harms which are mere vehicles to some end.

I might well be aware that some outcome is a vehicle to some end of my own, without intending that outcome as a means—and thus, without violating the constraint—if I have some altogether different reason for countenancing it. If my reason for refraining from warning the one about the cyanide tea is that his poisoner holds a gun to my head and threatens to shoot me if I speak, then I do not *intend* the death of the one—even if I realize that the death of the one will in fact be a vehicle to saving the two. Indeed, I may even be *glad* at the thought that the one will die, and thus save the two—so long as that is not my reason for keeping silent. (Of course the threat to my own life needn't be my only reason for keeping silent, and if another one of my reasons for keeping silent is in order to save the two, then I violate the constraint. Should I speak? Presumably the moderate thinks I should change my *reasons*, keeping the acceptable one, and dropping the morally offensive one. But an agent may not have that kind of easy control over what his reasons actually are.[5]) Restricting the constraint to prohibiting

---

[5] Imagine a crazed utilitarian doctor who frequently deliberately lets patients die when their organs can be used to save a greater number of patients who will otherwise die themselves. Imagine that a certain patient can be cured, but the doctor is tempted to let him die so as to save five others. However, the doctor is also

only the countenancing of harm where the agent's reason for so reacting is that the harm is a vehicle, prevents the constraint from being unacceptably strong for the moderate. Without the restriction, e.g., I would be required to warn the one in the cyanide tea case—where the poisoner holds a gun to my head—even though it would cost my life.[6] The constraint, then, only forbids countenancing harm which is intended as a means.

Finally, let me quickly indicate where the moderate might locate the moral offensiveness of intending harm. Two possibilities suggest themselves. First, the moderate might stress that when I countenance harm to another as a means, then I am *using* that person—and it might plausibly be claimed that the other person is not mine to use. Second, the moderate might stress that when I intend harm I have a *reason* for countenancing something evil.

tempted to *save* the one patient, for if the five patients die then their organs can be used to save twenty-five others. Given his motives, the constraint against intending harm forbids him to allow the one to die, for his reason for doing so would be to save the five. Yet it also forbids him to save the one, for his reason for doing that would be to allow the five to die so as to save the twenty-five. That is, the doctor's reason for allowing the five to die is not that this is the inevitable side-effect of saving the one (which would be a permissible reason), but that it is a means to saving the twenty-five. Since his reason for saving the one would be that by doing so he can countenance the deaths of the five and thereby save the twenty-five, if he saves the one, he will be intending harm (the deaths of the five)—and this is forbidden. Thus he can neither save the one nor allow the one to die. So what should he do? Presumably, he is supposed to save the one where his reason for doing this is strictly to *save* the one and not so that he can countenance the deaths of the five as a means. But if the doctor—utilitarian that he is—simply would *not* save the one, but for the fact that he can thus countenance the deaths of the five as a means of saving the twenty-five, then he cannot simply shuffle his reasons to suit the constraint—and so no matter what he does, he will violate it. This does not mean, of course, that the constraint will give inconsistent advice to everyone in this situation: many can simply save the one and be done with it. But the constraint prohibits reactions done for certain reasons, and for some individuals (who would inevitably act for the wrong reasons) this would mean prohibiting anything they might do. It would take us too far afield, however, to consider whether this is actually a flaw in the constraint.

[6] Indeed, a constraint which simply forbade countenancing any harm which was a vehicle to some desired end would probably be incoherent—forbidding all possible reactions whatsoever in various cases. In the organ example of the previous note, e.g., any doctor at all would find himself blocked on all fronts. There might, however, be a pro tanto reason not to countenance harm which is a vehicle—i.e., a moral *presumption* against profiting from the misfortune of others, even though the misfortune is not intended as a means. But I won't explore this possibility. Even if there were such a presumption, it would not be a constraint, and thus presumably it could occasionally be overridden by the appeal to cost. Such a presumption, therefore, would not be sufficient to enable the moderate to block options to do harm.

Thus, in a sense, my mind is *turned* to the bringing about or allowing of evil—and it might plausibly be claimed that one must not *aim* at evil. We will consider these two possible accounts of the constraint in greater detail. Here it is worth noting the difference in emphasis: the latter locates the offensiveness in the fact that I am *intending* harm as a means; while the former locates the offensiveness in the fact that I am intending harm as a *means*.

It is also worth noting that neither of these two possible accounts of the moral offensiveness of intending harm could be readily used in support of a constraint against *doing* harm. (This brings out, once again, the importance of distinguishing clearly between the two constraints.) On the one hand, the constraint against doing harm does not itself forbid cases of allowing harm, even when the harm is allowed because it is a means to some end. Yet if I deliberately allow the harm as a means—that is, if this is my reason for countenancing the harm—it seems that I am still *aiming* at the harm. Similarly, the person whose harm I allow is still being *used* by me, even though I haven't caused his harm; he is still being treated as a mere tool. Thus an appeal to the two accounts would not support the constraint's restriction to cases of doing harm. And on the other hand, the constraint forbids doing harm even when the harm is not done as a means. Yet if the person I harm is not being harmed as a means to some goal of mine, I am not treating him as a tool, as a way of gaining something; thus I may not be *using* him in the relevant sense. Similarly, since the harm is not a means to any of my ends, I am not *aiming* at it. Thus an appeal to the two accounts would not support the full scope of the constraint against doing harm. In short, in the two areas where the constraint against doing harm diverges from the constraint against intending harm, it appears that the two accounts support the latter rather than the former. Whether that support is adequate, however, is a question to which we will return.

With these brief explanatory notes out of the way, let us consider some of the difficulties facing the constraint against intending harm.

SELF-DEFENSE

Suppose that while innocently sitting in the park reading Kant, I am suddenly attacked by an evil aggressor, Schmidt, who is bent on taking my Kant and my life. Imagine that the only way to defend myself is to shoot and kill Schmidt with the elephant gun that I have prudently brought along. It is a clear case of self-defense. Am I permitted to kill him?

It seems that advocates of the constraint against intending harm must say that I am *not* permitted to kill Schmidt—even though I am the victim of an unprovoked attack. For if I shoot him, it is with the intent of harming him—wounding him or even killing him—as a means of securing my own safety. No doubt, noble spirit that I am, I do not intend harm to him as an end in itself. But surely I countenance his death as a *means* of saving my life. Therefore, I intend harm. And this is forbidden by the constraint.

Yet most moderates presumably want to claim that I *am* permitted to kill in self-defense. This is, of course, not a universally held belief, and those moderates who are complete pacifists need not be troubled by this objection (they won't escape the section after next as easily). But for the majority of moderates who believe that killing Schmidt *is* permissible, it appears that the constraint against intending harm condemns too much.

It clearly won't do for the moderate to reply that if I shoot Schmidt in self-defense I do not actually intend his death, only foresee it. That is, the moderate must not claim that all I *intend* is to protect myself, or to save my life, or perhaps to stop Schmidt from hurting me—while the harm to Schmidt is merely a foreseen side-effect of my doing so. Such a response won't do, for it seems clear that although saving my life is my *end*, harming Schmidt is a necessary *means* to that end: so I do intend harm, as a means, in violation of the constraint. It is hard to see how the moderate could give content to the notion of *means* without admitting that harming Schmidt is a means to my end. And if the moderate *could* defend his claim that the harm to Schmidt is not intended, then it would seem that a similar defense could be constructed for the claim that when I kill the one to save the two I do not actually intend harm, but merely foresee it as a side-effect of saving the two. (At least this could be argued for *some* versions of this case.) The moderate needs the constraint against intending harm to block my killing the one to save the two; yet the same constraint apparently blocks my killing Schmidt in self-defense.

Nor will it do for the moderate to reply that Schmidt is an evil aggressor—a far cry from the innocent souls that the constraint against intending harm was meant to protect. Of course he is; but so what? I still intend harm to him as a means of achieving some desirable end, and this is forbidden by the constraint. It is true that Schmidt himself plans to violate that very constraint, but this does not seem to make *my* reaction any less of a violation. If the moderate admits—what seems clearly true—that I am intending harm when I defend myself, and yet nonetheless wants to claim that I am permitted to do so, then he must either abandon the constraint or modify it.

Modification may seem a plausible enough route. Roughly, the constraint would be restricted to forbidding intending harm to the innocent. (This won't quite do: even an evil person can't be harmed intentionally for *any* old end. The punishment must fit the crime, so to speak. But let this pass.) Schmidt is not innocent, and so is not protected by the constraint.

Making the modification may be easy; defending it is not. It is difficult enough to explain what it is about intending harm that justifies a constraint against such reactions; it is all the more difficult to see how the exception for the guilty is to be justified—for if the exception is not to be *ad hoc*, it will have to be compatible with the grounds for the constraint itself. And it is, to say the least, not obvious that such modification can be justified. (Pacifists may well be moderates who see the force of this.)

The moderate believes that in normal cases there are forceful reasons which oppose intending harm—reasons powerful enough to ground a constraint. That is, in normal cases these reasons are thought to be morally decisive. If, nonetheless, intending harm to Schmidt is to be permissible, then the moderate must point to special countervailing considerations that prevent those reasons from generating a requirement in such cases; the moderate must explain why there is no morally decisive reason not to intend harm to Schmidt. Following the discussion of Chapter 2, we can say that there are, in principle, three basic approaches that might be available to the moderate. First, he might argue that the reasons that normally oppose intending harm are not generated in cases where it is harm to the guilty that is intended. Second, he might argue that those reasons do still arise, but they are overridden by countervailing reasons which actually support harming the guilty. Finally, he might argue that although the *balance* of reasons still opposes intending harm—the original reasons are still generated, and they are not overridden by countervailing reasons—nonetheless that balance of reasons somehow fails to be morally *decisive*, and so it is not morally forbidden to intend harm to Schmidt. (Recall once more that in Chapter 2 I allowed for the possibility that an act might not be morally required, even though it was supported by the balance of reasons, if those reasons failed to meet other plausible conditions for moral decisiveness.) Let us consider each approach in turn.

The first approach seems the most promising, for intuitively we are inclined to say that Schmidt's guilt somehow *undermines* the constraint: it is not that his right not to be harmed is overridden, but rather that through his action he has lost or forfeited his right. It must be admitted, of course, that such talk is hardly unambiguous in its support for the first approach. But at any rate, the question is whether the moderate can defend the suggestion that the reasons that normally oppose intending harm fail to be generated when I face Schmidt. Obviously, the moderate cannot simply assert an exception for the guilty: he needs to show how the exception flows naturally from the account offered of how and why those reasons are normally generated in the first place. Thus the success of such a defense will depend on the particular account offered.

I would not want to claim that no plausible arguments for self-defense can be constructed along these lines. For example, in Chapter 1 there was a discussion of two types of indirect moral theories, the two-level approach and the contract approach. It would not be implausible to suggest that either of these approaches might yield the desired argument: the promulgation of rules permitting self-defense might well be optimal; parties to an agreement might well insist that specific protections under the contract are to be conditional on conformity to that contract. An argument in terms of one or another of these indirect theories would show why reasons that normally oppose intending harm would not come into play in cases of self-defense. But as I argued in Chapter 1, these indirect approaches provide overall support for the extremist rather than the moderate. The moderate, therefore, cannot turn to these theories now in support of self-defense; such an appeal would undermine the moderate's larger defense of ordinary morality. But how, then, is the moderate to support the permissibility of self-defense? Clearly, he must appeal to some favored account of the constraint against intending harm.

I have noted two plausible accounts of where the moderate might locate the moral offensiveness of intending harm: in aiming at evil, or in using the victim for one's own ends. It is hard to see how the second of these could justify making an exception for self-defense. For despite Schmidt's guilt, if I try to harm him it would seem to be just as much the case that I will be using him to further my own ends. There is no explanation of why the reasons that oppose using another should not be generated here as well. At first glance, however, the moderate appears to do better with the other account. It might be argued that when I harm Schmidt, although I am aiming at *harm*, I am not aiming at *evil*—for by virtue of Schmidt's evil intent and behavior, he deserves to be harmed, and thus the harm at which I aim is a good rather than an evil. Thus the reasons that normally are generated in opposition to intending harm fail to be generated here.

This does seem to be a possible line of defense, but most moderates will find that they cannot avail themselves of this argument. For if the argument is accepted, it will lead to what is for most moderates an overly minimalist interpretation of the constraint against intending harm: the justification of self-defense will excuse too much. Imagine that it is not necessary for me to harm Schmidt in order to escape from his attack. I can in fact capture Schmidt by coolly aiming my trusty elephant gun at him, and telling him to halt. However, what I do instead is coolly take aim and shoot to kill. All, or almost all, moderates will find this unacceptable. Self-defense may be permissible, but I am only permitted to use the minimal amount of force reasonably thought necessary to fend off the attack. (Let us assume that I am under no illusion as to the need to shoot Schmidt.) Yet it appears that the argument just given would provide a defense of my killing Schmidt despite the lack of need. If Schmidt's act of aggression makes it such that harm to him is a good rather than an evil, then I am not aiming at evil when I needlessly kill him. And if aiming at evil is the key to what is wrong with intending harm, then the constraint against intending harm must permit my act.[7] It seems that those moderates who wish to reject this conclusion as overly minimalist will have to reject either the premise that aiming at evil is the source of what is

---

[7] Might my unnecessary killing of Schmidt be forbidden by a principle ruling out 'gratuitous harm'? Perhaps, although it is far from clear that a plausible prohibition against gratuitous harm would come into play at all here, given that—on the line of argument being considered—harm to Schmidt is a good rather than an evil.

offensive in intending harm, or else the claim that Schmidt's guilt means that harm to him does not count as evil in the relevant sense. I do not know which course the moderate will find most plausible. But either way, this will involve abandoning the original argument for self-defense.

It seems, therefore, that for almost all moderates the first approach to the justification of self-defense is unsuccessful. It appears that the reasons that normally oppose intending harm will continue to oppose it, despite Schmidt's guilt. This, however, brings us to the second possible approach, which involves the claim that although the reasons that oppose intending harm to Schmidt are still generated, they are outweighed (or at least balanced) by countervailing reasons that *favor* Schmidt's being harmed. (For example, it might be suggested once more that Schmidt deserves to be harmed, and that there are reasons to help give people what they deserve.) Even if we put aside the problem that such a view would apparently still justify the use of unnecessary force in self-defense, the claim does not seem an especially plausible one for the moderate to make.

Recall just how powerful the moderate normally takes the reasons not to intend harm to be: I may not kill the one to save the two; indeed most moderates would insist that I may not kill the one even in order to save four, five, or a great many more. Yet if he is to take the second approach, the moderate must claim that these same reasons are nonetheless outweighed (or balanced) by the presumed reasons which favor Schmidt's being harmed; there is greater reason to see to it that the guilty Schmidt is harmed than there is to see to it that several innocent people are saved. Assuming, plausibly, that the moderate has no desire to make this claim, he can only hold that the reasons that favor Schmidt's being harmed outweigh the reasons that oppose intending him harm, if he holds that the latter reasons are considerably weaker than they normally are. But this is, in effect, to return us to the first approach, which we have already dismissed.

Nonetheless, here, as in general, my claim that a given principle would 'excuse too much' is compatible with the possibility that *some* further, additional principle would rule out the reaction that the initial principle fails to forbid. The charge is not that the original principle *guarantees* the permissibility of what should be forbidden, but rather that it itself simply forbids too little—i.e., that it fails to forbid some of what the moderate wants to have ruled out by an adequate principle of the kind in question.

The final possible approach was for the moderate to claim that although the balance of reasons still opposes intending harm to Schmidt, those reasons nonetheless fail to be morally decisive in this case, so they do not forbid self-defense. This suggestion can be quickly dismissed, for there is no particular reason to believe that Schmidt's guilt strips the balance of reasons of any of the other properties that may be necessary for being morally decisive: the reasons still have an appropriate subject matter, they still concern significant harms, and so on.

In principle, any one of these approaches might have enabled the moderate to justify his modification of the constraint against intending harm. But it appears that all three have failed. Despite its intuitive appeal, defending the permissibility of self-defense (while maintaining a prohibition on the unnecessary use of force) eludes the moderate. If the moderate cannot justify the modification of the constraint against intending harm, then he may have reason to abandon the constraint altogether. But, as we have noted, some moderates may be willing to embrace the constraint in its undiluted form. A few others may be willing to accept the loss of the prohibition on the unnecessary use of force. And still others may feel the problem of self-defense is too limited to merit great concern, or hope that the modification can be given adequate defense. So let us consider a related problem facing the constraint.

SHIELDS

Suppose that the indefatigable Schmidt is driving in a tank pointed at me and my family, bent on killing us. Luckily, I can destroy the tank with my anti-tank gun, killing Schmidt in an act of self-defense. We have already seen how difficult it will be for advocates of the constraint against intending harm to permit such acts of self-defense; but now let us add a new twist. Imagine that Schmidt has strapped an innocent bystander to the front of his tank: I cannot destroy the tank without thereby killing the person who shields it.

Let us call an innocent person who protects a threat in this way a *shield*.[8] Although it is no fault of the shield that he finds himself protecting the tank in this way, many moderates believe that I may nonetheless fire my gun—destroying the tank, Schmidt, and the

---

[8] Following Nozick, pp. 34–35, from whom the tank example comes as well.

shield as well. Yet harming the shield is not straightforwardly an act of self-defense, for the shield is not an aggressor. Thus, if the harm is intended it will evidently be forbidden by the constraint—and once more the moderate may have to conclude that the constraint condemns too much.

The moderate might reply that the harm to the shield is *not* intended, suggesting instead that it is merely a foreseen side-effect of destroying the tank. Yet even if this response is plausible in some cases—e.g., dropping a bomb on the tank—it will not suffice to excuse the agent in all those cases in which the moderate typically wants to permit harming the shield: for there are cases where it is more plausible to suggest that the harm to the shield *is* intended as a means to stopping the threat. Suppose for example, that the missile from my anti-tank gun must pass through the body of the shield in order to hit—and destroy—the tank. Unless I can get at the tank itself, I cannot stop it. Thus, digging a path through the body of the shield is a necessary *means* to accomplishing the end of stopping the tank. But having a missile go through a body is obviously a harm; therefore when I shoot at the shield in order to hit the tank, I am intending harm to the shield as a means. And so, when I fire the gun—destroying the tank, but also killing the shield—I violate the constraint against intending harm. If the moderate is to permit harming shields in the course of self-defense, he must either reject the constraint or modify it once more.

It is far from obvious, however, what the modification should look like. One possible approach, of course—although not the only one—would be to modify the constraint's prohibition of intending harm so that it explicitly excepted harm intended against shields. There would be difficulties with describing this exception precisely, however (were this our approach), for I do not think that it would be a trivial matter to demarcate the class of innocent shields of threats. Schmidt has strapped the innocent bystander to the front of the tank, putting him directly in the line of fire; the bystander's body is literally acting as something of a physical shield. But Schmidt is primarily thinking of the bystander as a moral shield: he hopes that others will hesitate to attack the tank, given that this cannot be done without harming the bystander. Thus, even if Schmidt had strapped the bystander to the back of the tank, or had merely lured him nearby, hoping that this would gain him protection against attack (e.g. from aerial bombing), it seems that we might still want to classify the bystander as a shield. But how, then, should we delimit the class of shields? Perhaps: all those bystanders who would be harmed in the course of attacking (disarming, incapacitating) the threat. Such an analysis, however, may be uncomfortably wide, classifying more people as shields than we intuitively think of as shields. The moderate may then find himself granting more exceptions to the constraint than he would like. I do not think that these difficulties are necessarily insuperable; but they do bring out how merely *stating* the modification in a helpful and intuitively acceptable form may be a problem.

Furthermore, even if a satisfactory modification can be formulated along these lines, it is far from obvious how the advocate of the constraint against intending harm is to *defend* it. After all, if I intend harm to a shield as part of my attempt to stop a threat, it still seems that I am intending evil (even if only as a means), and that I am using the shield to further my own ends. The fact that the shield is protecting the threat doesn't offer any clear explanation of why the shield should lose the protection of the constraint. Modification seems *ad hoc*.

Nonetheless, I would like to suggest what strikes me as a promising possibility. To motivate it, we need to appreciate that an intuitively acceptable modification will not always permit harming the shield. Consider this gruesome variation on our tank example: suppose I have no gun powerful enough to destroy the tank, but by shooting and killing the shield I can spatter his blood over the tank's window—blinding Schmidt, and allowing me to escape. Were it not for the shield conveniently located on the tank, I would be *unable* to escape. I think that most moderates will find killing the shield in this second case to be unacceptable, even though it was permissible to kill the shield in the original example. But what is the difference? The answer, I think, is that there are two ways that the harm to the shield can be a means to my end.

In the original case, the harm to the shield is a means to an end which I would have been able to achieve even were it not for the existence/state of the shield. All along I was capable of stopping the tank with my gun; now the shield blocks the tank—but harming the shield only puts me back where I would have been otherwise. The shield's presence—and eventual harm—doesn't make me any better off than I would have been without the shield altogether. It is different for the second case, where the presence—and eventual harm—of the shield itself *benefits* me. It makes me better off than I would have been without the shield altogether. Without the shield I would have been incapable of stopping the tank; harming the shield puts me ahead of where I would have been otherwise. Let us say, for cases of this second kind, that harm is a *strong* means to the desired end; in contrast, for cases of the first sort, the harm is merely a *weak* means to the end. Perhaps the moderate should modify the constraint so that it only forbids intending harm as a *strong* means. That is, the modified constraint would not rule out harm which is merely intended as a weak means.

The modified constraint apparently yields the intuitively correct judgments about shield cases. But since it does not explicitly mention shields at all (unlike the original suggested modification), it thereby avoids the difficulties that would be involved in specifying the class of shields. What we have instead is a more general modification of the constraint against intending harm, which has, as one consequence, the ability to handle cases involving shields. Yet the modified constraint is still capable of prohibiting typical cases of intending harm: e.g., it forbids my allowing a patient to die so as to use his organs to save five others—for in such a case the death of the one would be a *strong* means to my end.

What is more, the modification may even provide the moderate with a solution to the problem of self-defense as well. Consider first the treatment of innocent threats—innocent individuals who increase the danger to others (e.g., a young child who is unwittingly about to cause an explosion). Moderates typically want to permit harming innocent threats if this is the only way to avert danger, yet an unqualified constraint against intending harm would apparently prohibit such a response. The modified constraint, however, seems to yield permission: harming an innocent threat generally does not put the agent in any better position than he would have been had the threat never come along in the first place;[9] consequently the harm is merely a weak means to the end of avoiding the danger— and so it is permitted. Nothing here seems to turn on the innocence of the threat, however: it seems that even when the threat is posed by a deliberate aggressor, harming the aggressor will merely be a

---

[9] Might there be cases where harming the innocent threat in a particular way would reduce the danger even beyond what it would have been had the innocent threat never come along in the first place? If so, harming the threat in that way would be a strong means, and would presumably be forbidden.

weak means to avoiding the danger he poses; thus the modified constraint can apparently permit intending harm in typical cases of self-defense. In short, if the moderate can restrict the constraint to cases of intending harm as a *strong* means, then he may find himself provided with answers to the difficulties we have noted.

But can the modification be defended? It is not clear that it can be. If we locate the moral offensiveness of intending harm in the fact that the agent is aiming at evil—one of our two suggested accounts of the constraint—then it seems that we will be unable to accept the modification. For even in cases where the harm is merely a weak means, the agent will still be intending evil, and so the morally offensive feature will still be present. Nor does it seem promising to suggest, e.g., that although the reasons that normally oppose intending harm are still generated (the agent is still aiming at evil), they are overridden by countervailing reasons that favor intending harm in such cases. Aside from the obvious difficulties attending such a proposal (What could be the origin of such reasons? Can they really be as powerful as the argument would require? And so on), we would need an explanation of why these countervailing reasons are generated *only* when the harm would be merely a *weak* means. No such explanation seems forthcoming. It appears, then, that the account that locates the offensiveness of intending harm in aiming at evil will be unable to accommodate the suggested modification of the constraint.

However, we *may* be able to incorporate the suggested modification if we follow instead the second of our two accounts of the constraint, and locate the moral offensiveness of intending harm in the fact that it involves using a person. Perhaps an advocate of this account might argue as follows: 'Each agent has, or is able to acquire, certain abilities; he is capable of accomplishing certain goals, avoiding certain harms, and so on. Now in some cases— cases where harm is merely a *weak* means—some other individual has (unfortunately) become so situated that he will be harmed by the exercise of the agent's capabilities. In effect, however, the agent only accomplishes what he is already able to do: the harm to the other bestows no real benefit; it only frees the agent from the paralysis imposed by the presence of the other. In contrast, when harm is a *strong* means, the agent literally gains at the other's expense. His capabilities are *increased*: he is able to take what he could not otherwise take—by virtue of the loss inflicted upon the other. So it is only in cases where harm is a strong means that the other person is actually being used, only in such cases that the agent is genuinely profiting from the misfortune of another. Therefore the constraint against intending harm should be restricted to cases of intending harm as a strong means.'

I do not know what we should make of this speech. On the one hand, it isn't obvious that we only want to speak of a person being used in those cases where the agent gains what he could not gain were it not for the existence of the victim. So it may be that the modification cannot actually be incorporated by the second account of the constraint either. On the other hand, it seems *possible* that a view of sort sketched here could be developed—in which case the moderate would be able to make the suggested modification after all.

However, the modified constraint itself may have implications which are unacceptable to the moderate. Restricted to cases of intending harm as a strong means, the constraint may excuse too much. For example, imagine that the only way to avoid the tank racing toward me is to push an innocent bystander over the cliff— enabling me to stand in safety where the bystander is currently standing. Most moderates, no doubt, would forbid my pushing the bystander—and it seems plausible to think that the constraint against intending harm should rule out such a reaction. Yet on the account I have suggested, pushing the bystander apparently is merely a weak means to my end, for I am no better off for the bystander's presence: were he not there, I could simply move to the safe spot. Thus it seems that the modified constraint excuses too much, and the moderate will want to reject it. Yet as we have seen, without proper modification the constraint against intending harm will unacceptably condemn too much.

It is true, of course, that the bystander whom I push out of the way is not serving as a shield for the oncoming tank. This may suggest that the proper solution is to somehow combine the two modifications considered so far. Against shields, perhaps, it is only harm that is intended as a strong means that is forbidden; but for others, the constraint is to be restrengthened, so that it altogether forbids intending harm, even as a weak means. Although such a version of the constraint would succeed in forbidding the pushing of the bystander, the objections to using such a solution are apparent. First, such an approach would reintroduce the need to delimit precisely the class of shields. Second, such an approach would no longer provide a justification of self-defense. (Although, no doubt, one could add further clauses to the proposed modification to take care of this problem as well.) But most importantly, relaxing the constraint so that it permits harm intended as a weak means against shields—but only against shields—seems hopelessly ad hoc. As I have noted, the second account of the moral offensiveness of intending harm may have available a justification for recognizing the distinction between weak and strong means. This argument may or may not succeed, but I see nothing at all in the potential justification that could explain why the distinction between strong and weak means should come into play for shields and shields alone.

If the moderate is to distinguish properly between the different kinds of cases involving shields, it seems that something like the distinction between weak and strong means is called for. But if making such a distinction is appropriate, it is hard to see why it should not be used in its full generality; and, as we have seen, there are indeed advantages to doing so. Yet, given the particular account of the distinction that I have offered, it remains true that a constraint restricted to a prohibition of harm intended as a strong means apparently excuses too much.

Perhaps the moderate could suggest an alternative analysis of the distinction between weak means and strong means so as to avoid the unwelcome results. Unlike the account I have suggested, such an alternative analysis would have to yield the desired judgment that pushing the bystander is a strong means. This is certainly a possibility. I do not know, however, what the rival account would look like, nor whether it could be defended, so let us move on to a new problem.

PERMISSION

Consider this classic example. A hand grenade falls in the middle of a group of revolutionaries. In an unusual act of self-sacrifice, Manfred throws himself on the live grenade in order to shield his comrades from the explosion. He is killed, but his fellows escape unharmed.

Now this is a paradigm of the sort of act which ordinary morality believes to be governed by an option. What Manfred does is meritorious—but not morally *required*. Although he is free to do so, he need not sacrifice his own life to protect the lives of his comrades. This is, presumably, what moderates want to claim about Manfred's reaction.

Yet it seems that advocates of the constraint against intending harm—far from considering his reaction meritorious—must condemn Manfred's act as morally forbidden, for it apparently violates the constraint. Manfred harms himself as a means of protecting his fellow revolutionaries. But this means that he *intends* harm—and this is forbidden by the constraint.

If this is correct, then the constraint will clearly be unacceptable to the moderate. Countless saintly, heroic, and altruistic deeds will not be the living examples of moral ideals which they are normally taken to be, but will rather be examples of acts which are morally forbidden. If every self-sacrifice undertaken to help others is condemned by the constraint, then the constraint obviously condemns too much, and will be abandoned by the moderate.

Advocates of the constraint may try to argue that Manfred does not actually intend harm. They might suggest that the harm which he suffers—mutilation and death—is not itself a means to his end of protecting his friends. It is only covering the grenade which is the means of protecting the others: it is this which shields them from the explosion. The harm to Manfred which eventuates, it might be argued, is only a foreseen side-effect of covering the grenade. So harm is not intended, and the constraint is not violated.

Such a reply, however, would clearly be inadequate. Imagine that when the grenade falls, Manfred does *not* throw himself on it, but is instead *thrown* on it by his not so comradely fellow revolutionary, Annette.[10] Throwing someone on a live grenade in order to protect oneself and one's friends is obviously just the sort of act which the constraint is meant to forbid. Equally obviously, the fact that Annette throws Manfred, instead of his throwing himself, cannot alter whether harm is *intended*. In both cases, Manfred's body provides a shield for the others, by absorbing the impact of the exploding grenade; he is placed in a dangerous and harmful position as a means to a good end. From the point of view of what is intended, Annette's act of murder is indistinguishable from

[10] This case is noted by Duff, p. 79, although he fails to draw the obvious conclusion.

Manfred's act of self-sacrifice.[11] The moderate is unwilling to group the two acts together, but the constraint against intending harm seems unable to distinguish between them.

Now there is, of course, an obvious difference between the two cases. When Manfred throws himself, his sacrifice is voluntary; when he is thrown by Annette, the sacrifice is imposed on him, against his will. In both cases harm is intended, but in the former case alone the recipient of the intended harm undergoes the harm willingly: Manfred grants permission to himself (as it were) to impose the harm. This suggests that what the moderate may want to claim is that the constraint does not forbid intending harm when the agent has the permission of the recipient of the harm. Let us call this the *permission principle*.

Stated in this way, the permission principle does not distinguish between cases where the agent and the victim are one and the same person, and cases where they are different people. Manfred as victim gives permission to himself as agent—and does not violate the constraint. Equally permissible, however, would have been for Manfred to give his permission to Annette to *throw* him on the grenade; this too would have been within the bounds of the constraint. Some moderates may be unhappy with such symmetry, feeling that it is permissible for Manfred to sacrifice himself, but not permissible for Annette to act, not even with Manfred's permission. But so long as the permissibility of Manfred's act of self-sacrifice is explained in terms of the willingness of the recipient of harm, the symmetry seems unavoidable. Asymmetry could, of course, be created if the explanation were cast in terms of the agent's willingly harming *himself*: such an asymmetrical permission principle would rule out Annette's throwing Manfred; for even though she would have his permission, Manfred would not be doing the deed himself. Yet if we are going to assume that the willingness of the recipient of the harm can make a difference at all—and this is what any form of the permission principle must assume—then it is hard to see why it should matter whether the person is capable of performing the sacrificial act himself, or must resort to the use of an authorized assistant. So let us consider the permission principle in the symmetrical form.

---

[11] It is also worth noting that even if it is true that Manfred's mutilation and death are not themselves means of protecting the others, his exposure to the risk of mutilation and death clearly *is* a means, and surely the constraint must forbid such risky exposure as well. There is, however, no need for us to get involved in a detailed analysis of risks, harms and means.

The first thing to notice is that the permission principle may excuse too much for the taste of many moderates. Although ordinary morality praises deeds such as Manfred's act of self-sacrifice, it has often been taken to condemn such acts as suicide and euthanasia. Many moderates have wanted to forbid killing oneself; and an even greater number of moderates have wanted to forbid deliberately taking the life of another person, even when that person believes, e.g., that a swift painless death is preferable to a slow painful one. This attitude about suicide and euthanasia is not universal among moderates, of course, but it is widespread. And many moderates who hold it have believed that the constraint against intending harm explains why such acts are forbidden: harm (death of oneself or of another) is being intended as a means to some desirable end (the elimination of someone's suffering and misery).

If the moderate is going to accept the permission principle, however, then the judgments about suicide and euthanasia cannot be maintained. For in both sorts of acts, although harm is intended as a means, the agent of the harm acts with the permission of the recipient of the harm—and so would not be in violation of the constraint. Note, furthermore, that the permission principle does not merely yield the permissibility of suicide and euthanasia in extreme cases, e.g., where the victim suffers from intense and untreatable pain. Many moderates would be willing to endorse suicide or euthanasia in such extreme cases; but the effect of the permission principle is far more general: so long as the victim desires to die (provided that he is not irrational?), even if he is not in great pain or greatly incapacitated, it appears that the constraint against intending harm could not forbid suicide or euthanasia. For many moderates, then, the permission principle added to the constraint against intending harm excuses too much. But without the moderating influence of the permission principle, the constraint alone *condemns* too much. Thus the moderate faces a dilemma; and I am unaware of any other plausible alternative to the permission principle which will suit the moderate's purpose. (It should be noted that even for an asymmetrical version of the permission principle, the permissiblity of suicide seems to follow.)

This problem is quite a serious one for those who want to reject suicide and euthanasia. But as I have noted, such rejection is not at all universal; many moderates are inclined to accept the permissibility of such acts and so are willing (or perhaps eager) to embrace the implications of the permission principle. Such moderates, however, face another pressing difficulty: it is not at all clear that advocates of the constraint against intending harm can *justify* the permission principle. As with the suggested exceptions for cases of self-defense, the modification may provide better fit for intuitions, but it may be unacceptable from the point of view of the constraint itself.

Consider the two possible accounts of the moral offensiveness of intending harm which were briefly suggested earlier, i.e., that intending harm involves aiming at evil, or using another person. The first seems clearly incapable of accomodating the permission principle, for the issue of whether one's mind is 'turned' to evil when one intends harm does not seem to be affected by the recipient's having granted permission. If the moderate could claim that when permission is granted, pain, mutilation, or death are not actually harm, or not actually bad, then the exception could be accounted for: one would not really be intending *harm* after all; or at least, one would not be aiming at *evil*. But such a position cannot be maintained. Permission does not transform harm into nonharm.

Of course there may well be cases in which certain sorts of harm are not actually bad (and perhaps should not even be called 'harm' at all, on balance). It might be suggested, e.g., that the death of one who is in great pain, and who desires to die, is not bad, or not an evil. Now such cases might provide a limited justification for suicide and euthanasia, since, by hypothesis, one who intends the death of such a victim would not be aiming at evil. But such cases would not amount to anything like a defense of the permission principle, for it is not at all plausible to suggest that the mere presence of permission guarantees that harm is not evil, or that permission transforms pain, mutilation, and death into something not bad. On the contrary, special cases aside, such damage is still intrinsically bad, and the agent has a strong reason to avoid it—despite the recipient's permission. (Suppose that the agent finds a safe alternative means to the desirable end, but that the recipient foolishly continues to give permission.) Permission does not alter the extent to which the agent is incorporating harm into his course of action; it does not alter the extent to which the countenancing of harm as a means is an indication that the agent is aiming at evil. If the notion of aiming at evil is going to provide the center of the account of the constraint against intending harm, then the permission principle seems ruled out. But without it, the constraint condemns too much.

Once again, however, the moderate may do better with the second possible account of the moral offensiveness of intending harm—the account which stresses that when I intend harm as a means I *use* another person. It might be suggested that this flies in the face of the fact that the other person is not *mine* to use; no one else is mine to use. And so it is wrong to use people as a means in this way.

Such an account has a plausible way of yielding the permission principle. For although no other person is mine to use, it does not seem unreasonable for the moderate to hold that *I* am mine (so to speak), and so in using *myself* I am not using what is not mine. Therefore, it might be claimed, in cases of intending harm where the agent is himself the recipient of the harm, the morally offensive element is missing, and the constraint does not apply. So far, the argument only supports the permission principle in its asymmetrical form—where the agent's permission makes it permissible for the agent to intend harm to himself. But a somewhat similar line might support the entire, symmetrical permission principle. For if I have been given permission by some other person, then my intending harm is not an instance of my using another for my own ends. By granting permission the recipient reveals that he has taken on the ends as his *own*, and I can be viewed as merely being a duly authorized agent of the recipient, who is acting through me. Once more, the morally offensive element is missing, and the constraint does not apply. It is possible, therefore, that this second account of the constraint can be filled out in such a way as to incorporate the permission principle.

It is not clear whether the second account will actually be able to support the permission principle in this way. For the argument just sketched appears to involve the claim that an agent *cannot* misuse himself—i.e., that it is impossible for him to do so. It is the impossibility of using oneself in the morally offensive way that guarantees that the presence of the recipient's permission removes the morally offensive element from intending harm. But this view— that it is impossible for an agent to misuse himself, to treat himself improperly—is one which most moderates would reject, including many advocates of the second account. Most moderates would hold that it is indeed possible to use oneself in the morally offensive way, and that such behavior is, consequently, forbidden. In fact, one common way of expressing this point is to say that one may not treat oneself as a mere means. But if it is in fact possible for an agent to use himself in the morally offensive way, then the defense of the permission principle is unsuccessful. At the very least, more would need to be said to establish whether the complaint that intending harm uses the victim can be legitimately restricted to cases of using others. For if the restriction is illegitimate, the attempt to make room for the permission principle within the constraint against intending harm fails.

Another way to understand this point is to recast it in terms of autonomy, a notion that meshes well with the attempt to locate the moral offensiveness of intending harm in using another. It might be suggested that it is a violation of my autonomy for others to use me for purposes that I reject; thus an appeal to autonomy appears to support a constraint against intending harm. But at the same time, it might also be claimed that when I act freely—whether alone or in cooperation with others—for ends that I endorse, this is, in contrast, an expression of my autonomy. Thus, at first glance, an appeal to autonomy also supports the permission principle. But many advocates of autonomy have wanted to maintain that there are ways that an agent may treat herself which, far from expressing her autonomy, actually serve to oppose it or to violate it. Yet if this is correct, it would seem that one who appeals to autonomy will ultimately have to reject the permission principle as unacceptably strong.

Of course there may be ways to modify or restrict the permission principle so as to remove the unacceptable implications. And it is possible that a full explication of what is offensive about using someone may make clear how and when the recipient's permission eliminates the morally offensive element. It does not seem implausible for an advocate of the constraint against intending harm to hope that the second account can actually be developed so as to permit cases of self-sacrifice; but it is, at least, not obvious that this is so.

It is worth mentioning that the advocate of the constraint against *doing* harm may have been enjoying himself as we have rehearsed the difficulties that self-defense, self-sacrifice, and the like cause for the constraint against *intending* harm. If this is so, then the self-satisfaction is misplaced—for the same problems plague the constraint against doing harm. Indeed, it is even *less* obvious how a defender of that constraint would go about justifying incorporating the necessary modifications.[12]

DUE PROPORTION

The problems with the constraint against intending harm which we have considered so far suggest that the constraint may condemn too much. But this is not the only problem it faces. The constraint as we have described it also *excuses* too much; and it is not clear whether this problem can be satisfactorily corrected.

Imagine that a factory owner can increase his profit by altering the chemical processes used in production. Unfortunately, the new processes will release poisonous wastes into the nearby river which will travel downstream to the next town, resulting in a certain number of deaths. Unscrupulous profit-maximizer that he is, the industrialist orders the introduction of the new processes. Yet he quiets his slightly nagging conscience with the thought that he intends no harm at all—that the harm which he countenances is merely *foreseen*.

Surely the factory owner is right when he claims that the harm which befalls his victims is not a means to his end; the deaths of the townspeople are merely foreseen side-effects. His action, therefore, does not violate the constraint against intending harm. Presumably, however, moderates typically want to forbid the industrialist's reaction. Apparently, then, the constraint against intending harm excuses too much.

[12] Harming an aggressor or a shield is clearly still doing harm, and it is still interfering with the welfare of another. (It is, furthermore, distributing a good—e.g., the life of the aggressor or shield—in a manner opposed to the desires of those on whom it is dependent.) So how is self-defense to be justified? And harming someone—even with their permission—is still doing harm, and still interfering (although suicide is something of a gimmicky case). So how is self-sacrifice to be permitted? (It must be admitted, though, that when an agent has the permission of the recipient of the harm, he needn't be distributing a good in a manner opposed to the desires of those on whom it depends. Advocates of this approach, therefore, had better be willing to endorse an undiluted permission principle.)

The moderate will of course reply that the mere fact that the reaction is not forbidden by the constraint does not show that the reaction is *permitted*. And this is correct. A morally decisive reason opposing the industrialist's reaction, grounding a prohibition of that reaction, might well be provided by something other than the constraint. In particular, the moderate might note that the pro tanto reason to promote the good remains, and the factory owner might lack a morally acceptable countervailing reason.

But such a reply won't suffice, for by the moderate's lights the factory owner does have an acceptable countervailing reason. For the industrialist can make an appeal to cost—thereby grounding an option to do the unintended harm to the townspeople. Such an appeal would be illegitimate were the harm intended—for the constraint against intending harm is presumed to override the appeal to cost. But since the harm is *not* intended, nothing blocks the appeal. Yet the moderate does want to forbid the owner's reaction.

If the factory owner's appeal to cost is to be overridden, then the moderate will have to supplement the constraint against intending harm with some additional requirement. Without such supplementation, the constraint will be inadequate to cover the cases which the moderate wants covered.

It is for this reason that advocates of the constraint against intending harm have typically insisted on a requirement of *due proportion* between the various aspects of the outcome countenanced by the agent.[13] Unfortunately, little if anything is ever said to clarify the notion of due proportion, and as we shall see, this leads to serious problems. But roughly, the idea is that the good aspects of the countenanced outcome must be significant enough to justify the countenancing of the bad aspects. That is, even if the bad is unintended, its proportions must not be so great as to undermine the legitimacy of countenancing the good. The factory owner countenances a very great harm—the deaths of several townspeople—and only a very slight good—an increase in profits. Therefore, even though he does not violate the constraint, for he intends no harm, he falls short of the requirement of due proportion—and his reaction is forbidden.

With the added requirement of due proportion, then, the moderate can maintain his allegiance to the constraint against

[13] See, e.g., Mangan, p. 43 and passim; and Fried, pp. 52, 202–3.

intending harm, without fearing that the constraint may excuse too much. But I was deliberately vague in the previous paragraph as to just what relation between the good and bad aspects of the outcome is required in order that due proportion be satisfied. Making the notion of due proportion acceptably precise presents the moderate with considerable difficulties. Let's examine several possible accounts.

1. We might start with the plausible suggestion that due proportion is simply a matter of the good which is countenanced being objectively greater than the bad which is countenanced. The requirement of due proportion, then, would demand that when an agent reacts, the good aspects must outweigh the bad; and the constraint itself adds the requirement that none of the bad be intended. Our factory owner countenances more harm than good, and so fails to meet the requirement of due proportion.

The moderate, however, cannot accept such an account of due proportion, for it would require too much—leaving no room for the sort of options that he wants to endorse. An option to allow harm, for example, may permit an agent to promote his own interests in some manner, even though in doing so he fails to prevent some harm, where the harm he allows is objectively greater than the good he promotes. But this means that the outcome he countenances has both a good and a bad aspect—and the bad is objectively greater than the good. Thus, in acting on the option to allow harm, the agent fails to meet the requirement of due proportion as we have just specified it.[14]

If we maintain such an account of due proportion, then, we find ourselves endorsing an extremist's position: a system with constraints, but without options. (Remember that the extremist's position is compatible with the existence of constraints, even though—since it is also compatible with their nonexistence—I have placed the burden of defending constraints upon the moderate.)

---

[14] Does the requirement of due proportion as we have given it rule out *all* options? I believe so. Any option grants the agent permission to perform an act which is less than optimal from a neutral perspective. If he acts on the option, then, at the very least, he fails to promote the good as fully as he is able, promoting instead a lesser good. The nonobtaining of that greater good is a bad aspect of the outcome which he countenances, and it is greater in magnitude than the good which he does promote: so due proportion is not satisfied, no matter what the option. The nonobvious step here is the claim that the nonobtaining of some good should count as bad for the purposes of the due proportion requirement. I won't try to defend this nonobvious claim, however.

Since this account of due proportion would effectively eliminate options, accepting it would represent a victory for the extremist. Without any requirement of due proportion, however, the constraint against intending harm excuses too much for the moderate—yielding an overly minimalist position. If he is going to avoid both of these alternatives, the moderate must find a more modest account of due proportion.

The need for a second account of due proportion is reinforced by the fact that intuition seems to support a more complicated account than the one we have just considered. Intuitively, it seems that judgments of due proportion—despite the name of the requirement—are affected by factors other than simply that of the magnitude of the good and bad aspects of the outcome.

Contrast these two cases.

(A) In an effort to free my backyard of mosquitoes, I release a gas bomb—foreseeing that the poisonous fumes will waft into the home of my immovable invalid neighbor, causing his death.

(B) Killing the mosquitoes does not threaten my neighbor at all—but I realize that had I sent the money with which I purchased the smoke bomb to famine relief instead, some individual who will now die would have been saved.

In both cases the death which is countenanced is merely a foreseen side-effect of my reaction; in neither case is harm to another a means to accomplishing my end of freeing my yard of the insects. Consequently, in neither case is the constraint against intending harm violated. What about the requirement of due proportion? Since the corresponding magnitudes of the good and bad aspects are identical, on our original account the two cases would have to be treated equivalently. And since the bad aspect of the countenanced outcome (the death of some individual) is greater in magnitude than the good aspect (ridding my yard of mosquitoes), the requirement of due proportion would have been met in neither case. And so my reaction is forbidden in both.

Yet presumably moderates want to distinguish between the two cases, forbidding my reaction in (A), while permitting it in (B). (A) is of a piece with the sort of behavior displayed by the factory owner, which provoked the concern that the constraint against intending harm excuses too much, and prompted the introduction of the requirement of due proportion. (B), however, is an example of the sort of behavior which moderates typically want to protect with options; it may not be praiseworthy, but it is permissible. An account of due proportion adequate to the moderate's purposes, therefore, must find some way to discriminate between the two cases.

The obvious suggestion, of course, is the relevance of the distinction between doing and allowing. The harm is the same magnitude in both cases, and in neither case is it intended—but in (A) I do harm, while in (B) I merely allow it. It appears that the requirement of due proportion must be sensitive to whether the harm which the agent countenances is one he actually brings about, or merely allows. The requirement must be more severe in the former case than in the latter. Not only is this an obvious suggestion, it is difficult to think of any *other* suggestion which is at all promising.

If he follows this suggestion, however, the moderate is immediately faced with a number of difficulties. To begin with, it should not be overlooked that by incorporating the doing/allowing distinction into the account of due proportion, the advocate of the constraint against intending harm inherits the various problems which plagued the advocate of the constraint against doing harm. I argued in the previous chapter that it is not clear whether the doing/allowing distinction can be drawn in an intuitively satisfying manner without trivializing it for the moderate's purposes as a result of presupposing normative elements in the account. Providing a substantive requirement of due proportion will be equally difficult if the account of the requirement is to depend on the elusive distinction.

I also argued that, taken seriously, the constraint against doing harm appears to condemn too much, for there are various troublesome cases—e.g., cases of cutting off a process of aid—which must be classified as cases of doing harm, contrary to our intuitions. If due proportion is going to forbid doing harm—even though the harm is unintended—when the good countenanced is not significant enough to justify countenancing the bad, then the troublesome cases are going to return to embarrass the advocate of the constraint against intending harm. For imagine that we adopt a requirement of due proportion which is more demanding with regard to unintended harm which is brought about than it is with regard to unintended harm which is merely allowed. Such a requirement will find itself unwillingly forced to subject many cases to the more severe standards reserved for unintended harm which is brought about—cases which intuitively should have been subject only to the lenient standards reserved for unintended harm which is merely allowed.

Without incorporating the distinction between doing and allowing, then, it seems that an adequate account of due proportion cannot be provided. If the distinction is incorporated, however, there is a renewal of problems which the advocate of the constraint against intending harm hoped to leave behind.

Nor do the moderate's problems end here. The basic idea for a revised account of due proportion—sensitivity to the doing/ allowing distinction—may be clear enough. But it is rather obscure just how this idea is to be developed. All that is really established is that we have to make separate decisions about the standards which must be met when I bring about unintended harm and when I merely allow unintended harm; and that the former are to be more severe than the latter. But there is little guidance as to what due proportion should require within these two cases.

Let us start by considering the question of what due proportion will require for unintended harm which is merely allowed. Moderates, of course, do not believe that an agent's option to allow harm is unlimited. There are cases—e.g., the drowning child— where the good to be gained so vastly outweighs the cost to the agent, that the agent is forbidden to allow the (admittedly unintended) harm. Many moderates might even be willing to require significant sacrifices of the agent were the harms that could only be prevented in this way sufficiently overwhelming. In short, options to allow harm may have thresholds. From one perspective, then, to say what due proportion requires for unintended harm that is merely allowed is simply to describe the thresholds that these options have. This is certainly something that a full description of the moderate's position must provide. But it is, luckily, something that we need not consider further here.

There is, however, a question as to whether it is helpful to talk of a requirement of due proportion in describing the thresholds of such options. Not surprisingly, moderates differ as to how these thresholds are determined. Now on some views, the threshold—the limit to the harm that the agent can allow—is a multiple of the potential cost to the agent of preventing that harm.[15] On such views, then, there is a clear sense in which we can speak of a requirement of due proportion for unintended harm which is merely allowed: doing so draws attention to the fact that the harm allowed must be less than some given multiple of the good gained by the agent. On other views, however, the thresholds of options are not determined by any such simple multiple, and so talk of due proportion for unintended harm that is merely allowed does nothing but clumsily point to the very fact that options do have thresholds.

There is, in fact, some reason to say that due proportion will require nothing at all when it comes to unintended harm that is merely allowed. For it is the interplay of the pro tanto reason to promote the good and the appeal to cost that will yield a set of options and thresholds, determining when it is permissible to allow harm as a mere side effect, and when it is not permissible. The boundaries of permissible reactions in this area will simply be established in the course of justifying options. Talk of a requirement of due proportion here may mislead us, for it may suggest that some additional work is going to be done by something other than the appeal to cost and the pro tanto reason to promote the good. For this reason, it may be best to say that due proportion does not require anything for unintended harm that is merely allowed.

If the moderate does decide to say that for such cases due proportion requires nothing at all, this would *not* mean, of course, that it would be permissible to allow any harm at all, so long as the harm was not intended. It would simply mean that the appeal to cost would be legitimate in such cases, in contrast to cases where the allowed harm *is* intended as a means—in violation of the constraint—and so appeal to cost is illegitimate. Given that options to allow harm have thresholds, an appeal to cost in a particular case of allowing harm may not necessarily be successful, but it will not be out of order. As already noted, however, it is not pressing for us to determine precisely where the moderate locates the thresholds of options to allow unintended harm.

It is pressing, however, to specify what due proportion requires

---

[15] Scheffler describes such an option, I believe, p. 20. See my discussion of this passage in 'Does Consequentialism', pp. 250–1.

in those cases where the unintended harm is brought about. For here the moderate certainly does *not* want to give the appeal to cost such free reign. The moderate presumably does not want to leave the callous industrialist free to appeal to cost and thereby ground an option to poison the townspeople downstream. The requirement of due proportion is needed to override such an appeal. Therefore, it is important to see whether the requirement can be specified in an acceptable manner. What account should we give?

2. We might want to retain here the germ of our original account of due proportion—the notion that the good aspects of the countenanced outcome must be greater in magnitude than the bad aspects. On the revised account of due proportion, unintended harm which I bring about must be less than the good which I countenance. This would be enough to block both my reaction in (A) and that of the callous industrialist—for in both cases the harm which is brought about is greater than the good countenanced. According to this second account, however, due proportion *would* be satisfied in any cases in which the unintended harm that I bring about is *less* than the good.

3. Alternatively, we might want to make the requirement of due proportion even more demanding with regard to unintended harm which I bring about: we might simply erect a constraint against doing harm even when unintended. The force of the constraint could be tempered, if we liked, through the use of thresholds; or we could uncompromisingly keep the constraint absolute. (It is not clear that the requirement of due proportion would deserve its name if it simply amounted to a constraint, particularly if it were an *absolute* constraint—but never mind.) On this third alternative, it would not be sufficient for the unintended harm that I bring about to be less than the good which I countenance. The good might have to be several times the size of the bad (depending on the threshold)—or it might be forbidden to bring about any harm at all (if the constraint were absolute).

This third account is likely to be rejected by the moderate, however, for it would run counter to the intuitions on which advocates of the constraint against intending harm thrive. Consider a case typical of those which are likely to be appealed to when such moderates defend the claim that the constraint against intending harm captures our intuitions more adequately than a constraint against doing harm. It is a case in which the judgments of the constraint against doing harm and the constraint against intending harm diverge—and the former gives what is taken to be the wrong answer.

(C) Suppose that a meteor is racing toward a large city, and will cause a large number of deaths if its lands. However, if we first send out the appropriate sort of shock waves—say, by exploding certain missiles at a particular location high in the stratosphere—we can deflect the meteor. Unfortunately, we cannot alter the path enough to send the meteor safely crashing into the ocean—but we can at least guarantee that the meteor will only land in a small town, causing a smaller number of deaths. Should we create the shock waves, deflecting the meteor?

Those moderates who favor the constraint against *intending* harm will answer 'yes'. And they will emphasize that the constraint against intending harm permits deflection, for the deaths of those in the small town are an unfortunate but merely foreseen side-effect of saving the greater number in the large city. The constraint against doing harm, however, must forbid the deflection, for the small number of deaths are brought about if we alter the path, while the large number of deaths would be merely *allowed* if the meteor is not deflected. The ability of the constraint against intending harm to permit deflecting the meteor is taken to be an advantage of such a constraint over a constraint against doing harm.

If the requirement of due proportion were construed in keeping with our third account, however, this purported advantage would be lost. For this account suggests that we erect a constraint against doing harm, even when it is unintended. Since deflecting the meteor is bringing about harm, it would fail to meet the requirement of due proportion.[16]

---

[16] A defender of the third account might suggest that the threshold of the due proportion requirement may have been passed in (C)—and that is why it is permissible to deflect the meteor. But such a response to the objection won't suffice. For if the due proportion requirement does indeed involve a constraint against the unintended doing of harm, as the third account suggests, then there will have to be cases in which it is *forbidden* to deflect the meteor in situation (C)—even though more lives would be saved than lost—because the net gain would be too small to pass the threshold. Presumably, however, advocates of the constraint against intending harm believe it permissible to deflect the meteor in (C) no matter how small the net gain in lives saved. So due proportion must be understood in accordance with the second account.

If the moderate is going to retain the presumed advantage of the constraint against intending harm, then due proportion must be construed in such a way as to permit exploding the missiles and creating the shock waves, even though this results in bringing about unintended harm. Thus due proportion must be taken in the sense of our second account: the harm which is done must be smaller in magnitude than the good countenanced—but doing harm is not altogether forbidden. Since deflecting the meteor results in a smaller number of deaths, all of which are unintended, due proportion would be satisfied, and creating the shock waves will be permitted.

It appears, then, that the moderate will want to propose the second account. But this account of due proportion has its counterintuitive aspects as well. The third account appears to condemn too much; but the second account excuses too much. Consider a revision of example (C).

(D) Suppose that the meteor is racing toward the large city, and that, as before, shock waves can deflect it. This time, however, the meteor can in fact be deflected safely into the ocean. Unfortunately, the only way to create a shock wave of the correct size and direction is by exploding the missiles a few hundred feet directly above the small town, which would have otherwise escaped unharmed. The explosion of the missiles just above the town will, of course, unavoidably result in a great deal of destruction. The expected number of deaths is the same as in the original example. Should we explode the missiles above the town, deflecting the meteor?[17]

Many moderates will want to claim that we may not explode the missiles directly above the town, even though this is the only way to alter the path of the meteor. If we do explode the missiles, however, the ensuing deaths will not be a means to creating the shock waves (the presence of the town is irrelevant for that)—so the constraint against intending harm is not violated.[18] If exploding the missiles

---

[17] (C) and (D) are variations of examples given by Thomson in 'Trolley', p. 208.

[18] There may be a lingering belief that the harm to the townspeople *is* intended, contrary to my suggestion. Imagine, then, a range of cases, in which the shock waves are created by exploding the missiles at different heights directly above the small town. I suspect that for each moderate there is some height such that he will feel that the harm to the townspeople will be only a foreseen side-effect of creating the shock waves, yet it will nonetheless be impermissible to explode the missiles.

just above the town is to be forbidden, it apparently must be because due proportion is not satisfied. Yet on the second account due proportion *is* satisfied—for the unintended harm which is brought about is smaller in magnitude than the good which is countenanced.

The revised example, (D), therefore, supports the third account, according to which due proportion forbids the unintended doing of harm; for it is clear that exploding the missiles directly above the small town is a case of doing harm, even though the harm is unintended. That is, the third account of due proportion can accommodate our intuitions concerning the revised example, (D). Unfortunately, however, as we have seen, the third account fails on the original example, (C). In contrast, the second account succeeds for the original, but fails for the revised example.[19]

Clearly, if the intuitive judgments for examples (C) and (D) are to be retained, the moderate needs yet another account of due proportion. For in both cases the harm is unintended, brought about by the agent, and smaller than the good which is countenanced. It seems, then, that neither the doing/allowing distinction, nor the relative magnitudes of the good and bad aspects of the countenanced outcome provide sufficient material for creating an account of due proportion which will meet the moderate's needs.

[19] Not every moderate will agree with the intuitive judgments I have offered for the two examples. Although there is no room to marshal a long list of alternative examples, let me note two more (both come from Foot): (C) can be replaced with the classic trolley example, where I must choose between letting the trolley continue on its present track where it will kill five people, or switching the trolley to the other track where it will kill only one. Here the choice is between bringing about the unintended death of one or merely allowing the unintended deaths of five. Most believe it is permissible to switch to the track with one—contrary to the constraint against doing harm. A constraint against intending harm can permit switching to the track with one, since the death is unintended; but only if due proportion permits the doing of unintended harm, as our second account suggests. (D) can be replaced with the poison gas in the hospital case, where an operation to save five will unavoidably release poison gas killing a sixth patient who cannot be moved, but who otherwise would be fine. Most moderates believe one cannot operate in this case. Yet the death of the one is merely a foreseen side-effect of saving the five. Thus if the constraint against intending harm is to forbid operating, it seems that it will have to be because due proportion forbids the doing of unintended harm, as our third account suggests. These examples could be easily multiplied. I believe that (almost?) all moderates sympathetic to the constraint against intending harm will be able to find at least one intuitively compelling counterexample to each of these two accounts of due proportion. (Obviously, however, a given account will remain available to any moderate who finds no members of the relevant set of counterexamples intuitively troubling.)

No obvious fourth account presents itself for consideration.[20]
And this is a most serious problem for the advocate of the
constraint against intending harm. Without a requirement of due
proportion, the constraint against intending harm excuses too
much. But we have been unable to find an account of due
proportion with which the moderate can be happy—not even when
we have incorporated the troublesome doing/allowing distinction.[21]

Although it will require a short digression, I cannot resist
discussing one more case. When I distinguished between the
constraint against intending harm and the constraint against doing
harm, at the start of Chapter 3, I noted that advocates of each
constraint try to marshal cases in support of their claim that our

---

[20] One might suggest that due proportion permits deflecting an already existing
harm, but forbids *creating* a new harm (cf. Thomson, 'Trolley', pp. 208 ff.). This
seems to account for (C) and (D), as well as the classic trolley case and the poison gas
case mentioned in the previous note. But the suggestion won't do: advocates of the
constraint against intending harm typically want to permit strategic bombing of
munitions factories during war, where deaths to civilians are foreseen side-effects—
even though bombing the factory involves creating a new harm and not merely
deflecting an old one. (Lest it be suggested that the special circumstances of being at
war make it permissible to create harm—and that is why bombing the munitions
factory is permitted—bear in mind that moderates typically do *not* want to permit
the deliberate bombing of hospitals so as to dishearten the enemy. The constraint
against intending harm is used *within* the context of war to discriminate between the
permissible and the impermissible; an adequate account of due proportion had
better be available to do the same.)

[21] Two other complications in the requirement of due proportion should be
mentioned. (1) Sometimes unintended harm (to one or many) is countenanced
because the only way to avoid it would be by reacting impermissibly (e.g., intending
a smaller amount of harm to someone else). Should unintended harm of this sort be
counted when determining whether due proportion has been satisfied? It seems not.
For if it were counted, there might be cases in which due proportion would forbid
countenancing the unintended harm—thus requiring the agent to react in a way that
is, by hypothesis, impermissible (i.e., intending the smaller harm). It might be
suggested, however, that in any case apparently of this sort, if the unintended harm
is so large that due proportion rules out countenancing it, then the threshold for the
constraint against intending the smaller harm will have been passed, and so the
reaction needed to avoid the larger, unintended harm will be permissible after all.
But reflection on examples will establish, I believe, that even if this sometimes holds
true, it will not hold true universally. (2) A satisfactory requirement of due
proportion will still have to be supplemented by (or else incorporate) a prohibition
against gratuitous harm. For even if a particular good outcome is sufficiently
weighty to justify causing a certain harm as an unintended side-effect, an adequate
account will not permit causing that harm if it could be avoided (or at least
reduced)—while still achieving the good. There are several other points in ordinary
morality at which the need for such a prohibition of gratuitous harm may emerge as
well (e.g., whenever constraints have finite thresholds); an adequate statement of this
principle would, I believe, be surprisingly complex.

intuitions support one constraint rather than another. Examples are constructed for those areas where the two constraints diverge—i.e., where one constraint forbids the given reaction, while another constraint permits it. By checking our intuitions concerning the reaction in question, we can see which constraint better conforms to our intuitions. Now when a particular case is offered as an intuitive counterexample to a given constraint there are two basic possibilities. (1) Our intuitive judgment may be that the reaction in question is forbidden, and yet the constraint being criticized permits it. (2) Our intuitive judgment may be that the reaction in question is permitted, and yet the constraint being criticized forbids it. Of these two possibilities, the second is intuitively far more damaging.

When examples belong to the first type, they may show nothing more than that there is a need to supplement the constraint in question with other moral principles. Recognizing that a given moral principle fails to prohibit a particular forbidden reaction is still compatible with retaining that moral principle unchanged, so long as it can be supplemented with other principles that do manage to rule out the remaining forbidden reactions. The introduction of the requirement of due proportion is, in effect, a response to examples of this first type. It is an attempt to supplement the unadorned constraint against intending harm, prohibiting reactions that we intuitively take to be forbidden, but which the constraint by itself fails to forbid. Since I suggested, at the start of Chapter 3, that both the intend/foresee distinction and the do/allow distinction have intuitive weight, it is, perhaps, not surprising that advocates of the constraint based on the former distinction have felt the need to supplement that constraint. (What is somewhat surprising is that advocates of the constraint based on the latter distinction have not recognized a corresponding need— even though cases of allowing harm as a means often intuitively strike us as immoral, suggesting that the constraint against doing harm should be supplemented as well.) As we have seen, it is not an easy matter to find an intuitively adequate supplement, but those moderates who advocate the constraint against intending harm can proceed in their search with the hope that ultimately they will still be able to retain the constraint itself.

When counterexamples fall into the second class, however, the attack on the given constraint is far more threatening. For if the constraint forbids a reaction that we take to be permitted, the problem cannot be solved by supplementing the constraint. Rather, the constraint in question must be cut back, so that it no longer forbids the given reaction. If the example goes to the heart of the constraint, such surgery may not be possible, and the constraint may have to be abandoned. It is for this reason that cases like (C)—the original meteor example—have been especially emphasized by advocates of the constraint against intending harm. By exploding missiles high in the stratosphere and thereby deflecting the meteor, we prevent a large number of deaths, and bring about a much smaller number. Those who share the intuitive judgment that it is permissible to deflect the meteor onto the small town, will find that the constraint against intending harm can accommodate the intuition (for the deaths in the small town are unintended side-effects), while the constraint against doing harm cannot—for there is no question that the deaths in the small town are ones we bring about. Intuitively, cases of this sort are extremely damaging to the constraint against doing harm. There seems little hope of modifying the constraint to permit deflection of the meteor, and so those who want to retain the intuitive judgment seem faced with the necessity of abandoning the constraint against doing harm.

Examples like (C) provide extremely strong intuitive support for a constraint against intending harm rather than a constraint against doing harm. It seems only fair, then, to mention in this context an example which appears to support a constraint against doing harm over a constraint against intending harm (i.e., just the opposite of (C)). Imagine that someone will be hit and killed by a runaway trolley unless I warn him to get off the tracks. Normally, of course, I *would* warn him. But suppose that if he does get off the tracks, the trolley will kill five children further down, whom I cannot warn. However, if I keep silent and the one is killed, his body will stop the trolley and the five will escape. If I warn him, five die; if I keep silent, only one dies.

Many, I think, will feel it is permissible to keep silent. And silence is permitted by a constraint against *doing* harm—for I will merely be *allowing* the death of the one. (If I warn the one, and the five die, have I merely allowed their deaths, or brought them about?) A constraint against *intending* harm, however, will inappropriately forbid my keeping silent—for clearly I will be countenancing his death only because it is a means of saving the five.

Together with (C), this example seems to show that neither constraint can satisfy our intuitions. Each constraint appears to forbid some reaction that may intuitively strike us as permissible. If we were to believe that justifying a constraint is simply a matter of testing it against our intuitions, it would seem that we might be forced to abandon both constraints. As I have repeatedly urged, however, I do not believe that justification is a matter of intuitive fit. A position that strikes us as wildly counterintuitive, such as the extremist's view, may still be the most justifiable. And even if a given position managed to capture our intuitions perfectly, we would still need to know whether the position could be provided with a coherent justification. It is this question that advocates of the constraint against intending harm must now face.

RELEVANCE AGAIN

In the previous section I argued that the constraint against harm excuses too much, unless it can be supplemented with a requirement of due proportion—but that no satisfactory account of due proportion can be provided. In earlier sections I argued that the constraint also *condemns* too much, unless it can be modified in certain ways—but that the two suggested accounts of the constraint may be incapable of incorporating these modifications. For the most part, then, in our examination of the constraint against intending harm we have so far largely confined ourselves simply to considering the unpalatable implications of the constraint. But it is time to turn directly to the problem of justification, so let us bracket the previous objections, and pretend that the constraint against intending harm can be appropriately modified and supplemented, so that it neither condemns nor excuses too much.

As we have seen, the defense of a constraint against a given type of reaction can be understood as involving a series of three tasks. Therefore, to defend a constraint against intending harm, the moderate must do all of the following. First, he must establish (in a broad range of cases) the existence of a reason that particularly opposes intending harm. Second, the moderate must show that this reason is (typically) sufficiently powerful to override the countervailing reasons—in particular, the pro tanto reason to promote the good. Third, if there are any further conditions necessary for moral decisiveness, the moderate will have to show that the given reason meets these extra conditions as well. As with the discussion of the constraint against doing harm, however, I want to focus our attention on the first of these tasks. Let us assume that *if* the moderate can demonstrate the existence of a reason that particularly opposes intending harm, such a reason will be able to ground a constraint. Can the existence of the necessary reason be defended?

In Chapter 3, when we considered the justification of the constraint against doing harm, I noted three mysteries that the moderate is unable to dispel: why should doing be morally more significant than allowing; why should doing harm be more significant than doing good; and why should harm-doing generate agent-relative rather than agent-neutral reasons? As we shall see, similar mysteries shroud the constraint against intending harm.

The first question, of course, is why the distinction between intending and merely foreseeing should be thought to be morally relevant. Obviously enough, belief in the relevance of the distinction underlies the constraint. For if the moderate is to hold that intending harm is opposed by a morally decisive reason, there must be something especially offensive about it—something distinguishing it from merely foreseeing harm. Countenancing harm where this is merely a foreseen side-effect of one's reaction may well be a serious matter; but intending harm is a more serious matter. Presumably, this view is at the heart of the moderate's attempt to defend a constraint against intending harm: I cannot intend harm even in order to prevent some greater harm, for in such a situation I have to choose between actually *intending* harm and merely *foreseeing* harm—and the former is more significant than the latter. As with the distinction between doing and allowing, I conceded at the start of the last chapter that the moral relevance of the distinction between what is intended and what is merely foreseen probably has some intuitive support. Once again, however, the question is whether the moderate can *justify* this position.

I have briefly indicated two plausible suggestions for locating the moral offensiveness of intending harm: in the first, the thought is that the agent is *aiming* at evil; in the second the idea is that such an agent *uses* the person whose harm he intends. Let's consider each suggestion in turn.

If an agent intends a state of affairs, then that state of affairs is a *goal* of his—even if it is only a derivative goal, taken on only because it is a necessary means to achieving some intrinsically desired goal. The agent shapes his reaction so as to promote the goal. He reacts in such a way as to nurture it: he does what he can to bring it about; he takes steps to avoid eliminating it; he deliberately refrains from hindering it. If the state of affairs is only intended as a means, then the agent might gladly use other, better means were any available. But if they are not, he turns his mind to pursuing the necessary means—and his behavior is *guided* by the need to countenance the (possibly subsidiary) goal. We might say that the agent *aims* at the goal.

Therefore—the moderate may argue—when an agent intends harm as a means, he has a subsidiary goal of *harm*. The agent shapes his reaction so as to promote that goal—that evil. His mind is turned (even if only in part) to nurturing evil. It does not matter that he acts with a heavy heart; the agent's reaction is still *guided* by the need to countenance evil. He *aims* at evil. But it is the nature of evil that we should be *repelled* by it. It is of the essence of evil that it is not to be *aimed* at. Evil is not something we should be nurturing. Intending harm involves aiming at evil—and thus standing in a fundamentally incorrect relation to the essence of evil. When harm is merely a foreseen side-effect, however, one is not *aiming* at it—and so one does not stand in the essentially inappropriate relation. According to the first suggestion, this is the ground of the moral relevance of the distinction.[22]

We can grant the moderate the claim that to intend some state of affairs as a means is to have that state of affairs as a goal—to aim at it. Since harm is evil, it follows that to intend harm—even if only as a means—is to aim at evil, to have it as a goal. We can further grant that it is the nature of evil that we should be repelled by it. But it does not follow that it is always incorrect—let alone fundamentally incorrect—to intend evil; it does not follow that we should never aim at evil. This can be seen more clearly if we consider an example involving pain.

It is the nature of pain that we should attempt to repel it. Pain, after all, is not something that we want to nurture. Yet it does not follow from this that we should never aim at inflicting pain upon someone—that we should never have another's being in pain as our goal. For there could be cases in which causing someone to be in

---

[22] This account is borrowed from Nagel; his most recent statement of it is in *Nowhere*, pp. 181–82.

pain is a necessary means to preventing that person from undergoing even greater pain. Imagine a disease which has no painful symptoms for an initial period, but which—if left untreated—eventually erupts, regularly causing the patient excruciating pain, with no chance of remission or treatment. Luckily the disease can be cured, if treated during the initial, dormant stage. Treatment, however, requires inflicting a significant amount of pain upon the unfortunate patient: causing pain to the patient's body stimulates it to release certain hormones and antibodies (which cannot be otherwise produced) that destroy the disease-causing virus. Since the pain necessary for treatment, although significant, is far less than that caused by the disease itself, we may have good reason to deliberately induce pain in one who has recently contracted the disease.[23]

Note that the infliction of pain is no mere side-effect of providing the treatment; it is an essential means to curing the disease. If this is aiming at pain, having it as a goal, nurturing it—so be it. Arguably, it is the very fact that it is the essence of pain that it is not to be desired which justifies our decision to deliberately intend pain. At the very least, it does not follow from the essence of pain that it is fundamentally incorrect to aim at it. And this should help us to see, more generally, that it does not follow from the essence of *evil* that it is fundamentally incorrect to aim at it.

Of course, it may be objected that it was inappropriate to say that it is the *essence* of pain that we should repel it—given that pain can properly be used as a means to avoid pain. Depending on what we want to pack into the notion of essence, this may be so. But then it would be question-begging for the moderate to assume that it is the essence of *evil* that we should be repelled by it. All that could be uncontroversially claimed is that evil (like pain) is an intrinsically undesirable state of affairs; nothing would follow about its desirability in any given case, all things considered.

The negative nature of something does not entail that it is always incorrect to have some of it as a subsidiary goal. Intrinsic disvalue does not rule out the possibility of extrinsic value. Thus the realization that it is the nature of evil that it should repel us does not *entail* that evil should never be intended. And this means that the moderate has given us no reason to think that intending harm necessarily involves standing in a fundamentally incorrect relation

[23] I owe this example to Derek Parfit.

to evil. Indeed, the example of the painful disease shows that such a claim is incorrect. This first suggestion, therefore, fails to ground the moral relevance of the distinction between intending and merely foreseeing harm.

The moderate might try to salvage this first argument by suggesting that the pain that is inflicted upon the diseased patient is not *evil*, in which case he may be able to retain his claim that aiming at evil is always morally offensive. But how is this suggestion to be defended? The moderate might note that the painful treatment is presumably given with the permission of the patient; but as was observed in the discussion of the permission principle, permission does not turn harm into nonharm. The patient's pain is still intrinsically evil, despite the patient's permission. The moderate may reply, of course, that although the patient's pain is still intrinsically evil, it is on balance a good—for it has tremendous instrumental value as a means of avoiding much future pain. But if the moderate retreats in this manner to the claim that it is not aiming at intrinsic evil that is morally offensive, but rather aiming at what is evil on balance (i.e., including instrumental value)—then he has retreated too far. For if I kill the one to save the two, the death of the one—although intrinsically evil—is on balance a good (for it is a means of saving the lives of the two), and so the moderate would no longer have an explanation of what was morally offensive about intending the death of the one.

Presumably the moderate will want to emphasize the fact that when we inflict pain upon the patient, this is done for the sake of the patient's own greater good. In contrast, killing the one intends harm to the one for the sake of *others*. This difference between the two cases is certainly undeniable, but how does it help the moderate defend the relevance of the distinction between intending and merely foreseeing harm? Perhaps, armed with some version of the permission principle, the moderate will suggest that what is actually morally offensive is aiming at (an intrinsic) evil to one (without that one's permission) for the sake of others. No doubt something like this claim captures the moderate's intuitions reasonably well. But it seems clear that the notion that there is something fundamentally inappropriate about aiming at evil is no longer doing any real work here. The work is being done instead by the assumption that there is something especially offensive about evil to one serving as a means to the good of others. In effect, the first account of the moral offensiveness of intending harm has given way to the second account: intending harm is morally offensive because it involves *using* someone as a mere means.

It seems, then, that the attempt to defend the relevance of the distinction between intending and foreseeing harm in terms of the first account is ineffective. But before turning to see whether the second account fares any better, there is a further possibility that must be considered. For although the first account is inadequate taken by itself, perhaps it can be used to buttress a defense of the constraint which is based on respect. We have already considered attempts to ground constraints on the need to respect persons; and they have proved unsuccessful. But the feeling that respect for persons lies behind constraints is a persistent one, and so it is worth considering a new twist on the old argument.

There is certainly a strong temptation to insist that to intend the harm of another is to fail to accord that individual the respect which is his due. We are inclined to accept that intending harm is more disrespectful of the victim than merely foreseeing that harm. As before, the obvious reply is that to countenance harm which I could prevent—as when I fail to throw Maude the life preserver, and idly watch her drown—is to reveal straightforward lack of respect. (Such lack of respect seems even more in evidence when the harm is something I bring about, albeit as a side-effect.) Once again the moderate may note that cases of merely foreseeing harm are frequently motivated more from indifference than from contempt; and this will again prompt the reply that indifference to the fate of a person seems a sure sign of disrespect (or, at least, the absence of respect).

So far we have merely retraced familiar steps. But now the path changes. For previously—in the discussion of the constraint against *doing* harm—the extremist was able to continue with the observation that if indifference is *not* to be construed as a sign of disrespect, then the moderate will have to admit that many cases of violating the constraint against doing harm do not reveal disrespect for persons, for the harm is done out of indifference to the victim. This was a telling objection to the attempt to defend that constraint on the basis of respect. But no such objection can be leveled against the moderate now. For when an agent *intends* harm there can be no pretense that he is *indifferent* to it. This is what we learned from the claim that to intend is to aim, to have as a goal. An agent cannot be indifferent to what he intends: he necessarily has some sort of positive attitude to the obtaining of the intended state of affairs.

Thus if an agent intends the harm of another (even if only as a means), he has a positive attitude to that other's being harmed. And this—the moderate might argue—surely is a mark of greater disrespect than when the harm is merely foreseen, for in the latter case the attitude is at *worst* one of indifference. Even if such indifference reveals disrespect, a positive attitude to another's harm is a more significant type of disrespect—and so the distinction between intending harm and merely foreseeing it is morally relevant.

This new version of the argument from respect, however, is no more successful than the others. We might start by noting that the argument is incorrect in suggesting that an agent's attitude toward harm that is merely foreseen will at worst be one of indifference. As I pointed out at the start of this chapter, an agent may favor some harm without intending it, provided that the agent's *reason* for countenancing the outcome is something other than the fact that it will promote some end of the agent's. Thus the agent is not necessarily indifferent to harm that is merely foreseen: he may have a positive attitude toward it. So—it might be argued—even if having a positive attitude toward the harm of another is a sign of disrespect, the moderate will not have shown that the intend/ foresee distinction is morally relevant; the offensive attitude can be found on both sides of the line.

The moderate might insist, however, that these remarks do not undercut his claim to have established the moral relevance of the distinction. So long as it is granted that all cases of intending harm display the morally offensive positive attitude to the harm of others, the moderate can concede that some cases where harm is merely foreseen display the offensive feature as well. After all, the moderate never claimed that it is *only* the intending of harm that is forbidden. The claim was simply that the intend/foresee distinction is significant, since cases of intending harm are necessarily morally offensive, in a way that cases of foreseeing harm need not be. Given that a positive attitude toward the harm of another is always present when the harm is intended, but it cannot be argued that the positive attitude is always present when the harm is merely foreseen, the moderate may still claim to have established the relevance of the distinction.

The question to be asked of the moderate's argument, therefore, is whether it has established that cases of intending harm always involve a morally offensive attitude—in particular, always reveal disrespect. Now I think it must be conceded that there is a sense in which intending the harm of another always involves having a certain kind of positive attitude to that harm. But this, of course, does not yet establish the moderate's conclusion. For the argument also presupposes the claim that having a positive attitude to the harm of another is necessarily a mark of disrespect; yet the moderate has given us no reason to think that this is so.

Obviously there *are* cases where having a positive attitude toward another's harm is disrespectful: after all, it is disrespectful to mistreat a person, and it is disrespectful to have a positive attitude toward his mistreatment. But the moderate simply assumes without argument that there are no cases where the agent shows *no* disrespect even though he has a positive attitude toward another's harm—and this is the very point in question.

Now the example of the painful disease has already shown us that it needn't be disrespectful to intend harm to another person. So having a positive attitude toward the harm of another is not necessarily a sign of disrespect. Of course we can assume that the moderate means to restrict his claim to cases of intending harm to one for the sake of another. But the example of the painful disease still establishes an important point: having a positive attitude toward another's harm will *not* be a sign of disrespect if there is an adequate justification for intending harm to that person, and that is the agent's reason for intending the harm. It is because the moderate agrees that there is an adequate justification for intending harm to the diseased patient, that he admits that intending harm in this case does not reveal disrespect.

Thus, if the moderate assumes—as his argument requires—that intending harm to one for the sake of another always reveals disrespect for the one, he must be presupposing that there is no adequate justification for intending harm in such cases. But this is the very point of contention here between the extremist and the moderate—i.e., whether there is ever adequate justification for intending harm to one for the sake of others. The extremist holds that it is permissible to kill the one in order to save the two. The moderate thinks not. But it simply begs the question for the moderate to *presuppose* that there is no adequate justification for killing the one, for this is the conclusion that his argument is trying to *support*. Given the assumption that intending harm to one for the sake of others is unjustifiable, it no doubt follows that intending that harm, and having a positive attitude toward that harm, reveal disrespect for the person being harmed. But the moderate cannot *use* the premise that intending harm to one for the sake of others reveals disrespect, in an attempt to demonstrate that intending harm in such cases is always morally offensive: there is no reason to believe the premise unless we already believe the conclusion.

For all that the moderate has shown, there may be cases in which intending harm to one as a means of saving others from harm is justified—and if there are such cases there is no reason to thing that a positive attitude to the harm of the one must be a mark of disrespect. Thus the moderate has not actually supported the claim that intending harm necessarily reveals disrespect; and so the moral relevance of the distinction between what is intended and what is merely foreseen remains undemonstrated.

The first account of the constraint—which stresses that intending harm is aiming at harm—thus seems incapable of grounding the moral relevance of the distinction. Does the second account do any better? Recall that what is stressed here is that intending harm *uses* a person. When I intend harm to another as a means to some end of my own, I gain at the expense of the other. I profit from his misfortune; he is reduced to the status of a tool for furthering my goals. In contrast, it might be argued, when the harm to another is merely a foreseen side-effect, I do not use the other to further my ends. I do not profit from his misfortune, and he does not function as a mere tool. Thus the distinction between what is intended and what is merely foreseen marks a morally relevant line.

The suggested considerations, however, do not really point to the distinction between what is intended and what is merely foreseen. Talk of foreseen side-effects should not beguile us into thinking that what is merely foreseen must be causally irrelevant (at best) to promoting my ends. Recall once more a point made at the start of this chapter: it may be improper to call a harm a *means* to a given end unless the agent intends the harm; but that harm clearly can be a *vehicle* to that very end independently of what the agent intends. (For example, I may stand to profit from my rival's death, even though that fact is not my *reason* for countenancing her death. In such a case I do not intend her death as a means, but it is nonetheless a vehicle to my goal.) The mere fact that a countenanced harm is not intended does not mean that the harm cannot further my goals. Similarly, it may be improper to speak of 'using' a person unless the profiting from another's harm is intended; but the profiting itself can obviously occur even if it is unintended. And so there will be cases of unintended harm which nonetheless possess the morally offensive feature suggested by the second account. One can gain at the expense of another, and profit from the misfortunes of a person who may be effectively reduced to functioning as a mere machine which furthers one's goals—even when the harm is merely foreseen. If the morally offensive feature is the one suggested, then the distinction between what is intended and what is foreseen is not the morally relevant one. Instead, it seems that the relevant distinction will be between countenanced harms which are vehicles to the agent's ends, and countenanced harms which are not.

This distinction, however, will not suit the moderate's purposes. For as I noted at the beginning of the chapter, a constraint which simply forbids countenancing harms which are vehicles to one's ends—whether intended or not—will be unacceptably strong (indeed, it may be incoherent). The moderate must claim, therefore, that there is an important distinction *within* the class of countenanced harms which are vehicles. He must hold that there is something *particularly* significant about those cases where the harm is countenanced *because* of the fact that it is a vehicle. Only in this way can the moral relevance of the distinction between what is *intended* and what is merely *foreseen* be maintained. Nothing in the second account, however, suggests how this view might be defended.

The moderate might try to resurrect the argument from respect once again. Building on the previous attempt, he might suggest that when harm is intended the agent has a positive attitude toward it. Thus, even though it is true that there is always something morally offensive about profiting from the misfortune of another—whether the harm is intended or not—when the harm *is* intended the agent's reaction is particularly offensive. When an agent (merely) foresees that harm to another will be a vehicle to his ends, and he does not try to prevent this, his attitude may reveal a certain amount of disrespect. But having a *positive* attitude to the fact that one is gaining from another's misfortune is a far greater mark of disrespect—and this is what intending harm involves. Thus the distinction between what is intended and what is foreseen is morally relevant after all.

I recognized earlier that there are cases where having a positive attitude toward another's harm is a mark of disrespect. It seems plausible to suggest that having a positive attitude toward someone's mistreatment reveals such a lack of respect. Thus, if the moderate is right that there is always something morally offensive about harm to a person serving as a vehicle to goals other than her own, then the moderate may also be right to conclude that intending such harm may be particularly disrespectful. But in fact the moderate has offered no support for as bold a claim as this. The argument fails for the same reasons that the earlier argument failed. There are, obviously, all too many cases where an agent unjustifiedly harms another so as to make his own illegitimate gains. But it does not follow that there are never cases where the harm is justified and the gain legitimate. If there are such cases then the mere fact that a person's harm serves as a vehicle—or even a means—will not entail that the person has been mistreated; and a positive attitude to such harm will not necessarily be a sign of disrespect. The moderate, of course, thinks that all cases of intending harm constitute mistreatment[24]—but he has given no reason to think so, and thus no reason to think that intending harm will always be especially disrespectful.

Perhaps I should indicate why I think that all such attempts to buttress the argument from respect must fail. For most cases, I believe, an act is only disrespectful *because* of the fact that it involves mistreatment: by mistreating another, the agent reveals that he lacks due regard for that other—thus, that he does not respect him. The treatment's being unjustified is the *ground* of its being an expression of disrespect. In effect, disrespect is normally something of an epiphenomenon: an act's being disrespectful cannot typically be the ground of its being mistreatment—for generally it is the fact that an act is unjustified which *makes* its

---

[24] This is, of course, an overstatement. The moderate may well recognize cases in which someone has a special obligation to make some contribution to others (e.g., as a result of past promises, or through a principle of fair play). Should that contribution not be forthcoming, it may sometimes be permissible to coerce it—in effect, imposing a sacrifice as a means of aiding others. The existence of such cases obviously does not show that it is permissible to intend harm to one for the sake of others in the *absence* of such a special obligation. It is the latter sort of case that the moderate thinks always constitutes mistreatment, though he has not yet given reason to believe this.

performance disrespectful. In typical cases, then, an act can only be shown to be disrespectful if one *first* shows that it is unjustified.

Now this is not always the case: sometimes an act is meant as an *expression* of disrespect; it is intended to communicate to the receiver of the act (or to others) that the agent regards him with disdain or contempt. Such expressive acts may be conventional gestures of disrespect, or they may take on their communicative aspect in the given context. Other than the fact that the act is being done to communicate an attitude of disrespect, there need not be anything *else* about the content of the act that constitutes mistreatment. So in such cases it is (wholly or in part) the fact that the act expresses disrespect that makes the act unjustified. (Note that it need not always be improper to communicate disrespect; some scoundrels may deserve it. But for simplicity, let us assume that we are not dealing with such people.)

Now if, in a given situation, there were an adequate justification for performing a certain act, and that is why the agent does perform the act, then this intentionally communicative aspect does not come into play. In such cases an agent does not have, and is not trying to communicate, an attitude of disrespect. Of course, the agent's act may be *misinterpreted* as such an expression; but any act is open to misinterpretation. Except in extremely rare cases, the possibility of such misinterpretation will not be sufficient reason to forbid an act that there is otherwise good reason to perform.

Cases in which an act is meant to communicate an attitude of disrespect are unusual. In the typical case, as I have suggested, a reaction involves disrespect only *because* of the fact that it is unjustified. If there is good reason to perform an act, then the performance of the act will not reveal disrespect. It is *by virtue* of the justifiability or unjustifiability of a given act that performance of that act reveals or does not reveal disrespect. That is why the argument from respect must fail: it tries to claim that a certain kind of act's being disrespectful is the basis of its being unjustified. But I believe that the reverse is closer to the truth, that disrespect is typically epiphenomenal: the moderate must first show that harming is always unjustified; only then does it follow that it is always disrespectful. And what this means, of course, is that the moderate cannot hope to point to disrespect as the basis for harming having an especially morally offensive character.

Thus neither of the two accounts of the constraint is able to adequately defend the relevance of the distinction between what is intended and what is merely foreseen. Why the distinction should be thought relevant is, thus, a mystery. It corresponds to the first mystery surrounding the constraint against doing harm.

MORE MYSTERIES

The second mystery which shrouded the constraint against doing harm was the question why—even if we grant that doing is more significant than allowing—doing harm should be thought more significant than doing good. The corresponding question arises for the constraint against intending harm. It is, after all, possible to intend good as well as to intend harm. How does this affect the moderate's ability to defend the constraint?

If I kill the one as a means of saving the two, there is no denying that I intend harm to the one. But we must not overlook the fact that my *goal* is the saving of the two. That is, I intend good as well as intending harm. And there is no reason to think that the latter should be more significant than the former. If intending harm is especially morally offensive, then intending good should be especially morally pleasing; if there are powerful reasons that particularly oppose intending harm, there should be similarly powerful reasons that particularly support intending good. But if this is right, then the constraint against intending harm cannot get off the ground. When I kill the one to save the two, I intend both harm and good, and the magnification due to *intending* can simply be factored out: the situation seems to reduce to a choice between two lives and one—and the moderate has no reason to forbid killing the one.

After all, a constraint against intending harm requires the existence of a morally decisive reason. Thus it is not sufficient for the moderate merely to establish the existence of a reason that opposes intending harm. If that reason is to be morally decisive, it must outweigh the countervailing reasons—including any reasons there may be which support intending good. Now the moderate claims that the special character of intending (as opposed to merely foreseeing) generates a reason that particularly opposes intending harm. But unless the moderate can also show why the special character of intending should not equally generate a reason that particularly supports intending good, there will be no morally decisive reason not to intend harm.

This difficulty is most easily seen for the first account of the constraint—which argues that an agent who intends harm is aiming at evil. For a similar line of reasoning notes that an agent who intends good is aiming at good. Aiming at evil may cut against the normative grain, and therefore take on a special moral importance for the agent. But aiming at good cuts precisely *with* the normative grain, and should therefore take on a corresponding moral importance. If it is true that it is the essence of evil that it should not be aimed at, then it seems equally true that it is the essence of good that it *should* be aimed at. The notion of aiming is clearly incapable of discriminating between cases of aiming at evil and cases of aiming at good. And nothing that the first account offers suggests any reason for recognizing an asymmetry. But without an asymmetry between the importance of intending evil and the importance of intending good, the moderate is unable to defend the constraint.

Does the second account of the constraint fare any better? At first glance, at least, it seems as though this account may be able to escape the objection. Now the first account focused on the notion of aiming, and this prompted the recognition that one could aim at good as well as aiming at evil. But the second account suggests locating the moral offensiveness of intending harm in the fact that when I intend harm I am *using* another as a means; and this directs our attention to a different pair of corresponding relations. When I harm someone as a means I am using him. We must not, however, overlook the fact that it is also possible to use someone by *benefiting* him as a means. Of course, it may sound a bit odd to say that benefiting a person as a means is *using* that person, so let us adopt a more neutral sounding expression. Let us say that an agent *utilizes* a person when she benefits or harms him as a means. The relation that corresponds to harmfully utilizing someone, then, is beneficially utilizing someone.

The symmetry argument I used against the first account urges that when I kill the one to save the two, the positive relation in which I stand to the two corresponds to the negative relation in which I stand to the one—and that the very reasons which might support the claim that the negative relation is important equally support the claim that the positive relation is important. The notion which corresponds to aiming at evil, e.g., is aiming at good, and the moderate has to recognize that in killing the one to save the two I aim at good as well as at evil. This is why the first account is unable to justify the constraint.

But now the second account may appear to dodge the symmetry argument. For when I kill the one to save the two, although I *am* harming the one as a means, I am *not* benefiting the two as a means. That is, I harmfully utilize one, but I do not utilize the two at all. Consequently, even if the moderate concedes that both harming and benefiting as means take on special moral importance, it seems he needn't thereby abandon the defense of the constraint. Since the benefit to the two is not intended as a *means*, symmetry does not commit him to admitting that the magnification due to intending factors out. In killing the one to save the two I *use* the one; but I do not utilize the two. So a defense of the constraint which locates the moral offensiveness of violations in the fact that people are *used* does not seem undercut.

The symmetry argument fails to undermine the second account of the constraint, for that account is essentially limited to explaining what is wrong with intending harm as a *means*. As a result, that account cannot be forced by the symmetry argument into providing reasons for recognizing the significance of intending good as an *end*. But seeing why the symmetry argument fails in this way provides an indication of how the second account should be attacked. For as it stands, that account is fundamentally incomplete— offering no explanation of the moral offensiveness of intending harm as an end. The account will have to be supplemented. But once it *is* supplemented, the symmetry argument gains a footing once more: if intending harm as an end is morally significant, then intending good as an end must be equally significant. It is true that when I kill the one to save the two I intend harm (as a means). But I also intend good (as an end). The moderate will have no grounds for holding the former more significant than the latter—and so the defense of the constraint will collapse.

Thus, even if we grant that intending harm is a more significant category than merely foreseeing, the moderate has no reason to think that intending harm is morally more significant than intending good.[25] But without the latter assumption the constraint against intending harm cannot be maintained. As before, the moderate is left

---

[25] The moderate might offer a dischargeability argument, similar to the one given in Chapter 3 concerning doing harm and doing good; but it would be subject to objections analogous to the ones given there.

with the brute assertion that morality is more concerned with evil than with good. But the moderate has given us no reason at all to think that this is so. It is a second mystery.

Before turning to the third mystery, I want to indicate an extra embarrassment that greets the moderate. As just noted, the defense of the constraint is undercut by the fact that when I kill the one to save the two, I intend good as an end—and there is no reason to think that intending good (as an end) is less significant than intending harm (as a means). But as I also noted, it is not only intending good as an end which is possible: one can also intend good as a means. Now as we know, the moderate believes that there is an unusually weighty reason to avoid harming someone as a means. But by symmetry, then, shouldn't he also believe that there is an unusually weighty reason to attempt to benefit someone as a means? Obviously, however, the moderate believes in no such weighty reasons. Yet if harmfully utilizing a person is morally significant, then beneficially utilizing a person should be equally significant. Nothing that the moderate has said justifies the asymmetry—and it seems that the concept of intention is incapable of making the discrimination.

Consider, in this regard, the first account once more: if the moderate locates the moral offensiveness of intending harm (even if only as a means) in the fact that the agent is *aiming* at evil, then he will have to admit that even if an agent benefits another only as a means to achieving some end, that agent *aims* at the recipient's well-being (even if only derivatively). With the first account of the constraint, therefore, the moderate has no ground for holding beneficial utilization to be less significant than harmful utilization.

Thus the first account suffers from a double failure. On the one hand, it fails as a defense of the constraint (since it cannot explain why intending good to the two should not be as significant as intending harm to the one). And on the other hand, it cannot avoid the implausible view that there are unusually weighty reasons favoring benefiting a person as a means (corresponding to the weighty reasons opposing harming someone as a means).

What about the second account of the constraint? Can this account justify the asymmetrical treatment of the two forms of utilization? It is actually rather unclear what implications this account should have for the case of benefiting another as a means. It might be suggested, first, that if there is an especially weighty reason which opposes using a person to his detriment—as the second account claims—then it would seem that there should be an equally weighty reason which *supports* 'using' a person to his advantage—i.e., benefiting him as means. However, it might be stressed instead that what is especially offensive about using another person is his being treated as a tool, as a means. Thus it might be suggested that a person is still being treated as a tool even when he is being *benefited* as a means. On this view, the second account can avoid the implausible claim that there is an especially weighty reason to benefit people as means. Yet the account now seems to be saddled with the equally implausible claim that there are especially weighty reasons that *oppose* benefiting people as means. (Perhaps the implausibility of this claim could be mitigated somewhat with the help of the permission principle. Presumably people typically don't mind being benefited as a means, and so perhaps their permission may be assumed. Yet if someone withholds her permission, is it really as morally offensive to benefit her as a means as it is to harm her as a means?) Other suggestions might be made as well. Fortunately, we need not settle the question of how the second account will handle cases of benefiting as a means; for our purposes, it is sufficient to bear in mind its failure with regard to the second mystery. Like the first account, the second account cannot explain why—when I kill the one to save the two—my intending good should be any less morally significant than my intending harm.

Unless the moderate can point to a morally decisive reason not to intend harm, there will be no justification for a constraint against my killing the one to save the two. But the moderate's failure to dispel the second mystery undermines the claim that there is such a morally decisive reason. For unless intending harm generates weightier reasons than those generated by intending good, there will be no reason to believe that the reason that opposes killing the one will be significant enough to outweigh the reason that supports saving the two. And as we have seen, the moderate has given us no reason to believe that intending harm is more significant than intending good.

The third mystery can be quickly recalled: even if we grant that intending harm is morally more significant than intending good—the moderate is still far from justifying a constraint against intending harm. For he still needs to offer an explanation of why the importance of intending harm should be embedded in an agent-relative structure. Embedded in an agent-neutral structure there will be no constraint—for I will be permitted to kill the one, even though this is intending harm, in order to prevent the two would-be murderers from harming their victims as means. As I noted in Chapter 2, if a reason is to ground a constraint, that reason must be an agent-relative one; thus the moderate needs to argue that the reasons generated by intending harm are agent-relative rather than (only) agent-neutral. Yet nothing at all that the moderate has told us gives us reason to think that an agent's intending harm takes on a special moral importance for that agent alone, rather than being (what should be) the subject of equal concern for all agents who are in a position to do something about it.

The defense of a constraint against intending harm requires that the moderate establish the existence of a reason that opposes intending harm—a reason of exactly the right sort. This the moderate seems incapable of doing. Indeed, the same three mysteries which accompanied the constraint against doing harm haunt the constraint against intending harm: the moderate has not explained why intending is more significant than merely foreseeing; why intending harm is more significant than intending good; and why the intending of harm generates agent-relative rather than agent-neutral reasons. To these three we can add several more. For we have seen that without a requirement of due proportion, the constraint against intending harm excuses too much. Yet any attempt to justify the requirement of due proportion (a chore which moderates in general have simply overlooked) would be plagued by mysteries similar to the ones which plague the constraint itself. From start to finish, then, the constraint against intending harm is in desperate need of justification—justification which is never provided. Coupled with the realization that the constraint probably has unpalatable implications, this provides the moderate with excellent reasons for abandoning it.

5

Without Constraints

We have now examined in some detail two attempts to offer a constraint against harming: first, a constraint against doing harm; and second, a constraint against intending harm. I have argued for both cases that there are unanswered difficulties involved not only in *justifying* the given constraint but even in offering a satisfactory *description* of the constraint. Given the difficulties which surround the two attempts, I have suggested, the moderate has excellent reasons for abandoning them.

This puts the moderate in an uncomfortable position—for he needs a constraint against harming in order to maintain the defense of options based on the appeal to cost. And of course, even had they not been necessary for the defense of options, the moderate would have wanted to defend constraints in their own right—for constraints are one of the major features of ordinary morality. It seems that a constraint against harming would have to be included in any system which hoped to capture our ordinary moral intuitions—but the two most common attempts to articulate such a constraint are plagued with problems. So much the worse for our ordinary moral intuitions, we may conclude; and so much the worse for the moderate.

Are there other versions of the constraint against harming which fare better? I do not know of any. Indeed, it is difficult to think of *any* fundamentally different versions which have been seriously proposed. Frequently no specification at all is made of how the line is to be drawn in the constraint against harming. But when such specification is offered, it generally involves either the do/allow distinction or the intend/foresee distinction.

For example, it is not uncommon for moderates to express the existence of a constraint against harming by saying that individuals have a *right* not to be harmed: to harm another violates a

constraint, for it violates the victim's rights. Talk of rights may have
its advantages—but the need to specify which sorts of reactions
constitute harming another remains. Some systems may hold that
individuals have a right not to have harm *done* to them; other
systems may suggest that individuals have a right not to be the
victim of harm *intended* as a means. Obviously, however, these are
equivalent to the two constraints already discussed. Yet if there is a
third plausible way to describe the contents of the right, I do not
know what it is. From this perspective, then, a right not to be
harmed does not provide a genuine alternative to the two
constraints we have already considered.[1]

There is some reason to think that the two constraints exhaust
the field (except for minor variations). Recall the view that
constraints must be grounded in particular facts about the agent. It
is a common belief among moderates that constraints can only arise
when there is a particular connection between the agent and victim.
Without such connection the agent-relative nature of constraints
cannot be explained, for why should the agent be especially
concerned with the welfare of some particular individual if it is not
for the existence of some link forging a connection between that
agent and the individual? One way to spell out this view is to hold
that the appropriate sort of connection exists only when either the
agent or the victim has made a difference to the other. That is,
either the victim is altered because of the agent, or the agent is
altered because of the victim. Only when one of them has made
such a difference to the other is there ground for thinking that the
two are linked in the proper way: only in such cases does the victim
have a claim against the agent. But this suggests two fundamental
ways that constraints might be grounded—and thus two basic
approaches to the constraint against harming. First, one might
concentrate on the connection which arises when the victim would
be worse off because of the agent: i.e., when the agent brings about
harm to the other. Emphasis on such a connection suggests the
constraint against *doing* harm.

Alternatively, one might concentrate on the connection which
arises when the agent would be better off because of the harm to the
victim: i.e., when the victim's harm is a vehicle to some end of the
agent's. This suggests the presumption against profiting from the
misfortune of another mentioned in the last chapter. But since the

[1] We will return to rights, although in a different context, in Chapter 6.

moderate might hold that merely profiting from another is not in itself sufficient alteration in the agent for the appropriate connection to be forged, it may be that we should limit attention to those cases where the agent's *reason* for countenancing harm is that it will facilitate his ends. Emphasis on such a connection suggests the constraint against *intending* harm.

Thus we find ourselves presented with the two constraints we have considered at some length. The constraint against doing harm represents the realization that the agent can make a difference to the victim: the victim is worse off because of the agent. The constraint against intending harm represents the realization that the victim can make a difference to the agent: the agent's reaction is influenced by his ability to profit from the misfortune of another. On the one hand, this may account for the prevalence and intuitive appeal of the two constraints: both are attempts to capture the intuition that constraints must be grounded in a particular connection between agent and victim. And on the other hand, this may account for the dearth of fundamental alternative conceptions of the constraint against harming: for the proper connection, either agent or victim must make a difference to the other—and the two basic possibilities have already been covered.

If this is correct, then an intuitively satisfying constraint against harming will have to be construed either in terms of a constraint against doing harm or a constraint against intending harm (or some variation on these two). Even if this suggestion is incorrect, however, the fact remains that these two versions of the constraint are not only the most popular, but are also (as far as I know) the only versions which have been seriously proposed. And our discussion has shown the host of problems facing both of them. The moderate has reason to abandon both the constraint against doing harm and the constraint against intending harm; and this appears to involve abandoning a constraint against harming altogether.

Of course I have only been able to discuss a limited number of moves which might be made by an advocate of either of the constraints. Nothing like a general proof of the *impossibility* of a constraint against harming has been offered. This lack of a decisive counterargument may inspire some moderates to carry on the struggle—offering a new round of attempts to defend a favored version of the constraint. Obviously, these new attempts cannot be dismissed in advance; detailed criticism must wait until the new

defenses are presented. Nonetheless, the discussion up to this point
gives some grounds for a general attitude of scepticism.

After all, it is not simply that some particular defense of some
particular version of the constraint happens to be undercut by this
or that particular objection. Failures of this sort might still hold out
some reasonable chance of repairing holes in the defense, or of
supporting a slightly altered constraint. But many of the objections
we have considered have been of a more general sort. The same
kind of problems surrounded both the constraint against doing
harm and the constraint against intending harm; the discussion
revealed recurring shortcomings of a fundamental sort in the
defense of constraints. Now this is not, as I say, a proof that
constraints cannot be defended; but it is inductive evidence for the
belief that similar problems will plague any such attempt. Given the
lack of any indication of how the recurring objections might be
met, we have some reason to believe that an adequate defense of a
constraint against harming simply cannot be offered.

THE NEO-MODERATE

Without a constraint against harming, it seems that the moderate
must abandon the defense of options based on the appeal to cost.
For I have argued that an appeal to cost would support not only
options to allow harm, but also options to do harm—and this is an
unacceptably minimalist position for the moderate. Of course, as I
have noted, the moderate may actually be willing to endorse certain
extremely limited options to do harm. But most such options would
indeed be rejected by the moderate as unacceptably minimalist; and
the appeal to cost, I have argued, would support options of this
clearly unacceptable kind.

Now had he been able to defend the constraint against harming,
the moderate might have claimed that the considerations which
support the constraint are powerful enough to resist the appeal to
cost. That is, the moderate might have shown how the reasons
supporting the constraint manage to be morally decisive—despite
the countervailing considerations arising from the appeal to cost.
On balance, then, no option to do harm would have been
grounded. The moderate could have blocked the unacceptable
option to do harm while still using the appeal to cost so as to

ground the desired option to allow harm.[2] But as we have seen, the moderate has been unable to offer an adequate defense of the necessary constraint. And without the constraint, it appears that the defense of options must be abandoned as well.

Before putting the appeal to cost out to pasture, however, it is worth asking whether there is any way that its minimalist implications can be avoided without having recourse to the constraint against harming. As we know, the existence of an option turns on the absence of a morally decisive reason. So, clearly, to block options to do harm, there must be a morally decisive reason that—in the relevant cases—opposes the doing of such harm. And, as we have just noted, a constraint against doing harm would presumably provide such a morally decisive reason. But even though a constraint would be sufficient to block the option to do harm, it may not be necessary.

At least, it may not be necessary if we focus our attention on blocking the most unacceptably minimalist cases of doing harm— i.e., doing harm even when this results in an overall loss in the objective good. For the appeal to cost seems especially pernicious in its tendency to support permission in cases of this kind: e.g., permission to do significant harm to another merely so as to avoid some smaller cost to myself. Yet a constraint against doing harm blocks not only such cases of harm-doing with a net negative impact, it also blocks cases of doing harm even where, on balance, this would lead to better consequences overall. It seems possible, therefore, that there might be considerations which were not adequate to ground a *constraint* against harming but which nonetheless *were* able to resist the appeal to cost. If there were considerations with just this character, there would be no constraint against doing harm (for, by hypothesis, the considerations would not be sufficient to ground such a constraint); but the option to do (overall negative) harm would nonetheless be blocked (for the support generated by the appeal to cost would be overridden). Options to allow harm, however, might well be safe: some of the

---

[2] A corresponding argument could be offered, of course, with a constraint against intending harm: the option to intend harm could be blocked by such a constraint, while still leaving open the possibility of using the appeal to cost to defend an option to countenance harm which is merely foreseen. Although I will continue to cast the discussion in the text in terms of the do/allow distinction, the corresponding claims using the intend/foresee distinction should be borne in mind as well.

imagined considerations might specifically come into play only in cases of doing harm—not countenancing harm in general—and so the appeal to cost would be unhindered in its support of options to allow harm.

If there were such considerations, the system which would result would not be entirely satisfactory to the moderate. For I have portrayed the moderate as a defender of ordinary morality, and I have claimed that ordinary morality includes a constraint against harming. The system we are considering would have no such constraint—and so it would be somewhat misleading to call the advocate of such a system a moderate. Nonetheless, a defender of such a system would have significant areas of agreement with the moderate—so let us call her a *neo-moderate*. Like the moderate, the neo-moderate denies that agents are required to relentlessly pursue the good: she recognizes the existence of an option to allow harm. And like the moderate, the neo-moderate denies the minimalist's claim that agents are permitted to *harm* others even in those cases where this leads to a decline in overall good. Unlike the moderate, however, the neo-moderate believes that agents *are* permitted to harm others when doing so *promotes* the overall good.

The neo-moderate's system is a mixture of the strange and the familiar.[3] Its stance on the allowing of harm is easily recognized: agents are permitted to pursue their interests even when doing so allows a greater overall amount of harm. But the system's position on the doing of harm is somewhat unfamiliar. Agents are not altogether forbidden to do harm—but they are neither given a free hand to do harm whenever they choose, nor required to do harm whenever this would be optimal.

In a moment I want to give a somewhat technical description of the neo-moderate's system; but before doing that, it might be helpful if I gave some indication of what it is that might *attract* one to the neo-moderate's position. Such a system, I believe, can be profitably seen as the result of holding three potentially attractive views. First, agents are not generally required to promote the good—for such a requirement would demand undue sacrifice of an agent's interests. Instead, the appeal to cost generates an option to

---

[3] Scheffler described and defended a neo-moderate system—although in very different terms from the ones I am using here—in his doctoral dissertation; but he abandoned this precise position by the time he published his revision of that work. Despite the theoretical interest of the neo-moderate's view, I know of no other discussion of this type of moral system.

pursue one's interests even though this involves countenancing a greater amount of harm overall. Second, agents are always *permitted* to promote the greater good overall. Even though an agent need not pursue the good if she does not want to, if she *does* choose to promote the good, she may.

Now these first two views, obviously, are even acceptable to the minimalist—who feels that the agent is free to do *whatever* she chooses. But there is a third view involved in the neo-moderate's position: there is something particularly significant about *doing* harm. Because of this special significance, there is a limit to the agent's option. Although an agent may *allow* harm in the pursuit of her own interests, she is not permitted to *do* harm to others simply because this would be in her interests as well.

As we know, the moderate too holds the view that there is something particularly significant about doing harm. But he carries the view further: the moderate believes that the significance of doing harm creates a limit not only to the agent's option to pursue her own interests, but also to the permissiblity of promoting the good. There is a *constraint* against doing harm; one cannot do harm even to promote the greater good. The neo-moderate, however, does not go to this extreme. In rejecting the constraint, she takes the second view seriously: if an action will genuinely promote the greater good overall, then it is permissible to do it— even if it involves the doing of harm. Those who share this view— and the others I have ascribed to the neo-moderate—should find her system attractive: doing harm is significant enough to limit the agent's option to pursue her own interests; but it will be permitted when necessary if the agent freely chooses to promote the greater good.

In the neo-moderate's system, then, there is neither a constraint against doing harm, nor an option to do harm. Yet it would also be correct to say that the system has a zero threshold constraint against doing harm coupled with a zero threshold option to do harm. These concepts, however, require some explanation.

A constraint against doing harm with an infinite threshold would be an absolute constraint: it would prohibit harming another even if there were no other way to prevent a moral catastrophe involving the deaths of millions. But as I have noted, the threshold of a constraint need not be infinite; one might believe that the typically prohibited reaction would be permissible if enough were at stake.

For example, the constraint might have an extremely high threshold—prohibiting harming in all typical situations, but permitting it if this were the only way to prevent catastrophe. Now normally the constraint against harming is thought to have quite a high threshold—but there is in principle no reason why the threshold could not be more modest. With a high threshold, one cannot do harm even though the gain in overall good which would be brought about might be fairly significant. With a low threshold, the minimum gain in overall good which would be necessary before the constraint would lower its barrier would be correspondingly smaller. As the threshold gets lower and lower, it takes less and less for the constraint to be relaxed. Thus, as the threshold approaches zero, the constraint provides less and less of a barrier to promoting the good. With a zero threshold, the constraint against harming would provide no barrier to promoting the good at all.

What this means is that with a zero threshold an agent would be permitted to do harm in any case where this will result in an overall gain in the objective good. Unlike ordinary morality, there would never be cases in which the agent is forbidden to harm another even though it would be optimal for him to do so. But this does *not* mean—as the minimalist would have it—that the agent is simply free to harm another whenever this is in his interests. A zero threshold constraint against harming would still require that there be no overall *loss* in objective good as a result of the agent's doing harm. The agent would still be forbidden to harm others in all those cases—surely the most common—in which greater overall good would be countenanced by his refraining.

The notion of a zero threshold constraint appears to be perfectly intelligible—but is it appropriate to call it a *constraint?* Perhaps not. Constraints prohibit various reactions even when it would be optimal for the agent to react in those ways. Since zero threshold constraints provide no barrier to promoting the good, it may be improper to claim that they are genuine constraints. But as long as we are clear about the points of similarity and the points of difference, it is of less importance whether we consider them degenerate constraints, or decide that they are not constraints at all.

The notion of a zero threshold option is similar; for options too can have thresholds of various sizes. An option to do harm might have an infinite threshold, which would permit doing harm no matter what the outcome. Or it might have a finite threshold—

permitting the agent to do harm so long as the overall loss in objective good were within some limit. As the threshold approached zero, the privilege to do harm would decrease. A zero threshold option would never allow doing harm at the expense of the overall good. But it would not rule out doing harm altogether: agents would still be permitted to do harm in those cases where this would result in the overall promotion of the good. A question similar to the one we asked about zero threshold constraints can be raised: are zero threshold options genuine options? Perhaps not— for they do not give the agent permission to react in a nonoptimal manner. But it does not seem important whether or not we consider them degenerate options, so long as we remain clear about their differences from typical options.

When I suggested earlier that the neo-moderate's system contains neither an option to do harm nor a constraint against doing harm, clearly what I had in mind were constraints and options with finite or infinite (i.e., nonzero) thresholds. What the neo-moderate's system *does* contain is, on the one hand, a zero threshold constraint against doing harm coupled with a zero threshold option to do harm, and on the other hand, an ordinary option to allow harm. Like the straightforward extremist position, then, the neo-moderate's system prohibits doing harm when this will lead to a decline in the overall good—but permits doing harm when this will lead to an increase overall. Unlike the extremist, however, the neo-moderate does not *require* the pursuit of the good. Agents are permitted to promote the good if they choose—even if this involves doing harm—but they need not promote the good if they do not want to. They can pursue their own interests at the expense of the overall good, provided that they do not harm others in doing so.

Since the notion of a zero threshold option or constraint is rather unfamiliar, the combination of these elements into the neo-moderate's system may merit some further discussion. As we have seen, the zero threshold constraint against doing harm forbids doing harm in those cases where this will lead to an overall loss in objective good. It does not, however, provide any barrier to doing harm in those cases where this will result in an overall gain. To resort to our familiar example, it does not rule out killing the one if this is the only way to save the two. I am permitted to kill the one. But I am not *required* to kill the one. For my killing of the one is covered by the zero threshold option to do harm—which permits me to do harm where this would result in the overall promotion of the good, as in this case, but does not require me to do it. As with a more typical option, I am permitted to react or to refrain from reacting in the given manner, as I choose. Of course, if I do refrain from killing the one, then I have allowed a harm—the death of the two. But this is permissible, since the neo-moderate's system also includes an option to allow harm. (This brings out—what will come as no surprise—that the various elements of the neo-moderate's system are not altogether independent of one another.)

The neo-moderate permits the agent to do harm if this is the only way to promote the good. It is worth noting, furthermore, that under the neo-moderate's system the agent is permitted to do harm even in many cases where he fails to use that harm to perform the optimal act open to him. That is, so long as the harm brings about *better* consequences overall, it need not bring about the *best*. For so long as the suboptimal act of harm-doing will, on balance, bring about more good than harm, it will not be ruled out by the zero threshold constraint. Similarly, since the zero threshold option to do harm permits the agent to do harm provided that there is a net gain in the overall good, it will permit such suboptimal (but overall positive) acts of harm-doing. Admittedly, in failing to do harm in the optimal manner, the agent is failing to prevent a certain amount of avoidable harm; but this, of course, is permitted by the familiar option to allow harm.

Such is the neo-moderate's system. Although it is a small digression, it may also be of some interest if we briefly consider a few other possible combinations of the elements we have been discussing. Now for the neo-moderate, as I have noted, although the agent is permitted to do harm that leads to better consequences overall, he is not required to do so: this last is guaranteed by the zero threshold option. We could, however, imagine a system (no longer the neo-moderate's) which kept the zero threshold constraint, but lacked the zero threshold option. The agent would still be permitted to do harm that increases the overall good—this much is guaranteed by the zero threshold constraint—but he would no longer be permitted to refrain from doing harm in such cases. That is, he would be *required* to promote the good where he was able to do so through harm-doing. Such a system would be like that of the extremist in this regard: agents would be forbidden to do harm when this would lead to worse consequences overall, and would be required to do harm when this would promote the good overall. Obviously, all of this would in turn require a restriction of the option to allow harm (agents cannot allow harm that could be prevented by harm-doing). Oddly enough, however, such a system wouldn't inevitably reduce to that of the extremist: one could still keep *some* of the option to allow harm (agents could allow those harms—and, bizarrely enough, only those harms—that cannot be prevented by harm-doing).

If we add to the zero threshold constraint against doing harm a zero threshold constraint against allowing harm, this will give us, in effect, a zero threshold constraint against *countenancing* harm, which will bring us all the way to the most straightforward version of the extremist's system. With such a zero threshold constraint, an agent can countenance a given harm only if the good promoted by his reaction is greater than the harm he thereby countenances. Such a system, as we should expect, would have no options at all—not even zero threshold ones. The agent would simply have to do as much good as possible—for otherwise he would be countenancing more harm than he needs to, in violation of the zero threshold constraint.

If we return to the neo-moderate's system—with its zero threshold constraint against doing harm, zero threshold option to do harm, and ordinary option to allow harm—we might wonder what the effect would be of removing the zero threshold constraint against doing harm. Such a system would no longer forbid harm-doing, not even when this leads to an overall loss in the objective good. There could, however, be two such systems: a particularly repugnant version might actually require the agent to perform such harmful acts (thanks to a constraint against forgoing harmful acts—perhaps subject to some threshold); a somewhat less repugnant, but nonetheless thoroughly minimalist system might instead merely grant agents permission to perform such harmful acts if they so choose (thanks to an option to do harm with a nonzero threshold).

There are other variations that might be worth exploring as well. We have not yet, for example, considered the possibility of constraints and options with *negative* thresholds. (An option to do harm with a negative threshold would permit the agent, if she chooses, to do harm, but only if the overall gain was greater than the given threshold; a constraint against doing harm with a negative threshold would permit doing harm provided that the loss in overall good was less than the specified threshold.) But the discussion has already taken us far enough afield. For our present purposes, our interest lies only in the neo-moderate's system, which promises to resist the undesirable aspects of the appeal to cost without having recourse to a constraint against doing harm, while nonetheless retaining the option to allow harm.

I have suggested that a system of this kind might be the result if there were reasons that opposed doing harm—in the relevant cases—which were unable to ground a constraint against doing harm, but which nonetheless *were* able to overcome the appeal to cost. The appeal to cost would be able to ground the acceptable option to allow harm, but would be overridden insofar as it supported options to do harm. The neo-moderate's system would exclude the (nondegenerate) option to do harm without including a (nondegenerate) constraint against doing harm. Thus it seems that the defense of options based on the appeal to cost could be maintained even though one was unable to justify a constraint against doing harm—provided, of course, that considerations adequate to ground a neo-moderate system could in fact be found.

AVOIDING THE CONSTRAINT

The purported advantage of the neo-moderate's system is that it is able to block an unacceptable option to do harm without committing itself to a *constraint* against doing harm. Since no way has been found to defend such a constraint, the neo-moderate seems to offer an attractive alternative to the moderate which still stays clear of the excesses of the minimalist and the extremist. Yet although the logical possibility of a structure such as I have described seems clear, it is *not* clear that there is any way that such a system could be plausibly maintained. It may be that the neo-moderate's system is an illusory alternative.

The neo-moderate accepts an option to allow harm, but opposes an option to do harm. Options of both sorts, however, are supported by the appeal to cost. Thus, if the neo-moderate is to block options to do harm she must claim that the appeal to cost is overcome, or resisted, in such cases—but not in cases of allowing harm. Now how such a position is to be maintained will depend, obviously, on the details of the appeal to cost; that is, it will depend on which specific countervailing considerations are generated by the appeal to cost. Of course, we have not yet attempted to spell out the appeal to cost; but it should nonetheless be clear that the logical possibilities are themselves determined by the list of conditions necessary for moral decisiveness. For if the appeal to cost is to prevent various reasons—which would otherwise ground requirements—from being morally decisive, how it accomplishes this will clearly depend in part on just which conditions must be met for moral decisiveness.

I have, of course, suggested that at least one condition that a (morally acceptable) reason must meet in order to be morally decisive is that of outweighing any opposing reasons. Consequently, one plausible suggestion of how the appeal to cost prevents the pro tanto reason to promote the good from grounding a requirement is the following: when the promotion of the good would involve a significant sacrifice of an agent's interests, this generates weighty reasons for the agent not to promote the good. If so, the pro tanto reason to promote the good will frequently fail to be morally decisive, for it will be outweighed by (or, at least, fail to outweigh) the countervailing reasons that arise from the appeal to cost. No general requirement to promote the good will be generated; instead there will be an option to allow harm.

What prevents these same countervailing reasons from grounding an option to *do* harm? Of course the pro tanto reason to promote the good still opposes doing harm in those cases where this will lead to an overall reduction in the objective good. But by hypothesis this reason cannot by itself outweigh the countervailing reasons arising from the appeal to cost. The most straightforward solution is to claim that there are further, especially weighty reasons, which particularly oppose the doing of harm. If one takes this approach, one can then go on to claim that the special, further reasons that oppose harm-doing—together, perhaps, with the pro tanto reason to promote the good—are sufficient to outweigh even the countervailing reasons generated by the appeal to cost. These reasons, therefore, might well provide a morally decisive reason not to do harm in such cases, blocking the option to do harm.

So far, the account we have been sketching seems to be equally acceptable to both the moderate and the neo-moderate. But if she does take this approach, a problem immediately arises for the neo-moderate. For if there are indeed weighty reasons not to do harm, why don't these reasons generate a *constraint* against doing harm?

Imagine a case where doing harm will lead to better results overall. Doing harm in such a case will, of course, be supported by the pro tanto reason to promote the good; but it will be strongly opposed by the special reasons adverse to harm-doing. If the latter reasons are as weighty as the neo-moderate must claim, surely there will frequently be cases in which those reasons outweigh the pro tanto reason to promote the good. It would seem to follow, then, that the reasons that oppose harm-doing will often be morally decisive, even though greater good might come from doing harm. In short, there will be a constraint against doing harm. But the neo-moderate, as we know, hoped to avoid such a constraint; unless she can, she has not actually offered an alternative to the moderate. Yet if the neo-moderate takes the approach we have been discussing so far, how is the creation of a constraint against doing harm to be avoided?

There are three basic possibilities, for, as I have previously noted, there are three basic ways that a given reason might be prevented from grounding a requirement. First, the reason itself might be undermined, in the relevant cases. Thus the neo-moderate might argue that in those cases where harm-doing leads to better results overall, something prevents the generation of the special reasons that typically oppose harm-doing. Obviously, if the special reasons are not even generated in cases where the doing of harm leads to better overall consequences, there is no danger that a constraint will be established. Second, the reason might be overridden. Thus the neo-moderate might try to show that the special reasons that oppose harm-doing are, in principle, *always* outweighed by the pro tanto reason to promote the good, no matter how weak. If so, those reasons will be unable to ground a constraint against doing harm. Third, it should be recalled that there may be further conditions necessary for moral decisiveness beyond that of outweighing any opposing reasons. If so, the neo-moderate might claim that although there are weighty reasons that especially oppose harm-doing, taken on their own these reasons fail to meet some further condition necessary for moral decisiveness; once more, then, they will be unable to ground a constraint against doing harm.

In principle, any of these strategies might be available to the neo-moderate. With sufficient ingenuity each could be incorporated into some version of the neo-moderate's system. Of course, each strategy also comes with its own unique difficulties. But rather than pursue the problems specific to each strategy, let's focus on a general objection to this entire approach.

According to the line of argument we have been considering, the pro tanto reason to promote the good is prevented from grounding a general requirement by the countervailing reasons arising from the appeal to cost. If, nonetheless, there is no option to do harm that is because there are also further reasons that especially oppose harm-doing, and these special reasons (together with the pro tanto reason to promote the good) are sufficient to outweigh the appeal to cost's countervailing reasons. Now as we have just noted, the neo-moderate must resort to one or another strategy to explain what prevents those special reasons from generating, in turn, a constraint against doing harm. These strategies involve qualifying, in various ways, the strength, character, or range of these reasons; but whatever the details, the fact remains that the entire approach is committed to the existence of these special reasons that oppose harm-doing.

The general problem, therefore, that faces the neo-moderate is this: when we previously noted the moderate's inability to defend a constraint against doing harm, it was, in fact, the very existence of reasons of just this sort that the moderate was unable to prove.

A constraint is based on the existence of a morally decisive reason of just the right kind. In principle, a complete defense of a constraint would have to establish (1) that the relevant kind of reason exists, (2) that the reason has sufficient strength to outweigh the opposing reasons (in particular, the pro tanto reason to promote the good), and (3) that the reason satisfies the further conditions, if any, that must be met for moral decisiveness. It will be recalled, however, that when I challenged the moderate to defend his constraint I did not require him to demonstrate (2) or (3). Instead, the discussion focused on the moderate's inability to establish (1)—the very existence of the reasons in question. If, as I argued, no way can be found to defend the existence of such special reasons that particularly oppose the doing of harm, this obviously calls into question not only the moderate's defense of constraints, but also the neo-moderate's somewhat more modest use of those same reasons.

The neo-moderate might hope, of course, that a review of the problems that faced the moderate's attempts to defend the existence of special reasons for an agent not to do harm would reveal that some of the objections were specific to the use that the moderate hoped to make of those reasons. Perhaps, given the slightly different use to which the neo-moderate wants to put the reasons in question, a demonstration by the neo-moderate of the existence of those reasons could escape the previous criticisms. In fact, however, I do not think that such an attempted demonstration will meet with any greater success than before (although certain objections, no doubt, would have to be altered somewhat); and since the discussion was, of course, rather a lengthy one, I will not take the trouble to rehearse the arguments once again.

In short, despite the fact that the neo-moderate manages to avoid the *constraint* against doing harm, she seems unable to escape the difficulties that led us to introduce her system in the first place. At least this is so if the neo-moderate tries to defend her system along the lines we have been considering. It is worth noting, therefore, that the neo-moderate may in fact have an alternative approach available. In the preceding discussion we have been assuming that, in order to block the option to do harm, the neo-moderate must argue for the existence of special reasons that oppose harm-doing. But this is not the only way that the option to do harm might be resisted. Instead, the neo-moderate might try to argue that there is something about the doing of harm that prevents the countervailing reasons that normally arise from the appeal to cost from being generated in the first place.

If she takes this line, the neo-moderate must argue that although considerations of cost normally generate reasons for the agent to pursue his own interests, when this can only be accomplished through the doing of overall negative harm, no such reasons are generated. This claim would need to be defended, of course, but consider its implications. There would be a morally decisive reason not to do harm which would lead to worse results overall: for the pro tanto reason to promote the good will oppose harm-doing in such cases, and the appeal to cost will fail to generate any countervailing reasons. So the option to do harm will be blocked. But there will still be no general requirement to promote the good, for when the agent can pursue his interests without doing (overall negative) harm, the appeal to cost *will* yield countervailing reasons which prevent the pro tanto reason to promote the good from being morally decisive. Note, finally, that since—on this approach—there is no need for the neo-moderate to introduce any special reasons that particularly oppose doing harm, she is in no danger of inadvertently grounding a constraint. Indeed, since such reasons simply play no role in the neo-moderate's system at all—that is, if something like this second approach can in fact be defended—it seems that the neo-moderate may finally escape the difficulties that plague the attempt to defend such reasons. Here, at last, the neo-moderate may offer a feasible alternative to the moderate.

A potential complication must be mentioned. So far, we have been operating under the assumption that the appeal to cost works solely through the generation of countervailing reasons, reasons that are often able to outweigh (or, at least, cannot be outweighed by) the pro tanto reason to promote the good. But as I have already observed, there may be further conditions necessary for moral decisiveness other than that of outweighing any opposing reasons. Consequently, the possibility must be noted that the appeal to cost might work through one or another of these further conditions as well (or instead). That is, the claim may be that when promotion of the good would require a significant sacrifice of an agent's interests, the pro tanto reason to promote the good will fail to meet some other particular condition necessary for grounding a moral requirement.

Obviously, the details of such a position would depend on the particular further condition through which the appeal to cost is supposed to work. But a few general remarks can still be made. We are assuming that the pro tanto reason to promote the good frequently fails to meet the further condition necessary for moral decisiveness; this is what creates the option to allow harm. What, then, rules out the option to do harm? Presumably the neo-moderate's answer must be that the doing of harm which would lead to worse results overall is opposed by a morally decisive reason, even though it might be costly to the agent to be unable to do such harm. In particular, this reason—if it is truly to be morally decisive—must meet the specified further condition.

Most straightforwardly, the neo-moderate might appeal, once again, to the existence of special reasons that oppose harm-doing; if she can show that such reasons meet the given further condition, even when acting on these reasons involves a significant sacrifice of the agent's interests, then those reasons (together, perhaps, with the pro tanto reason to promote the good) might well be morally decisive—despite the appeal to cost. The difficulty with this straightforward suggestion is, of course, the very fact that it makes use of the special reasons, for the attempt to demonstrate the existence of such reasons has been unsuccessful.

A more interesting suggestion, therefore, would be this: the neo-moderate might argue that although the pro tanto reason to promote the good does not *generally* meet the particular further condition in question (at least, when the cost to the agent of promoting the good would be significant), it nonetheless *does* meet that condition when the pursuit of the agent's interests would require doing harm that leads to worse results overall. In such cases, therefore, the pro tanto reason to promote the good might well provide morally decisive opposition to doing harm. In effect, the pro tanto reason's ability to meet the further condition would be 'boosted' in the relevant cases; the option to do harm would thus be blocked. But when the agent *was* able to pursue his interests without doing (overall negative) harm, the pro tanto reason to promote the good would frequently fail to meet the further condition necessary for moral decisiveness; and so the option to allow harm would still exist.

This line of argument has obvious affinities with the second of the two approaches sketched above; the neo-moderate avoids the difficulties of proving the existence of special reasons that oppose doing harm by simply doing without such reasons altogether. Indeed, the two lines of argument might be combined, if the appeal to cost works through a morally decisive reason's double need— i.e., the need both to outweigh any opposing reasons *and* to meet other conditions as well. The neo-moderate might try to show that although countervailing considerations prevent the grounding of a general requirement to promote the good, they do not arise in cases involving the doing of overall negative harm. In such cases there is something that undermines the generation of the countervailing reasons and that 'boosts' the pro tanto reason to promote the good's ability to meet the further conditions necessary for moral decisiveness.

A defense of the neo-moderate's system along these lines would avoid the constraint against doing harm by making no use at all of the reasons out of which such a constraint might be erected. By dispensing with them outright, it would obviously escape the need—central to the moderate's failure to defend constraints—to establish the existence of such reasons. And yet, even without making use of such reasons, it would avoid the option to do harm while at the same time preserving the option to allow harm. In short, even if—as I have argued—the moderate proper is unsuccessful in his attempt to simultaneously fend off both the minimalist and the extremist, it seems as though the neo-moderate may hold out the possibility of success.

AVOIDING THE DISTINCTION

But a problem still remains. In the neo-moderate's system, as we are now construing it, there is no reason to avoid doing harm per se, no special reasons that particularly oppose harm-doing. This is clearly an advantage, since no way has been found to defend such reasons. And yet, for all that, the neo-moderate is committed to the special moral significance of harm-doing nonetheless. For the heart of this approach to the neo-moderate's system is, roughly, the claim that the countervailing considerations that normally arise from the appeal to cost just do not arise in cases involving harm-doing.

This statement needs to be qualified slightly. On the current interpretation, the neo-moderate isn't actually making the claim that in *all* cases involving harm-doing the countervailing considerations fail to arise. Rather, it is only in cases involving harm-doing with worse results overall. This restriction is necessary to preserve the agent's option to do overall positive, but nonetheless suboptimal harm. For the neo-moderate holds that harm-doing is permissible provided that it leads to *better* results overall; it need not lead to the best results available to the agent. If this feature is to be preserved, however, there must be no morally decisive reason opposing the doing of suboptimal but overall positive harm. Apparently, then, even though such suboptimal acts of harm-doing are opposed by the pro tanto reason to promote the good, the appeal to cost must generate countervailing considerations that prevent that reason from being morally decisive. Thus the appeal to cost must yield its countervailing considerations even in cases involving overall positive harm. It is only where harm-doing leads to worse results overall that the countervailing considerations normally generated by the appeal to cost do not arise.

Consequently, it may seem incorrect to suggest that the neo-moderate is committed to the moral significance of the distinction between doing harm and allowing harm. For, as we have just seen, the neo-moderate does not hold that there is something about cases involving harm-doing *per se* which somehow prevents the generation of the countervailing considerations (in contrast to cases merely involving the allowing of harm). Rather, what are somehow unique are cases involving overall negative harm-doing (in contrast to cases involving either the allowing of harm *or* overall positive harm-doing).

Yet the neo-moderate seems committed to the relevance of the do/allow distinction nonetheless. After all, she does not hold that the countervailing considerations fail to arise in *all* cases involving the countenancing of overall negative harm. This only happens if the countenancing takes the form of *doing* harm, not if it merely takes the form of *allowing* harm. It seems, in short, that the neo-moderate is actually committed to the relevance of two distinctions—both the overall positive/overall negative distinction, and the do/allow distinction. And the mere fact that the neo-moderate is committed to the relevance of the former does nothing to alter the fact that she is also committed to the relevance of the latter.

This conclusion—that a defense of the neo-moderate's system presupposes the relevance of the do/allow distinction—will hardly be a surprising one. After all, the neo-moderate was introduced as someone who holds that the doing of harm is significant in a way that the allowing of harm is not. Even though the neo-moderate does not go so far as to embrace a constraint against doing harm, the importance of the do/allow distinction is clearly at work in her insistence that although the appeal to cost will yield an option to allow harm, it cannot create an option to do harm.

If this is correct, however, then the neo-moderate has not escaped after all from the problems that surrounded the moderate's unsuccessful attempt to defend constraints. For I argued that the moderate was not even able to defend the mere *relevance* of the distinction. Indeed, why the do/allow distinction should be thought to carry any moral significance at all was the very first of the three mysteries that shrouded the defense of constraints. Since the neo-moderate's system essentially relies upon the significance of the do/allow distinction, and given that no way has been found to support the claim that the distinction has any intrinsic moral significance, it appears that in the final analysis the neo-moderate's system cannot be given an adequate defense. (Once more, of course, it might be suggested that—given the somewhat different use that she wants to make of it—the neo-moderate might escape some of the objections that undermined the moderate's defense of the distinction; I believe, however, that although certain of the objections might need to be modified slightly, the defense of the distinction would remain unsuccessful.)

In short, it is not sufficient for the neo-moderate to have avoided the constraint against doing harm. Nor is it sufficient for the neo-moderate to avoid commitment to the existence of special reasons that particularly oppose harm-doing. If the neo-moderate is to completely escape the objections that plagued the moderate, she must avoid commitment to the moral relevance of the do/allow distinction altogether. But this, I think, the neo-moderate is unable to do; for it seems that this commitment is at the very center of the neo-moderate's system.

What if the neo-moderate did try to make do without the do/allow distinction? It seems that she might alter her system in either of two ways. First, she might move to the claim that indeed in *all* cases of countenancing overall negative harm, the appeal to cost is unable to generate countervailing considerations. But such a system will yield no option to allow harm at all; the neo-moderate will thus have conceded victory to the extremist. Alternatively, she might move to the claim that the appeal to cost can indeed generate countervailing considerations even in cases involving overall negative harm-doing. But such a system will be unable to resist the unacceptable option to do harm; the neo-moderate will thus have conceded victory to the minimalist.[4] Clearly, neither alternative is acceptable to the neo-moderate.

The neo-moderate held out the possibility of maintaining the appeal to cost and the option to allow harm, while avoiding the option to do harm—without having recourse to a constraint against doing harm. Given that the moderate's defense of constraints was unsuccessful, the neo-moderate seemed an attractive alternative. It seems, however, that an adequate defense of the neo-moderate's system would inevitably run up against many of the same objections that sank the moderate's defense of constraints. Apparently, then, the moderate and the neo-moderate must founder together.

---

[4] Interestingly, in preparing his work for publication (see previous note) Scheffler modified his views in just this way, apparently unaware of the minimalist implications.

6

Avoiding the Appeal

It is time to consider where the discussion has brought us. The extremist believes that an agent is morally required to perform—of those acts not otherwise forbidden—that act which can be reasonably expected to lead to the best consequences overall. Up to this point we have portrayed the extremist as sceptical of the existence of constraints—i.e., as holding that no reaction which would best promote the overall good is forbidden. This most straightforward version of the extremist's position thus amounts to the claim that an agent is always required to promote the best consequences overall. The position is based on the recognition of a pro tanto reason to promote the good, and the denial of the existence of any countervailing considerations.

In contrast, the moderate believes that morality is less demanding than the extremist claims. Although the moderate himself recognizes the pro tanto reason to promote the good, he also believes that countervailing considerations can prevent that reason from generating a requirement. The moderate believes that there are agent-centered options granting permission to perform acts which from a neutral perspective are less than optimal. These options are not unlimited—only the minimalist holds that—but they significantly curtail the extent to which an agent is required to promote the good.

Chapter 1 argued that the most plausible defense of options requires an independent demonstration of the existence of constraints. For without constraints, the appeal to cost would support not only options to allow harm but also options to do harm—and the latter are unacceptable to the moderate. That is, given that the moderate does *not* believe in the existence of options to do harm, we knew that he would have to reconsider his commitment to the appeal to cost if he could not also establish constraints in order to limit its effect. The conclusion of Chapter 1 examined general arguments for constraints, and found them inadequate. After Chapter 2 further clarified the structure of ordinary morality, Chapters 3 and 4 turned to more detailed examinations of the two most plausible versions of the constraint against harming, and showed the problems undermining each. The combined result was to call into question the existence of constraints, and this in turn threatened the moderate's ability to provide a satisfactory justification for options. Chapter 5 therefore reexamined the possibility of grounding the appropriate sorts of options without constraints, but ultimately concluded that the attempt to do so was unsuccessful. This reconfirmed the moderate's unhappy position: without constraints he must either abandon his defense of options, and grant victory to the extremist—or recognize a more far-reaching range of options than he finds acceptable, and grant victory to the minimalist. Either way, the moderate's own position cannot be defended.

The belief in constraints is apt to be a difficult one to eliminate, however—for the intuitions which support it are slow to disappear. Many moderates, although embarrassed by their inability to *justify* constraints, are likely to remain convinced of their *existence*. And they will persist in their belief in options as well—for once the constraints are assumed, the objection to grounding options in the appeal to cost vanishes.

Now I have already argued that one must not rest content with intuitions which cannot be given more adequate justification—for the slaveholder too may be supported by his intuitions. But there is no point in denying that the belief in constraints is likely to be retained. Yet suppose we were to *grant* the moderate his constraints—what would actually follow? In Chapter 1 we bracketed the question of whether options *could* actually be justified, noting only that the most plausible defense was unavailable to the moderate unless there were constraints. Even if we *assume* that there are constraints, however, it is by no means *obvious* that there are options as well. The extremist, after all, is prepared to deny this. Recall the previously dormant qualification in the extremist's claim: the agent is only required to perform the optimal act of those *not otherwise forbidden*. As we noted earlier, the extremist can admit the existence of constraints and still offer a morality radically more demanding than the moderate's. That is, the extremist can allow constraints and nonetheless deny options. In granting constraints, therefore, we put aside a powerful objection to the moderate's position; but the question still remains whether the moderate can provide an adequate defense of options. This is the issue which we will begin to examine in this chapter. Let us see whether the moderate can justify options.[1]

THE SELF-CONSTRAINT ARGUMENT

We have granted the existence of constraints so as to silence what would otherwise be a crippling objection to the moderate, thus enabling the moderate to return to the task of attempting to construct a positive defense of options. Even given constraints, however, it does not seem likely that the task of defending options will be a trivial one. Indeed, as we shall see, examining the appeal to cost will occupy us for three chapters. But some moderates may hold that in granting constraints we have given the moderate all that he needs—contrary to the belief of the extremist. Such moderates may suggest that the existence of options follows fairly directly from the existence of constraints.

In the present chapter we shall be concerned with a few arguments which such moderates might offer. As it happens, even if they are sound, the arguments may not so much offer explanations of *why* there are options as simply demonstrate *that* there are options. Thus they lack some of the potential depth of the appeal to cost: they would not necessarily help us to *understand* why agents are not required to promote the good (within the limits of constraints—a qualification which should be hereafter understood, unless context indicates otherwise). But at the same time, the (relative) modesty of the objective of these arguments may be seen as an advantage: after all, the mere demonstration of the *existence* of options would be sufficient to refute the extremist. If a fairly brief argument can settle this score, while avoiding the more arduous task of spelling out the appeal to cost, it is worth considering.

---

[1] It will be observed that the notes to my discussion of the defense of options contain next to no references to particular moderates. This is mostly because almost nothing is ever said by way of *defending* the existence of options, except perhaps for passing vague gestures in the direction of the appeal to cost. Scheffler's work, however, is a valuable exception. And, although it is less explicitly a defense of options, Williams' work is important in this regard as well.

How might the moderate pursue the suggestion that the existence of options follows from the existence of constraints? As we know, constraints typically prohibit agents from standing in certain relations to people. The constraint against harming, for example, means that it is forbidden to force various sacrifices upon individuals, even though it might promote the good to do so. Such thoughts may suggest the following argument. If it is in general forbidden to force a sacrifice upon an individual on the mere grounds that such a sacrifice would promote the good, then it seems clear that a general requirement to promote the good must be ruled out as well. For such a requirement forces sacrifices upon individuals—that is, it forces individual *agents* to make sacrifices— and it does it for what the constraint holds to be inadequate grounds: the mere fact that such sacrifices would promote the greater good. Thus a requirement to promote the good seems in some sense incompatible with the constraint against harming; it appears to involve a violation of the constraint. Hence, once we assume the existence of the constraint, we can rule out the existence of a requirement to promote the good; and we can, therefore, infer the existence of options.[2]

This is an obscure argument. Who, or what, is it that is supposed to violate the constraint against harming, when an individual agent is required to promote the overall good? Three possibilities suggest themselves. First, it might be society that would violate the constraint, by *enforcing* a requirement to promote the good. Second, it might be morality that would violate the constraint, by *including* a requirement to promote the good. Third, it might be the agent herself who would violate the constraint, in certain cases of *acting* on a requirement to promote the good.

The first suggestion is the most straightforward. We have several times entertained the possibility that it is impermissible for others to force a given individual to make various sacrifices for the greater good. Presumably, if there is a constraint against harming, it will typically (although perhaps not always) be forbidden for the members of society to coerce a given member into making such a sacrifice. For society to enforce a requirement to promote the good—to back up such a demand with the threat of various social sanctions, or the use of force—may well violate the constraint. But such considerations would do nothing toward establishing the

[2] See, e.g., Heyd, pp. 174–5.

existence of options. The impermissibility of one or more individuals *imposing* a sacrifice upon another is completely compatible
with that other person's nonetheless being morally *required* to
make the sacrifice herself. So even if it is true that society may not
enforce a requirement to promote the good, this does not show that
morality does not include such a requirement.

What of the second possibility, i.e., that it is morality that would
violate the constraint, by the mere fact of including a requirement
to promote the good? After all, isn't there a sense in which the very
existence of the requirement to promote the good forces individuals
to make sacrifices? No doubt there is such a sense, but it seems that
here we have a case in which the personification of morality can
lead us into error. Constraints forbid various sorts of reactions. But
strictly speaking, morality itself does not react at all. It is not the
right *kind* of entity to violate a constraint; it is not an agent (nor a
group of agents). For the most part, morality is rather a system of
reasons for action, a set of guides for behavior. If morality includes
a requirement to promote the good, then there is a morally decisive
reason for an individual to promote the good. But the *existence* of
such a reason can hardly force the agent to make sacrifices, in the
sense of 'force' that a constraint against harming prohibits.
Provided that she is not forced by others, if an agent makes a
sacrifice, it is only the agent herself who *imposes* the sacrifice.

Perhaps, then, the final interpretation of the argument can be
developed. Can a requirement to promote the good be ruled out on
the grounds that in certain cases an agent's imposing sacrifices upon
herself violates the constraint against harming, and so there can be
no requirement to make such sacrifices? This is a possibility worth
exploring. We should bear in mind, however, that if the moderate is
to demonstrate the existence of a genuine *option*, his argument that
there can be no requirement to promote the good must somehow be
compatible with his belief that sacrifices for the greater good are
nonetheless permitted (i.e., despite the constraint). If an account
along these lines is to avoid outright contradiction, it will have to
bring in the assumption that the constraint can be waived.

As I have noted, constraints typically prohibit agents from
standing in various relations to people. Each individual is therefore
protected by a given constraint: because of the constraint, agents
are forbidden to treat the person in various ways. Presumably for
most constraints, however, the protection offered can be waived by

the individual in question (recall the discussion of the permission principle in Chapter 4). It does not violate the constraint for an agent to treat the person protected by the constraint in the otherwise prohibited manner if the agent has the permission of that individual. Perhaps not all constraints can be waived in this way, but many can be. At the very least we can suppose this is so: let us assume that the constraints we have granted the moderate are, in the main, waivable.

The moderate might then argue in this way: suppose it violates a constraint for an agent to treat an individual in a certain way unless the agent has the permission of that individual. Then this is true regardless of who the agent is; so it is true even if the agent is the given individual himself. If forcing a certain sacrifice upon a person without his permission is forbidden, then it is forbidden for that person to force the sacrifice upon himself against his will. Thus, if an agent does not desire to make that sacrifice, he need only withhold his permission qua patient from himself qua agent. Making the sacrifice in such a situation is forbidden—for it violates the constraint. A fortiori, it is not *required*. Therefore, if the agent does not want to make the sacrifice, it is not required.

On the other hand, if the agent is willing to make the sacrifice, then he need only grant himself permission to do so—and it will no longer violate the constraint. That is, if the agent wants to make the sacrifice, he is permitted to do so. Putting these two results together, we find that the agent is permitted to make the sacrifice if he wants to, but is not required to make the sacrifice if he does not want to. That is, the agent has an *option* permitting him to refrain from making the sacrifice, even though it would be optimal for him to make it. Therefore, if the constraint exists, so must the option.

This argument is an unfamiliar one, and so it may be worth running through it a second time. It tries to show that if there is a *constraint* protecting the individual from having various sacrifices forced upon him, then there must be a corresponding *option* permitting the individual to refrain from taking on the sacrifice. Suppose that there is such a constraint. Then—the argument claims—the agent must be permitted to refrain from making the sacrifice if he does not want to make it. We know that he is *permitted* to refrain, because in fact it would violate the constraint *not* to refrain. The constraint, after all, prohibits forcing the sacrifice upon the individual against his will—even if it is the individual himself who does the forcing. That is, if the individual does not want to make the sacrifice, he withholds permission, retaining the protection of the constraint—and therefore qua agent he is forbidden to force the sacrifice upon himself qua patient. Thus, given the existence of the constraint, we know that the individual need not make the sacrifice if he does not want to make it.

However, if the individual *wants* to make the sacrifice he can give himself permission to do so: forcing the sacrifice upon himself will no longer violate the constraint; and so the individual will not be required to refrain from taking it on—i.e., he will be permitted to make the sacrifice. What all of this means is that *if* there is a constraint, then the agent is permitted to make the sacrifice, or not make the sacrifice, as he chooses. But obviously this is equivalent to the claim that if there is a constraint then the agent has an option. That is, if we are given the existence of the constraint, it will follow that the corresponding option must exist as well. Since the heart of the argument, in effect, lies in the notion of an individual turning the constraint which protects him back upon himself, let us call this the *self-constraint* argument.

Establishing the existence of an option in this way is, of course, conditional upon there being a constraint protecting the individual from having the sacrifice forced upon him against his will. But we have granted the moderate the existence of such constraints; so the existence of options appears to follow. There are options permitting me not to treat myself in those ways which others—thanks to constraints—are forbidden to treat me.

Of course, since options, and the protection offered by constraints, can be waived, and waived selectively, there will be artificially created cases in which an agent is protected by a constraint although he now lacks the option. Nothing in the self-constraint argument rules out this possibility. But if sound, the argument shows that an agent who is protected by a constraint naturally possesses the corresponding option. And this is obviously all that the moderate would care to claim. (For simplicity, let us leave artificial cases to one side.)

If successful, what does the argument accomplish? A bold claim would be that the argument actually *explains* the existence of the various options which it yields: the options literally derive from the constraints; they exist *because* of the constraints. A more modest claim, however, would be that the argument does not itself explain options but rather simply demonstrates that there must *be* options (if there are constraints). On the modest view, options and constraints might well have some common basis of which they are coproducts. But on the bold view it would be more appropriate to see options as a mere corollary of constraints. Since refuting the extremist only requires that the moderate establish the *existence* of options, we need only ascribe the *modest* view to the moderate.

It should be noted, even if only in passing, that the self-constraint argument's ability to defend a given option will obviously depend upon whether we recognize the existence of the necessary corresponding constraint. And it seems that no set of coherent constraints could yield all of the options which the moderate desires.[3] But this should not necessarily trouble the moderate. He can observe that this is not in itself any reason to think the self-constraint argument unsound—nor any reason to deny the existence of those options which *can* be derived. That is, the moderate might admit the need to find additional arguments if he is going to establish all of the options he desires: nothing in the self-constraint argument suggests that the *only* options are those which can be established through it. Yet the moderate can still claim to have successfully proven the existence of those options which can be derived from constraints. To prove the existence of *any* options, after all, is to refute the extremist; and it is not an insignificant range of options which the argument yields.

What, then, are we to make of the self-constraint argument? The appropriate reply, I believe, is simply this: the argument just doesn't work. Talk of my violating, qua agent, constraints which protect me, qua patient, provides us with an image. It may even be a suggestive image. But it is no more than that; and it will not bear the weight which the moderate's argument places upon it.

Suppose I am in a situation in which I can impose a sacrifice upon

---

[3] Imagine a situation in which I have the resources to save either one of two individuals, both of whom will otherwise die; and imagine that I am one of the two. The moderate presumably believes that I am free to save myself. Yet the only way such an option could be derived through the self-constraint argument would be if there were a constraint prohibiting others from *allowing* me to die. But since I could be either of the two, the necessary constraint would have to prohibit allowing *either* of us to die: that is, agents would have to be required to save both—even though they lack sufficient resources to do so. Obviously there could be no such constraint. Thus the self-constraint argument will necessarily fail to yield all of the options which the moderate wants to grant. (It is probably worth mentioning as well that given certain commonly accepted constraints, the argument may also yield some options which are unacceptable to the moderate.)

myself—say, by making certain movements—and where it would violate a constraint for others to force the sacrifice upon me, without my permission. The self-constraint argument insists that I am not required to make the sacrifice, if I don't want to—for I need only withhold permission from myself: forcing the sacrifice upon myself in this case would be to violate the constraint which protects me. Yet clearly I am *capable* of imposing the sacrifice upon myself: I can still perform the necessary movements, and so on. Suppose I *do* force the sacrifice upon myself: can there be any such cases in which I have managed to do so while withholding my permission? Or does permission automatically follow?

Suppose, first, that performing the act constitutes, or guarantees, permission. Then I needn't worry, when I impose the sacrifice upon myself, about violating the constraint protecting myself. I need only proceed to impose the sacrifice, and the necessary permission will come 'in tow'. Thus I will have done nothing forbidden in taking on the sacrifice: I cannot *possibly* violate the constraint which protects myself. But the reason that the self-constraint argument gave for thinking that it was permissible to *refrain* from taking on the sacrifice if I did not want to make it, was that *making* the sacrifice while I withheld permission would violate the constraint. If, however, I *cannot* violate the constraint protecting myself then the self-constraint argument will have provided no reason for thinking that taking on such a sacrifice cannot be required. And so no option will be established.

More interestingly, then, suppose for the moment that permission does not automatically follow. In this case it is possible to impose the sacrifice upon myself where I do so unwillingly. But it seems absurd to say of such cases that my action is *forbidden*. This is not to say, of course, that there are no cases in which it is forbidden for an agent to mistreat himself in various ways. There may well be so-called duties to oneself, and there is nothing absurd in the suggestion that if there are such duties, violation of those duties would be forbidden. But presumably genuine requirements concerning one's treatment of oneself would not be *waivable*; and so the case at hand cannot involve such a requirement. For as we have seen, if the self-constraint argument is to generate options, the constraints upon which it operates must be such that the person protected by the constraint is able to waive that protection—i.e., in particular, he must be able to waive the requirement that he treat himself in conformity with the constraint. What is bizarre, then, is the suggestion that I can violate a *waivable* constraint by imposing sacrifices upon myself unwillingly—that to do so is forbidden.

Perhaps there is something morally undesirable about imposing sacrifices upon myself against my will (still assuming that this is possible)—but it seems totally inappropriate to say that such reactions are prohibited. And I take it that moderates would not want to make such an outlandish claim. Yet the self-constraint argument asserts that I *would* be doing what is forbidden if I were to impose the sacrifice upon myself against my will. But once we drop the inappropriate claim that making sacrifices unwillingly is forbidden, then the self-constraint argument loses its ground for concluding that taking on such sacrifices cannot be required. And this means that the argument will give no reason for thinking that it is *permissible* to refrain from making the sacrifice. Once again, no option will be established.

Thus neither answer is acceptable. Whichever way the moderate answers, the self-constraint argument is undercut. We might still wonder, however, why it *isn't* the case that imposing the sacrifice upon myself against my will violates the constraint protecting me from having such sacrifices forced upon me. After all, I *am* an agent; why don't I fall under the scope of the constraint? Presumably the answer is the obvious one: although I fill the role of both agent and patient, I am one and the same individual. I am not simply one agent among others as far as my treatment of myself is concerned. It is not possible for me to interfere with myself, or to show disrespect for myself, and so on, in all the ways that I can do these things to others. Once again, this is not to say that it is impossible to show disrespect for myself: there may well be duties to oneself. But if the constraints upon which the self-constraint argument is supposed to operate are waivable—as the argument requires—then this is presumably because for such constraints the morally offensive feature that underlies violations of the constraint cannot be displayed in cases where the patient is a cooperating partner. In such cases, then, the constraints in question will not protect me from myself. They cannot, therefore, be used in any general way to yield options. The self-constraint argument fails.

There are, perhaps, cases in which an individual might violate some code if she performs some act, even though that very act would be permissible if she gave herself permission. Imagine a situation in which a person holds two institutionally defined offices—each office sharply limited as to its legitimate powers and the considerations which are to be taken into account in making decisions. There may be some act which the person who holds the first office is able to perform, but only permissibly so if she has the permission of the person who holds the second office—who, as it happens, is the very same person. In her capacity as holder of the second office, however, it would be improper to grant permission, and so she withholds it. If the person went ahead and performed the act anyway, she would act impermissibly. Merely considering the complexity of such a case, however, reveals how implausible it is to think anything similar could happen in the typical, noninstitutional case. Despite the talk of the individual in his roles of agent and of patient, the person is not at all compartmentalized in the way that would be necessary in order to construct an analogous conflict. To suggest otherwise is to impute a disjointed and multiple personality to the individual which is obviously lacking. Unlike the institutional case, there is nothing to correspond to the withholding of permission once the *person* has chosen to perform the act.

I have been suggesting that the unity of the person typically rules out the kind of conflict within the individual that the self-constraint argument requires. There is, however, an important qualification to this claim that should be considered. In many cases, my reaction at a given time can affect me not only at the very time of the reaction, but also at a significantly later time. In such cases it is far easier to understand talk of my imposing sacrifices upon myself against my will, for I may react *now* in such a way as to impose a sacrifice upon myself *later*—a sacrifice that I may later oppose (but be unable to undo). And regardless of the appeal of other purported duties to oneself, given such conflicts between a particular individual now and the same individual later it is easier to take seriously the possibility that the individual as agent is restricted by constraints protecting her as patient.[4] It might be suggested, therefore, that in these cases, at the very least, the self-constraint argument can succeed in demonstrating the existence of options.

[4] This is because the relation of an individual now to herself later is somewhat more akin to the relation of that individual to others. How significant we find this fact, however, may depend, in part, on our views concerning the nature of personal identity across time. A discussion of the connection between conceptions of personal identity and the application of moral principles to such intrapersonal but intertemporal cases can be found in Parfit, Chapters 14 and 15, and in Wachsberg.

Note, however, that even if we assume (as the self-constraint argument requires) that the relevant constraint can be waived (unlike more typical duties to oneself) it is only the individual at the later time who is in the position to waive the protection of the constraint. That is, the approval or disapproval of the individual agent *at the time of acting* is, strictly speaking, irrelevant. What makes the decision to sacrifice (or to refrain from sacrificing) her later interests permissible is the fact that she will *later* come to approve (or disapprove) of such a sacrifice. But this means that the agent's approval or disapproval at the time of acting does not suffice to guarantee the permissibility of her reaction. Thus it is not in fact the case that the agent may permissibly make the sacrifice or refrain from making the sacrifice *as she sees fit*—i.e., as she sees fit at the time of acting. So the argument has not succeeded in grounding a genuine option.

It is true of course that the individual's decision now may well causally influence her attitude later; but the possibility, or even the likelihood, of such influence does not suffice to ground an option. By hypothesis, the individual may later disapprove of the sacrifice that she earlier imposed upon her later self; so the agent's earlier imposition of the sacrifice may well violate the constraint, and hence be forbidden, despite her decision at the time of the reaction. Thus it may not be permissible for the individual to make the sacrifice, regardless of what she wants at the time. What's more, if the individual will later approve of the sacrifice, it may have been forbidden earlier for the agent to refuse to make that sacrifice, regardless of what she happened to want then. Since making, or refusing to make, the sacrifice may well be forbidden—regardless of the desires of the agent at the time of acting—it can hardly be claimed that a genuine option has been established.

In short, when we focus—as we did initially—upon the relatively standard cases in which I act now to sacrifice my current interests, it is difficult to see how to make sense of the notion of my acting against my own will. But even if we focus instead upon cases in which I act now to impose a sacrifice upon myself later, although we can make sense of the notion of my imposing a sacrifice upon myself against my (later) will, the self-constraint argument fails to ground an option nonetheless.

Perhaps, however, another objection to the argument is even simpler. According to the self-constraint argument, it can be permissible for me to refrain from making a sacrifice, if I so desire, for it would violate the given constraint to force the sacrifice upon myself when I withhold permission (however this notion is best understood). However, even if we grant that failure to make the sacrifice would be permissible were I to withhold permission, the self-constraint argument may *still* fail to establish the existence of options. For the moderate has given no reason to think that it is permissible for me to withhold my permission when it would be optimal for me to give it. (This is so, regardless of whether the relevant permission is at the time of acting, or at some later time.) If it is not permissible, then I am required to waive the protection which the constraint gives me from myself—and so that protection cannot be used to prove the existence of an option. If the moderate is to establish options, he needs another approach.

RIGHTS

The self-constraint argument promised to establish the existence of options directly from the existence of constraints, while avoiding the need to spell out the appeal to cost. Although that argument was unsuccessful, there are two other arguments that I want to consider which, I believe, can also be understood as trying to fulfill that promise. As it happens, however, the two basic arguments we will examine are typically cast, not in terms of constraints, but rather in terms of *rights*. Now this is a notion of which we have not made much use previously, but there is no obvious reason why it should be avoided. Rights do the work of constraints in many moral systems: the presence of a constraint against harming, e.g., is expressed by saying that people have a (negative) right not to be harmed. And so on. (A distinction is often made between negative and positive rights: the right not to be harmed is an example of a negative right—for others are required to *refrain* from doing something; a right to be given some sort of aid, on the other hand, is an example of a positive right—for others are required to *do* something.) Whether all talk of constraints can plausibly be reformulated in terms of rights is a question which need not detain us here. It is at least plausible to think that in granting the moderate his constraints, we have granted him the means to speak of various rights. So let us examine the arguments in their common, seductive form.

Suppose in some situation my reacting in a certain way would be nonoptimal. The reaction might consist in keeping or obtaining some personal good, remaining or becoming such and such, and so on. The moderate will note that it will often be the case that I nonetheless have a right to react in this nonoptimal way. We can see this, he will argue, by considering the fact that it would be forbidden for others to force me to give up the personal good, prevent me from obtaining it, stop me from becoming such and such, etc.

For example, I may have a certain amount of money which would receive optimal use if donated to charity. But—the moderate argues—it would violate my rights to be *forced* to give money to charity. Thus, I have a right to keep my money. That is, in keeping my money I act within my rights. But obviously what I have a right to do, I am permitted to do. So—the moderate may conclude—I am morally permitted to keep the money. That is, I have an option: I am permitted to perform a less than optimal act. (The argument could be offered for either negative or positive rights. Here I shall concentrate on negative rights. For positive rights, the argument would say that since I have a right to receive certain aid, I am permitted to accept it.) Stripped to its essentials, the moderate's argument can be reconstructed as follows—argument schema A:

A   (1) I have a right to do X (e.g., keep my money).

     (2) If I have a right to do X, then I am permitted to do X.

∴ (3) I am permitted to do X.

Presented in such bare form the argument may lose much of its appeal. Since I do not think the argument can establish the existence of options, I will not attempt to dress it more attractively. Yet it is not without its charms, for both (1) and (2) have a certain uncontroversial air about them. After all, on the one hand, if it would violate my rights to prevent me from doing X, it seems obvious that I have a right to do X. And on the other hand, if I *do* have a right to do X, then it seems clear that I am *permitted* to do X. Given (1) and (2), the conclusion certainly seems to follow—and so argument A may be thought to establish the existence of options. I do not think the argument is sound, but before examining it more closely, let me introduce a second argument from rights.

Suppose that it would be optimal for me to perform some act; let us say that by giving a certain amount of money to some needy individual I will do more good than by keeping it. The extremist would insist that I am required to provide the aid. The moderate, however, might reply on my behalf that the individual in need has no *claim* against me; I am not violating anyone's *rights* if I fail to help him (in particular, I am not violating any positive right of the individual against me). But this means that failure to aid is committing no *injustice*; so it can't be that I am *required* to help.

It is easy to get entangled in this web. The moderate, in denying the requirement to aid, moves from 'no right violated' to 'no injustice done' to 'not immoral'. How many (or which) of these links are legitimate may depend on what we mean by 'justice'. If, on the one hand, we take justice in a narrow sense to be the respecting of the rights of others, then the claim that since no one's rights are violated no injustice is done will clearly be true. But then we will want to know why we should think that justice is all of morality. If, on the other hand, justice is used more broadly so that it trivially follows that an act is morally required if and only if it is required by justice, then we will want to know why we should think that justice requires nothing beyond respecting rights.

In actual practice the word 'justice' is apt to be used imprecisely, masking the moderate's slide from 'doesn't violate a right' to 'not morally required'. The slide can be masked even more thoroughly by introducing terms such as 'duty'. (Is it a trivial truth or a substantial claim that all duties are grounded in rights? Is it trivial or substantial to claim that one's moral duty is exactly equivalent to what one is morally required to do? And so on.) In order to avoid the temptation to make such slides, let us reconstruct the moderate's argument so that it moves directly from 'no right violated' to 'not required'. We then have argument schema B:

B   (1) I am required to do Y (e.g., to aid another) only if someone has a positive right to my doing Y.

(2) No one has a positive right to my doing Y.

∴ (3) I am not required to do Y.

Argument B complements argument A. Argument A moves from the *presence* of a (negative) right (on the part of the agent) to the lack of a requirement to do the optimal act. Argument B moves from the *absence* of a (positive) right (on the part of the needy individual) to the lack of a requirement.

The two arguments are apt to be found together. This is probably due to the fact that A suggests B: for A appeals to the presence of a negative right, and given the plausible sounding view that you can't have a positive right to what I have a negative right to—i.e., the thesis that corresponding negative and positive rights *conflict*—then it would follow that others must lack the corresponding positive right—and this is used in argument B.[5]

There is something surprising about arguments A and B. Both attempt to establish the existence of options merely by noting the presence or absence of various rights. That they should try to do so is somewhat curious, for we initially permitted the introduction of rights-talk as a mere substitute for constraint-talk; yet—given the failure of the self-constraint argument—it doesn't seem at all likely that the mere presence or absence of a constraint should entail the existence of an option. What arguments A and B make obvious is that the notion of a right involves greater conceptual complexity than we have so far recognized. In order to get clear about where the arguments go wrong, it is necessary to distinguish various elements of rights.

THE ELEMENTS OF RIGHTS

When people claim that they have a right to do X, they may be ascribing to themselves all or some of a variety of elements. We can say that a *full negative right* consists of these parts: (1) an *option* for the agent to do X (or not do X, as he chooses); (2) an *injunction* protecting the agent's decision—i.e., it is wrong for others to force the agent not to do X (to interfere as he tries to do X, to cause him to not do X, to punish him for doing X, etc.; there is no need here for us to distinguish various forms injunctions may take); (3) an *enforcement privilege*, giving the agent the right to enforce the injunction.

[5] Examples of both A and B can, I think, be found in Thomson, 'Abortion'—although she appeals primarily to B. This article also displays two of the features I have mentioned. First, I believe that Thomson makes some illicit slides of the sort I have criticized. Second, she appears to use the conflict thesis in the way I have suggested: she moves from my having a negative right to my body to the claim that others lack a positive right to it—evidently basing her case on the conflict thesis (although there is also plenty of simple, unadorned *assertion* that others lack the positive rights in question).

The option is, of course, a familiar notion: it grants the agent permission to react in a certain way (or refrain from so reacting) if he chooses—even though the choice may not be optimal. But the other two concepts require more commentary. The injunction provides moral protection for the agent's decision—protection from others, that is. With a negative injunction, others are forbidden to force the agent not to do X (and so on). An injunction is thus equivalent in its effect to a requirement that others not react in certain ways. Indeed it *may* be that to speak of an agent's being protected by an injunction is simply another way of speaking of there being such a requirement binding upon others. On some views, however, although there is such a *correspondence* between injunction and requirement, the two are not actually one and the same thing. And in some cases, at least, it may be thought that the existence of the injunction helps to *explain* the existence of the requirement. All of this is a controversy into which we need not enter.

A second matter concerning injunctions, however, will be of more importance to us. As I have described the notion, there is an injunction whenever it is wrong for others to force the agent not to do X (etc.). In this sense, then, even consequentialists—and other opponents of constraints—can accept the existence of injunctions: for obviously *sometimes* it will be wrong for others to force the agent not to do X, e.g., perhaps when the agent is going to do the optimal act, etc. Thus an injunction needn't correspond to a *constraint*. Typically, however, when a moderate speaks of a right he means to suggest the existence of an injunction of a more substantial sort than would be acceptable to consequentialists. This is a matter to which we shall return in the discussion of argument B.

The enforcement privilege gives the agent the right to enforce the injunction—i.e., the right to react in various ways against those who try to force the agent not to do X. Different accounts may vary as to the details of the enforcement privilege: for example, on some views the right to enforce the injunction may include not only a right, e.g., to use force against those who are trying to violate the injunction, but also a right to punish those who have already succeeded in violating the injunction; similarly, it may be not only the agent who has the right to enforce the injunction, but also the agent's duly authorized deputies (e.g., the government). For our purposes, however, there is no need to pursue these matters; the general characterization—i.e., that the enforcement privilege gives the agent the right to enforce the injunction—should suffice.

The presence of the word 'right' in this characterization of the enforcement privilege shows that the enforcement privilege can itself be decomposed: it consists of an option to enforce the injunction, and an injunction protecting the agent against others forcing the agent not to enforce the injunction. Indeed there looms before us a hierarchy of higher order enforcement privileges: for the enforcement privilege will consist not only of an option and an injunction, but also of an enforcement privilege, which can itself be decomposed, and so on. We will thus find such subparts as an option to enforce one's right to enforce, an injunction against others trying to force one not to enforce one's right to enforce, and the like. Despite the logical distinctness of these higher order enforcement privileges, it won't generally be clear what might constitute defending one's right to enforce one's injunction as distinguished from simply defending one's injunction. But such fine points won't concern us.

On some views the enforcement privilege isn't actually a component of a given right itself. It is rather a second, distinct right. On some of these views a given right is always backed up with its corresponding enforcement right (which in turn is always backed up with its corresponding right); while others may hold that it is always an interesting question whether a given right is backed by an enforcement right. But for simplicity's sake I shall assume that in a *full* right the enforcement privilege is included.

A full negative right, then, consists of an option, an injunction, and an enforcement privilege. Similarly, a full positive right consists of the same sorts of parts: (1) an option to do X; (2) a positive injunction—making it wrong for others to fail to help the agent to do X in various ways; and (3) an enforcement privilege.

In calling rights that have all of these parts *full* rights, I do not mean to suggest that all rights are full rights. Nor do I mean to suggest that in most cases when someone speaks of a right, the right they have in mind is thought to be full in this sense. I do not think that talk of rights is generally carefully enough fixed to make such a claim. Basically I believe that when someone says he has a right he has *some* of these parts in mind, and he isn't being very clear about which of them it is—or whether it is all of them. For the parts are detachable: one might have some and not the others—and the word 'right' is loosely used to cover any of them.

In contrast to a full right, we might talk of a *thin* right. A thin right is an injunction. It is, I think, the thin right which is the heart of most rights-talk. When someone complains that it was a violation of her rights to have her property appropriated, arm chopped off, or for so and so to fail to return her car—what makes this true (when it is true) is her thin right. For regardless of whether the other elements of a full right are present, provided that the individual is indeed protected by an injunction against such behavior on the part of others, it seems appropriate to speak of her having a right. To ascribe to someone a thin right, then, is simply to ascribe possession of the relevant injunction, without committing oneself on the question of whether the other elements necessary for a full right are present as well.

It is clear that once we assume the existence of constraints, we assume that there is a prohibition against treating individuals in certain ways, and thus that people are protected by *injunctions* forbidding such treatment. Therefore, in granting the moderate the existence of constraints, the extremist is in effect granting the existence of a significant group of thin rights. Now if it can be shown that the extremist has also committed himself to the existence of *full* rights (or even of only one full right), then the extremist will have undercut his own position—for a full right contains an option as one of its elements. But it is far from clear that in granting the existence of thin rights, the extremist has also thereby committed himself to the existence of full rights. Unfortunately, however, it is easy to confuse thin rights and full rights. Such confusion lies behind argument A.

It is possible to have a thin right without having a full right. In particular, it is possible to have an injunction without having the corresponding option. It is this possibility which undercuts argument A. Recall that the moderate argued that to be forced to give up my money, e.g., would be to have my rights violated. In this way he hoped to establish the truth of (1)—I have a right to do X. But all that this uncontroversially establishes is the existence of a thin right. If we take 'right' in the argument to refer to thin rights, then (2)—if I have a right to do X, then I am permitted to do X—is not a logical truth, and the extremist is free to doubt it. Logically, that is, one might have a negative injunction without having the corresponding option; and so the extremist needn't accept (2). If we take 'right' to refer to full rights, however, then although (2) is a logical truth, the moderate hasn't demonstrated the truth of (1): he has only shown the existence of a thin right, and illicitly assumed he has shown the existence of a full right.

The moderate might reply that although it is a logical possibility for the various parts of a full right to be detached, it is not an actual *moral* possibility. In particular, then, an agent never merely possesses a thin right and nothing more: if he possesses a *thin* right, then in fact he possesses the *full* right. Making this claim explicit, we can revise argument A as follows:

A' (1) I have a thin right to do X.
    (*) If I have a thin right to do X, I have a full right to do X.
    (2) If I have a full right to do X, then I am permitted to do X.

    ∴ (3) I am permitted to do X.

In the revised argument, (2) is uncontroversial and the extremist must accept it; and (1), as we know, follows from the recognition of constraints. If the various parts of a full right cannot actually be detached, then (*) will be true as well—and the argument will be sound.

But the moderate would be wrong to claim that the various parts of a full right cannot in fact be detached. We can quickly run through a few cases to show how one might have some of the parts without others. For the sake of generality, let me begin with some cases which contradict the thesis that the parts of a full right cannot be detached, but which are not themselves counterexamples to the *specific* claim that one cannot have a thin right without having a full right.

Suppose I have a right not to do X, but I release you from my injunction ('I hereby waive my right that you not try to force me to do X'). Presumably in some such cases it is no longer wrong of you to try to force me to do X—but I do not thereby become *required* to do X, so I do not automatically lose my option. Thus I have an option without an injunction. I can *also* give up my right to enforcement ('I promise that if you do try to force me, I won't fight back')—or I can *retain* the right to enforcement ('It won't be *wrong* of you to try to force me; but I'll still have the right to try to stop you if I want').[6]

More to the point at hand, there are cases where there is an injunction without an option. I can contract with you that I am to

---

[6] It may be odd to speak of 'enforcement' here—since there is no longer an injunction to be enforced. Perhaps a more neutral term is called for: the *response* privilege gives the agent the right to react in certain ways to various forms of treatment at the hands of others. But I'll stick to 'enforcement'.

do X, and then you can sell back to me my former injunction against your *forcing* me to do X, without releasing me from the obligation to do X. Or I might promise you to do X *provided* that you don't try to force me—but if you do try to force me then the promise is void and I'll enforce my right not to do X. Here we have an injunction and enforcement privilege, without an option.

What these cases show is that the various parts of a full right *can* be detached from the other parts. Thus the moderate has given us no reason to think that one can move from the existence of a thin right to the existence of a full right—and so (*) is unjustified. The moderate might respond by noting the artificiality of these examples. He might assert that although a given agent can *detach* various parts of his rights, they never come separate *naturally*. If this is correct, then in those cases—surely the most common—in which the agent has *not* somehow waived some portion of his right (nor artificially *gained* some portion of a right), it is legitimate to infer the existence of a full right from the presence of an element of a right.

If the moderate can make out this claim—concerning the natural attachment of the various parts of a full right—then some version of argument A would go through. But obviously such a thesis is a controversial one, and would need elaborate defense; and I am not sure how the moderate is to provide such a defense.[7]

The moderate will note that it *might* be possible to establish the natural attachment of the parts of full rights without actually being able to defend the existence of any given part. In particular (given the needs of argument A), the moderate might attempt to show that *if* there are certain sorts of injunctions, then there *will* be corresponding options. Then, once we have granted the moderate the existence of a particular injunction, the existence of the corresponding option would follow. The self-constraint argument can be viewed, or reinterpreted, as one attempt along these lines.

---

[7] Nor am I sure that all moderates want to defend the thesis, even in its qualified form. For example, sometimes people say that they have a right to do X, when apparently all they are ascribing to themselves is an option: they are merely asserting that they are *at liberty* to do X—that they have no requirement not to. Such rights—sometimes called liberties for that reason—don't seem to entail the existence of any injunctions, and thus they apparently provide a counterexample to the thesis that the parts of a full right never are naturally detached. However, it isn't obvious that such rights involve *no* injunctions at all: it may seem plausible to suppose, e.g., that others are prohibited from wantonly interfering with the exercise of my liberties.

Had it succeeded, it might have provided a defense of the essential core of the moderate's claim that the various parts of a full right naturally come attached. This claim could then be used in order to buttress argument A. (Of course, had it been successful, the self-constraint argument would have established the existence of options on its own—even without the scaffolding of argument A.) But the self-constraint argument failed.

Now this still leaves A in the lurch: without the thesis of the natural attachment of the parts of full rights, argument A is undermined. But the moderate is not in the position to defend the thesis—and so the extremist, obviously, is free to reject it. Thus the moderate cannot resort to argument A to prove the existence of options: a crucial presupposition is unsupported.

Yet the thesis that the various parts of a full right naturally go together is not without its intuitive plausibility. One might well wonder what is the *point* of granting someone protection against interference from others, if she herself is not morally free to take advantage of that noninterference and perform the protected act. Quite similarly, one might wonder what could be the point of granting someone permission to perform a nonoptimal act, if others are not to be at all restrained from interfering with the performance of the act. And one might wonder what is the point of granting moral protection against interference, if the agent is unable to enforce the claim to noninterference against those who would trample upon it.

To feel the force of these questions is to see the plausibility of thinking that the various parts of a full right naturally come in one package. And it should be noted that one can feel the force of these questions even while rejecting any suggestion that morality has been *designed* by some artificer, who 'grants' constraints and options, and so on. The questions simply evoke the intuition that, ultimately, all the elements of full rights must share a common underlying basis. The moderate may therefore hope that in providing an adequate defense of one element of full rights one would see how the very same grounds provide a basis for the other elements.[8]

It is, as I say, easy to feel the force of this intuition. But this is not

---

[8] Given such a common basis, we would typically expect to find corresponding options and constraints. But we would also have to be open to the possibility that in some cases although the option can be generated, the corresponding constraint

yet an argument. Without actually being provided with an account of the purported common basis, we do not have adequate reason to assume that the intuition will be borne out. As noted, the moderate may hope that justification of one of the elements will reveal the underlying basis. But we have only *assumed* the existence of constraints; we have not justified them. Since the moderate must concede that he has been unable to provide us with an adequate account of constraints, I take it that he will also have to admit that he has not given us (sufficient?) insight into what might be the common grounds for the basis of the various elements of full rights. Consequently, the moderate is not yet in a position to assert that the various elements of a full right are never naturally divided. And until such time as the moderate is able to give us more adequate insight into the purported common basis, the idea is perhaps better left to one side.

POSITIVE RIGHTS

Without a defense of the thesis that the various parts of a full right naturally come attached, argument A must be abandoned. And this, obviously enough, means that the moderate cannot use that argument for a defense of options. I began the discussion of rights, however, by presenting *two* arguments from rights—and we have not yet examined the second. Even if A fails, B might still establish the existence of options; so let us consider it more carefully. Recall how the argument goes:

B   (1) I am required to do Y (e.g., to aid another) only if someone has a positive right to my doing Y.

      (2) No one has a positive right to my doing Y.

    ∴ (3) I am not required to do Y.

I suggested that a plausible way for the moderate to argue for the truth of (2) is via the thesis that positive and negative rights *conflict*:

cannot be. One such case might be the example considered in n. 3, in which the corresponding constraint would be impossible to discharge. It might be suggested, in effect, that although the common base would have yielded the constraint if it could—it cannot. For the corresponding option, however, there is no such problem of dischargeability, so nothing prevents the common ground from yielding the option. Vague as such a suggestion may be, the moderate may hope that it nonetheless offers a glimpse of why constraints and options do not always appear hand in hand.

if, in many cases, it would violate my negative rights to force me to do Y, it seems reasonable to conclude that in such cases no one has a *positive* right to my doing Y. Since it seems plausible for the moderate to defend (2) in this way, it is worth noting that this thesis may not be true. A *full* negative right and its corresponding *full* positive right will conflict.[9] But as we have seen, it is far from obvious that all rights are naturally full rights. If the given positive right lacks an enforcement privilege, and if the given negative right lacks an option, then there doesn't seem to be any conflict after all. In such a situation, e.g., it would be wrong of the agent not to give aid (for the needy individual possesses a positive injunction)—and yet it would *also* be wrong of the needy individual to *take* the aid with force if it isn't offered (and this is all that is guaranteed by the agent's negative injunction). Only if the positive right contains an enforcement privilege (e.g. permitting the needy in our example to take the money if it isn't offered), or if the negative right contains an option (permitting the agent to keep the money), is there an obvious conflict between my having a negative right and your having a positive right to the same thing.

Without the thesis that the various portions of a full right come naturally attached, it is unclear how the moderate hopes to argue for the truth of (2); although the moderate might be able to establish its truth in some other way. But there is no need to settle this matter now—for we can grant, for the time being at least, the plausibility of (2): no one's positive rights are violated if I fail to aid.

How are we to understand (1)? I do not think the positive right referred to in (1) should be taken to be a full positive right. Rather, I think we should probably interpret (1) to mean that I am required to do X only if someone has (at least) a *thin* positive right. For a thin positive right alone would be sufficient for me to be required to do X. Even if the moderate believes that any naturally arising positive right will be a full positive right, he loses nothing by accepting this more modest interpretation of (1).

Thus we can take (1) to be claiming that I am required to aid another, e.g., only if someone has (at least) a thin positive right to

---

[9] Actually, even this claim may not be true on some views, according to which the genuine existence of a right in a given case is completely compatible with that right's nonetheless being overridden in that case by someone else's right. Advocates of such views would need to replace my talk of 'rights' with talk of 'rights that are not overridden', and make the corresponding alterations in my discussion of A, B, and the elements of rights; but the substance of my remarks should not be affected.

my providing aid. I am required to aid another only if he has the corresponding positive injunction.[10] How might the moderate argue for (1)? He might note that I am required to aid another only if—obviously—it is morally wrong for me to fail to (try to) aid that other. But this is exactly what constitutes grounds for asserting the existence of a positive injunction. That is, a positive injunction states that it is wrong for some individual to fail to provide aid (of the appropriate sort). So—the moderate argues—it is *true* that I am required to aid another only if he has a positive injunction—i.e., has a positive right to my aid. Therefore (1) is correct, and (2) has already been granted—so the argument is sound.

But the moderate has moved too quickly. When I introduced the notion of an injunction, I noted that even consequentialists can concede their existence—for to speak of an individual's injunction, in effect, is to say no more than that others are required to react in certain ways toward that individual. In this sense, injunctions can be fairly 'flexible'; an injunction needn't correspond to a require-ment as restricting as a constraint, for example. It is this noncontroversial aspect of injunction-talk which makes (1) plaus-ible. But I also noted that when moderates speak of rights they tend to suggest the existence of an injunction of a fairly 'substantial' sort. And it is only when we have such substantial injunctions in mind that (2) remains uncontroversial.

There is no need to get very precise about what sorts of injunctions qualify for talk of a 'right' according to the tastes of moderates. What is fairly clear is that not all injunctions will so qualify. For example, moderates are apt to think that if an agent is morally required to provide aid to some individual merely because the causal nexus has so worked itself out that it happens that aiding that individual will best promote the good, then the situation does not merit speaking of a positive *right* to aid: the injunctions underlying rights must be of a more stable sort, perhaps being grounded more essentially in the nature of the individual himself, or what have you. Leaving the task of demarcating this class of injunctions to rights theorists, let us simply label its members

---

[10] Here is a possible complication. Mightn't Harpo have a positive injunction requiring Chico to aid Groucho—even though Groucho lacks it himself? It does matter, after all, whether the ability to waive Chico's requirement to aid Groucho resides with Harpo or with Groucho. But let's keep things simple and assume that the only relevant positive rights—if such there be—reside with the individual to be aided.

substantial injunctions—and thus distinguish them from those injunctions which are not substantial, the *flexible* injunctions.[11]

Once we distinguish flexible and substantial injunctions, however, argument B no longer seems plausible. If we decide to use 'right' broadly enough so as to include flexible injunctions, then (1) retains its uncontroversial status. But in this case (2) can no longer be granted to the moderate without begging the question in his favor. For to assert that no one has (at least) a thin positive right to my aid will be to assert that no one has a positive injunction requiring that I aid—not even a flexible one. And this will be to assume what was to be shown: that I am not required to give the aid.

On the other hand, if we restrict talk of rights to those cases where the individual has a substantial injunction, then it remains plausible to contend that typically no one has a positive right to my aid—so (2) is true. However (1) will no longer be plausible with this restriction—for surely flexible injunctions would be sufficient to ground a requirement to aid, and the moderate has given us no reason to think the class of flexible injunctions is actually empty. Thus argument B fails.

Indeed, it seems that the moderate himself might want to admit that the argument fails. For he does want to recognize a requirement to aid the drowning child. Yet a minimalist might appeal to argument B and claim that the child has no *right* to his assistance—concluding that he is not required to throw the child the life preserver. So far as I can see, the moderate has only two ways out of this problem. First, he might try to defend the claim that the drowning child *does* have a positive right to a passerby's assistance. But the moderate would then have to explain why he

[11] Not all rights will correspond to constraints: e.g., in the system without constraints discussed in Chapter 5, it still seems appropriate to speak of rights. Ultimately, whether an injunction qualifies as a right may be more a matter of the character of the particular reasons grounding the given injunction. At the very least it seems likely that consequentially grounded injunctions will not be substantial. (One might suggest that a requirement that substantial injunctions be waivable will yield this result—for consequentially grounded injunctions will not typically be waivable. However, there can be no such general requirement that substantial injunctions be waivable—at least, not if we want to leave open the possibility of inalienable rights.) It is also worth noting that substantial injunctions may have to be grounded in facts essentially about the injunction-holder. Thus if for some independent reason you have a special *duty* to serve me (perhaps arising from your job), my positive injunction may not qualify as substantial: it may be inappropriate to speak of my *right*. But let us leave all these matters aside.

does not recognize similar positive rights in all those cases where an individual's receiving aid would best promote the overall good. Presumably the moderate would have to resort to the appeal to cost. Yet the point of considering the arguments presented in this chapter was that they purported to avoid the need to fill in the details of the appeal to cost. Thus argument B might be saved from the counterexample—but all the work would remain to be done. Second, of course, the moderate might abandon argument B altogether, and consider the appeal to cost directly. Either way, then, it is the appeal to cost to which we must turn.

7

The Appeal to Cost

The appeal to cost provides an intuitively plausible basis for a defense of options. Such a defense appears to have several advantages. First, it represents one of the replies we are actually inclined to make when pressed to justify our failure to provide aid. That is, appealing to cost is something we frequently do when explaining why we do not take on some given sacrifice which would promote the good.[1] Basing the defense of options on such an appeal thus has the virtue of being true to what we actually say.

Second, the appeal to cost appropriately discriminates between cases which the moderate wants to distinguish. To see this, contrast a different response which the moderate might initially be tempted to make. If called upon to make some significant sacrifice in the pursuit of the good, an agent might very well refuse with the explanation that she simply does not want to. Whatever the force of this reply, it is not one which the moderate can accept by itself as justifying the refusal to provide aid—for such a reply, if acceptable, would ground options of a more powerful sort than the moderate wishes to grant. The moderate, after all, believes that I am required to save the drowning child; and the mere response that I do not want to do so would not provide sufficient excuse.

Obviously enough, the moderate must believe that there is something special about the various cases where he does believe my refusal to provide aid is permissible. He must find a feature which

---

[1] I have written as though the point of all options is to grant the agent permission to pursue his interests at the possible expense of the overall good. But in fact a moral system might include options which grant relief from other would-be requirements as well. For example, a system might have a strong presumption in favor of punishing the guilty, but grant agents permission to refrain from carrying out such punishment (if they so choose) if it would involve a significant sacrifice of their interests. Presumably, however, the defense of such options would still be in terms of the appeal to cost. I will not consider them further.

provides justification for refusal only in those cases where the moderate wants to recognize options. The appeal to cost appears to indicate such a feature: aiding the drowning child requires no significant sacrifice of one's interests—it costs little or nothing; therefore, providing aid in such a case will still be required. But providing famine relief, say, could involve a significant drain on one's resources. Therefore, one will not be required to do all that one can toward fighting famine (although providing a modest amount to famine relief may well be required). Thus grounding options in the appeal to cost will apparently provide limited options of the sort desired by the moderate.

Third, the appeal to cost appears to offer an *explanation* of options, and not merely a defense of their existence. This is in contrast to the two arguments from rights given in the previous chapter, for example, which would not have gone very far—even if successful—toward explaining the various options whose existence they hoped to demonstrate. The appeal to cost goes deeper. It seems to help us understand *why* agents are not required to promote the good: agents needn't pursue the good because of the *cost* of doing so. (A reminder: since we have granted the moderate the existence of constraints, what is at issue here is only why agents need not pursue the good even within the *limits* of those constraints; generally, however, I'll leave this qualification implicit.)

But this last point is not as simple as it may seem. Even if the appeal to cost provides the *heart* of an adequate explanation of options, an unadorned indication of the cost involved in any given sacrifice will not by *itself* constitute a satisfactory explanation of why the agent is permitted to avoid the sacrifice. We need to know *why* the cost is an acceptable excuse. Obviously there is no question about the fact that promoting the good typically involves significant cost to the agent; but the extremist will clearly demand to be told *how* this fact is supposed to fit into a justification for options. Why does cost provide an *excuse*? Developing the appeal to cost so as to answer this question is not a trivial matter. Indeed, it will take us several chapters to consider various attempts. But the deep intuitive appeal of grounding options in considerations of cost gives us reason to think that it is worth undertaking the investigation.

As a first attempt, then, let us suppose that the moderate offers the following argument. Promoting the good can involve a significant drain on my resources. Money, time, effort, and life itself can be consumed in the course of my reacting in an optimal manner. This primary sacrifice of my resources will almost always take a secondary toll: the ensuing sacrifice of my ability to promote my interests. If my resources are being devoted to the promotion of the good, then I will generally be unable to favor those things with which I might be particularly concerned. These might include my own welfare, or the welfare of various other individuals whom I love or with whom I am friends. They might also include various projects, goals, or other endeavors to which I am committed. The pursuit of the good may leave me no time to tend my garden or to study philosophy. If all my spare cash is being sent to famine relief, I cannot support the local astrological society, or take my family on vacation. Worse still, in a situation in which I must choose between saving some loved one, or two strangers, I apparently must choose to save the strangers.

The moderate might plausibly argue that all of this is an intolerably heavy burden to place upon an agent. Requiring that an agent promote the good effectively cuts off the possibility of his molding his own life. It demands that he be ready to sacrifice all that to which (and all those to whom) he has devoted himself. But surely there is something undesirable about asking an agent to abandon that to which he is committed. Under a moral system without options agents will repeatedly be required to sacrifice their interests. This is an unacceptable feature, and the only way to avoid it is by the introduction of options—permitting agents to favor their interests, even though it may not be optimal for them to do so.

In this way the moderate might attempt to spell out the appeal to cost.

THE SACRIFICE OF INTERESTS

The moderate's argument—as I have just given it—turns upon the complaint that promoting the good requires the agent to sacrifice his interests. That is, I have been assuming that when the moderate offers the appeal to cost as a defense of options, it is the agent's sacrifice of his interests that constitutes the basic cost in terms of which the argument is ultimately to be understood. It is not, for example, the sacrifice of *resources* per se which is problematic, but rather the fact that the sacrifice of resources curtails the agent's ability to promote his *interests*.

Now it is important to remember that one's interests (as I am using the term) need not be limited to what is in one's self-interest narrowly construed. An agent may take an interest in the welfare of another person, e.g., even though he does not expect that person's well-being to lead to a more immediately personal benefit for the agent himself. Indeed, an agent may take an interest in various states of affairs which do not 'personally' affect him at all. Thus an agent's interests need not (and often will not) coincide with his self-interest. It is, in fact, a possibility that in some situations an agent may best promote his interests by sacrificing his own life or his overall self-interest.

Given this potential divergence between an agent's interests and his self-interest, the question arises whether it is indeed the sacrifice of interests per se that is relevant for the appeal to cost, or only the sacrifice of one's self-interest. Typically, no doubt, there is extensive overlap between an agent's interests and his well-being; but still, it might be suggested that ultimately it is only the latter that is of direct importance for the appeal to cost. That is, it might be suggested that the sacrifice of an agent's interests is itself only of importance for justifying options insofar as it involves a sacrifice of the agent's self-interest.

On this second proposal, the mere fact that the pursuit of the good would involve a significant sacrifice of an agent's interests would not necessarily trigger the appeal to cost, justifying an option to refrain from making the sacrifice. Rather, it is only if the sacrifice would involve a sacrifice of the agent's overall well-being that the appeal to cost would come into play. In contrast, on the original proposal, options would be generated by the appeal to cost whenever pursuit of the good would involve a significant sacrifice of the agent's interests—even if the promotion of those interests would not promote the agent's own well-being.

It might be urged, in defense of the second interpretation of the appeal to cost, that the sacrifice of an agent's well-being has a clear moral significance which may be lacking in cases where the agent merely sacrifices interests that do *not* contribute to his well-being. For in the latter kind of case—where the given interest does not promote the agent's self-interest—there is an obvious sense in which the sacrifice of the interest in question does not leave the agent any worse off. Accordingly, or so it might be argued, the agent can hardly claim that promoting the good in such cases involves an intolerably heavy burden. It is only when promotion of the good would involve a sacrifice of the agent's self-interest that he can defend an option by pointing to the cost involved in making that sacrifice.

Nonetheless, I believe that the moderate would do better to pursue the original interpretation of the appeal to cost, according to which options will protect an agent's interests even if (some of) those interests are unconnected to the agent's overall well-being. Two related considerations point in this direction. First of all, despite the fact that a given interest may be unconnected to the agent's personal welfare, in principle it might still be among the agent's most significant concerns—i.e., it may be one of the things of greatest concern to the agent. Even if there is *some* sense in which the sacrifice of such an interest may not lower the quality of the agent's life, it seems equally clear that it may constitute a significant loss or sacrifice for the agent nonetheless. Thus it seems plausible to hold that the appeal to cost should be concerned with the sacrifice of interests, and not merely with the sacrifice of self-interest.

So interpreted, the appeal to cost will generate a wider range of options than would follow were it only self-interest that was protected.[2] But this brings us to the second point, for it also seems plausible to hold that it is in fact this wider range of options that is recognized by ordinary morality. Intuitively, ordinary morality appears to grant the agent the option to refrain from significantly sacrificing his interests, regardless of whether the pursuit of those interests would itself contribute to the welfare of the agent himself. As the defender of ordinary morality, then, the moderate will prefer a defense of options which is not restricted to those cases where the agent's self-interest is at stake. Thus the appeal to cost must be understood broadly, in terms of interests in general, rather than narrowly, in terms of self-interest alone. And this is the way that I have presented the argument.

But this last response suggests in turn a different objection. It might be argued that interpreting the appeal to cost in terms of the agent's interests—far from being too broad—is itself still too narrow, failing to account for the full range of options recognized by ordinary morality. In particular, it might be argued that the

---

[2] Strictly speaking it may also be narrower as well: since there is the logical possibility of an agent who takes no interest at all in his self-interest, an interests-based approach will not necessarily yield all of the options generated by an approach based on self-interest.

options embraced by ordinary morality permit an agent to react nonoptimally not only when this promotes her interests, but even when the reaction in question does *not* promote the agent's interests. That is, although typically the agent is permitted to promote her interests (at the cost of the greater good), and permitted to promote the greater good (at the cost of her interests)—she is *also* permitted to react in a manner which *neither* promotes her interests *nor* the greater good. But the permissibility of this last possibility cannot be explained by a defense of options that views those options as serving to protect the agent's interests (against any general requirement that they be sacrificed for the greater good); since reactions of the kind in question do *not* promote the agent's interests, such a defense seems incapable of justifying this aspect of the relevant options. If this is correct, however, then a defense of options based on an appeal to the cost involved in the sacrifice of interests will not suffice for the moderate's purposes.[3]

It might be suggested, therefore, that the appeal to cost should be understood even more broadly still. Whether or not an agent's interests are at stake, when a given reaction is forbidden, her freedom of choice is curtailed. If she is going to conform to morality, each additional moral requirement diminishes the agent's ability to mold her life by her own lights or in accordance with her own plans. We can speak of an agent's *moral autonomy* being limited or diminished by further moral requirements. The suggestion, then, is that to capture the full range of options recognized by ordinary morality, the moderate should understand the appeal to cost not in terms of the sacrifice of interests, but rather in terms of the loss of or reduction in the agent's moral autonomy.

At first glance, this new view appears to offer a plausible and powerful motivation for options: options protect and thus serve to express the value of moral autonomy. Upon closer examination, however, it becomes unclear whether talk of moral autonomy provides any sort of justification for options at all. After all, to say that an agent's moral autonomy—in the present sense—is greater or smaller is simply to say that a larger or smaller set of reactions is morally available to the agent. That is, moral autonomy is simply a matter of whether a given reaction is permitted or forbidden. But

---

[3] This argument comes from Slote, as does the suggestion—about to be noted—that options should be viewed instead as protecting moral autonomy. See pp. 23–34.

this means that talk of moral autonomy cannot explain or justify options; such talk is simply an alternative way of referring to the exact same facts that we are already referring to when we speak of the existence of options in the first place. For example, the claim that options protect moral autonomy—despite the appearance that this expresses a substantive insight—amounts to nothing more than the trivial truth that if a given act is covered by an option then it is permitted (but not required). Nothing has been gained here by introducing the notion of moral autonomy, except for the illusion of progress. (In contrast, note that the rival claim—that options protect the agent's interests—is not trivial in this way.)

Similarly, the claim that options express the value of moral autonomy amounts to nothing more than the question-begging assertion that there is value in a given reaction's being permitted rather than required or forbidden. In even simpler terms, it comes to the assertion that options are a good thing by virtue of being options. Here too, it seems, the point can easily be stated without recourse to the notion of moral autonomy, and nothing has been gained through its use. For the moderate to provide a genuine justification for options along these lines, he would still need to explain *why* it is better (other things being equal) that a given reaction be permitted. And we seem no further along the path to discovering the necessary explanation.

It might be argued, however, that thinking of the problem in terms of moral autonomy actually does direct our attention to a promising line of thought. For moral autonomy can be seen as a particular instance—within the moral domain itself—of the more basic value of autonomy in general. Intuitively, we place considerable value on freedom from interference within, say, the political or social domain. Similarly, then, freedom from moral interference should be seen as having significant value as well. But moral interference is constituted by the presence of moral requirements and prohibitions; freedom from such interference requires the presence of options. In short, by understanding moral autonomy as one more instance of the same basic value which underwrites the importance of political autonomy, or personal autonomy, we can see options as expressing—within the moral realm—a value which is of general and pervasive significance.

I think, however, that it is in fact a mistake to view moral autonomy as of a piece with these other types of autonomy. Moral 'interference' is so unlike political or social interference, e.g., that it is inappropriate to understand the former as essentially similar to the latter. This point is basically the same as one I made in Chapter 6, where I argued that morality itself cannot violate a constraint by requiring that agents make some sacrifice—for morality cannot literally coerce the agent or *force* her to make the sacrifice. A moral requirement exists when there is a morally decisive reason for an agent to react in a given way. But the mere *existence* of such a reason hardly forces the individual to react appropriately. Thus moral requirement is quite unlike external interference or coercion; and, for that matter, it is also quite unlike internal (physical or psychological) disability, or other limiting or disabling factors (such as the lack of resources). The existence of a moral requirement per se simply does not limit our abilities.

This is, perhaps, a slight overstatement. After all, given the existence of a morally decisive reason to react in a certain way, the agent is unable to react in some different way without going against the morally decisive balance of reasons. But it would be implausible to claim that *this* 'loss of freedom' is genuinely offensive or undesirable. (One is similarly unable to violate the laws of logic, e.g., or the canons of theoretical reasoning, without going against the balance of theoretical reasons; but this too hardly constitutes an undesirable loss of freedom.)

Now if, as I have just argued, the restriction of moral autonomy cannot be criticized by appeal to the more basic value of autonomy in general, then the moderate still has no defense for the claim that it is better (other things being equal) that a given reaction be permitted rather than forbidden or required. So let me mention one other possible argument for this claim.

If an agent performs some act that benefits another (and does not benefit himself), and this act is not one that is morally required, clearly the agent is not reacting in this way because he must; rather, he is doing it because he *wants* to. That is, his act is not done from duty—but rather out of concern for the individual he is aiding. And it might be argued that this is an especially valuable kind of motive, one that would be lost if the given reaction had been morally required. Since it is freedom from moral requirement that makes possible this higher form of motivation, all other things being equal it is better if a given reaction is covered by an option.[4]

[4] Heyd may have something like this argument in mind at pp. 9, 179; cf. pp. 41, 175, 177.

Unfortunately, this argument assumes that if the given beneficial act were in fact morally required (or, more generally, if there were a requirement to promote the good) it would be harder, or perhaps even impossible, to act out of this higher kind of motive. But there is no good reason to believe this claim. The existence of a moral requirement, and indeed the recognition of this requirement, is perfectly compatible with acting out of direct concern for the relevant individuals. Neither the existence of such concern nor the motivational force of such concern need be reduced by the realization that there is in fact morally decisive reason to provide the aid in question.

There is, then, no clear support for the claim that it is better (other things being equal) if a given reaction is permitted rather than required or forbidden. An appeal to the general value of autonomy seems unsuccessful, as does an appeal to the higher value of certain forms of motivation. I cannot think of a more promising line of defense for this claim, and so I think that the proposal to view options as an expression of the value of freedom from requirement per se should be resisted. The moderate will do better if he sticks to the suggestion that options protect the agent's interests, rather than protecting his freedom from requirement per se.

Yet even if no adequate defense of options can be mounted in terms of the value of moral autonomy, and the like, doesn't the fact remain that ordinary morality recognizes a wider range of options than can be accounted for in terms of protecting the agent's interests? It was, after all, this unanswered objection that originally prompted the search for some alternative, broader basis for options. The proposed alternative defense may fail, but isn't it true nonetheless that according to ordinary morality agents have options to react in ways that neither promote the good nor promote their interests?

I suspect, however, that this is in fact a point concerning which defenders of ordinary morality will differ. Despite the initial plausibility of the claim, it is not, I think, completely clear that ordinary morality *does* recognize options to react in ways that neither promote the good nor promote one's interests.

One reason for scepticism is this. We often make statements concerning the permissibility of reacting in one or another nonoptimal way. And it must be admitted that—taken literally—statements of this kind may well assert that the agent *is* permitted to react in the given nonoptimal way—i.e., without regard to whether this promotes her interests. Yet it seems possible that such assertions should not be taken quite so literally. For a statement that a given reaction is permissible will often be made on the implicit assumption that the agent would only choose to react in that particular way if it were conducive to her interests to do so. Thus, the statements in question may instead be loose and convenient ways of conveying the point that the relevant act *would* be permitted—i.e., if it were to promote the agent's interests; the unstated qualification is 'understood' or presupposed. If something like this is correct, then typically the evidence of such statements is at least ambiguous as to whether ordinary morality genuinely includes permission to react in ways that neither promote the good nor promote one's interests.

Furthermore, there is some reason to think that ordinary morality may actually *reject* options to react in nonoptimal ways that do not promote one's interests. Recall an example I gave in Chapter 1, in which I enter a burning building and choose to save a caged bird rather than a young child. Intuitively, I have done something wrong. According to ordinary morality, of course, I probably need not have entered the building in the first place—for this involved a significant risk to my safety, and similarly endangered my ability to promote my various interests. However, once I had decided to take the risk—had decided to sacrifice, or to risk the sacrifice of my interests—it seems intuitively wrong of me not to have promoted the greater good by saving the child. What this case suggests (and others would reinforce the conclusion) is that although ordinary morality grants me the option to refrain from promoting the good in the pursuit of my interests, I do *not* have the option to react in a manner that neither promotes the good *nor* my interests.

It must be admitted that neither of these two considerations demonstrate conclusively that ordinary morality only recognizes options that protect the agent's interests. As I have already stated, I think defenders of ordinary morality will differ over this point. But in the absence of clear evidence that ordinary morality recognizes a wider range of options than can be accounted for in terms of interests, it does not seem pressing to continue looking for an alternative account. What all of this adds up to, I believe, is a reasonable case for sticking to our original proposal and interpreting the appeal to cost in terms of the sacrifice of interests. As far as I can see, at any rate, this still provides the most plausible line of argument for the various options recognized by ordinary morality.

OTHER OPTIONS

I have been arguing that the appeal to cost should be understood in terms of the sacrifice of interests rather than more broadly (in terms of, say, the sacrifice of moral autonomy). On the other hand, I also argued that an interpretation of the appeal to cost which viewed it as restricted to the sacrifice of self-interest would itself be overly narrow. Agents can take significant interest in matters which do not themselves contribute to their own personal well-being (or do so, at best, incidentally). Since the cost to the agent of sacrificing such interests for the sake of the greater good can still be considerable, the appeal to cost is most plausibly understood as protecting interests in general, and not merely self-interest.

It should be noted, however, that this argument by itself does not suffice to show that *every* interest of the agent is in principle relevant for the appeal to cost. Even if it is granted that options should be viewed as protecting the agent's interests—regardless of their connection to the agent's self-interest—there is still room for uncertainty as to whether *all* of an agent's interests are relevant for the appeal to cost, or only some crucial subset of those interests.

Now when the moderate complains that promoting the good requires the sacrifice of interests, it is fairly natural to understand him to be referring specifically to the various long term concerns which inform an agent's life. (In the argument sketched at the start of this chapter, e.g., the examples given are of this sort.) Let us extend the notion of *projects*[5] to cover all these central concerns, i.e., the various goals, endeavors, and the like, which have taken on a central significance in the agent's life—including the well-being of loved ones, as well as the advancement of favored causes, and so on. It might be suggested, then, that options are necessary because without them an agent is unable to promote his projects. This is, as I say, a natural way to understand the moderate's argument.

Alternatively, the moderate might prefer an approach which did not particularly focus on the agent's ability or inability to promote

---

[5] Roughly following Williams. See, e.g., 'Persons', pp. 5, 12–14.

his projects per se. Instead, the moderate might understand the appeal to cost more broadly, as sensitive to the sacrifice of all interests, and not only those interests that constitute an agent's projects. On such an approach, the moderate might note that without options an agent will frequently be unable to do what he wants to do. That is, in countless cases promoting the good will require the agent to sacrifice his *wants*. Of course an agent will generally want to promote his projects—and so the sacrifice of projects will involve the sacrifice of wants. But the latter has a broader extension than the former: promoting the good will sometimes require an agent to react in some way that he does not *want* to react, where nonetheless it would be inappropriate to claim that it would require a significant sacrifice of the agent's *projects*.

In short, if options are viewed as protecting only the agent's projects, then not all of an agent's interests are relevant for the appeal to cost. For many of an agent's interests will be too fleeting or peripheral to be counted among his projects; we might speak of these other interests as mere desires, or mere wants. And this raises the question whether, when the moderate complains that promoting the good requires the sacrifice of interests, he should be concerned with the sacrifice of *all* interests, including even the sacrifice of mere wants, or whether instead he should only be concerned with the sacrifice of projects.

One obvious reason for thinking that options are grounded in the undesirability of the sacrifice of projects is that it seems plausible to suggest that projects are more *important* than wants. An agent's projects have a centrality to his life that cannot be matched by many mere wants. If we hope to leave the agent room to shape his life as he chooses, then it seems plausible that the *central* features of that life have a greater claim to protection from the demands of the good. Thus it is easier to see why an agent should be permitted to refuse to sacrifice his projects than it is to see why such permission should be extended to cover such inessential and peripheral concerns as various fleeting wants.

Yet there are reasons to think that the moderate should not restrict himself to a concern with projects. It is true that the sort of option which is most frequently discussed is supported by consideration of the need to protect projects: a life spent promoting the good—say, by fighting famine—leaves little time for such projects as the study of early modern painting. So the protection of projects will support options to refrain from sacrificing those projects. But there are other options which are less comfortably handled by concentrating on the sacrifice of projects; and these options suggest that it is the need to protect all interests—including mere wants—with which the moderate should be concerned.

Consider, first, options to refrain from doing small favors and other trivial beneficial acts. If someone asks me the time, e.g., it seems likely that typically the gain to the stranger would objectively outweigh whatever inconvenience I might suffer if I stop, look at my watch, and answer. Telling the time thus better promotes the good than refraining—and if there are no options then I am required to meet the stranger's request. Many moderates, however, believe that such small favors are *not* required: in normal circumstances I have an option to hurry on my way or to stop and tell the time—as I see fit. But it is not clear that the moderate will be able to ground such 'trivial' options if his argument is centered on the protection of projects. For it doesn't seem at all plausible to suggest that a requirement to tell a stranger the time will involve any significant sacrifice of my projects.

If the relevant sacrifice of interests is construed as encompassing even the sacrifice of mere wants, however, then the moderate is in a better position to ground the desired option: if I don't *want* to take the (slight) trouble to tell the time, then an option is necessary to free me from the intrusive requirement that I do something that I don't want to do. If the moderate is to give a unified account of both typical options and such trivial options then it seems that he must be concerned with protecting interests in general—that is, even mere wants.

The point is not decisive. Some moderates may actually believe that agents *are* required to do such small favors; such moderates, obviously, need not trouble with the point at all. But even those moderates who do believe in the existence of options to refrain from small favors may be able to find a way to ground such options in the potential sacrifice of projects. They might suggest, for example, that although any particular favor would not affect one's ability to promote one's projects, the cumulative effect of a general requirement to do such favors *would* be significant. I do not know how successful such a suggestion would be. (Why wouldn't it lead to a requirement to do small favors except in those unusual cases where the burden of doing them grows excessive?) But whatever the success, it certainly seems that construing the appeal to cost in terms of all interests—however trivial—provides a more *natural* basis for these options: the agent need not do the favor simply because he does not want to.

It is possible, however, that trivial options can be handled in another way. As I argued in Chapter 2, the existence of an option turns on the absence of a morally decisive reason. (After all, in any given case, there can only be an option to refrain from reacting in a certain way if there is no *requirement* to react in that way. Thus, if there is to be an option, either there must be no reason at all in support of reacting in the given way, or else that reason must fail to meet some condition necessary for being morally decisive.) Now the most obvious condition which must be met for a reason to be morally decisive is that it outweigh any opposing reasons. But I also noted the possibility that there may be further, less obvious conditions necessary for moral decisiveness as well. One such potential extra condition is the following: it might be suggested that a reason can be morally decisive only if its strength is greater than (or equal to) a certain minimum.

If such a condition is appropriate (and assuming that the minimum is set above a totally negligible level), typically there will be no requirement to do small favors. For in such cases, presumably, the reason supporting doing the favor will be a weak one—below the minimum necessary for moral decisiveness. Even if the reason which supports doing the favor outweighs the reasons that oppose it, that reason will nonetheless fail to be morally decisive, and so will not ground a requirement.

Now such an argument—if successful—would provide a defense of only a limited range of options: those where the good that could be done is fairly trivial. It would, therefore, need to be supplemented by an account adequate to establishing options in those common cases where the agent pursues his interests even though he could instead make a rather significant contribution to the overall good. But this is not, in itself, an objection. For in the latter sort of case—where the good at stake is not trivial—the moderate can try to defend options by turning to the appeal to cost.

Indeed, it should be noted that the suggested defense of options involving small favors does not introduce the appeal to cost at all. Since the sacrifice of interests plays no role in explaining such options, the account is equally available however we understand the relevant sacrifice of interests—whether in terms of all wants or only in terms of projects. And this means that the existence of trivial options would provide no particular difficulties for those who want to understand the appeal to cost in terms of projects. That is, if the moderate can defend the suggested extra condition on moral decisiveness, he can reserve the appeal to cost for cases where the sacrifice would indeed be significant; and so the moderate may still be able to base his account of that appeal on the importance of protecting projects.

However, it is difficult to see what reasons there could be to accept the suggested extra condition on moral decisiveness. Why should we accept the claim that moral requirements can be grounded *only* in reasons greater in strength than a given minimum? No doubt, if the reason supporting a given reaction is below a certain minimum in strength, it will typically be unable to outweigh the opposing reasons which may support alternative reactions open to the agent. But if there are cases (rare as they may be) in which the given reason does indeed outweigh any opposing reasons, why should the fact that the reason is less strong than some given minimum automatically rule out the possibility of that reason grounding a moral requirement? Why should minimum strength be a *condition* on moral decisiveness?

The advocate of the proposed condition may suggest that it is inappropriate to bring out the 'big guns' involved in labeling something a moral requirement if there is only a fairly weak reason to perform the reaction in question. But such a reply seems to presuppose that it is always a weighty matter to fail to react as one is morally required; and this is a dubious claim. After all, we frequently assess the relative moral significance of different requirements facing agents—typically, for example, killing someone is worse than breaking a promise—and in some cases, it seems, failure to do what morality requires is a fairly minor matter.[6]

One could, of course, simply *stipulate* that the term 'moral requirement' is to be reserved for those cases where the reason involved is greater in strength than some minimum. But such a

---

[6] Of course if one held that there will always be a pro tanto reason to *punish* failures to react as morality requires, then one might reasonably believe that morally decisive reasons must be fairly strong; but this view about punishment is itself implausible. On the other hand, if the view is simply that *some* form of social sanction is always appropriate for failure to meet moral requirements, then this might be so even for morally decisive reasons that are not especially strong.

terminological move is inadequate to defend the substantive view behind the claim that there is an option to refrain from small favors. It will now be true—by stipulative definition—that one is not 'required' to do small favors; but it may still be true that failure to do the small favor is a moral shortcoming of exactly the same kind (although on a smaller scale) as failure to do what *is* required. (Stipulatively restricting the word 'larceny' to theft of items worth more than $100 entails that theft of $50 is not larceny; but that does not make it any less of a theft.) The view of ordinary morality, however, is that there is a difference in kind between mere failure to promote the good, when this is backed by an option, and failure to do what is genuinely required. If this view is to be captured, the claim that it is a condition on moral decisiveness that the reason in question be stronger than some minimum will have to be defended as the substantive claim that it is, rather than being made true by definition. Yet, as I have indicated, I can see no reason to accept this substantive extra condition on moral decisiveness. And this leaves us back where we were before the suggestion was made—i.e., trying to defend trivial options through the appeal to cost. In short, if trivial options are to be defended, and if (as it seems) the defense is to be conducted in terms of the appeal to cost, there is some reason (although hardly a decisive one) to think that the sacrifice of interests should be understood in terms of all wants—including mere wants—rather than only projects.

There is a second kind of option which is handled more naturally by wants than by projects. Consider situations in which an agent takes on a significant sacrifice so as to provide a lesser benefit for *someone else*. Such situations differ from the more frequently discussed case in which an agent fails to promote the overall good as a result of his promoting his *own* projects. In the latter sort of case, roughly speaking, the agent favors himself over others; while in the former sort of case he favors others over himself. Now in both sorts of cases the agent's reaction is to the detriment of the overall good, and so the reaction is permissible only if there are options. But a distinction between the types of option needed for the two sorts of cases seems worth making: for the unusual case of favoring others at one's own greater expense we might speak of options of *generosity*; and for the more typical case of favoring oneself at the greater expense of others we might uncharitably speak of options of *selfishness*. (The terminology is uncharitable, since one's projects needn't be particularly selfish. Still, there is a distinction to be drawn between promoting one's projects, at the expense of the greater good, and sacrificing one's projects for the sake of promoting someone else's interests, at the expense of the greater good.)

Options of selfishness grant permission to refrain from promoting the interests of others in various cases in which pursuit of the good would require making a significant sacrifice of one's own projects. Thus such options can be straightforwardly handled by an account which centers on the sacrifice of projects (leaving aside the difficulties which may arise for *trivial* options of selfishness.) But it is not obvious how such an account is to handle options of generosity. For these options grant permission to *sacrifice* one's projects so as to bestow a lesser benefit upon another. If options are defended as necessary to permit an agent to *protect* his projects, then it seems that the moderate will be unable to ground options of generosity.

The moderate does better, however, if his account focuses on the need to protect interests per se rather than projects alone. For it seems plausible to suggest that in cases where options of generosity come into play the agent wants to benefit another—even though this involves a sacrifice of his own projects. If the agent can make the sacrifice, this is not because this protects his projects (on the contrary!), but simply because he wants to. Thus, protecting interests in general—including mere wants—grounds options of generosity. But since typically we would expect an agent to want to protect his projects, an account of options centered on interests in general will be able to ground options of selfishness as well. (Indeed, on such an account, the distinction between the two kinds of options may be of no particular significance.) Thus if the moderate is to give a unified account of both options of generosity and options of selfishness it seems that he must be concerned even with the sacrifice of mere wants.

Once again the point is not decisive. Moderates who favor an account in terms of projects may be able to find a way to ground options of generosity. They might suggest, for example, that in such cases—despite appearances—the agent is actually promoting his projects overall.[7] After all, an agent's projects needn't be limited to

---

[7] Or, at least, his *present* projects. But this raises a new question: regardless of whether one thinks that the relevant interests should be understood in terms of projects or wants, are options to be understood as protecting *all* of an agent's (relevant) interests—regardless of when they are held—or only an agent's *present* interests? This is a matter concerning which theorists might disagree and on which I hope to be neutral. (But some related issues are raised in the discussion of prudence in Chapter 8.)

matters which are in his self-interest. As before, I do not know how successful such a suggestion would be. (Is it really plausible to suggest in all those cases where an agent makes a sacrifice so as to bestow a lesser benefit upon another that he has a greater on-going concern for that other person's well-being than for his own?) But whatever the success, it still seems that an account in terms of interests in general provides a more natural basis for these options.

There is, once more, a different line of argument open to the moderate. Options of generosity might be explained instead by introducing yet another purported condition on moral decisiveness. An option of generosity involves permission to sacrifice one's own interests for the lesser benefit of others. Now presumably there is a reason which opposes making that sacrifice—namely, the fact that it will hurt one's interests. If, nonetheless, that sacrifice is to be permitted, then that reason must not be a morally decisive one. Let us say that reasons generated by the fact that a given reaction will promote (or harm) a given agent's interests have *self-regarding content* for that agent. It might be suggested, then, that reasons with self-regarding content cannot be morally decisive for the agent in question. If this is indeed an extra condition on moral decisiveness, then even though the balance of reasons may oppose sacrificing one's interests for the lesser benefit of others, such reasons cannot be morally decisive, and so one will be permitted to make the sacrifice.

This argument is, of course, similar to the one considered for trivial options. Like that original argument, the defense of the further condition on moral decisiveness would only provide an account of certain options—in this case, options of generosity. Options of selfishness would still need to be defended, presumably through the appeal to cost. Furthermore, since the appeal to cost would not be involved in the defense of options of generosity, the suggested account would again be equally available however we understand the relevant sacrifice of interests. Thus, if the further condition could be defended, the moderate would be able to reserve the appeal to cost for cases involving options of selfishness; and apparently, in such cases, the sacrifice of interests could be understood in terms of projects.

I believe, however, that the similarity goes further: once more, I do not see how the further condition on moral decisiveness is to be defended. Why should we believe that the mere fact that a reason has self-regarding content automatically rules out the possibility of that reason being morally decisive? After all, those moderates who believe in the existence of duties to oneself will rightfully resist the claim that we should build the suggested condition into the very account of what it is to *be* morally required. And even those moderates who deny the existence of such requirements presumably do not think that the issue is to be settled by appeal to the notion of moral requirement itself. There may or may not ever actually be moral requirements to protect one's interests, but it is difficult to see what ground there could be for simply ruling out the possibility by insisting that lacking self-regarding content is a necessary *condition* for moral decisiveness.

Rejecting this as a condition on moral decisiveness, however, leaves us where we were before the suggestion was made—i.e., trying to defend options of generosity through the appeal to cost. In short, if options of generosity are to be defended, and if (as it seems) the defense is to be offered in terms of the appeal to cost, there is some reason (although hardly a decisive one) for thinking that the sacrifice of interests should be understood in terms of all wants, rather than only projects. And this conclusion, of course, parallels the one we reached concerning trivial options.

Trivial options and options of generosity may thus give some reasons to think that the defense of options should be construed in terms of the protection of interests per se rather than the protection of projects alone. But we have already seen one consideration which supports the opposite conclusion. At the start of this chapter I noted the moderate's need to exclude an overly minimalist option which would grant permission to refrain from aiding the drowning child. If options protect projects then the moderate will be able to avoid such an unacceptable option: throwing the life preserver involves an insignificant sacrifice, presumably posing no threat to projects whatsoever. But if options protect mere wants then it seems as though the moderate may not be able to exclude the unacceptable option: an agent may shrug off the request for aid with the reply that she simply does not want to throw the life preserver; if interests are to be protected even when projects are not at stake, the moderate may find himself grounding the minimalist option.

Yet this point, too, may not be decisive. On the one hand, the advocate of protecting even mere wants might hope to demonstrate that in the case of the drowning child the threshold for the option has been passed: the want is trivial enough, and the danger significant enough, so that the option to avoid aid is curtailed. And, on the other hand, there may well be cases in which the drowning child must be thrown the preserver even though this *would* involve a sacrifice of the agent's projects: if so, even the advocate of protecting projects might find himself embarrassed by his difficulty in excluding the unacceptable option altogether. I will not pause to examine either of these possibilities: initially, at least, it seems as though the advocate of projects is in a stronger position than the advocate of interests in general for avoiding the minimalist's option.

If the advocate of interests per se is in danger of grounding too lenient an option, however, it may be that the advocate of projects is in danger of grounding too *restricted* a set of options for the tastes of many moderates. For if options are grounded in the need to protect projects, then they will fail to excuse agents from sacrifices which would not seriously endanger their projects. This means that an agent's requirements to provide aid will vary with the extent of her resources. A wealthy individual, e.g., could give away a sizable portion of her income without seriously curtailing her ability to promote her projects. (Of course, an increase in wealth tends to be accompanied by taking on increasingly expensive projects; and in some cases one's project simply is to amass as much wealth as possible. But in most cases it would be implausible to suggest that *all* of the agent's wealth is tied to her projects.) It would seem to follow that she is required to devote that sum of money to the promotion of the good.[8] Yet many moderates believe that there is no such requirement: the agent has an option to do with her income as she wishes. Such options may be available to the advocate of protecting interests—where it is the mere fact that the wealthy woman does not *want* to part with her money which

---

[8] What sorts of options are yielded by the projects account? (a) It might be that the options only protect a 'basic grant' of resources—sufficient to meet essential needs and minimally enabling the agent to promote a reasonable set of projects. Any resources beyond the basic grant would be subject to the demands of the overall good. (b) It might be that beyond this basic grant (or instead of it) options protect a certain proportion of the agent's resources which are devoted to her projects (or perhaps protect against sacrifice a certain proportion of the projects themselves). Beyond this protected portion, the agent would be subject to the demands of the good. Either way, it seems that a wealthy individual will have to devote more of her resources to the pursuit of the good. Perhaps there are other plausible suggestions.

grounds the option—but it is not clear how they are to be defended by the advocate of protecting projects.

There are, in short, considerations in support of both sides. There are reasons for the moderate to defend options in terms of projects, and there are reasons to defend options in terms of interests in general—including mere wants. I do not know which line the moderate should take: either way, it seems that there will be difficulties. I propose, therefore, to be neutral. The moderate can continue to couch his argument in terms of the sacrifice of interests—thereby avoiding explicit commitment regarding whether he is concerned with protecting interests in general, or only projects. It should be noted, however, that moderates sometimes take undue advantage of this ambiguity. Often they will speak as though options are a response to the need to permit the agent room to do as he *chooses*: agents should have some freedom to react in various ways simply because they *want* to. When pressed as to the importance of such freedom, however, moderates will often resort to observations about the centrality of projects in an agent's life, and the need to protect them. Rarely is there a recognition of the possible tensions between projects and other wants. Nonetheless in typical cases the two accounts will largely coincide: an agent will want to promote his projects, and pursuit of the good would require that they be significantly sacrificed. Options are necessary if the agent is to be able to avoid the sacrifice of his interests.[9]

THE NEIGHBORHOOD OF THE ACCOUNT

However we settle the issue of the previous section, the moderate's argument comes to this: promoting the good can require a

[9] One other complication worth noting: suppose that the relevant interests include all of the agent's present interests—including mere wants—but *only* his present interests (see n. 7). It may then be unclear as to whether it is even *possible* for an agent to (knowingly, voluntarily) sacrifice his interests overall. For however the agent chooses to react, won't this necessarily be what the agent most wants to do? So how can it genuinely be an overall sacrifice of his interests? But then what content can be given to the complaint that promoting the good may require the agent to sacrifice his interests?

I will not try to answer these questions here, except to note two relevant points. (1) Agents who *fail* to promote the good presumably have interests that might indeed have to be sacrificed if the agent *were* to promote the good. (2) And even those agents who *do* promote the good have, in a relevant sense, sacrificed the interests they *would* have had—i.e. but for their recognition of the morally decisive reasons to promote the good.

significant sacrifice of an agent's interests; and there is something intolerable about placing such a burden upon an agent, something undesirable about an agent's losing the ability to mold his own life. To avoid the undesirable feature, we must introduce options.

The extremist, of course, has a ready answer to the moderate's complaint. He will concede that there is something undesirable about an agent sacrificing his interests—indeed, the extremist will insist upon the point. But he will reply that the disvalue of the given agent's loss is more than compensated by gains to others: were this not so it would have been incorrect to say that the agent's sacrifice promotes the good. Although considered in itself the sacrifice is bad, all things considered it is preferable to the alternative of the agent avoiding the sacrifice and thereby countenancing a greater overall harm. Therefore, the extremist will contend, the moderate has given no reason not to require the sacrifices.

This is, by now, a familiar argument. Previously the extremist noted that constraints could not be erected on considerations of badness—for objectively the bad which would result from my harming my potential victim might well be less than the bad to others which would ensue if I refrained. The extremist is now making an analogous point: options too cannot be erected on considerations of badness. By hypothesis, the bad which will result from my sacrificing my interests while promoting the good will be less overall than the bad to others which I would countenance if I avoided making the sacrifice. Thus considerations of badness do not support the moderate's plea for options. Consequently the moderate cannot ground options by focusing on the badness of an agent's sacrificing his interests.

The moderate, however, has a reply. He never claimed that the undesirableness of the agent's sacrificing his interests should be construed as being a matter of its *badness*. He simply located the undesirable feature—the sacrifice of interests—and noted that the only way to eliminate it would be to grant options. Presumably the extremist is correct that if we take it to be the badness of the agent's sacrifice of his interests which is what is undesirable about this feature of the situation, then we will be no closer to justifying options. (More generally, the inadequacy of an appeal to the badness of the sacrifice of interests shows that the necessary account, whatever it is, will not turn on the claim that the sacrifice of interests generates agent-neutral reasons that oppose the undertaking of the sacrifice; such reasons cannot justify the agent's permission to favor his own interests over that of others.) But the moderate need not hold that it is the *badness* of the sacrifice which justifies the existence of options (although, no doubt, such sacrifices do have disvalue, as the extremist has agreed). Rather it is something *else* about the fact that the agent is sacrificing his interests which accounts for the need for options.

Let us adopt yet another neutral expression and put the moderate's claim this way: the sacrifice of interests is *problematic*. Of course, the moderate still needs to develop an account of what is problematic about the sacrifice of interests *other* than the disvalue of such sacrifices—an account which will ground options. (Labeling the sacrifice of interests 'problematic' simply allows the moderate to leave open—for the moment—the details of that account.) But, to repeat the basic point, the mere fact that the problematic feature cannot be construed in terms of the *badness* of the sacrifice does not altogether rule out the moderate's chances of grounding options. For the time being, then, the moderate's claim is simply that the sacrifice of interests is morally problematic, and that by virtue of this a general requirement to promote the good must be rejected.

The next point to bear in mind is this. What the moderate wants to claim, of course, is that the problematic nature of the sacrifice of interests somehow rules out the requirement that one make such sacrifices. But since the moderate's goal is the defense of an *option*—that is, an option to make or to refrain from making the various sacrifices, as one chooses—the sacrifices themselves must be morally permissible. Whatever the ultimate account of the problematic nature of the sacrifice of interests, if that account is to be of any use to the moderate, it cannot have the implication that the given sacrifice is morally forbidden.

This is not to say, of course, that the sacrifice of one's interests is *never* forbidden. Many moderates would want to claim, for example, that I am forbidden to save two strangers rather than, say, my child: there is a special obligation to aid one's family. So, if we assume that (unsurprisingly) I have a significant interest in the welfare of my child, this might well provide a case in which I am forbidden to sacrifice my interests. However, even if there are special duties requiring an agent to do what will protect his interests in certain cases, the moderate presumably does not believe that in *typical* cases (provided that the agent has met those duties, and other constraints) the agent does something forbidden if he does decide to sacrifice his interests. Furthermore, it is obvious enough that in those cases where the moderate does want to say that the sacrifice of interests is forbidden, because one has a special obligation to aid one's family (or what have you), if such aid is indeed required by a constraint, then it is not covered by an option—which would merely *permit* the favoring of one's family without requiring it. Clearly, then, the claim is not that the moderate can never consider the sacrifice of interests forbidden, but only that he cannot do so in those cases where what he is trying to do is to establish the existence of an *option*.

There is a second sort of case worth noting where the moderate may well want to claim that the sacrifice of interests is forbidden. I have in mind cases of gratuitous sacrifice, that is, cases where the agent sacrifices his interests for no reason at all, or for a grossly inadequate reason. Many moderates—although, no doubt, not all—would want to claim that such pointless sacrifices are forbidden. (Of course, it might be difficult to demarcate precisely which sacrifices should be classified as gratuitous; grossly inadequate reasons shade smoothly into mildly inadequate reasons and on into reasons that are barely outweighed. At some point, for example, the moderate will want to speak not of gratuitous sacrifice, but rather of options of generosity. But put this problem aside.) Once again, however, it is obvious that if a given sacrifice is forbidden, since gratuitous, then the sacrifice is not covered by an option. So the point still stands: in those cases where what the moderate hopes to defend is the existence of an option, if that defense is to be in terms of the problematic nature of the sacrifice of interests, that defense had better not have the implication that the given sacrifice is itself forbidden.

Even if cases of these two kinds are of no use to the moderate in establishing the existence of options, mightn't they still be helpful for resisting the extremist's claim that there is a general requirement to promote the good? After all, if a given sacrifice is indeed forbidden, the extremist can hardly be correct in requiring it. But such a suggestion rests on a misunderstanding of the extremist's position. For the extremist only claimed that we are required to perform the optimal act of those acts not otherwise forbidden. Thus, for example, if there are constraints, we are only required to promote the good within the confines of those constraints. So if constraints do sometimes require an agent to promote his interests (as in the case of special family obligations), it is a mistake to think that the extremist would require the sacrifice of interests in the cases in question—once we have granted the existence of constraints. Similarly, the moderate may hold that gratuitous sacrifices are prohibited. But it must be remembered, once more, that the extremist never required such sacrifices in the first place; on the contrary, since a gratuitous sacrifice will fail to promote the good (if a given sacrifice did promote the overall good, it would not be gratuitous), not only isn't it required, it is indeed forbidden.

To take issue with the extremist, then, the moderate must focus on cases involving the sacrifice of interests where, on the one hand, the sacrifice will genuinely promote the good and, on the other hand, the sacrifice is not otherwise forbidden. The moderate must claim that the sacrifice is somehow problematic and that this rules out the sacrifice's being required (despite the fact that it will promote the good). And yet, at the same time, the moderate must also resist the conclusion that the sacrifice is forbidden (despite the fact that it is problematic).

This suggests a third point. There is a danger that in speaking of the problematic nature of the sacrifice of interests, we will assume that the moderate is necessarily committed to the claim that the sacrifice of interests is *somehow* morally objectionable in itself. Now such a claim may or may not turn out to be an ingredient in a successful defense of options; but at this stage we are still trying to be neutral on such questions. Thus talk of the 'problematic' nature of the sacrifice of interests must be understood as a claim about why the promotion of the good cannot be *required*, rather than as a claim to the effect that the sacrifice of interests is in itself somehow morally objectionable. The moderate should hold that in labeling the sacrifices of interests as problematic, he is not thereby claiming that the sacrifice of interests is in itself objectionable, but only that there is something about the sacrifice of interests that prevents the generation of a requirement to make such sacrifices. Perhaps, therefore, we should shift terminology slightly, and have the moderate put the point this way: it is not the sacrifice of interests *per se* which is problematic, but rather the *requirement* of such sacrifices.

Now none of this, obviously, takes the moderate very far toward a defense of options; but neither does it bring him back to where he began—simply insisting that morality must not require the pursuit of the good. The initial steps of a defense still remain: attention is still focused on the sacrifice of interests. The moderate must maintain that there is something problematic about requiring an agent to sacrifice his interests. There is something about the sacrifice of interests which rules out a requirement to promote the good—without at the same time ruling out the permissibility of making the sacrifices.

For the most part, the points we have just been discussing are of a negative nature. I have, in effect, been noting potential pitfalls that must be avoided by the moderate's argument: his account cannot be based on considerations of badness; it cannot imply the impermissibility of making the sacrifices; and so on. Such remarks help give us a better idea of what the moderate's position must be, even if only indirectly. But not much has been said of a positive nature about the moderate's position, beyond the rough outline sketched above. We have, at best, indicated the neighborhood in which the moderate's account must be located. But now we must ask how the details of that account are to be provided. How, exactly, is the moderate to spell out and defend his position? Why *is* it problematic for a moral code to require the sacrifice of interests?

I think we would do well to remember the analysis of moral requirement suggested in Chapter 2. A given reaction is required if and only if there is a morally decisive reason to react in the given way. Therefore, when the moderate claims that there is something about the sacrifice of interests that rules out a general requirement to promote the good, he is claiming that there is something about the sacrifice of interests that (typically) prevents the pro tanto reason to promote the good from being morally decisive. In short, the sacrifice of interests somehow generates countervailing considerations sufficient to prevent the pro tanto reason to promote the good from grounding a requirement.

Now the details of how the moderate might best argue that these countervailing considerations block the generation of a requirement to promote the good will obviously depend in part on exactly which conditions are necessary for moral decisiveness. For each such condition there is a possible line of argument according to which the pro tanto reason to promote the good fails to meet the given condition in cases involving the sacrifice of interests (and hence fails to ground a requirement). As we shall see, more than one such line of argument can be pursued with some plausibility.

It should also be clear, however, that all such arguments will need an account of why the sacrifice of interests should be thought to generate such countervailing considerations in the first place. On the one hand, there must be something about the sacrifice of interests that explains why it gives rise to countervailing considerations at all. And, on the other hand, it is presumably this relatively general explanation that, in turn, determines which specific countervailing considerations are actually generated.

Let me put the point another way: if the moderate is to reject a requirement to promote the good, it is inevitable that he must argue for the existence of countervailing considerations that prevent the pro tanto reason to promote the good from generating a requirement. What is not inevitable is the moderate's choice of what to point to as the *source* of these countervailing considerations. Now what we are exploring, of course, is the suggestion that it is the appeal to cost which provides the most plausible basis for a defense of options. But, as we have seen, spelling out the appeal to cost focuses our attention, in turn, on the sacrifice of interests. Thus, if options are to be defended through the appeal to cost, the moderate needs to offer an account of the sacrifice of interests that makes it clear why this is a plausible place to identify as a source of countervailing considerations. This account, in turn, will guide the moderate's further claims about the specifics of those countervailing considerations. But first we need the account itself: what is it about the sacrifice of interests that makes it plausible to think that it does, in fact, generate countervailing considerations?

Presumably, the moderate's account should turn on the significance of the fact that in asking an agent to sacrifice his interests, it is his *interests* that he is being called upon to sacrifice. After all, we must recall just what it is that the agent is being asked to do. It is not simply any old action which is being required: the agent is being asked to sacrifice those things which he favors the most, to override his desires and to react in ways that he does not want to react. The moderate might plausibly suggest, therefore, that when we consider the connection between an agent and his interests it becomes clear that there is something problematic about requiring an agent to sacrifice his interests. But how, exactly, is the moderate to defend this claim? The most promising suggestion is that the moderate should base his claim upon a thesis about the nature of persons.

THE PERSONAL POINT OF VIEW

Persons have a point of view.[10] It is a significant fact about us that each of us views the world from a particular perspective. We act out of this perspective, evaluate changes in the world from it, and are affected by those changes at it. It is from this point of view that we undertake plans and projects, and develop interests and desires. We live life—both in its active and its passive aspects—through this perspective, and indeed it is the presence of this point of view which gives our interests and plans a unity, molding them into a single life.

From this point of view persons assess the world, weighing the relative benefits and disadvantages of various actual or potential changes. The evaluation is relative to the particular person, for it is relative to his particular personal perspective; it is a judgment of what is good from his point of view. Typically it will differ from the agent-neutral evaluation of the impersonal perspective, i.e., an evaluation of what is good objectively. For when persons assess events from their point of view, they assign weights to those events in which they take interest out of proportion to the weights which an impartial perspective would assign: for example, the impersonal evaluation tells us that one death is objectively better than two; but the subjective evaluation made from my personal perspective may differ, if I am the one. The weight we assign to an event reflects a bias in favor of the objects of our desires. Matters which are near to us, both psychically and physically, loom large; we consider them more important. And since our reactions reflect our assessment of the various possible outcomes, our actions too typically reflect this bias to what is near to us.

It is a contingent matter, perhaps, what interests a particular agent may have. But it is part of our very nature as persons that we care more about the objects of our desires—whatever they might be—than about other matters which might be just as important from the objective perspective. We are built so that we care more about our wants being satisfied than about other things.

Obviously a good deal more would need to be said to fill in the holes in this hasty sketch, and to make what has been said here

---

[10] The moderate's argument given in this and the following section is a direct descendant of the defense of options presented by Scheffler. I have not, however, been completely faithful to the original. (A more careful rendition of Scheffler's argument is examined in my essay 'Does Consequentialism', pp. 249–54.)

more precise. But that it *is* a significant fact about us that we are built in roughly the way just described, certainly seems to be the case. It is, at least, a highly plausible description of us—and we may grant the moderate that it reflects a deep fact about the nature of persons.[11]

It might be reasonably objected, however, that this way of putting things treats a trivial truth as though it were a substantive truth. After all, the claim that we care more about our wants than about other things is just a tautology, saying nothing more than that we care about what we care about. It is hardly a deep truth about us that we care more about our wants being satisfied; that's just what it *is* for something to be one of our wants. But there are, of course, substantive truths here as well, that could be expressed more explicitly with greater care (and, ultimately, with greater awkwardness, were this done in every case). Consider the various specific objects of someone's particular desires—call them X, Y, and Z. It may be a trivial truth that this person cares more about his wants being satisfied, but it is not a trivial truth that he cares more about X, Y, and Z. More importantly, it is not a trivial truth that he cares about X, Y, and Z out of proportion to their objective importance. And more generally, it is not a trivial truth that people *have* concerns and interests such that we give the objects of our desires greater weight than they merit from an objective perspective.

This is the substantive truth about the nature of persons to which the moderate is pointing. Persons have a point of view from which certain objects (the objects of their desires, concerns, interests) take on an importance and are assigned weight disproportionate to the weight an impartial perspective would assign. Once this substantive point is understood, however, no harm should be done if it is sometimes expressed through the use of phrases that can be given a trivial reading. I do not, in fact, think that the trivial readings of the phrases are inevitable; but at worst, such phrases provide a

[11] It should be noted, however, that I think we can grant all of this—i.e., that people have a point of view, from which they give disproportionate weight to their own interests, and so on—without committing ourselves to any particular metaphysical diagnosis of the facts in question. In particular, talk of persons 'having' a point of view does not commit us to reifying this point of view—i.e., conceiving of it as (in some sense) a distinct entity. (On the other hand, this is obviously not to say that metaphysical investigation of these matters could not be illuminating. We might like to know, for example, what impact (if any) the fact that we are physically located in one place—and thus that we act and are acted upon in one location—has upon the fact that we are biased toward our own interests. And so on.)

convenient shorthand. (Explicitly substantive paraphrases can be substituted by those who prefer them.) To repeat the moderate's point, then, it is part of our nature as persons that we care more about our wants being satisfied than about other things.

This means that it is harder to motivate us to look after matters which are not the objects of our wants. If a certain reaction is necessary so that our desires may be satisfied, the necessary motivation comes naturally and quickly. But if a similar reaction is necessary in order to promote some goal which we do not already want to promote, then the motivation is slow to arrive, if it comes at all. And if there is a *conflict* between our wants and the promotion of that other goal—then it will be particularly difficult to muster the motivation to react in the way that we do not want to react: for even if the considerations in support of countenancing that goal objectively outweigh the considerations in support of acting in accordance with our wants, the latter will weigh heavily for us, creating a powerful presumption in their favor. If it is possible to motivate us at all to promote the goal, it will only be because we come to recognize especially *compelling* reasons to react in that particular way.

The relevance of this to the promotion of the good is evident. As I have noted, the pursuit of the good will frequently require significant sacrifices of interests. Not surprisingly, these are sacrifices which an agent will usually not want to make—indeed, she will strongly desire that she *not* make a given sacrifice. And these wants will forcefully pull her in the direction of avoiding it. Even if she recognizes that the considerations for making the sacrifice objectively outweigh those for refraining, this will not typically be sufficient to motivate her to undertake it. Thus we will rarely be motivated to make the significant sacrifices which a requirement to promote the good would demand of us.

Similar although less drastic failures of motivation would arise for many of the small favors which would be demanded of us if the pursuit of the good were required. Here, typically, there will be no *conflict* with our wants (except perhaps for a desire to be left alone), for no significant sacrifice would be involved in doing the favor. Nonetheless often there will be a simple *absence* of a desire to do the small service, and so sufficient motivation may still be lacking. Thus even in these trivial cases we will frequently fail to promote the good.

If the facts in question are as the moderate suggests then it is natural for us to weigh our own interests more heavily than they objectively merit. More than this: given the nature of persons we think it reasonable of ourselves to assess the world and to react to it in this way. We are not troubled by our failure to promote the good, for this is simply in keeping with our nature. And indeed, from our point of view the fact that we act in keeping with that point of view is perfectly legitimate. From where we are, so to speak, where we are appears to be a perfectly legitimate place to be.[12]

If something like this account is correct, it offers an explanation of why agents fail to promote the good. Although there may arise a rare individual whose fundamental wants simply *are* to promote the good, for all the rest of us our interests and the objective good will not be in such harmony. Given the nature of persons, therefore, most agents will frequently fail to react in the optimal manner: they will simply lack sufficient motivation to do so.

It is perhaps worth noting that an account along these lines is available to the moderate regardless of whether or not he thinks that the recognition of reasons can directly motivate an agent. According to some views, an adequate explanation of how an agent comes to react in a given way will crucially refer to the presence (or absence) of the relevant kind of desire; to say that recognition of a reason motivates (or fails to motivate) the agent will be elliptical for a fuller explanation which spells out how the necessary motivation is (or fails to be) derived from previous desires, and so on. It is relatively straightforward to see how the moderate's position can be explicated in terms of such a view: given the disproportionate concern that agents have for their own interests, sufficient desire to sacrifice those interests for the greater good will generally be lacking.

On other views, however, indicating the presence of the relevant desire will sometimes be explanatorily superfluous; in principle, the very recognition of the reason itself may be able to directly explain the agent's having reacted. At first glance, such a view may seem to leave the moderate unable to explain why agents will often fail to promote the good even when they recognize that there is objectively greater reason to do so. But even on views of this second kind, the

---

[12] Cf. Parfit, p. 142: 'Why may not *my* point of view be, precisely, *my* point of view?'

recognition of a reason *need* not be adequate to motivate the agent. And so the moderate can plausibly claim that, unless the reasons recognized are unusually compelling, agents will—on balance— typically be motivated to favor their own interests rather than the overall good.

Thus, as far as I can see, nothing in the current discussion, or in what follows, should turn on which of these two views is correct. Either way, the moderate's basic position should be unaffected: given the nature of persons, agents will frequently fail to be motivated to react in the optimal manner. Appeal to the nature of persons allows the moderate to explain why agents do not generally promote the good.

But the moderate, of course, hopes to do more than merely *explain* this behavior: he wants to justify it.

If he is to do this, however, more will have to be said, for even the extremist could accept all that has been claimed so far. After all, the extremist recognizes that agents do not generally promote the good; if he likes he can accept the moderate's explanation of why this is so. Yet he might still maintain that agents are nonetheless *required* to promote the good. We understand why they do not do so—but their behavior might still be unjustified for all that. It may be true that from the perspective of the personal point of view the influence of such a point of view is legitimate—but the extremist needn't accept this self-accreditation. What the moderate has given us, then, will not suffice. It is only the first step in the argument.

REFLECTING THE NATURE OF PERSONS

The next step in the argument is for the moderate to suggest, plausibly, that an acceptable system of morality must adequately reflect the nature of persons. For once he is armed with this meta- ethical principle, and the substantive view about the nature of persons just presented, the moderate stands ready to evaluate moral systems: An adequate moral system must reflect the fact that the agents care more about (the objects of) their wants than they do about other matters; it must recognize that agents have a personal, subjective point of view from which they assess the importance of the promotion of their own interests out of proportion to the weight which those interests carry from the objective standpoint.

The moderate will argue that a moral system with options reflects these facts about the nature of persons, for it grants agents permission to react in ways which do not promote the good. That is, it frees them, in a range of cases, to do as they want to do—even though this may not be optimal. It allows them to devote a disproportionate amount of energy and attention to those matters with which they have the greater concern, and to justify their decisions with a simple appeal to their own wants. Options provide room for the agent to favor his interests; and this is in keeping with the priorities of the particular agent's point of view. In thus reflecting the nature of persons—taking cognizance of the fact that persons *have* a subjective point of view—a system with options passes the suggested requirement for adequacy.

In contrast, the moderate will continue, a system which requires the promotion of the good will not reflect the nature of persons. It demands that agents devote only that amount of energy to satisfying their wants which those wants could command from the objective point of view. It does not recognize the disproportional importance which an agent's point of view assigns to his own interests. In asking agents to react as if they lacked this subjective standpoint, such a system overlooks the legitimacy which the personal point of view has by its own lights. The requirement to promote the good leaves the agent no room to favor what he wants to favor, nor does it permit him to justify any of his decisions simply through an appeal to his wants. In all of this the requirement to promote the good is at complete odds with the existence of a personal point of view; thus a system which requires pursuit of the good fails to take account of the nature of persons. For this reason, the moderate concludes, it can be rejected as unacceptable.

The extremist will respond that this argument trades on an ambiguity in the notion of *adequately reflecting*. He will claim that there are two senses in which a system might reflect some set of facts and that it is only in the first sense that the meta-ethical principle to which the moderate appeals is uncontroversially true, yet it is only in the second sense that a moral system which includes the requirement to promote the good uncontroversially fails to reflect the nature of persons. If this is correct, then the moderate's argument is not sufficient as it stands.

Intuitively, the distinction the extremist is after is this: a system *minimally* reflects a set of facts if it does only what it *must* about those facts; it *fully* reflects the facts if it does all that it *can*. In the former case the system is something of an adversary—taking on only those features which are *forced* upon it by the recognition of the facts. In the latter case, however, the system is freely and more thoroughly shaped by the facts: it takes on not only those features which are necessitated by the recognition of the facts, but also those various optional features which might put the system more fully in harmony with the facts. We might say that a set of facts often implicitly involves both demands upon a system and appeals to it. If the system recognizes the facts, the *demands* cannot be neglected; and provided that they are met, the system can be said to minimally reflect the facts. The appeals, however, *can* be neglected; the mere recognition of the facts does not force the system to comply with the appeals. To fully reflect the facts, however, the system must go beyond what is forced upon it: the appeals too must be met.

An analogy might be helpful. The decor of a room may, in various ways, reflect some particular piece of furniture. And in some cases, inclusion of a striking piece of furniture may aesthetically dictate various other features of the decor. The decor of the room may be said to minimally reflect the given piece of furniture provided that the decor possesses whatever features are aesthetically forced upon it by the presence of the given object. However, there may also be further decorative features which are suggested—although not necessitated—by the piece of furniture, ways in which the decor of the room could be more fully shaped by the desire to reflect the object in question. The decor of the room can be said to fully reflect the given piece of furniture only if the decor possesses these various optional features as well. We can imagine the piece of furniture as making certain demands upon the decor, as well as making further requests or appeals for various additional features. The latter need not be met; minimal reflection is a matter of meeting the demands alone. For full reflection, however, the decor must meet the appeals as well.

In many cases, perhaps, the distinction will not, in the last analysis, do much work: it might turn out in a particular case that it would be inappropriate for a system not to possess *all* of the features which would reflect the given facts. (A given piece of furniture might dictate the *entire* decor of a room.) In such a case even in order to minimally reflect the facts the system would have to fully reflect them. But in the abstract, at least, we can envision the possibility that a system might be able to minimally reflect the facts without being required to fully reflect them. Thus full reflection might be optional. Minimal reflection, however, is not optional: it is a requirement of adequacy. For a system will clearly be inadequate if it fails to recognize the facts (assuming, of course, that the facts are relevant in the right way), or if it lacks the various features which recognition of the facts necessitates.

How does the extremist's distinction between minimal and full reflection apply to the moderate's argument? The moderate appeals to the meta-ethical principle that an acceptable moral system must adequately reflect the nature of persons. If this principle is understood to require only minimal reflection, then it is uncontroversial, and the extremist will accept it. For it seems clear that the nature of persons *is* relevant to a moral theory, and any moral system with an incorrect view on this matter will be unacceptable. Furthermore, if there are any features which are forced upon a moral system by the recognition of the nature of persons, then clearly any system which lacks those features will also be unacceptable.

The extremist denies, however, that moral systems which require promotion of the good fail to minimally reflect the nature of persons. As I noted earlier, it seems to be open to the extremist to accept the moderate's account of the nature of the personal point of view—and to use this account, in turn, as an explanation of why agents fail to promote the good. A system which requires the pursuit of the good can acknowledge the facts about the nature of persons which the moderate has stressed; it needn't be found unacceptable in that regard.

Now such a system might still fail to minimally reflect the facts in question if recognition of those facts *necessitates* certain features, and those features are lacking from the system. The extremist, however, sees no reason to believe that there *are* any such features mandated by the recognition of the nature of persons. At the very least, the moderate has given no reason to think otherwise. It is not that the extremist thinks that a particular view of the nature of persons *couldn't* possibly necessitate certain features: the extremist admits, e.g., that if the nature of persons entailed that agents could not recognize or act on considerations of a certain sort, then any moral system which expected agents to act on such considerations would be unacceptable. It is simply that the moderate has given no reason to think that the nature of persons as we have described it *does* rule out any particular feature.

The extremist, of course, can readily grant the importance of bearing in mind the fact that agents naturally tend to favor their own interests. For this may affect decisions about how to best maximize the overall good that agents will produce: for example, it might support structuring rewards and punishments so that an agent can best promote her own interests by promoting the overall good. But the fact that the nature of persons may have such implications for the *application* of an underlying requirement to promote the good does not indicate any incompatibility between the two. Therefore, the moderate has not shown that a moral system which requires promotion of the good will necessarily fail to minimally reflect the nature of persons. And if this is to be the test for adequacy, then the moderate has given no reason to think such a system unacceptable.

What the moderate *has* given is reason to think that a system without options does not *fully* reflect the nature of persons. For there are features which a system might possess which would make for greater harmony with the nature of persons—features which a system which requires promoting the good admittedly lacks. The feature which the moderate has noted, of course, is the presence of options. The extremist can readily concede that a system with options, by giving the agent room to favor his interests, more fully reflects the nature of persons than a system which lacks options. But this concession costs the extremist nothing, for the moderate has given no reason to think that any acceptable moral system must fully reflect the nature of persons. Nor would it be promising for the moderate to understand his meta-ethical principle as requiring full reflection, for such a principle would be controversial, and require support of a sort that the moderate has not provided.

Let us review the argument so far. Armed with his meta-ethical principle, the moderate claimed that only systems with options reflect the nature of persons. The extremist, however, distinguished between minimal and full reflection—in particular, between (a) possession of only those features that are dictated by recognition of the nature of persons and (b) possession, in addition, of the various further features with which a system can more fully reflect the nature of persons. Now if the moderate is merely saying that only a system with options does all that it *can* to reflect the nature of persons, the extremist is prepared to grant this. But so what? No reason has been given to think that it is a flaw in a system if it fails to reflect the nature of persons fully. So presumably the moderate is saying, rather, that only a system with options does all that *must* be done to reflect the nature of persons. In effect, the moderate is committed to the claim that the nature of persons—the existence of the personal point of view and the bias in favor of one's own interests that this creates—generates countervailing considerations which prevent the grounding of a general requirement to promote the good. Thus only a system with options minimally reflects the nature of persons. Yet, despite the moderate's claim, no reason has been given to think that a requirement to promote the good actually does fail to minimally reflect the nature of persons. Thus, although the extremist will readily admit that it would indeed be a flaw in a system for it to fail to minimally reflect the nature of persons, the moderate has not shown that minimal reflection requires options.

The extremist's response might be summarized in this way. Because of the nature of persons, agents naturally favor their wants. This much has been granted to the moderate. We might say that there is an implicit request in the nature of persons that the agent be given room to do what he wants to do, simply because he wants to do it. But a system which lacks options can recognize the existence of the request just as well as a system which possesses options. The question is whether the request is a demand or an appeal. If it were a demand then a system without options would admittedly be inadequate, for such a system does not grant the request. The moderate of course may *claim* that it is a demand, but he has given no reason to think so. As far as the extremist is concerned, the request is a mere appeal which needn't be satisfied (although, of course, the *existence* of the request should be recognized—that is, a moral system should have an accurate view of the nature of persons). Requiring the promotion of the good, therefore, is not unacceptable, and the moderate's argument fails.

At this stage the moderate might be tempted to offer a conciliatory reply. He might suggest that although his argument does *not* show that systems including the requirement to promote the good are unacceptable, it does at least show that systems which include options *are* acceptable. Options are an attempt to fully reflect the nature of persons in a moral system; and this is surely one reasonable response to these facts. Thus the moderate might claim that he has at least succeeded in offering an *explanation* of why a moral system might include options, and it is this, after all, which has been his primary concern. The moderate would thus offer a fairly modest claim: he would abandon his attempt to demonstrate the *unique* acceptability of systems with options, being content merely to establish the *legitimacy* of such systems. Both the inclusion and exclusion of options would be plausible responses to the nature of persons: which sort of moral system one adopted would be determined by how fully one wanted the nature of persons to be reflected in one's moral system.

The extremist should not be impressed by the modesty of the moderate's reply; the moderate is still claiming more than is warranted. The moderate suggests that we view the inclusion and the exclusion of options as equally legitimate responses to the nature of persons: the two sorts of systems differ in the degree to which they reflect the facts in question—and the choice between systems is something of a matter of taste. But such an attitude would only be appropriate if there were no other relevant differences between the two sorts of systems, and in particular if reflection of the nature of persons were the *only* relevant criterion for choosing between systems. For if there are other relevant factors, the moderate cannot assume without further argument that a system with options will be equally acceptable when these additional factors are taken into consideration as well. Now it would not, in fact, be plausible for the moderate to suggest that adequately reflecting the nature of the personal point of view is the only factor of relevance in choosing between moral systems. So, at the very least, there is no reason to accept the moderate's claim to have shown the acceptability of a system with options.

This way of expressing the argument, while conveying the intuitive force of the moderate's proposal and the extremist's objection, may once again appear to presuppose that morality is a matter of deliberate design or choice. So let us restate the argument in such a way as to eliminate this appearance.

The moderate's meta-ethical principle states that an acceptable moral system must adequately reflect the nature of persons. For our present purposes we can think of this as equivalent to an indirect necessary condition for moral decisiveness: a reason is morally decisive only if it is part of a system of reasons that (jointly) reflect the nature of persons. Originally, the moderate suggested that only a system with options would meet this condition: the pro tanto reason to promote the good could not typically be morally decisive, for a system with a general requirement to promote the good would not adequately reflect the nature of persons. Lacking a defense for this position, however, the moderate retreated to the more modest suggestion that both full and minimal reflection were equally good ways to reflect the nature of persons. That is, the indirect condition on moral decisiveness could be equally well met by systems that included options and by systems that included a requirement to promote the good. But it was a mistake for the moderate to move from this premise—that both kinds of systems equally satisfy one particular condition on moral decisiveness—to the conclusion that both systems are equally acceptable when all other factors are taken into account as well. The modest premise does not support the desired conclusion.

What's more, ironically enough, in retreating to his modest position, the moderate has effectively cut himself off from a defense of options. The moderate is left with no account of the presence of options within his own system. Originally, of course, the moderate introduced the appeal to cost in the belief that it would help him defend options. In particular, the fact that promotion of the good would typically require the sacrifice of interests was supposed to generate countervailing considerations sufficient to prevent the pro tanto reason to promote the good from grounding a requirement. Reflection on the sacrifice of interests was going to reveal how and why the pro tanto reason to promote the good would frequently fail to meet some condition necessary for moral decisiveness. But the only condition which has emerged from the moderate's discussion is the requirement that the nature of persons be adequately reflected. Now a system with options might very well reflect the nature of persons, but by itself this does not constitute an adequate *defense* of these options. Such a defense requires that the moderate be able to indicate the countervailing considerations (within the system) that prevent the pro tanto reason to promote the good from being morally decisive. Had the moderate insisted that only a system with options could adequately reflect the nature of persons, he might have gone on to indicate how the personal, subjective point of view generates the requisite countervailing considerations. Yet once the moderate has retreated to his modest position, and has admitted that a requirement to promote the good does indeed adequately reflect the nature of persons after all, there is no longer any reason to believe that there *is* any condition for moral decisiveness that the pro tanto reason to promote the good fails to meet.

In short, in retreating to the modest position, the moderate has left himself with nothing with which to support his claim. He has no account of the generation of options within his own system. In effect, he has no explanation of the presence of options in ordinary morality. Therefore, once the moderate has retreated to his modest position, there is no reason to think that a system with options is an acceptable alternative to a general requirement to promote the good.

Thus the moderate's modest reply will be rejected by the extremist. (Why do you think they're called extremists?) If the moderate is to demonstrate the legitimacy of systems which include options, he must point to some inadequacy in systems which lack them. He must return to his original claim that systems which require promotion of the good do not adequately reflect the nature of persons. But the claim will have to be supported by a more aggressive argument.

8

The Negative Argument

In the last chapter, the moderate charged that systems which require promoting the good fail to reflect the nature of persons adequately. The extremist's response was twofold. On the one hand, he conceded the need to minimally reflect the facts, but denied the claim that such systems fail in this regard. On the other hand, he conceded that systems which lack options do not fully reflect the nature of persons, but denied that this marked such systems as inadequate. This suggests two ways the moderate might attempt to bolster his original argument—one of them more ambitious than the other. First, the moderate might maintain that systems without options do indeed fail to reflect the nature of persons even minimally. Second, the moderate might maintain that it is indeed inappropriate for moral systems to fail to reflect the nature of persons fully. (The second line may appear to involve collapsing the distinction and maintaining that minimally reflecting the nature of persons is impossible without fully reflecting it. But we shall see.) If either of these approaches can be developed, then by the extremist's own concessions, systems without options will be inadequate.

The first argument adopts an essentially negative attitude toward the nature of persons, for the question is what sorts of features are *forced* upon a moral system in order for it to achieve minimal reflection of the relevant facts. We might picture morality as *regretting* the nature of persons, but realizing that it must recognize the facts for what they are, and asking what is the minimum number of concessions that must be made to them. The extremist objected that he has not been shown that any concessions at all need be made to them. The moderate must argue that concessions to our nature are indeed necessary, and that these concessions are incompatible with the requirement to promote the good.

The moderate, of course, need not actually hold the negative attitude toward the nature of persons adopted by this first argument. His claim is simply that even *if* such a negative attitude is appropriate, as the extremist may believe, it is *still* the case that certain concessions to our nature are unavoidable. Let us call this the *negative* argument.

As I have just noted, however, the moderate may feel that in fact it is inappropriate to hold such a negative attitude toward the nature of persons. This view is developed by the second argument. On this line, the moderate must argue that it is actually a positive attitude which is called for; and this in turn will suggest that it is appropriate for a moral system to *fully* reflect the nature of persons. Since the extremist concedes that fully reflecting the nature of persons requires options, such an argument would provide a more ambitious way to demonstrate the inadequacy of systems which lack them. Let us call this the *positive* argument.

The two arguments seem to have similar conclusions: systems which lack options are unacceptable. Their primary difference seems to be one of tone: the first adopts a negative attitude toward the nature of persons, and concludes that nonetheless an adequate moral system must (unfortunately!) include options; the second adopts a positive attitude, and concludes that it is *desirable* for a moral system to include options. As we shall see, however, the difference between the two arguments is actually greater than this. Although both arguments point to countervailing considerations that prevent the generation of a general requirement to promote the good, they point to different countervailing considerations—and this difference is significant. If it is successful, the positive argument is much more far-reaching in its implications. But let us begin with the more modest negative argument. We shall return to the positive argument in the next chapter.

Given the nature of persons it is difficult to motivate us to do things that we do not want to do. Our interests carry tremendous motivational force, but other considerations weigh on us quite lightly.[1] This means that an agent must be convinced that there exist especially compelling reasons to react in some way which is

---

[1] Yet if a consideration has any weight with us at all, however light, doesn't it automatically qualify as an interest (in my broad sense of the term)? So isn't it a trivial truth that we are only motivated to act on our interests? Perhaps, but there is a substantive point being made here as well. Consider the interests that we have prior

not supported by her interests—and all the more so if the agent's interests *oppose* her reacting in that way. If the agent is not convinced in such cases of the existence of especially compelling reasons, then the considerations which favor her reacting in the particular way—despite their overall merit—will be unable to motivate the agent sufficiently, and she will not react in the given way. Thus the mere fact that there is, overall, greater reason supporting a particular act may not be sufficient, if the agent does not want to perform the act: unless she finds that the reasons are especially compelling, they won't be able to motivate her.

It may be helpful to point out, once again, that an account along these lines is available to the moderate regardless of whether or not he believes that recognition of reasons can directly motivate an agent. For simplicity, I have spoken—and will continue to speak—of an agent's being moved (or not being moved) to sacrifice her interests by her recognition of a given reason. Such talk is, perhaps, most straightforwardly understood in terms of the view that recognition of a reason can (although it need not) directly motivate an agent. But nothing in the argument turns on adopting this view. Consequently, those who hold that an adequate explanation of an agent's reaction must refer to the presence (or absence) of the relevant kind of desire can understand my talk of an agent's being moved by the recognition of reasons as shorthand for more perspicuous but cumbersome locutions which would speak instead of the agent's being moved by the appropriate desire, the derivation of which (from previous desires, and so on) is to be explained in part by her recognition of the given reasons. One could recast the entire discussion in these terms, but for obvious reasons I have chosen to use the simpler form of expression.

For our purposes, then, it does not matter which of these two views the moderate holds. Either is compatible with the basic claims of the account that we have sketched (although some moderates may prefer to state those claims in slightly different terms): given the nature of persons, the mere fact that the balance of reasons supports a particular reaction will often be insufficient to

to (or independently of) our recognition of various moral reasons. Since the recognition of a reason can sometimes alter what we are motivated to do, it can modify our interests. Generally, however, our prior interests have tremendous motivational weight, while often enough the recognition of other considerations, such as moral reasons, is able to modify our motivation (and our interests) only weakly, or not at all. (Cf. Chapter 7, n. 9.)

motivate the agent to react in that way; if it would not promote the agent's interests, then unless the reasons supporting the given reaction are especially compelling they simply won't be able to motivate her.

Now all of this—the moderate might argue—has direct implications for what a moral system can require of an agent. A moral requirement must be supported by considerations powerful enough to motivate us to obey it. At a minimum, obviously, this means that sufficiently motivating considerations cannot be lacking. There must be considerations the appreciation of which are capable of motivating us to react in the required manner. But more than this, it means that the potentially motivating considerations must be the very considerations that make the requirement pertain to a given situation. That is, if a requirement to act obtains because of certain features of a situation then it must be those very features which are powerful enough to motivate the agent to meet the requirement. The grounds of the requirement—considerations internal to the foundation of the requirement—must be capable of motivating us to obey the requirement. Of course, there may be additional—external—considerations present which happen to motivate an agent to act in conformity with the moral requirement as well (for example, fear of punishment), but such external considerations must not be essential for motivating the agent: for a genuine moral requirement, it must be possible for conformity to be motivated by appreciation of the considerations that ground the requirement in the first place.

This does not mean, of course, that we always *will* obey any given genuine moral requirement; far from the case. It is all too common for us to fail to do what we are required to do. But we must be *capable* of being sufficiently motivated by the considerations which underlie the requirement. One cannot require just anything of an agent: he must be capable of being *moved* to satisfy the particular demand. Otherwise the 'requirement' is mere bluster; it is no requirement at all. For agents to be under a moral requirement, they must be capable of being motivated by it.

Now as the extremist is fond of observing, there is a pro tanto reason to promote the good. From this perspective perhaps we might like to require as much of agents as we can; we might like to require the pursuit of the good. But given the essential connection between moral requirements and motivation, and given the motivational character of persons, we find that we cannot require all that we might like to. In effect, a moral system must *sell* itself to an agent—for it is the agent who will react or not react in the way that the system desires. But given the nature of persons, unless the agent finds that there are especially compelling considerations in support of his doing what he does not want to do, he will not be capable of being sufficiently motivated to go against his interests. Thus we must tone down the demands we make on agents; we must make concessions to the nature of persons. Therefore, the moderate argues, to speak of requiring agents to promote the good will be mere pretense: there can be no such requirement. Agents can be required to do what they do not want to do only when there are particularly compelling reasons.

This first argument might be summarized in this way: morality would require promotion of the good if it could; but it cannot.

In effect, the moderate's negative argument turns on the claim that we must recognize a further condition which must be met for moral decisiveness: a reason to react in a given way can be morally decisive—thereby grounding a requirement—only if it is capable of motivating the agent to react in that way. Even if a reason meets the various other conditions necessary for moral decisiveness, if it fails to provide the necessary motivational underpinning, it will not ground a requirement. Given the nature of persons, the moderate argues, the pro tanto reason to promote the good will frequently be unable to motivate agents to sacrifice their interests. Thus in many cases the pro tanto reason to promote the good will fail to meet the motivational condition on moral decisiveness. In such cases, therefore, the promotion of the good will (usually) not be backed by a morally decisive reason. So there can be no general requirement to promote the good. By ensuring that the necessary motivational underpinning is typically lacking, the nature of persons prevents the pro tanto reason to promote the good from grounding a requirement.

Of course, as we have previously noted, the defense of options requires more than the rejection of the requirement to promote the good. For although, under an option, the promotion of the good is not required, it is nonetheless permitted. Thus, to complete the defense of options, the moderate would also have to demonstrate that in a broad range of cases there is no morally decisive reason that *opposes* pursuit of the overall good, no morally decisive reason requiring, say, the protection of one's own interests.

It is worth observing, therefore, that there is nothing in the negative argument that implies that an agent will typically be forbidden to sacrifice her interests. (Since it offers an additional condition that a reason must meet before it can be morally decisive, the argument cannot make it *more* likely that the sacrifice of interests is prohibited. It thus avoids one of the pitfalls mentioned in the previous chapter.) Of course, in certain cases, perhaps involving special obligations or other constraints, the moderate may indeed want to admit that the reaction that would best promote the overall good may be forbidden. But it does not seem implausible for the moderate to hold that in a broad range of typical cases the promotion of the good (at least, within the confines of constraints) will in fact be permissible. At the very least, such a view is not going to be challenged by the extremist. So let us assume that if the negative argument is successful, the moderate will indeed be able to complete the defense of options. This will allow us to focus our attention instead on the argument that must be rejected by the extremist—i.e., the argument that there can be no general requirement to promote the good, for it would lack the necessary motivational underpinning.

Note that this negative argument makes no claims at all about the balance of reasons. In particular, it does not challenge the extremist's claim that the pro tanto reason to promote the good outweighs any opposing reasons. The moderate is, in effect, conceding that for all he has shown, the balance of reasons may well support promoting the good. But he is insisting that even if this is so, there is no *requirement* to promote the good, for the pro tanto reason to promote the good fails to meet a further condition necessary for moral decisiveness.

Of course, as I also noted, the moderate may want to say more than this. The moderate may want to go on to claim that the personal point of view is of positive value in its own right—generating reasons that can outweigh the pro tanto reason to promote the overall good: this is the heart of the positive argument, to be considered in the next chapter. But in the negative argument itself no such claim is being made. Here the point is simply that even if a negative attitude toward the nature of persons is appropriate, certain concessions must be made. Even if there is greater reason overall to promote the good, the nature of persons prevents the generation of the corresponding requirement. Given the nature of persons, the pro tanto reason to promote the good cannot meet a motivational condition necessary for grounding a genuine moral requirement.

The motivational condition being appealed to by the negative argument should not be confused with the principle that 'ought implies can'. This latter doctrine states that for genuine moral requirements it must be possible for the agent to react in the required manner. Now on at least one standard interpretation of the principle, this condition will be satisfied provided that the agent could react in the given manner *if* he wanted to. On such an interpretation, at least, the question of whether the agent *could* be motivated to react in the given way simply does not arise. The proposed motivational condition, however, is in that sense more demanding. It insists that, for a genuine moral requirement, it must be possible for the agent to be *motivated* to react in the required manner. Furthermore, it insists that the considerations capable of moving the agent must be the very reasons that ground the requirement.

This motivational condition on moral decisiveness—the demand that the reasons grounding a requirement must be capable of moving the agent—is one version of what is sometimes called *internalism*.[2] It is a controversial doctrine, and is denied by many, including many extremists. Those who reject the doctrine charge it with conflating questions of justification with questions of motivation. They insist that it may well be an open question whether a given agent can be motivated to do what he has morally decisive reason to do. One possible response to the negative argument, therefore, would be for the extremist to reject the motivational condition on moral decisiveness. Without this condition the negative argument would collapse: despite the nature of persons, the pro tanto reason to promote the good might well be morally decisive, grounding a requirement.

It should be noted, furthermore, that internalism is rejected by many moderates as well. Such moderates, obviously, cannot avail themselves of the negative argument (at least in anything like the form I have developed it here). If they are to defend options, they

---

[2] See, e.g., Frankena; and Nagel, *Altruism*, pp. 7–12.

must instead point to some other countervailing consideration which prevents the generation of a requirement to promote the good (such as that to be proposed by the positive argument). Nonetheless, many other moderates will be sympathetic to the motivational condition, and will be prepared to appeal to something like it as a basis for the negative argument. Given the nature of persons, and given the motivational condition—such moderates will argue—there can be no general requirement to promote the good.

I do not intend to evaluate the arguments for and against internalism here. In particular, I do not intend to investigate the merits of the proposed condition on moral decisiveness. Instead I want to consider whether there are any other replies that can be made to the negative argument. Let us, therefore, grant the motivational condition on moral decisiveness (which, in any event, many extremists would be inclined to accept anyway). Once the extremist grants that a moral requirement must possess the corresponding motivational underpinning, does the conclusion of the negative argument follow inevitably? Must the requirement to promote the good be rejected, on the grounds that—external considerations aside—agents cannot generally be motivated to sacrifice their interests?

The moderate, of course, does not believe that there are no requirements at all demanding that agents do what they may not want to do. Constraints, for example, require agents to react in ways that may involve the sacrifice of interests. But this is compatible with the argument the moderate has just given—for presumably the moderate wants to claim that agents can and often *do* recognize the existence of especially compelling reasons for not violating constraints; thus the necessary motivational underpinnings of the requirement are provided. The moderate was unable to tell us the reasons for constraints; but we can take it that in granting their existence we assumed that the considerations which support constraints are of a particularly powerful and motivating sort.

Similarly, the moderate believes that agents are sometimes required to make minimal sacrifices in the course of aiding others: I am required to save the drowning child. Presumably in such cases as well the moderate would claim that I am capable of recognizing the existence of reasons to act sufficiently compelling to motivate me. In countless other cases, however, even though some reaction would promote the good, the moderate maintains that the reasons for so reacting are not sufficiently compelling: the motivational underpinning is absent; and so there is no general requirement to promote the good. (When *enough* is at stake, of course, the reasons may become especially compelling, and hence meet the motivational condition for moral decisiveness; this is why options have thresholds.)

The extremist might respond to the negative argument by insisting that there *are* especially compelling reasons to promote the good. He might insist that agents generally *can* recognize that the reasons to promote the good are of a compelling nature; and that these reasons *are* capable of motivating us. As the moderate would have to concede, the mere fact that we do not always *obey* a requirement does not show that the necessary motivational underpinning is absent. Thus it seems open to the extremist to contend that there can be a genuine requirement to promote the good. The moderate of course will simply deny that agents generally can find the reasons for promoting the good to be sufficiently compelling—and he will thus maintain his claim that the motivational underpinning for a requirement is absent.

The argument therefore appears to be at something of a standoff—but I think that the moderate has the better of it. Although the moderate has not altogether eliminated the possibility that a requirement to promote the good may have the necessary motivational underpinning, it does not strike us as particularly plausible to suggest that it does. The extremist must point to something more than the bare logical possibility that he does not run afoul of the nature of persons.

PRUDENCE

A more adequate response might begin by noting that the negative argument must be extended even further than the moderate proposes. The moderate's argument is based on the realization that the agent must be capable of being motivated by the considerations which underlie a moral requirement, for it is the agent who will react or fail to react as the system desires. But apparently the argument is capable of launching an attack not only against a requirement to promote the good, but also against prudence.[3]

As we have seen, because of the personal, subjective point of view, individuals care more about their own interests than about other matters; this—the moderate suggests—must be reflected by granting options. But individuals also care more about their present interests and desires than they do about their future interests and desires. This too follows from the nature of persons; and if minimally reflecting the personal point of view involves making concessions to the biases of agents in the case of options, it will also involve freeing agents from the requirement that they have equal regard for their future interests.

It seems fairly clear that a system which requires agents to act prudently will fail to make the concessions to the nature of persons which the negative argument appears to support. When agents assess the world from the personal perspective they assign weights to their own interests out of proportion to those weights which would be assigned from the objective standpoint; agents have a bias in favor of their interests. But even within the set of interests of the agent himself, there is a further bias, for agents do not weigh all of their own interests over time equally. Instead, they assign even greater weight to their *present* interests, at the expense of their future interests.

For contrast we might consider a *semi-objective* standpoint which readily grants the extra weight which the agent wants to assign to his own interests, but which tries, within that framework, to evaluate the satisfaction of the agent's various interests 'objectively', i.e., without regard to whether they are present or future interests.[4] If an agent were to act in keeping with this semi-objective standpoint, he would act prudently. The important point to be noted, however, is that the personal point of view typically is even

---

[3] Prudence is an important card to be played by the extremist against the moderate. Its use in this regard goes back at least to Sidgwick, Book 4, Chapter 2, paragraph 1; but I am especially indebted to Nagel, *Altruism*. Also see Parfit, Part 2. (Note that 'prudence' as I am using it here is a matter of giving equal weight to one's interests across time; it is not a matter of cautiousness or frugality per se. A careful analysis of the concept can be found in Bricker.)

[4] The problem of the connection between prudence and *past* desires and interests is a complicated one that I intend to ignore. But see Parfit, Chapter 8. I have discussed Parfit's arguments in 'Present-Aim', pp. 754–7.

less objective than the semi-objective standpoint. It is the nature of persons to be biased in favor of what is near—not only physically and psychically, but also temporally. Thus, although disregarding one's future interests so as to achieve a fairly trivial present satisfaction is acting imprudently, it is acting in keeping with the nature of persons. This suggests that a requirement that agents act prudently will lack the necessary motivational underpinning. And so the negative argument seems to imply that if a system is to minimally reflect the nature of persons, it must abandon the requirement of prudence.

But we do not regard it as reasonable for agents to act in an imprudent manner[5]—and so there must be some way to defuse the impact of the negative argument. (The most straightforward way, of course, would be to reject the moderate's internalist assumption that requirements must have the corresponding motivational underpinning; what we are asking, however—here, and throughout this chapter—is what alternatives would remain open if we were to grant this assumption.)

Three possible complications should be mentioned. First, it may be claimed that whatever the status of requirements of prudence, they are not moral requirements, for morality only governs an agent's interactions with others. We briefly considered one version of this view in the last chapter, in the form of the claim that a morally decisive reason cannot have self-regarding content; so a *moral* requirement could never be based on prudential consider-ations. I suggested in that earlier discussion that I could see no reason to accept this view. But for the extremist's present purposes it is irrelevant whether or not prudence is part of morality. Even if it is not, we can conceive of both as being portions of a larger, more encompassing system: a complete theory of reasons for action. The negative argument claims that a system must make concessions to the nature of persons; the extremist need only note that the moderate can give no reason for restricting this demand to what is properly called 'morality'.

The second complication is that it may sound odd (for reasons relating to the first point) to speak of *requirements* of prudence. But this too—even if it is correct—poses no problem for the extremist's argument. After all, it is surely possible, at least, that in our

---

[5] At least as long as the interests of others are not involved. For simplicity, assume that this is the only sort of case that we are considering.

complete system of reasons for action, we might want to recognize reasons for an agent to have equal regard for his future interests, reasons of a sufficiently overwhelming sort—decisive reasons—so that an agent who fails to act prudently is unreasonable, or perhaps even irrational. Whether or not we call this a *requirement* to act prudently is a matter of no moment.

The third complication arises from my broad use of the term 'interests' to cover not only self-interest but also the various other objects of the agent's desires and concerns. Some may deny, therefore, that there is any requirement of prudence to have equal regard for one's future interests in this broad sense. For on many traditional accounts, at least, prudence is concerned only with one's overall *self-interest*, one's personal well-being. However, the negative argument seems to pose just as much of a problem for this more narrow conception of prudence as it does for the broader conception. Even if we restrict our attention to cases where one's future self-interest is at stake, it remains the case that the nature of persons creates a bias in favor of one's current desires and other current interests.

The extremist's objection, then, is this. If a complete system of reasons for action is to require prudence, then—according to the negative argument—there must be reasons for prudent behavior sufficiently compelling for the agent to be able to overcome his motivational bias in favor of his present interests. The moderate must indicate how he proposes to defend prudence against the challenge posed by his own negative argument.

It is not sufficient to note that from the semi-objective standpoint (or from the objective one) there may be greater reason overall to sacrifice some present interest so as to promote some future interest. For the personal point of view typically is not the semi-objective one, and the agent must be capable of being motivated from his *actual* point of view. If the complete system is to judge an agent unreasonable for acting imprudently, then it must point to considerations which the agent is capable of appreciating from his personal perspective. The mere fact that objectively the reasons for promoting some future interest are greater than the reasons for promoting some present interest is not necessarily an indication that those reasons are sufficiently compelling to be able to motivate the agent. Given the nature of persons, we would expect otherwise.

Yet most of us do consider imprudent behavior unreasonable,

and not only in extreme cases. So we must believe that the agent *is* capable of appreciating and being moved by the considerations which support his having equal regard for his own future interests. As before, this does not mean that the agent will always act prudently: we know that this is not the case. It is not that the considerations always *will* motivate, but rather that the agent is *capable* of appreciating them so that they *can* motivate him.

VIVID BELIEF

How does this happen? One plausible suggestion, I believe, is this.[6] We must distinguish between two ways that beliefs can be represented in the mind: a belief can be *vivid*, or it may only be *pale*. Pale beliefs are genuine beliefs, and they may well be deeply entrenched beliefs—but they are displayed to the mind in such a way that the individual does not fully appreciate their import. We might say that they are beliefs to which we only pay lip service— meaning by this not that we do not actually hold the beliefs in question, but only that they are little more than propositions which we have tagged with the label 'true'. In contrast, vivid beliefs are displayed in such a way that the individual *does* fully appreciate their import. Vivid beliefs are beliefs whose significance we fully comprehend. Similarly, we might distinguish between vivid and pale understanding, vivid and pale knowledge, and likewise for other, related concepts.

The distinction I am after is, I think, one with which we are all acquainted. Let me give two examples. It is sometimes said that no one really appreciates what a billion dollars amounts to. Now in one sense, of course, this is obviously false. We know that a billion is a thousand million; it is 10^9. We know that one billion dollars is enough to give each of 125 million people $8 each. And so on. I want to call this pale understanding. But there is another sense— equally obvious—in which the claim may well be true. One billion dollars is so large an amount that we lose our grasp on its

[6] Versions of this suggestion, and the use of similar distinctions in this and related areas, have a long history in the philosophical literature, going back to Aristotle, 1146b25–1147b20, and perhaps even to Plato, 355e–356e. A recent use of the distinction can be found in Brandt, pp. 58–64 and passim. For a nontechnical discussion of some of the psychological literature, see (in addition to Brandt) Nisbett and Ross, pp. 43–62.

magnitude, and cannot feel about it much differently than we do about one million or one trillion dollars. To help give us a sense of what one billion dollars really comes to, someone may contrast the length of one million dollar bills stuck end to end with the corresponding span of one billion dollars—or offer other, similar aids to the imagination. To the extent that these attempts are successful, we come closer to having vivid understanding of the notion of one billion dollars; and if I am told that this is what some policy will cost the economy, my belief to this effect may be a vivid one. And so on.

Similarly, if you are asked whether you learned anything at a lecture, you might reply, 'She didn't convince me of anything I didn't already believe—but I didn't really *believe* it before.' Previously your beliefs were pale; now they are vivid.

Obviously, the dichotomy between vivid and pale beliefs is a simplification. It would be more appropriate to speak of a continuum: relatively pale beliefs can become more vivid, while still leaving room for further improvement. (Things get fuzzy at the ends: How pale can a belief be and still be a belief? Is there such a thing as complete vividness? Can beliefs be *too* vivid?) But for our purposes there is no need for a more fine-grained vocabulary.

We might well wonder what makes a previously pale belief vivid. Typically, no doubt, the transformation accompanies an influx of information concerning the subject of the belief. As we learn more details, the belief takes on flesh and blood, so to speak, becoming more vivid in our minds. It seems possible that vividness simply *is* a matter of having a wealth of details. Or it might be more directly a matter of how adequately the belief is displayed in the representational system of the mind—where the influx of information simply acts as a stimulus for more adequate representation of the belief itself. These are tricky issues. (Are they to be settled by philosophy of mind? By cognitive psychology?) But I believe that we can leave them to one side without ill effect.[7]

Sometimes an individual may deliberately seek out information so as to make a pale belief more vivid. A smoker may know that he

---

[7] The naturalness of speaking of vividness in terms of mental images is obvious. And for many of us, it seems, mental images do in fact play a role in affecting the vividness of a belief. But this is certainly not true for all of us (after all, some people cannot form mental images); and, of course, in many cases many of the facts that need to be vividly appreciated cannot literally be *pictured*. Here, such talk is only a handy metaphor.

damages his lungs with each puff he takes—but this is likely to be no more than a pale belief. A photograph of a dissected lung may make the knowledge vivid: at last the individual becomes truly aware of what he has been doing to himself. Whatever the precise relation between information and vividness, an increase in the latter can often be purchased with an increase in the former.

It is important to note, however, that an individual may be able to transform a pale belief into a vivid one without the aid of external stimulation. For in some cases, at least, all that may be required is for the individual to pay more attention to the belief in question than she has previously; to contemplate its implications, or to consider seriously what it amounts to. It may be sufficient to try to picture the relevant state of affairs, to imagine it more fully, supplying details from similar previous experiences or related areas of expertise. Where previously she had only considered a scene sketched hastily in the broadest of outlines, the individual may be able to bring herself to see that it is a genuine landscape teeming with life. In doing this it may be unimportant if the fine points are erroneous, so long as they successfully help the individual to appreciate the significance of her beliefs. My belief that someone is crying may be pale if I picture no more than a stick figure; it may become vivid if I give that figure a human face.

It may be worth noting, if only in passing, that vividness is no guarantee of accuracy. Vivid understanding is a matter of fully grasping the force and content of a proposition being entertained. It is a distinct question whether one's judgmental attitude toward that proposition—whether one accepts it or rejects it—is correct or not. One can vividly believe a claim, therefore, even though that claim is false. (Of course vivid *knowledge* can't be inaccurate, but that has nothing to do with vividness per se.) Little in our discussion, however, should be affected by this point. The fact will still remain: given that someone believes such and such, it matters whether that belief is pale or vivid.

The relevance of the distinction between vivid and pale beliefs to the discussion of prudence is this: individuals typically have only pale beliefs concerning their future. This is not simply to note the obvious—i.e., that there are *gaps* in any given individual's knowledge of his own future. Rather, even those beliefs about his future interests which are plausible and well-grounded are apt to be only pale beliefs. Vivid beliefs tend to be limited to the present.

When considering the possibility that satisfying some present desire will take a more significant toll later, the agent envisions his future dissatisfaction in only a pale manner—while the present desire is felt vividly. If he believes he will suffer in the future for what he does now, the belief in the future suffering is a genuine one—but it is not a vivid one. (Of course, in many cases it would actually be more accurate to say that what is involved is a conflict between vivid beliefs about the immediate or *near* future and pale beliefs about the distant or *further* future; but I'll leave this complication aside.)

Agents are not doomed, however, to having only pale beliefs about their future interests. Frequently they can make the beliefs vivid simply by taking the time to think about them. I may know, e.g., that if I do not leave my study and purchase a pineapple today I will be hungry tomorrow; yet typically my belief that I will be hungry tomorrow is pale. But if I pause to imagine myself in pain from hunger, recalling from previous occasions what it is like, the belief becomes more vivid: the reality of my future suffering is driven home to me, and I finally begin to appreciate what it is that I am risking.

When an agent's beliefs about his future interests become more vivid, it becomes easier for him to give them the weight that they deserve from the semi-objective standpoint.[8] As the beliefs become more vivid, it becomes easier for the agent to appreciate their compelling nature. Indeed, it does not seem implausible to suggest that the bias in favor of present interests and desires is simply a function of the fact that our knowledge of our present interests is generally fuller and more vivid than our knowledge of our future interests. Initially, my present desire not to leave my study so as to purchase the pineapple is vividly presented to my mind: the pro tanto reasons for staying are given their full weight. But my knowledge of my future distress is pale: the pro tanto reasons for leaving are barely felt. When my belief in my future hunger becomes more vivid, however, the reasons for purchasing the pineapple come into their own: I am capable of appreciating the relative weights of the various considerations pro and con. In this way, I am able to overcome the bias in favor of my present interests.

[8] I take it to be a substantive claim that vividness affects an agent's propensity to act on a given consideration; the notion of vividness, I believe, has sufficient content (independent of its motivational impact) for the claim to avoid triviality.

As it happens, in many cases it is not particularly difficult to acquire vivid beliefs about one's future interests. (Given how well we know ourselves, this is, perhaps, not particularly surprising.) This provides the basis of the explanation of many acts of prudence. Vividness increases our *appreciation* of the reasons generated by our future interests. And it does this in two ways. First, although we typically recognize that our future interests generate *some* reason for our acting, we often fail to assess the weight of these reasons accurately (and thus fail to act prudently, not realizing in particular cases that this is supported by the balance of reasons). A more vivid understanding of how one's future interests can be affected in a given case can lead one to better assess the proper weight of the reasons generated by that fact. Second, and perhaps more importantly, in other cases we may well already judge that the balance of reasons favors acting prudently, but we may not be *moved* by this realization. Vividness helps here too: we are better able to give reasons their proper influence on our behavior when we have vivid beliefs. Thus, by making our beliefs vivid, we may be led to react more prudently.

Often, of course, it will not be sufficient, strictly speaking, that we make our beliefs—that is, the beliefs we *already* have—vivid; for we may also have to acquire *new* beliefs. (And, of course, erroneous beliefs may need correcting as well.) Suppose—to take an extreme case—that in some situation I have no belief at all concerning my future; I simply have not considered the impact that my present action will have on my future interests. In such a case, making the beliefs I do possess vivid might do nothing to make me appreciate the reasons generated by those future interests. Here, if I do come to give my future interests the influence they merit, part of the explanation will obviously turn on my having come to realize that (and how) those interests will be affected. More generally, prudent behavior will often be explained by my coming to have various relevant beliefs about the possible effects of my reactions on my present and future interests. In short, it is not sufficient that my beliefs be vivid: I must possess the relevant beliefs.

In many cases, then, acts of prudence can be explained through some combination of these two factors: 1) I have or come to have the appropriate beliefs about the relevant facts; and 2) the relevant beliefs themselves are or become vivid. From an analytical perspective, perhaps, it might be helpful to keep these two factors clearly distinguished; indeed, there are probably other factors that might be profitably distinguished as well (e.g., we might distinguish between the vividness of a belief, and my *attending* to that belief). But for our purposes I do not think this will be necessary. We can let talk of vividness serve double duty: in what follows—unless context indicates otherwise—references to making our beliefs vivid should be understood to encompass not merely the increase in vividness of our beliefs, but also (when necessary) the supplementing and correcting of those beliefs. With this convention in mind, then, let me repeat the point that has been made so far: in many cases, by making our beliefs vivid we may be led to react more prudently.

There is a limit, however, to how much most of us are able to transform our pale beliefs into vivid ones. Vivid knowledge of tomorrow's hunger may be fairly easy; indeed with practice it may become second nature (felicitous expression!). But a young man's knowledge of his needs in old age is likely to stay relatively pale— and so prudent behavior in such a case is going to require a deeper explanation.

The key to explaining the difficult cases, however, lies with the simple cases—or more precisely, with the agent's ability to consider the implications of simple cases. Each of us can reason in this manner: 'When my beliefs about my future interests are vivid I tend to act in keeping with the semi-objective standpoint. Now it is true that there are limits to my ability to transform my pale beliefs into vivid ones; but it seems plausible to extrapolate from the simple cases. It seems likely that were I able to entertain vivid beliefs about my future interests even in those cases where I am presently unable, I would tend to act in accordance with the semi-objective standpoint there as well. That is, it is only because of my inability to make all of my beliefs vivid that I am tempted to favor my present interests. But I am already in the position to recognize that when my beliefs are vivid I am better able to give opposing considerations the influence they merit. Thus, recognition of the importance of vivid beliefs enables me to see that I have something of a blind spot with regard to my future interests. In the light of this, it seems plausible to hold that decisions concerning actions that will influence my future interests should conform to those I would make were I able to remove the blind spot—i.e., were my beliefs vivid. That is, I should accept as the correct judgments about the overall balance of reasons the judgments that I would make were my beliefs vivid. Furthermore, I find that my ability to act on my future interests is enhanced by my bearing these realizations in mind; I am now moved by the thought that I *would* be moved. So despite my pale beliefs, I am already in a position to conclude that it is reasonable to try to react in the way I would were my beliefs about my future interests vivid: and this realization moves me to act in keeping with the semi-objective standpoint.'

I do not mean to suggest, of course, that many of us go through an interior monologue of this sort. But we do recognize that our inability to vividly imagine our future is a handicap whose effect upon us it is best to minimize. As I undertake an imprudent act, someone else may warn me: 'You don't really appreciate what you are getting yourself into. You *will* know better later—but then it will be too late.' I am capable of taking this admonition seriously and recognizing that if I knew more I would make a different assessment of the balance of reasons than the one that I am tempted to make now. Even this belief may not be as vivid as it might be, but it is frequently enough to enable me to act in a prudent manner. Or such an admonition may force me to admit that although my assessment of the balance of reasons is in fact already correct, I would be more readily moved to act on that judgment were my beliefs vivid—and this realization may itself move me. In short, I am capable of recognizing that through my cognitive shortcomings I am inclined to underplay the importance of my future interests— but this is, in its own way, to recognize the importance of my future after all.

In order to act prudently the agent must be capable of recognizing reasons sufficiently compelling to overcome the bias in favor of his present interests. When an agent does act prudently, the reasons that he recognizes are simply those which on balance support sacrificing his present interest for the sake of his future interests—coupled with the realization that if he is tempted to assess the balance differently, or is tempted to refuse to act on that assessment, that is because some of the reasons are portrayed less vividly in his mind, and so will be given less than their due influence unless care is taken.

This is not to say that it will always be easy to act prudently. The temptation to indulge some present desire may be quite great, and may be overcome only with difficulty—even when the agent has a fairly vivid appreciation of his future interests. When his understanding of his future interests is pale it will be even harder to act prudently. The realization that the lack of vivid beliefs contributes to the difficulty of acting prudently may give the agent motivation to overcome his bias, even when he cannot acquire the vivid beliefs themselves; but it is still harder to act prudently in the absence of those vivid beliefs. Nonetheless, despite the difficulty of acting prudently, the bias *can* be overcome—whether it is through acquisition of vivid beliefs about one's future, or through realization of how one would act if one *did* have such beliefs.

It should be noted, of course, that there may well be prudential reasons *not* to make all of one's beliefs as vivid as possible. If the agent were forever trying to maintain a vivid appreciation of her future, she might have little ability or time to act effectively. Prudentially, she might do better if she were to retain various pale beliefs, but guide herself in typical circumstances with general principles for promoting her interests overall. Similarly, in many cases it might be best prudentially if the agent uses *other* means to motivate herself than thinking about her future. Obviously, these possibilities do not undercut the account given. The point is simply that the prudential considerations *can* motivate the agent—directly, through vivid understanding, or indirectly, through appreciation of the significance of the lack of vividness. There is no claim that appreciation of prudential considerations is always the most efficient way to provide motivation. Clearly, however, there will also be situations in which it *will* make sense to try to acquire vivid beliefs about one's future—for this may well be the easiest way to motivate oneself to sacrifice one's present interests.

Once again it should be stressed that there is no suggestion that agents always do act prudently. Even those individuals who recognize that failure to have equal regard for their future interests may spring from lack of vivid beliefs may not always take the pains to correct the situation as far as they are able. Often there is an air of self-deception, as agents try to assure that their beliefs about the future stay pale—lest they find themselves concluding that they must forgo the present temptations after all. But in doing so they reveal an awareness that were it not for their blissful semi-ignorance, they themselves would probably recognize the existence of compelling reasons for altering their behavior. Agents are *capable* of overcoming their bias in favor of their present interests—even if they do not always do so.

The moderate's negative argument, concerning the necessity of minimally reflecting the nature of persons, entailed that a complete system of reasons for action could only hold imprudent behavior unreasonable if the motivational underpinning necessary for such a judgment existed. Despite the fact that it is in the nature of persons to be biased in favor of their present interests, consideration of our ability to recognize the importance of vivid beliefs explains how the necessary condition is satisfied. Further consideration of the same point may help the extremist to reinstate the requirement to promote the good.

OTHERS

The extremist's defense of the requirement to promote the good against the moderate's negative argument can be constructed in rough parallel to the defense of prudence which has just been suggested. The relevance of the distinction between pale and vivid beliefs seems clear: most of my beliefs concerning the interests of others are pale, while beliefs about my own interests are relatively vivid. In the discussion of prudence, it is true, it was noted that my beliefs about my own future interests are pale in contrast to my beliefs about my present interests—but typically there is an even greater degree of contrast in the vividness of beliefs in the interpersonal case than in the intrapersonal case. It is generally fairly easy for me to increase the vividness of my beliefs about my future interests—while bringing about a similar increase in vividness in my beliefs about the interests of others is fairly difficult. And since aiding others frequently requires a sacrifice of present interests, the contrast is often particularly great. It is not inappropriate, therefore, to make the rough generalization that when sacrifices of my own interests are at stake I will envision this possibility fairly vividly, while the plight of others will be entertained rather palely.

Agents, of course, are not altogether limited to having pale beliefs about the interests of others. In some cases, at least, knowledge of another's needs can become relatively vivid. This is perhaps most obviously the case when the other individual is a loved one or a close friend. The intimacy of the interchange between the agent and the friend may provide the agent with the wealth of detail which commonly produces vivid belief. Such knowledge can sometimes be recalled, even in those cases where initial awareness of the potential harm to the friend's interests is fairly pale, so as to transform that belief into a vivid one. With time and practice, vividly contemplating the interests of loved ones may become something of a second nature.

It is rare, however, to have such intimate rapport with more than a few individuals. For the vast bulk of humanity my knowledge of their sufferings is a pitiful, pale belief. As always, we should recognize that the beliefs are genuine ones: it is not as though I harbor secret doubts that there actually are, e.g., millions of people starving to death. It is simply that the suffering of those on the other half of the globe—or indeed a few blocks away—is displayed so dimly in my mind, that I utterly fail to appreciate the magnitude and horror of the state of affairs I am contemplating.

The extremist suggests that were my beliefs more vivid I would find it easier to sacrifice my own interests for the sake of others. In a better position to evaluate the competing claims for and against undertaking some sacrifice, my behavior would tend to approximate the objective standpoint. Once again, continues the extremist, it does not seem implausible to suggest that an agent's bias in favor of his own interests may simply be a function of the fact that his interests are more vividly represented than are the interests of others. Typically, if some sacrifice of my interests is necessary so as to prevent or cure some greater loss to another, I am vividly aware of the cost to myself: the pro tanto reasons for avoiding the sacrifice are given their full weight. My belief in the cost to the other, however, is pale: the pro tanto reasons for undertaking the sacrifice are barely felt. It is not surprising, then, if I fail to take on the sacrifice. But were the interests of others vividly presented in my mind, I would be able to give them the weight they objectively merit.

Roughly, then, the extremist's thesis is that were all my beliefs vivid, I would tend to act in accordance with the objective standpoint. Strictly speaking, however, this statement of the extremist's view is slightly inaccurate. For the extremist is not really committed to the claim that it is the *objective* standpoint with which I would tend to act in accordance were all my beliefs vivid. Rather, the claim is only that I would tend to act in accordance with an *impartial* standpoint—having an equal regard for the interests of all individuals. (Even this last formulation is somewhat inaccurate, since the objective importance of the different interests of different people can vary. But the standpoint will be impartial in that no one's interests will be given more weight than they objectively merit.) It should be noted that an agent's occupying such an impartial standpoint does not rule out the possibility that he might sometimes (appropriately) recognize reasons—perhaps even morally decisive reasons—for refraining from countenancing the outcome which is objectively best overall. Thus, if—as we are assuming—there are constraints, the standpoint in question would not be completely equivalent to the objective standpoint. It would be more accurate to say, therefore, that the extremist's thesis is that, were all my beliefs vivid, I would tend to act in accordance with the objective standpoint—within the confines of constraints (or: except insofar as departures are mandated by constraints). Once again, however, none of the issues we are now discussing should be affected by this complication. So, for simplicity, I will hereafter leave off the qualification, and write as though the intended standpoint were the objective one simpliciter. Qualifications aside, then, the extremist claims that with vivid beliefs I would tend to conform to the objective standpoint.

At this point a reminder may be in order as well. To understand the extremist's claim properly, it is important to recall that talk of my having vivid beliefs is intended to cover not merely an increase in the vividness of the beliefs I already have, but also (if necessary) the supplementation of those beliefs with additional beliefs, concerning various relevant facts, as well as the correction of any erroneous beliefs I may have. Now in cases of the kind we are currently considering, the acquisition of such additional beliefs will often be of crucial importance. For when it is a matter of sacrificing my interests for the sake of others, obviously enough, a great deal of information about the lives of those others will be relevant. Typically I will not possess much of this information, and so it is not sufficient to ask how I would react if the beliefs I already have—and only those beliefs—were made vivid. The extremist's claim, rather, is that I would tend to conform to the objective standpoint if my beliefs were suitably supplemented and corrected— as *well* as being made vivid. It is important to keep this point in mind; generally, however (once more, for the sake of simplicity) I will continue to express the extremist's thesis in terms of vividness alone.

Now this counterfactual thesis—that if all my beliefs were vivid I would tend to act in accordance with the objective standpoint—is the heart of the extremist's response to the moderate's argument. And it is, of course, a controversial claim. I do not know of any decisive argument that can be brought in its favor or in opposition to it. The range of cases in which we do have vivid knowledge of the sufferings of others is so limited that it is perhaps inevitable that *any* attempt to extrapolate from these cases will be controversial. Yet several striking bits of evidence can be offered which seem to support the extremist's claim.

I have already mentioned the fact that an agent can often acquire vivid knowledge of the needs of friends and loved ones. It is not uncommon to find that as his appreciation becomes more vivid, it becomes easier for the agent to sacrifice his own interests for the sake of those of others. Of course, one's interests may include the welfare of some favored individual (interests are broader than self-interest); so not every act of aid to that individual will be an overall sacrifice of one's own interests. Yet it remains true that people *do* sometimes sacrifice their overall interests for friends and loved ones—i.e., make sacrifices greater than can be accounted for by the agent's interests alone—and it is this which can be explained by recourse to vivid belief. As the agent's beliefs become more vivid, he more fully appreciates the reality of the interests and desires of those to whom he is close; he becomes better able to recognize the potentially compelling nature of the pro tanto reasons for promoting those interests, and better able to act on those reasons.

Second, there is the remarkable difference that distance makes for motivating an agent. If I find myself in the presence of someone whose life is in danger, I will often be prepared to make some sort of sacrifice so as to provide aid. Yet I am rarely moved to make a comparable sacrifice when I am not faced with the individual himself, but merely have the knowledge that there *is* a person in similar need of my aid. A starving person in my living room has an altogether different effect on me than a similarly starving individual a few miles away—even when I am armed with the knowledge of the latter's plight. This is such a commonplace of our experience that we rarely stop to contemplate just how remarkable it is, or to consider its implications. Why is it that we do not feel equally compelled to act when the individual in need is out of sight?

One relevant consideration, to be sure, is that the probable effectiveness of a course of action frequently falls off when the distance between the agent and the intended recipient increases. But this can hardly be the complete explanation: even when we take into account the smaller probability of successfully aiding the individual who is not in my presence (and it is easy to exaggerate the likely reduction in probability of success), we still fall far short of accounting for the marked divergence in my responses. A more far-reaching explanation is necessary.

A second relevant factor, perhaps, is that often when the needy person is some distance from me, there will be many other individuals who are just as well situated to provide the aid as I am (or maybe even better situated). But this too cannot be a complete explanation. For the presence of others who could help is no guarantee that others *will* help. A deeper explanation is still needed.

A very plausible suggestion is this: distance affects response because it affects vividness. When the needy individual is directly in front of me, my awareness of his suffering is fairly vivid. I can see the pain on his face, and hear the plea in his voice. I can look around and fully appreciate the fact that if I do not act, there is no one else who will. In a thousand ways the reality of his need—and the necessity of my action—is driven home to me, and I am able to feel the force of the considerations which support my making the sacrifice. In unfortunately sharp contrast, when the needy individual is not in my presence, my awareness of his suffering is all too pale. Even though I may know of the individual's need, I may only picture a stick figure, if I do that—barely appreciating the fact that it is a genuine human being who faces a real death. Even though I may know that if I do not act no one else will, I do not pause to consider what this actually means about the inevitability of his suffering if I turn my attention to other matters. My belief in his need is genuine—yet there is indeed something of an air of unreality: his suffering is barely anything more to me than something I read about in a storybook. The situation is made all the worse when there is not a specific individual of whom I am aware, but simply an anonymous crowd of needy individuals—where any one of them might receive aid from some other donor, but where inevitably someone or the other will suffer unless I act. In such cases an already pale belief becomes even more pale.

It is unclear why distance should make a difference as to what effect an agent's awareness of the needs of others will have upon his actions—*until* we recognize the impact of distance upon the vividness of the agent's beliefs. Then the explanation becomes simple: distance affects vividness, and vividness affects an agent's ability to give due weight to the interests of others. Consideration of the influence of distance, then, is an important piece of evidence in support of the claim that were all our beliefs vivid we would tend to act in keeping with the objective standpoint.

It might be thought that the ease with which we pass by beggars gives the lie to the extremist's claim. For in such cases we are in the presence of the beggar, his need is presumably vividly felt—and yet we rarely offer aid. But the testimony of such cases is far from clear. The extremist can begin with the observation that many people doubt—whether correctly or not—that giving money in these situations actually does more good than harm. Even if such people are in error (perhaps even a self-serving error), they would not provide counterexamples to the extremist's thesis. More important, however, is the extremist's reply that it should not surprise us if a fleeting moment in front of the agent is insufficient for the beggar's needs to become vividly represented, and to have any significant effect on the agent's behavior. Indeed, even if recognition of the other's needs flashes vividly for an instant, another step or two and the agent is beyond him, the belief pales, and it is soon forgotten. It would only be surprising if such a flash of vividness *were* commonly sufficient to enable the agent to better appreciate the reasons for aid.

It is worth noting in this regard that even *prolonged* physical proximity is, of course, no guarantee of vividness. We are all acquainted with cases in which the agent has only the palest appreciation of the needs of individuals with whom she comes into regular contact. The common practice of attributing the indifference of such agents to the fact that they have no real appreciation of the needs of those others, points again to the suggestion that if their beliefs were more vivid the agents would act less callously.

The third bit of evidence in support of the extremist's thesis is the impact which movies, photographs, literature, personal accounts, and so on, can have upon an agent's responsiveness to the needs of others. All of these things increase the vividness of an agent's beliefs about the interests of others and enable him to recognize the full weight of the considerations which support promoting their interests. We frequently find it easier to make some sacrifice of our own interests after we are thus made sensitive to the significance of another's. This too, then, provides some support for the thesis that if our beliefs were vivid our actions would tend to be in accord with the objective standpoint.

Finally, consider the nature of one of the most basic of moral arguments: the request that the agent think about what it would be like to be treated in the manner in which she intends to treat another. Often such an appeal is effective—and the agent alters her behavior. But how does it work? The extremist's suggestion is that by pausing to sincerely contemplate what it is she is about to do, the agent transforms her pale belief into a more vivid one. By recalling past experiences in which the agent herself has been mistreated, or by having recourse to her fairly well-developed ability to imagine herself in such situations, the agent finds herself providing the details and coloring which make her more fully aware of how her intended victim will be affected. Her belief may become more vivid, and perhaps unwillingly she may find herself moved by her recognition that the reasons for not reacting in her intended manner outweigh the reasons for doing so. The argument of course is not always effective; but when it is, it may be the increased vividness of belief which enables the agent to act in a more objective manner. This too, therefore, provides some support for the extremist's thesis.

All of these pieces of evidence represent cases in which the agent is able to overcome somewhat his strong natural bias in favor of his own interests; increase in vividness involves an increase in the agent's ability to recognize and act in keeping with the objective weight of reasons. On the basis of these, and similar considerations, the extremist may be willing to offer his general thesis that were all of our beliefs vivid our actions would tend to be in accord with the objective standpoint.

It must be admitted, of course, that this counterfactual thesis is an extrapolation: generalizing from cases in which I have a limited amount of vivid belief concerning some determinate area, it moves to a conjecture about my behavior under a scenario which *never* arises—namely, one in which all relevant information whatsoever is within my possession and all my beliefs are vivid. Indeed, it should probably be admitted that not only does this scenario never in fact arise, it *could* not arise, given human limitations. After all,· there are billions of other people that one's reactions might affect, and the amount of potentially relevant information is unbounded. It may not even be possible for all of my *present* beliefs to be simultaneously vivid; it certainly is not humanly possible for me to have full and vivid beliefs about the interests of all others.

But this does not reduce the counterfactual thesis to meaningless fantasy. For although it may be impossible for me to have complete vivid knowledge, we can meaningfully 'construct' such an idealized version of myself and intelligibly conjecture about what my behavior or judgment would be. (More generally, for every given agent we can construct such an idealized counterpart, and ask how she would behave.) Such a construction, as I have noted, extrapolates from our own behavior, that is, the behavior of individuals who only imperfectly approximate this ideal. But consideration of this behavior can be illuminating nonetheless. For there are, e.g., cases in which the interests of only a few people are at stake, and agents do sometimes attain relatively vivid knowledge of the interests of these few, relevant individuals. Reflection on the impact of vividness in cases of this kind (as well as the others I have discussed) provides evidence for the extrapolation to cases involving many others, cases in which vivid knowledge is not attained, and may even be humanly impossible.

It may also be worth observing, however, that appeal to this limiting case of an individual with perfect information and all of whose beliefs are vivid is largely eliminable from the extremist's argument. In any given situation, it is only the directly relevant beliefs that need to be vivid; accordingly, the extremist need only argue that if those *particular* beliefs were vivid I would tend to react in keeping with the objective standpoint—that is, in the particular case in question. Such case-specific counterfactuals should suffice for the extremist's purposes (and, it may be noted, their conditions will be more generally fulfillable); they would allow the extremist to argue, on a case by case basis, that a requirement to promote the good will possess the necessary motivational underpinning. However, appeal to the limiting case of full and vivid belief allows the extremist to argue for this conclusion in a general way, which in turn helps us to focus our attention on the central features of that argument. Consequently, although it may be helpful to keep in mind the availability of case-specific counterfactuals, in what follows I will present the discussion in terms of the general counterfactual thesis.

Now the extremist would gain nothing by denying the controversial nature of this thesis. The considerations I have mentioned may offer some support—but they are hardly decisive. Eventually I want to consider two objections which the moderate might offer: first, it may be that not every agent will find his motivation affected by vividness; and second, it may be that an agent's bias in favor of his own interests would not be entirely eliminated even were all his beliefs vivid. But before presenting these two objections, it is important to see what use the extremist will make of his thesis if it is granted.

Since the argument for the requirement to promote the good parallels the argument on behalf of prudence, the next step should not be unexpected. Each of us can reason in this way: 'There are severe limits to my ability to have vivid beliefs concerning the interests of others; but this does not stop me from recognizing this as some sort of cognitive shortcoming—a handicap whose effects I should minimize. Since I would tend to act in accordance with the objective standpoint were all my beliefs vivid, it is only because of my inability to *make* all of my beliefs vivid that I am tempted to favor my own interests. But I am already in a position to recognize that when my beliefs are vivid I am a better judge of the relative weights of opposing considerations. So I am already in the position to see that it is reasonable to try to react in the way I would were I to have vivid beliefs about the interests of others. Furthermore, when I ask why I often fail to act on this considered judgment about the balance of reasons, I find that it is due to my lack of vivid beliefs about the interests of others. But this very realization helps move me to act in accordance with the objective standpoint.'

According to the negative argument, the pro tanto reason to promote the good fails to meet a necessary condition for moral decisiveness; the requirement to promote the good is unacceptable because it lacks the necessary motivational underpinning. For a genuine moral requirement, the agent must be capable of recognizing reasons sufficiently compelling to overcome the natural bias in favor of his own interests. When the moderate offered this argument the suggestion was clear that because of the natural bias of agents there would be many cases where the reasons for an agent's sacrificing his interests failed to be *sufficiently* compelling—even though admittedly they had greater objective weight overall. At best it would be only for some subset of those cases where the objective standpoint supported the agent's sacrificing his interests that the reasons would be *capable* of motivating the agent to take on the sacrifice. So although there would be exceptional cases where the promotion of the overall good would be supported by a morally decisive reason, grounding a requirement in those particular cases, there would be no *general* requirement to promote the good.

The extremist's response is that in *all* cases where there is greater objective reason overall for taking on some sacrifice the agent is *capable* of being appropriately motivated. Thus the motivational underpinning necessary for a general requirement to promote the good is present after all. This began as bald assertion on the extremist's part, but consideration of the importance of vivid belief may render it more plausible. When an agent promotes the good at cost to himself, the reasons he recognizes for doing this are simply those which on balance support his taking on some sacrifice for the sake of the overall good—coupled with the realization that if he is tempted to assess the balance differently, or if he is tempted to fail to act on this more considered judgment, this is because some of the reasons are portrayed less vividly, and so will not be given their due influence unless care is taken. The realization that the lack of vividness can lead to failure to act on the balance of reasons can itself motivate the agent to give the various reasons their proper influence.

Thus the extremist seems to be able to meet the negative argument—*if* he is granted the counterfactual thesis. The moderate argued that an acceptable moral system must minimally reflect the nature of persons. The extremist accepted the moderate's description of the natural biases of agents—but went on to argue, in effect, that agents have in themselves resources to overcome those biases. If the counterfactual thesis is correct, then apparently agents *can* be motivated to overcome their natural biases; and so the extremist's response to the negative argument is complete. If the moderate is to retain his argument, he must either deny the extremist's thesis, or challenge the use he makes of it.

HYPOTHETICAL JUDGES

The moderate might suggest that even if the extremist's counterfactual thesis is true, this does not imply that agents have reason to try to overcome their natural bias in favor of their own interests.

There are, after all, countless counterfactuals which are plainly irrelevant to what I should actually do. It might be true that if I had wings I would fly. But it hardly follows that in my present wingless state I should try to fly as best I can; nor does it seem that my recognition of the truth of the counterfactual could possibly improve my ability to fly.

Similarly, the moderate might argue, even if it is true that were all my beliefs vivid I would tend to act in accordance with the objective standpoint, it is far from obvious how it follows that in my present state of partially pale beliefs I should try to follow the objective standpoint. On the one hand, it is unclear why we should think it appropriate for me to act the way I would were I so radically different. And on the other hand, even if it had such an implication, it is hard to see how appreciation of the counterfactual would help me to overcome my natural bias. Obviously enough, knowing how I would act with vivid beliefs is not the same thing as actually having them.

Of course not all counterfactuals are irrelevant. Thus the success of the extremist's argument seems to depend upon his ability to explain the relevance of his particular counterfactual. The extremist will suggest that if we are clear about what the counterfactual asserts, we will understand why it is not simply one more 'What if?' to be noted and forgotten. Our discussion of vivid and pale beliefs suggested that an individual with pale beliefs fails to appreciate fully the significance of the state of affairs she contemplates. Therefore, to imagine how I would react were all my beliefs vivid is to consider what I would decide to do if I lacked a particular feature which I am already able to recognize as a cognitive shortcoming: the possession of pale beliefs. It thus involves imagining an improvement in my cognitive capacities; but it does *not* involve imagining gratuitous alterations in my interests or desires. Thus the extremist's counterfactual does not relate to a choice wildly irrelevant to my own. Rather it indicates what I would decide about my present choices were my ability to decide unhampered by pale beliefs which are largely a product of my lack of knowledge. It is a guide to how I would decide were I in a recognizably superior position to judge what to do.

Roughly, then, the counterfactual fits into an argument of this form: 'If I were a better judge, I would decide to do such and such. Knowing this, I should decide to do such and such—even though I am not such a judge.' The claim that I would tend to act in keeping with the objective standpoint were all my beliefs vivid, is a claim about what I would do were I a better judge. It is true that I am not such a judge; but I know what I would do if I *were* such a judge—and so I should try to do the same. Therefore, even though my beliefs may remain pale, consideration of the effect that vivid beliefs would have indicates that it is appropriate for me to act in keeping with the objective standpoint.

Arguments similar to this are not unfamiliar. Consider, first, the situation in which I know that another is more knowledgeable than I am concerning some matter about which I must make a decision. Suppose that left to my own devices I decide to act in a particular way; but then I learn that the expert advises me to act differently—even though she cannot explain her reasons to me. Knowing that she is a better judge in this matter than I, it would be reasonable for me to follow her advice. I need not be an expert myself for it to be appropriate for me to do what an expert would suggest.

Closer to the case at hand, consider situations in which I must make a decision and am forced to rely on general principles which I have evaluated and endorsed previously. For example, I may not have time to make the specific calculations relevant to my decision, but I might well recognize the sort of situation I am in, and know that if I *did* have the time to make the calculations I would decide to do such and such—for I have previously discovered that this is the course of action which is always appropriate to such situations. I might then reason in this way: 'If I had the time to deliberate from scratch, I would decide to do such and such. I lack the necessary time; but I know what I would decide—so I should act in accordance with it.' Given the pressures of the situation, I might in fact find myself initially tempted to act otherwise. But recognition of how I would act if I were a better judge—i.e., if I had the time to deliberate from scratch—tells me what the appropriate decision should be, and enables me to act on it.

There is, of course, a sense in which if I am able to reason from my knowledge of what I would do were I a better judge, I must already be a perfectly competent judge—albeit one who is dependent on the recognition of his own shortcomings. Similarly, the extremist suggests, my ability to recognize and compensate for the cognitive shortcomings involved in the lack of vivid belief means I am already in a position to make and act on competent judgments about my actions: I should try to act the way I *would* act were my beliefs vivid. The fact that I am not actually able to make all my beliefs vivid does not make consideration of the counterfactual situation irrelevant to my decisions. On the contrary: it makes it all the more important to bear it in mind.

Now the moderate might object that sometimes considering the decisions of such hypothetical judges can be dangerously misleading. For in imagining the situation in which the superior judge makes his decision, we may also be imagining alterations in various details of the situation; and it may be inappropriate to take the judge's decision how to act in that altered situation and apply it to our own case. For example, it might not be appropriate to do what I would decide to do if I had the time to deliberate fully, if the very lack of time or the very lack of full deliberation were relevant to the choice to be made. The moderate might suggest that in imagining the decisions I would make were all my beliefs vivid, I overlook the fact that the very lack of vividness in my actual situation is essentially relevant to what I should do.

But why should we believe the moderate's suggestion? The hypothetical self we are conjuring up is not one whose interests differ gratuitously from my own. If 'he' decides to make a sacrifice, there is of course a sense in which his interests are not completely the same as the ones I presently have; but any changes are simply a result of his fuller appreciation of the various implications of the choice 'we' face. And if my hypothetical self would choose to promote the interests of others, this will still be a sacrifice; for it is a sacrifice of the particular goals in which I *would* have retained an overall interest—would have, that is, but for my coming to better appreciate the reasons that support *sacrificing* these 'prior' interests. Thus, altering the vividness of my beliefs does not alter the fundamental choice. What it does is put me in a better position to evaluate directly the competing claims which I already face. Consequently, if it is true that I would tend to act in keeping with the objective standpoint were all my beliefs vivid, it does not seem unreasonable for the extremist to conclude that it is appropriate for me, even as I am, to try to do the same.

I take these remarks about hypothetical judges to show the plausibility of using my hypothetical behavior—how I *would* act were my beliefs vivid—as a guide to what I have reason to do now, in my actual situation. If, with vivid beliefs, I would regard the balance of reasons as supporting a certain reaction, that fact is evidence as to the actual balance of reasons confronting me now. (Indeed, some might want to go further, and claim that such facts— about my behavior under vivid beliefs—are partly *constitutive* of my having reasons. But let's stick to the evidential claim.)

It must be admitted, however, that there are examples that could be offered that appear to be exceptions to this generalization— cases in which many would be intuitively inclined to say that the judgment I would form under vivid beliefs might well be an erroneous one, or at least would be erroneous if taken as evidence of what I would have reason to do in the absence of completely vivid beliefs. Perhaps these apparent counterexamples can be disarmed. But maybe not. So the decisions that I would make were all my beliefs vivid may very well not be infallible guides to forming judgments about the relative weights of reasons facing me in actual situations.

In a full discussion of vividness, such examples would have to be examined, and the evidential role of vividness would have to be carefully analyzed. Luckily, however, for our purposes the issue is not an important one to settle. For even if there are cases in which attention to vividness can be misleading, this is not something that the moderate is in a position to argue with regard to the cases involving the promotion of the overall good. The moderate himself recognizes the existence of the pro tanto reason to promote the good; and, as noted at the start of this chapter, nothing in the negative argument challenges the extremist's claim that the balance of reasons supports promotion of the overall good. Of course the moderate could abandon the confines of the negative argument, and try to defend the claim that there are indeed countervailing reasons which override the pro tanto reason to promote the good. But this would be to move on to the positive argument, which we have yet to consider. For the time being, the question before us is whether the negative argument can stand on its *own*, offering sufficient ground for rejecting a general requirement to promote the good.

The negative argument turns on the claim that a requirement to promote the good would lack the necessary motivational under-pinning. To refute the negative argument, therefore, all that the extremist needs to show is that agents are capable of being motivated to overcome their natural bias in favor of their own interests. Now if the counterfactual thesis is true, the appeal to vividness is indeed sufficient to show that agents *can* be properly motivated. Thus, if we limit ourselves to the consideration of the negative argument, the question of the evidential role of vividness is, strictly speaking, irrelevant. Even if there are cases in which vividness (or consideration of the effects of vividness) would motivate an agent to react in a way not supported by the balance of reasons, the fact remains that vividness would motivate the agent; and it is only the presence or lack of potential motivation that is at issue in the negative argument. So if the counterfactual thesis is true, it seems that the extremist can show that the pro tanto reason to promote the good can meet the motivational condition on moral decisiveness after all.

If the moderate is to maintain his charge that a requirement to promote the good would lack the necessary motivational under-pinning (without moving on to the positive argument), it seems he has two alternatives. He can either deny the truth of the extremist's counterfactual thesis, or he can maintain that even if the thesis is true this does not suffice to show that the motivational condition has been met. To repeat an earlier observation, it may be difficult to see how appreciation of the counterfactual can help me to overcome my natural bias in those situations in which my beliefs are not, in fact, vivid.

Of course the moderate is correct when he notes that knowing what I would do if I had vivid beliefs is not the same thing as actually having them. The extremist will readily concede that this means that it will be much more difficult for me to sacrifice my interests for the sake of others than it would be for me to make the same sacrifice were my appreciation of the needs of others more vivid. Vivid beliefs would make it easier to overcome my natural bias; it is harder without them. But the moderate may claim that there is a greater difference than this: the mere realization of how I would act were my beliefs vivid, it may be suggested, cannot itself provide any motivation. So except for those cases where I actually *make* my beliefs more vivid, I will not normally be able to overcome my natural bias. Realization of how I *would* act with vivid beliefs will not itself be able to motivate me.

One reply that the extremist might make is that even if the moderate's latest bit of scepticism is correct, it too is irrelevant. After all, suppose that the counterfactual thesis is in fact true, but that realization of its truth simply has no effect whatsoever on the motivation of the agent. That is, the agent would be motivated to conform to the objective standpoint were his beliefs vivid, but the mere recognition of this fact cannot motivate the agent whose beliefs are *not* vivid. Now the moderate claims that, if this is so, a general requirement to promote the good would not meet the motivational condition that must be met by genuine moral requirements. (For this motivational condition demands that the reasons that ground a requirement must be capable of motivating the agent.) Remember, however, that we are supposing that the counterfactual thesis itself is still true. That is, if the agent's beliefs were vivid, so that he could vividly appreciate the reasons for sacrificing his interests for the greater good, he would indeed be motivated to conform to the objective standpoint. But this means that if the counterfactual thesis is true the motivational condition *is* satisfied: the very reasons that ground the requirement *can* motivate the agent—when vividly appreciated. It is irrelevant that these same reasons may not be capable of motivating the agent when they are not properly (i.e., vividly) appreciated; and it is irrelevant if the agent cannot be motivated by the mere realization that he *would* be motivated if he better appreciated the relevant reasons.

The moderate might insist, however, that these last points are not irrelevant at all. He might claim that the reasons grounding a requirement must be capable of motivating the agent from her *actual* point of view. Given that the agent's beliefs are not in fact vivid, it is not sufficient to demonstrate that motivation would be available if they were. (Indeed in some cases, as we previously noted, vivid possession of all the relevant beliefs may not even be a genuine psychological possibility.) Thus the extremist has relied on too modest a version of the motivational condition. It is the more demanding version—which requires that agents can be motivated from their actual point of view—that genuine moral requirements must meet, and here it is quite relevant to ask whether an agent whose beliefs are not vivid can in fact be motivated by the mere recognition of how she would react if only her beliefs were vivid.

It would not be an easy matter for the moderate to offer anything like an adequate statement of this more demanding version of the motivational condition. (Surely an agent does not escape from a moral requirement simply by virtue of having a headache, or by refusal to attend to the relevant reasons; yet either of these might keep the agent from being motivated. Exactly which features, then, of the agent's actual point of view can be discounted in determining whether she is capable of being motivated?) Nor is it clear that this more demanding condition could be defended; there may be no justification for moving beyond the modest version of the motivational condition. However, since I have not attempted to evaluate arguments for any version of the motivational condition in the first place, let us once more simply grant the moderate his premise. Suppose, then, that an adequate formulation of the more demanding version of the motivational condition could be found and defended. Details aside, the moderate's claim would then be that this condition is still not met: even if the counterfactual thesis is true, mere recognition of how I would act if my beliefs were vivid will not be able to motivate me.

I am not sure how the extremist should respond to this latest claim except to say that it simply does not seem correct. We do seem capable of being moved by a recognition of our shortcomings. More specifically, it does seem easier to act on the interests of others if we believe that the natural tendency to fail to do so persists because of a failure to vividly appreciate their needs. More should be said about how it is that an agent's recognition of his own failure to feel the compelling nature of a consideration increases his ability to act on that consideration—but that this is so seems borne out by experience. At the very least, the moderate has not given reason to think otherwise.

It seems plausible, then, for the extremist to conclude that if his counterfactual is true agents can be motivated to act in keeping with the objective standpoint. If the counterfactual thesis is true, the moderate's negative argument fails—for a requirement to promote the good will possess the necessary motivational underpinning after all. Therefore, if the moderate is to preserve his argument, apparently he must deny the claim that were our beliefs vivid we would tend to act in accordance with the objective standpoint.

ABANDONING UNIVERSALITY

Given the evidence offered in support of the extremist's counterfactual thesis, it would not be plausible for the moderate to suggest that a typical agent would be *unaffected* by increased vividness. Indeed, in my own case, at least, I know that I *am* affected by changes in the vividness of my beliefs; and it seems clear that typically an increase in vividness does increase the ease with which we approximate the objective standpoint. But the moderate might concede this, while still denying that it holds true for *everyone*. That is, the moderate might insist that there are certain individuals who would remain unaffected by an increase in the vividness of their beliefs concerning the interests of others, or—worse still— individuals for whom such an increase in vividness makes it *less* likely that they will react in keeping with the objective standpoint. To take one stock example, it might be objected that some people are sadists; for such people, vivid awareness of the sufferings of others may only reinforce their unwillingness to sacrifice their own interests so as to aid those others.

Conclusions drawn from the existence of such people must be viewed with caution. Arguably, some of these callous or hateful people—appearances to the contrary notwithstanding—do not genuinely possess a vivid appreciation of the suffering that they impose on others: they may have, e.g., only a pale belief in the reality of their victims. Nonetheless, the moderate can plausibly insist that at least some of these individuals provide genuine and thoroughgoing counterexamples to the extremist's general counter- factual thesis. And the extremist, it seems, will have to admit to at least the possibility of such people.

But this means that there are, or could be, agents who frequently cannot be motivated to sacrifice their own interests out of vivid appreciation of the interests of others. For these agents, then, it appears that in countless cases a requirement to promote the good would lack the necessary motivational underpinning.[9] Thus—the moderate argues—there can be no general requirement to promote the good.

So far, the moderate is only entitled to the (relatively) modest conclusion that there can be no general requirement to promote the good which is binding upon the particular, evil individuals under discussion. But if we add the widely accepted assumption that

---

[9] Strictly speaking, however, this conclusion does not actually follow from what has been granted. Even if the appeal to vividness fails to show it, conceivably some different type of argument might still succeed in establishing that even sadists are capable of being properly moved by the interests of others. See n. 11.

fundamental moral requirements are universal—i.e., binding upon all agents if they are binding upon any—then the moderate can make the more sweeping assertion that even for the rest of us there can be no general requirement to promote the good.

This last conclusion is, of course, quite unacceptable to the extremist, representing the abandonment of his position. But if he is to avoid this sweeping conclusion, his alternatives are limited. He must either reject the view that fundamental moral requirements are universal, or he must find a way to resist the original, modest conclusion.

Now I have admitted that the extremist must concede the existence, or at least the possibility, of individuals who cannot be appropriately moved by vivid appreciation of the interests of others. But the conclusion that such individuals are not faced with a general requirement to promote the good only follows given the further assumption that having the relevant motivational under-pinning is a necessary condition of moral decisiveness. This assumption, of course, is the basis of the moderate's negative argument, and although it is controversial, we granted it at the start of the chapter for the sake of assessing that argument. But it may be worth recalling, once more, that many extremists (and, for that matter, many moderates) would want to reject this motivational condition on moral decisiveness; and if they were to do so, even the modest conclusion could be resisted.

Suppose, however, that we continue to grant the motivational condition. The extremist is then saddled with the conclusion that there are, or could be, some individuals upon whom no general requirement to promote the good is binding. And so, if he is to avoid the sweeping conclusion that even for the rest of us there is no general requirement to promote the good, the extremist must reject the universality of moral requirements. He must claim, that is, that there can be genuine moral requirements, binding upon many or most agents, but not necessarily binding upon all agents.

Such a move on the part of the extremist may tempt the moderate to object that no acceptable moral theory can deny the universality of fundamental moral requirements. But this temptation should be resisted, for it seems likely that the moderate himself will find that many of the requirements of ordinary morality can only be preserved if moral requirements need not be universally binding.

To see this, let's begin by noting that from a formal point of view there is nothing especially troubling about the rejection of universality. As I argued in Chapter 2, an agent is morally required in a given case to react in a given way if there is a morally decisive reason in that case for that agent to react in that way. Nothing here guarantees that the presence or absence of a morally decisive reason will be constant for all agents facing the same type of situation. Whether this is so or not will depend on one's particular theory of how and when reasons are generated, and which conditions are necessary for moral decisiveness. If two agents in relevantly similar situations can find themselves confronted with different reasons (different in terms of kind, character, or strength, and so on) then one of these agents may well have morally decisive reason to react in a given manner, while the other may lack such morally decisive reason. Similarly, even if the two agents are confronted with the same reasons, if it is possible for some other condition necessary for moral decisiveness to be met in the case of one agent while remaining unmet in the case of the other, then it might well be that for the one agent that reason is morally decisive while for the other agent it is not. If either of these possibilities were realized, it would involve a breakdown in universality: the one agent would be morally required to react in the given manner, while the other agent—despite being in the relevantly similar situation—would not be so required.

It is the second of these two possibilities that is at work here. The force of the motivational condition is that a reason can be morally decisive only if the agent can be (appropriately) moved by consideration of that very reason. Yet whether a reason possesses that kind of motivational capability may depend not only upon the particular reason in question, but also upon the particular agent in question. For in some cases, at least, a given reason may be incapable of moving some atypical agent, although it is capable of moving the rest of us. Thus it is the very introduction of the motivational condition that guarantees the *possibility* that some moral requirements may not be universally binding.

The moderate, then, cannot object to the mere possibility of a breakdown in universality. Nor can he argue, on behalf of ordinary morality, that in his own system, at least, no such failures of universality arise. For it seems quite likely that the sadists and the like, appealed to by the moderate against the extremist's requirement to promote the good, will also be unmoved—and incapable of being moved—by the considerations that underlie many of the requirements of ordinary morality. Indeed, one might offer the empirical conjecture that for (virtually) every plausible moral requirement there are at least some individuals who, in at least some cases, cannot be moved by the considerations that underlie the given requirement. Perhaps this empirical conjecture is false; but I see no good reason to think it holds true for the extremist but not for the moderate.

Suppose the moderate were to insist on universality. (We could, in fact, introduce it as a further condition on moral decisiveness: a given reason can be morally decisive only if all other conditions necessary for moral decisiveness are equally met by all agents in similar situations.) Then, together with the motivational condition, if anything close to the empirical conjecture is correct this would effectively force the moderate into the minimalist's camp. Few or no purported requirements will be able to meet the motivational condition for *all* agents, and so—given universality—there will be few or no genuine moral requirements. If he is to avoid this overly minimalist position, the moderate's choices are limited. He can deny that the empirical conjecture holds true for the requirements of ordinary morality; but his own examples render this implausible. He can abandon the motivational condition; but to do so is to give up the crucial premise of the negative argument. Finally, he can admit that fundamental moral requirements need not be universal. This last alternative may be the most attractive way for the moderate to avoid the minimalist; it means, however, that the moderate cannot complain if the extremist concedes the possibility that the requirement to promote the good may not be universally binding upon all agents. Apparently the requirements of ordinary morality too cannot be held to be universally binding.

Perhaps the moderate's sense of disappointment at abandoning universality can be diminished somewhat if we note that this move may actually put the moderate into a better position with regard to at least one feature of ordinary morality. Although, as we know, the moderate insists that options free agents from having to sacrifice their interests for the sake of the greater good, it is a striking fact that agents who have made such significant sacrifices often report that as far as they themselves are concerned, morally speaking they had no choice. What may seem especially puzzling is that such individuals are often unwilling to say of others who do not make similar sacrifices that those other people are similarly required to promote the good; rather, it is as though these people view themselves as individually bound by more stringent moral requirements. Now the moderate is in a somewhat uncomfortable position with regard to the testimony of such people. Although he can, of course, simply dismiss it out of hand, he may be understandably hesitant to do this, given that such people are often held up as models of moral behavior. But once the moderate has admitted that moral requirements need not be universally binding, he can at least allow for the possibility that these people may be substantially correct when they hold that they themselves were required to do what the rest of us are not required to do.

What's more, something like this position is actually suggested by the negative argument. As we know, the basic idea of this argument is that there can be no general requirement to promote the good, for it would lack the necessary motivational underpinning. Whether this is so or not is, of course, being contested by the extremist. But even if the moderate is correct in his claim that the natural bias in favor of our interests typically leaves most of us unable to make the significant sacrifices that may be necessary for promoting the overall good, it cannot be denied that some individuals *do* make such sacrifices out of concern for the interests of others. Since these people are indeed moved it can hardly be claimed that the necessary motivational underpinning is lacking, and so nothing in the negative argument rules out the possibility that these people may in fact be morally required to make the sacrifices in question. And this could be so, even though for the rest of us there is no general requirement to promote the good—not even in relevantly similar situations—since the motivational condition is not and cannot be met.

Of course it is also true that nothing in the negative argument *forces* the moderate to take this position. The moderate can insist that even those individuals who do in fact make significant sacrifices for the greater good are not required to do so; and he can dismiss, where necessary, the claims to the contrary sometimes made by those individuals. Even though the negative argument by itself cannot succeed as a defense of options in these cases, this is completely compatible with the moderate asserting that some *other* argument (e.g., perhaps, the positive argument) will succeed in establishing options here too.

I suspect that moderates will differ among themselves as to whether it is, on balance, an advantage or a drawback of the negative argument that it allows for this failure of universality with regard to options. Luckily, there is no need for us to settle the point here. For our purposes, what is most important about this feature of the negative argument is that it underlines the fact that introducing the motivational condition opens the door for such failures of universality. If the moderate insists on retaining the motivational condition on moral decisiveness—and without this condition the negative argument as we have been developing it cannot get started—such failures of universality are only to be expected.

With this point in mind, let's reconsider the status of the moderate's original objection. The moderate has argued for the existence of certain thoroughgoing counterexamples to the counterfactual thesis, individuals who, in general, simply could not be appropriately motivated by the vivid appreciation of the interests of others. Obviously enough, if the existence of such individuals is granted, the extremist can no longer claim that his counterfactual holds true universally. Thus, if we continue to grant the motivational condition on moral decisiveness, the extremist may have to concede at least this much to the negative argument: the general requirement to promote the good may not be universally binding; certain sadistic individuals, and the like, may escape it.

Such a breakdown in universality may well be disappointing to the extremist (and he may harbor the hope of eventually disarming the apparent counterexamples); but it does not constitute a flaw in his position that can be criticized by the moderate. For as I have argued, it seems quite likely that the moderate himself will be forced to recognize a similar lack of universality in the requirements of ordinary morality. Sadists aside, then, the pressing question is this: what requirements are binding upon the rest of us?

It is important to note, therefore, that for all the moderate has shown, the extremist's counterfactual may well hold true for the rest of us—i.e., those who are not unusually evil or corrupt, and so on. And if a *typical* agent would tend to act in keeping with the objective standpoint were his beliefs vivid, then the extremist has an adequate reply to the moderate's negative argument. The general requirement to promote the good may not be universally binding, but so long as the extremist can claim that the typical agent is indeed required to promote the good, the moderate's defense of ordinary morality is unsuccessful.

Let us, therefore, put the possibility of sadists and the like aside, and restrict our attention to more typical agents. Apparently, the moderate must claim that even for typical agents the counterfactual thesis does not hold true. At least, this is what the moderate must claim if he is to preserve the substance of the negative argument.

THE CORE OF THE BIAS

The negative argument holds that there can be no general requirement to promote the good, for such a requirement would lack the necessary motivational underpinning. In response, the extremist has argued for the counterfactual thesis that were our beliefs vivid, we would tend to react in accord with the objective standpoint; given the truth of this counterfactual, and given our ability to be motivated by our recognition of the truth of this counterfactual, a general requirement to promote the good would possess the necessary motivational underpinning after all.

Faced with this defense, the moderate initially tried to deny the relevance of the counterfactual. When this objection proved unsuccessful, the remaining alternative was to deny the counterfactual's truth. As we have just seen, however, the mere fact that the counterfactual may be false for certain evil individuals will not really suffice for the moderate's purposes; rather, he must claim that even for typical agents the counterfactual thesis does not hold true. Now at first glance, at least, this may not seem a promising line to take. For as I have noted, it would not be plausible for the moderate to suggest that a typical agent would be unaffected (or inappropriately affected) by increased vividness; indeed, it does seem as though greater vividness increases the ease with which we approximate the objective standpoint.

Nonetheless, there is still room for the moderate to deny that agents would conform to the objective standpoint if only their beliefs were vivid. (In what follows, talk of agents is to be understood as referring to typical agents.) For the moderate might suggest that even if all of an agent's beliefs were made vivid, the bias in favor of his own interests would not be *eliminated*. That is, the moderate might concede that agents with vivid beliefs would be far more ready to take on various sacrifices for the sake of the greater good—and yet insist, for all that, that even with vivid beliefs agents would not overcome their natural bias altogether. The bias would be significantly diminished, to be sure, but a residual bias would persist.[10]

If this is correct, then the extremist has not succeeded in defending the requirement to promote the good against the negative argument. For the extremist will not have shown that the agent is capable of recognizing the existence of reasons sufficiently compelling to motivate him to sacrifice his interests in *all* those cases where such a sacrifice is supported by the objectively greater balance of reasons. Even with vivid beliefs, agents would assign their interests more weight than they objectively merit. (Alternatively, even if the agent correctly assessed the objective balance of reasons, the agent's interests would retain some of their disproportionate influence on his behavior.) Therefore, even with vivid beliefs, agents would not be motivated to act completely in keeping with the objective standpoint. The motivational underpinning necessary for the requirement to promote the good will still be lacking, and an adequate moral system will apparently have to grant options.

The moderate might back this conclusion up with a second, related objection. We have allowed the moderate to assume that it is the more demanding formulation of the motivational condition—according to which it must be possible for agents to be motivated from their actual point of view—that must be met. The question, therefore, is what motivation is available to an agent whose beliefs are not, in fact, vivid. Now the moderate, I have suggested, will have to concede that even an agent without vivid beliefs can be motivated by the recognition of how he would act if his beliefs were vivid. Nonetheless, it would still be plausible for the moderate to insist that such motivation would typically be considerably weaker than the motivation that would be provided by the vivid beliefs themselves. Consequently, even if the counterfactual thesis were true, recognition of this fact might not provide agents who lack

---

[10] Obviously, this position would also involve rejecting the earlier suggestion that the natural bias may simply be a function of an agent's typically having more vivid beliefs about his own interests than about the needs of others. (A similar scepticism might be voiced concerning the requirement to act prudently. There too, it might be suggested, vivid beliefs would not totally eliminate the natural bias—in this case, the bias in favor of one's present interests. See Parfit, pp. 161–62, for an argument to this effect.)

vivid beliefs with sufficient motivation to overcome their entire natural bias. On the other hand, once we suppose that the counterfactual thesis is actually false, as has just been suggested, then even with vivid beliefs an agent would not be motivated to act in complete accord with the objective standpoint. If so, then even when agents who fail to have vivid beliefs are motivated to act the way they would if their beliefs *were* vivid, it is not the completely objective standpoint that those agents will be motivated to act in keeping with—regardless of the strength of the motivation thus provided.

These two points reinforce each other: mere recognition of the need to correct for the lack of vividness might not be capable of providing sufficient motivation to enable the agent to overcome the entire natural bias; and, at any rate, correcting for the lack of vividness may not actually enjoin overcoming the entire bias in the first place. Therefore—the moderate concludes—the objection is as plausible, or even more so, when we appropriately focus on agents who lack vivid beliefs: even when the significance of vividness is taken into account, there will still be cases in which agents cannot be motivated to sacrifice their interests despite the fact that such a sacrifice is supported by the balance of reasons. Since the motivational underpinning necessary for the requirement to promote the good will be missing, morality will have to grant options.

It is well worth noting how comparatively little the moderate will have won even if these objections are sound. The size of the options which a moral system must grant will be a reflection of the size of the motivational bias which the agent cannot be moved to overcome. When the moderate first presented his argument that a moral system must minimally reflect the nature of persons, it was plausible to believe that the motivational bias was quite large, and so options would have to be rather significant. But despite the large natural bias, consideration of the importance of vivid beliefs suggested that agents are capable of being motivated to overcome that bias. Now even if the moderate's current objections are correct, and agents have inadequate motivation to overcome their natural bias completely, the untouched remnant is probably fairly small—at least, in relation to the original bias. For it surely seems plausible to suggest that agents would come considerably *closer* to the objective standpoint if their beliefs were vivid; and recognition of this fact, I believe, *can* be a relatively powerful source of motivation. Thus even if there would be a residual bias, it would probably be substantially less than the natural bias. Accordingly, it seems likely that the options which are necessary for minimally reflecting the bias would be rather insignificant in comparison to the options embraced by ordinary morality. The options would have relatively low thresholds and would give the agent only a modest amount of room in which she could permissibly favor her interests. Given the rather sweeping options which moderates typically like to claim, the victory over the extremist would be of little practical effect: morality would still be vastly more demanding than most people care to recognize.

Nonetheless, if the moderate's objections are sound, technically it would still be a victory over the extremist. However modest the options might be, they would still offer *some* relief from the otherwise relentless pursuit of the good. Moral systems which included a general requirement to promote the good would have to be rejected as unacceptable. Therefore it is worth asking if the moderate is correct when he suggests that even when the importance of vividness is taken into account, a residual bias will remain that the agent cannot be motivated to overcome.

Now the moderate gave two reasons for accepting this claim: first, he suggested that the counterfactual thesis may well be false; and second, he suggested that recognition of the need to correct for the lack of vivid beliefs may not itself provide a sufficiently powerful motive. It will be helpful if, for the time being, we put aside the second of these two points (we can return to it after discussing the first). Let us temporarily assume, then, that the second point can be adequately answered, and agents can be sufficiently motivated to react as they *would* react if their beliefs were vivid. We still need to know, obviously, whether the moderate is right to reject the counterfactual thesis. We need to ask whether the moderate is correct when he suggests that some bias would remain even if all of the agent's beliefs were vivid.

Both sides, I think, will have to admit that the evidence offered simply does not settle the question. On behalf of the moderate, it can be noted that the various pieces of evidence which the extremist adduced in support of his thesis only represent cases where agents undertake *some* sacrifice of their interests as a result of their beliefs becoming more vivid. There are (probably?) no cases where the agent comes anywhere near assuming a completely objective standpoint and maintaining it. This fits well with the moderate's suggestion that bias would remain even if beliefs were vivid. On behalf of the extremist, however, it can be noted that there are (probably?) no cases where the agent's beliefs about the interests of many others are nearly as vivid as his beliefs about his own interests, or where such uniform vividness is maintained for any appreciable period of time. It is to be expected, then, that agents will generally fall quite short of assuming and maintaining the objective standpoint. Thus the evidence is compatible with the extremist's suggestion that *if*—what is never the case—the agent's beliefs *were* vivid, he would tend to act in keeping with the objective standpoint.

The evidence does not decisively support either hypothesis against the other. Both moderate and extremist have plausible suggestions about the ultimate effect of vivid belief. On the one hand, I think that this means the moderate must recognize that the extremist's thesis is a reasonable hypothesis; and this in turn means that despite the moderate's negative argument the requirement to promote the good cannot be rejected on the grounds that it is clearly unacceptable. (At least this is so if, as we are temporarily assuming, agents can in fact be adequately motivated to react as they would react were their beliefs vivid.) But on the other hand, I think it also means that the extremist must recognize that the moderate's thesis is a reasonable hypothesis as well. And this seems to imply, given the negative argument, that the extremist must admit that systems with options (at least, weak ones) may be an appropriate response to the nature of persons; in some cases, at least, the pro tanto reason to promote the good may fail to meet the motivational condition for moral decisiveness, and so fail to ground a requirement. Apparently, then, each side must recognize that the other can be grounded in a reasonable appraisal of the facts. For the moderate, at least, such an acknowledgment of legitimacy from the extremist may be sufficient.

Perhaps, however, the extremist can push his attack on the negative argument even further.

It may be helpful, though—before we allow the extremist to renew the attack—to review where the discussion has brought us so far. According to the moderate's negative argument, there can be no general requirement to promote the good, for agents are incapable of recognizing the existence of reasons sufficiently compelling to enable them to overcome their natural bias in favor of their own interests. The strategy of the extremist's response has been to argue that agents *are* capable of being motivated to overcome their natural bias; for agents are capable of recognizing that pale beliefs are a cognitive shortcoming whose effects should be minimized. The extremist has suggested, plausibly, that trying to correct for the effects of pale belief is tantamount to trying to act in accordance with the objective standpoint: were all our beliefs vivid, no bias would remain. But the moderate has replied, equally plausibly, that even *with* vivid belief a residual bias would remain, and that the presence of such a residual bias is all the more likely in agents whose beliefs are not, in fact, vivid. If this is so, the moderate argues, an acceptable moral system will have to grant (weak) options.

The moderate, of course, is making a significant concession when he agrees that an agent would be able to overcome even the bulk of his natural bias. Obviously, however, there is still an important difference between the extremist and the moderate. The extremist claims that agents have sufficiently compelling reason to overcome their *entire* bias. But the moderate insists that even if much of the bias would be eliminated if beliefs were vivid, a residual bias—a final portion—would remain. It will be helpful to have a name for this contested portion of the bias: let us call it the *core* of the bias. The extremist claims that agents can be motivated to overcome even the core of the bias; and it is just this which the moderate denies.

Now the extremist, I think, will have to admit that the status of the core of the bias is still unsettled. The discussion of vividness was unable to establish the truth of the the extremist's counterfactual thesis. Furthermore, there remains the point that we previously put aside—the moderate's claim that even if the counterfactual thesis were true, mere recognition of this fact might not provide sufficient motivation to those agents whose beliefs are not actually vivid to enable them to overcome their entire bias. The moderate argues that for those agents who are merely motivated to try to correct for their lack of vivid belief, it is all the more plausible to hold that a final portion of the bias—a core of the bias—would remain. In this regard as well, I think, the extremist will have to admit that the discussion of vividness has left open the status of the core of the bias.

These are, of course, serious concessions. But the extremist can grant all of this, I think, without necessarily conceding the legitimacy of options. Although the discussion of vividness has failed to establish the extremist's claim that even the core of the bias can be overcome, there may be other considerations on behalf of that claim that the extremist can offer as well.

One way that the extremist might try to strengthen his claim that even the core of the bias can be overcome would be to identify further factors that can influence an agent's ability to appreciate—and hence be moved by—the various reasons that support a given reaction. The present discussion has, in effect, stressed the significance of two factors: the possession of (correct) beliefs about the relevant facts, and the vividness of those beliefs. It seems clear, however, that in a fuller account of deliberation other conditions necessary for the proper appreciation of reasons would be identified as well. Some of these would be straightforwardly cognitive, such as the need to attend to the relevant reasons. Other factors might be less clearly cognitive in nature. For example, such an account might also stress the need to eliminate various distorting influences, arising from certain passions, prejudices, and the like.[11]

Armed with a more adequate list of these conditions, the extremist might argue for an expanded version of his counterfactual: he might admit, on the one hand, that if the agent only meets some of these conditions, he will fall short of conformity to the objective standpoint; but he might also insist, on the other hand, that were the agent to meet *all* of the various ideal conditions—vividness, full information, attention, freedom from prejudice, and so on—even the core of the bias would be overcome. Furthermore, given a more adequate account of the ideal nature of these various conditions, the extremist might be more successful in establishing the strength of their motivational attractiveness even to those who do not themselves meet all of these conditions; that is, the extremist might be better able to support his claim that the very recognition of the truth of the counterfactual can itself provide motivation to agents who do not meet some of the conditions—motivation potentially sufficient to enable them to overcome even the core of their natural bias.

---

[11] Conceivably, once we correct for some of these noncognitive disturbing influences, even sadists and the like might come to be appropriately moved by vivid awareness of the interests of others. So a general requirement to promote the good might be universally binding after all. But I will not argue the case.

Now I am, in fact, inclined to think that an argument along these lines holds out a fair promise of success. Of course, until we are actually given this fuller and more adequate theory of practical deliberation, the moderate can hardly be faulted if he remains unconvinced of the extremist's prediction that the completed theory would indeed support the claim that even the core of the bias can be overcome. Unfortunately, however, providing the desired theory would obviously be a tremendously complex and controversial task. I will not attempt to undertake that task here.

Instead, I want to pursue a different line of argument. Rather than introducing new elements into an already complex discussion, I want to reconsider whether the extremist can construct an answer to the negative argument from pieces already on the table. To do this, however, we will have to reapproach the question of the core of the bias from a slightly different angle.

OVERCOMING THE BIAS

To meet the negative argument completely, the extremist must argue that the agent is capable of appreciating reasons sufficiently compelling to enable her to overcome even the core of the bias. It may be helpful if we separate the substance of what the extremist must show into two components. First, he must establish the existence of a reason to overcome the core of the bias. Second, he must show that this reason is sufficiently compelling to provide adequate motivation. If the extremist can indeed successfully perform both of these tasks, he will have refuted the negative argument.

As a first step, then, the extremist must claim that agents have reason to overcome their entire bias. Can he indicate such a reason? I believe so. I think the extremist can plausibly point to the pro tanto reason to promote the good. To see why this is so, let us consider the moderate's position once again. According to the moderate, an agent motivated to correct for her lack of vivid beliefs would still retain the core of her bias, even if much of the natural bias would be eliminated. Imagine such an agent: she will frequently sacrifice her own interests for the greater good—but not always. For example, she may avoid taking on the sacrifice if the overall gain in objective good is slight—for this will be a reflection of the remaining bias. Similarly, she may avoid overwhelming sacrifice of her own interests—for this too may be an expression of the residual bias.

Nonetheless, the moderate thinks that there is *some* reason for the agent to sacrifice her interests, even in these cases. (Indeed, moderates generally think that it would be *meritorious* for the agent to take on such sacrifices.) For the agent would be making the sacrifice for the sake of the greater good, and as we have seen, the moderate is himself committed to accepting the pro tanto reason to promote the good. (The moderate cannot deny the existence of this reason without ruling out the possibility of various judgments that he wants to make.) Thus, if the agent decides to act in accordance with the objective standpoint, even in those cases where the core of the bias comes into play, she is not acting without good reason. The moderate must admit, that is, that the agent *has* a reason to act in accordance with the objective standpoint: promoting the good.

But if the agent has a reason to act in accordance with the objective standpoint, then she has a reason to overcome her natural bias to favor her own interests—including the core of that bias. That is, she has reason to overcome not just the bulk of the bias, but the entire bias. The same is true even for those agents who choose not to sacrifice their interests in those cases where this is an expression of the core of the bias. Here too the moderate must accept that agents nonetheless have *a* reason to overcome their entire bias: the pro tanto reason to promote the good.

This argument must not be misunderstood as begging the question against the moderate. It is, rather, an attempt to spell out part of what the moderate himself must be committed to. All that the extremist has urged so far is that the moderate must admit that the agent has *some* reason to act in accordance with the objective standpoint—namely, the pro tanto reason to promote the good. Believing in options, of course, the moderate must also believe that typically this reason is not morally decisive. But for the extremist's present purposes, the point is simply that the moderate evidently must admit that there *is* a reason to act in accord with the objective standpoint.

In short, the moderate himself seems forced to acknowledge that agents are capable of recognizing the existence of a reason to overcome their natural bias in favor of their own interests. And, as we know, showing the existence of such a reason was the first of only two steps that the extremist had to take to refute the negative argument. But this means that if the moderate is to preserve that argument it seems he must block the second of the two steps. That is, he must claim that this reason is not always sufficiently *compelling* to enable agents to overcome the entire bias. Thus the motivational underpinning necessary for a requirement to promote the good will still be lacking.

I can think of two ways that the moderate might try to support his claim. First, he might insist that even though agents are capable of recognizing the existence of the pro tanto reason to promote the good, this reason itself is not *sufficiently* compelling for most agents to enable them to overcome the core of the bias. Second, he might suggest that the force of the pro tanto reason to promote the good is countered in part by considerations which support *maintaining* the core of the bias—so that *on balance* agents will not always be presented with sufficiently compelling reasons to motivate them to sacrifice their interests. Let's consider each possibility.

The moderate might suggest that it will be relatively difficult to overcome the core of the bias. That is, he might suggest that the last remnant of the bias will be the hardest to remove, and so a fairly powerful reason for doing so would have to be indicated; and the moderate needn't concede that the pro tanto reason to promote the good has *that* kind of motivating force. Perhaps for some agents it will have greater force—and these agents will obviously be justified if they act on it. But not *all* agents will find the reason sufficiently forceful to enable them to overcome the core of the bias. And so there can be no general *requirement* to promote the good.

It is easy to be misled by misanalogies here, however. In considering the moderate's suggestion that the core of the bias will be extremely difficult to overcome, we are apt to imagine, e.g., an authoritarian government striving to strip its protesting citizens of the very last of their possessions. In such a situation, perhaps, it would not be implausible to suspect that the citizens' greatest resistance might be offered in defense of the last few shreds. And they would correctly feel that they were being wronged. But the extremist is talking about an altogether different situation. Here, if agents sacrifice the greater part of their interests, it is *freely* done, either because they vividly appreciate and therefore directly respond to the needs of others, or else—indirectly responding to those needs—because they recognize the importance of compensating for the lack of such vivid appreciation. It does not seem implausible for the extremist to suggest that even the last part of the bias could eventually be overcome if agents came to appreciate a reason for taking that last step.

Suppose, however, that the moderate is correct, and it would take a significant effort to overcome the core of the bias. Suppose, in fact, that the moderate is correct when he claims that agents will typically *lack* sufficient motivation to enable them to overcome the core of the bias. Even if this is so, the extremist can still note that all agents are able to *try*. They may lack sufficient motivation to actually overcome the entire bias, but they will possess the motive to try to do so.

It needs to be recalled, once again, that the negative argument does not itself challenge the extremist's claim that the balance of reasons supports promotion of the overall good. The idea, rather, was that even if the extremist was right about the balance of reasons, and even if an essentially negative attitude toward the personal point of view was appropriate, it still remained the case that certain concessions had to be made to the nature of persons. But we need to consider more carefully the implications of adopting such a negative attitude toward the nature of persons.

The difficulty of overcoming the core of the bias pulls the agent toward acquiescence—but it is a pull with a peculiarly unstable motivational status. For although the core of the bias is a barrier to promoting the good, it is—at least within the confines of the negative argument—one without any justificatory weight in its own right. Considered on its own it is, at best, a neutral source of resistance to certain sorts of reactions. Therefore, once the agent recognizes any motivating reason for opposing the bias—and this much, it seems, is provided by the pro tanto reason to promote the good—it appears that there is motivation for him to do so so far as he is able—unless he recognizes a positive reason for *endorsing* the bias. That is, in the absence of any reason to consider the bias a source of positive value, it is simply a hindrance, nothing more. The agent's motivation may not be adequate to enable him to overcome this barrier—or so the moderate claims—but he will nonetheless have a motive to *try* to overcome the barrier.

At this point, however, the moderate might object that it is illegitimate to assume that the pro tanto reason to promote the good will necessarily have even this much motivational force. That is, in cases involving the core of the bias, the moderate might claim that recognition of the pro tanto reason to promote the good will not even be sufficient to motivate the agent to *try* to overcome the bias. In such cases—or, at least, some such cases—the pro tanto reason to promote the good will simply have no motivational force whatsoever.

It is important to see that there is nothing inconsistent in the moderate's taking this position. I argued in Chapters 1 and 2 that the moderate is committed to the *existence* of the pro tanto reason to promote the good; that is, the fact that a given reaction would promote the overall good always provides *some* reason for reacting in that way. But, so far as I can see, nothing in those arguments committed the moderate to any particular position concerning the motivational force of that reason. In principle, that is, it would have been compatible with those earlier arguments—although, of course, quite implausible—for the moderate to hold that the pro tanto reason to promote the good never has any motivational force whatsoever. Similarly, then, it is open to the moderate to hold the less extreme position that although the pro tanto reason to promote the good often has motivational force, it has none at all in cases involving the core of the bias.

Nor is this position rendered incoherent by the moderate's embrace of the motivational condition on moral decisiveness. To accept this condition is to hold that a reason cannot ground a requirement unless it is capable of moving the agent. Obviously enough, this suggests (although, strictly, it does not entail) that, in at least some situations, some perfectly genuine reasons will lack adequate motivational efficacy. It is, then, quite compatible with this for the moderate to hold that in some cases there is indeed reason to promote the good, but this reason has no motivational force at all.

Of course, one might offer a further motivational condition—not a condition on being morally decisive, but rather a condition on being a genuine *reason*. That is, one might argue that a genuine reason for action must possess at least some motivational force in any situation in which the reason exists (although this force may be overridden by that of opposing reasons, and so on). Clearly, if the moderate were to adopt this new motivational condition, something else would have to give: the moderate would either have to retract his acceptance of the claim that there is always some reason to promote the good (endangering some of the judgments of ordinary morality), or he would have to admit that the pro tanto reason to promote the good does have some motivational force even in cases involving the core of the bias (endangering the negative argument). However, so far as I can see, nothing in the moderate's position requires him to accept this motivational condition on being a reason; all he needs for the negative argument is the logically distinct motivational condition on moral decisiveness. Thus, logically speaking, the moderate can consistently continue to embrace the pro tanto reason to promote the good, while claiming that in some cases this reason has no motivational force at all.

Nonetheless, even though there is nothing *inconsistent* in the moderate's taking this position, it seems rather implausible. For as I have noted, within the confines of the negative argument the core of the bias must be viewed by the agent as a regrettable *barrier*— hindering action in accordance with what the agent himself recognizes to be the balance of reasons. All that the extremist is claiming is that once the agent comes to see that this is the correct way to view the situation, the agent is capable of being moved to try to overcome that barrier. This is an extremely modest claim. The agent need not succeed, he need only try. Indeed, he need not even try: it suffices that the agent is *capable* of being moved to try. To reject this claim, then, the moderate has to hold that even if the agent were to view the core of the bias in this way as an unfortunate hindrance, he would be utterly incapable of being moved to so much as try to overcome this barrier. It is difficult to see how the moderate could hope to defend this position—or that he would want to.

It seems, then, that the moderate will have to admit that the pro tanto reason to promote the good is capable of moving the agent to try to overcome the barrier. And on the face of it, at least, this seems to satisfy the motivational condition necessary for moral decisiveness. But if the motivational condition has indeed been met, then the extremist has succeeded in answering the negative argument: despite the natural bias in favor of our interests, the general requirement to promote the good apparently possesses the necessary motivational underpinning.

The moderate, of course, may yet again try to refine his formulation of the motivational condition. He may claim that for there to be a genuine moral requirement to react in a given way, the agent must be capable of being motivated to *react* in that way; it is not sufficient for the agent to be motivated to *try* to react in that way. If this is correct (and I shall, once more, avoid evaluating these claims concerning the motivational condition), then it is not sufficient for the extremist to have demonstrated the existence of a motive to try to overcome the core of the bias. There can be no requirement to promote the good when this involves overcoming the core of the bias, for such a requirement will in fact still lack the necessary motivational underpinning.

This last position, however, should bring the moderate no comfort. The extremist can reply that even if there can be no requirement to promote the good when this involves the core of the bias, there can still be a requirement to *try* to promote the good—to try to overcome the core of the bias. This will, perhaps, involve 'options' of a peculiar, feeble sort: an agent who fails to sacrifice his interests for the sake of the greater good will not fail to meet the moral requirement—provided that he was utterly unable to muster within himself sufficient motivation, although he tried as best he could. I do not think the extremist needs to be bothered much by such a 'concession'.

Admittedly, there would be no straightforward general requirement to promote the good. There would, however, be a general requirement that (a) in cases not involving the core of the bias, one should promote the good, and (b) in cases that do involve the core of the bias, one should *try* to promote the good. Less awkwardly, we might speak of a general requirement to (try to) promote the good. Indeed, I do not think it would be seriously misleading if we dropped the notational reminder altogether and continued to refer to a general requirement to promote the good, simpliciter. For it might plausibly be suggested that a moral system which includes a requirement to promote the good can recognize that agents may be psychologically incapable of adopting a totally objective standpoint— so long as it is reasonable for agents to strive to come as close to this standpoint as they are able. But however we resolve the issue of nomenclature, I think that such a requirement is likely to satisfy the extremist.

The moderate, on the other hand, will hardly find this a satisfactory position. If he is to maintain anything like ordinary options he must claim that agents are not even required to *try* to promote the good. And if this claim is to be based on the negative argument, the moderate must, of course, show that agents lack the corresponding motivation. That is, he must argue that agents do not even have motive to *try* to overcome the core of the bias. But the presence of such a motive seemed secure—given the pro tanto reason to promote the good—in the absence of any reason to view the bias as anything more than an unfortunate hindrance. Thus what the moderate must argue is that there are positive reasons for endorsing the bias after all.

It seems, then, that the moderate's response must be that the extremist has overlooked the existence of reasons for maintaining the core of the bias. If the moderate can demonstrate the existence of such reasons, then it may be that on balance the agent does *not* have sufficient reason to try to overcome his bias—contrary to the extremist's suggestion.

But this means that the extremist has succeeded in shifting the burden of proof. Apparently, unless the moderate can indicate reasons for endorsing the core of the bias, he must abandon the charge that the requirement to promote the good lacks the necessary motivational underpinning. (Some may prefer to say that, strictly speaking, the moderate *has* in fact shown that the requirement to promote the good may lack the necessary motivational underpinning—but what the moderate has not shown is any corresponding shortcoming in the requirement to (try to) promote the good. But I'll stick to the easier formulation.) However, if the moderate *can* demonstrate the existence of reasons for maintaining the bias, then the requirement to promote the good may yet be unacceptable. After all, the extremist can only offer the pro tanto reason to promote the good as a relevant consideration—one which supports trying to overcome the core of the bias. The moderate can concede that this is indeed a consideration which favors overcoming the bias—but insist that there are other, greater considerations which favor maintaining the bias. By indicating these opposing considerations the moderate hopes to defend his suggestion that the agent lacks sufficient motivation—all things considered—for trying to overcome the core of the bias.

Upon reflection, furthermore, it seems clear that the same sort of answer may be available to the moderate for the *entire* natural bias. The examination of vividness yielded a motive for agents to overcome a significant portion (at least) of their natural bias. But the extremist offered no argument that this stance was unopposed by *other* considerations. Thus the moderate might concede the existence of the pro tanto reason based on vividness for trying to overcome the natural bias, and yet still suggest that there are reasons for maintaining the bias such that, all things considered, the agent lacks sufficient motive for trying to overcome it at all. Considerations which tend to support maintaining the core of the bias—if there are any—may also tend to support maintaining the entire natural bias.

If they are significant enough, then it may be that despite the claims of vividness the agent does not have overall general motive to try to overcome even the bulk of his natural bias. Indeed, if the moderate can show that the balance of reasons actually supports maintaining the bias, this would further call into question the extremist's counterfactual thesis altogether. With vivid beliefs, agents are more inclined to give reasons their due weight; but if the balance of reasons actually supports maintaining the bias, it becomes implausible to claim that an agent with vivid beliefs would come anywhere close to conforming to the objective standpoint. (And even if the counterfactual were true, agents would have to discount it as being an inaccurate guide to the balance of reasons.) Consequently, agents trying to correct for their lack of vivid beliefs will not find themselves with a motive for trying to act in keeping with the objective standpoint. So if the moderate can point to significant enough reasons for maintaining the natural bias, the agent may largely lack motivation to overcome the bulk of that bias—or even to try. Thus the moderate's negative argument would return in full force and an acceptable moral system would have to grant a significant range of options.

What this suggests is that ultimately the negative argument must turn into the positive argument, which we earlier set aside for the next chapter. Demonstrating that there are powerful considerations in overall support of maintaining the bias—and this is what is necessary to shore up the negative argument—will basically amount to demonstrating that it is desirable overall that we tend to follow our subjective points of view—and this is the backbone of the positive argument. That is, it turns out that in order to defend the negative argument's claim that agents are incapable of recognizing sufficiently compelling reasons for overcoming their bias, one must defend the bolder claim of the positive argument that a positive attitude toward our biases is appropriate. For if such a positive attitude is *not* appropriate, agents will be able to recognize that on balance they should try to *overcome* the bias. But if the positive attitude is appropriate, then the considerations which support adopting a totally objective standpoint will be on balance uncompelling.

Thus, unless the moderate can offer reasons for endorsing the agent's bias, the extremist will have succeeded in countering even the more modest, negative argument—and the defense of options will be undercut. On the other hand, if the moderate *can* offer reasons for endorsing the agent's bias, then the more ambitious, positive argument will be available. And as I suggested at the start of this chapter, of the two arguments, the positive is more far-reaching in its implications. It is time, therefore, to examine it more carefully.

9

The Positive Argument

At the start of the last chapter I noted two ways the moderate might try to base a defense of options on the nature of persons. First, the moderate might argue that a system which lacks options fails to minimally reflect the nature of persons. Since minimal reflection of the nature of persons is a condition of adequacy, a system without options would be shown to be unacceptable. Second, the moderate might argue that it is in fact full reflection of the nature of persons which is appropriate for a moral system. Since systems without options admittedly fail to reflect the nature of persons fully, this too would show the unacceptability of a requirement to promote the good.

For the purposes of the first argument, the moderate was willing to adopt an essentially negative attitude toward the nature of persons. The moderate himself need not actually have held such an attitude; it was adopted simply to show that certain features of a moral theory are unavoidable: even if the motivational bias toward an agent's interests is something to be pandered to as little as possible; even if concessions to it are to be made only where necessary. If successful, the negative argument would have shown that even minimally reflecting the nature of persons places restrictions on a moral theory—restrictions which rule out the requirement to promote the good.

But the negative argument was not successful. For the extremist was able to point to the existence of motivating reasons for the agent to try (at least) to overcome his bias so as to act in keeping with the objective standpoint. Since the agent is able to recognize and be moved by these reasons, it seemed that the requirement to promote the good might possess the necessary motivational underpinning after all. As I noted at the end of the last chapter, the only way for the moderate to preserve the impact of his argument would be for him to claim that there are considerations which support maintaining the subjective point of view—considerations powerful enough to undermine the extremist's suggestion that on balance the agent is presented with sufficiently compelling reasons to promote the good. If the moderate can point to such considerations, then the requirement to promote the good will not possess the necessary motivational underpinning and will have to be rejected. By indicating reasons for endorsing the subjective standpoint, the moderate's argument would of course be abandoning the negative attitude toward the nature of persons which it had initially adopted, but it would still be claiming that systems without options fail to minimally reflect the nature of persons.

If the moderate can point to such positive considerations for endorsing the subjective standpoint, however, then he will have done more than merely salvage his first argument: he will also have provided the basis for offering the second argument—the positive argument. All along, the moderate may well have felt that a negative attitude toward the nature of persons was inappropriate. If he is able to support this view forcefully enough then it may follow that it is inappropriate for a moral system to limit itself to minimal reflection of the nature of persons; rather, it may be desirable for moral systems to reflect the nature of persons *fully*. After all, the moderate might argue, we do not consider it a flaw—something to be put up with—that we tend to act in keeping with our subjective points of view. Instead, the fact that persons are engaged in their subjective standpoints adds to the distinctive value and quality of our lives. This suggests that it is inappropriate for a moral system to try to disregard and circumvent the nature of persons so far as this is possible. Instead, it is fitting for a moral system which is to govern the conduct of persons to attempt to reflect the nature of persons fully—integrating, where feasible, features which are in harmony with the existence of subjective points of view. And one such feature is the inclusion of options.

Before we turn to see whether the moderate can actually justify such a positive attitude toward the nature of persons, let us consider the character and implications of the second argument more carefully. We can begin somewhat intuitively. The positive argument gives the nature of persons a pride of place which it has not previously had. In the negative argument, the person's natural bias in favor of his interests was viewed as an encumbrance which hinders morality from achieving goals which are independently set. But in the positive argument, the nature of persons itself largely forms the ends of morality. The argument stresses the desirability of adopting features which are in harmony with the nature of persons; rather than belittling the agent's engagement with the subjective point of view, and asking him to strive to overcome his natural bias, the features of morality should try to enhance the agent's ability to act in accordance with his nature.

This means that it is desirable for moral systems to give agents room to favor their interests—in keeping with the priorities of their subjective points of view. The negative argument entertained the suggestion that morality should require as much as it possibly can by way of promoting the good; it merely insisted that there was a limit to how much can be required. But on the present suggestion, morality should strive to avoid—as far as this is feasible—the undesirable feature of requiring agents to act contrary to their points of view by sacrificing their interests. There may or may not be reasons stemming from the nature of persons itself for requiring certain reactions. But as far as the general, externally grounded pursuit of the objective good is concerned, morality should require as little as it can—no more than is necessary.

By granting options, a moral system more fully reflects the nature of persons—and this is a desirable characteristic in a moral system. In contrast, systems which lack options needlessly restrict the agent's ability to favor his interests. They fail to reflect the nature of persons as fully as they might—and this marks them as inadequate.

The positive argument might be summarized in this way: morality shouldn't require promotion of the good unless it must; and it needn't.

In terms of our framework of morally decisive reasons, the positive argument can be understood as follows. If the appropriate attitude toward the nature of persons is a positive one, this implies that there are reasons for endorsing the subjective point of view. (To be sure, the positive value of the nature of persons may very well imply more than this; but it certainly implies at least this much.) Now as we have seen, from the subjective standpoint an agent is inclined to give greater weight to his own interests than those interests might merit from the objective point of view. But if the fact that persons are engaged in their subjective standpoints possesses a kind of moral value in its own right, then there are reasons for the agent to act in keeping with his subjective point of view. That is, there are reasons for the given agent to promote his interests—in keeping with the greater weight they possess from the subjective standpoint—beyond the level indicated solely by the objective importance of those interests.

On this view, then, there are special *subjective* reasons for a given agent to pursue his interests. Obviously, calling these reasons 'subjective' is not meant to imply that they are in any way illusory or morally illegitimate. Rather, it brings out the fact that these reasons are directly grounded in the subjective standpoint and thereby differ from reasons based solely on considerations of objective value. Indeed, it should be helpful to note some further contrasts between these subjective reasons and the pro tanto reason to promote the good.

Note, first of all, that these special subjective reasons go *beyond* the pro tanto reason to promote the good. They give the agent greater reason to promote his interests than would be yielded strictly on the basis of the objective importance of those interests. They are, in effect, additional reasons that an agent has for promoting his interests. Second, these subjective reasons are agent-relative. Each agent has a reason to promote *his* interests; he does not have similar reason to promote the interests of others (i.e., others in whom he does not independently take an interest). Of course, each person does have *some* reason to promote the interests of others: the pro tanto reason to promote the good. Since that reason—an objective reason—is generated for all agents, regardless of their particular interests, it is an agent-neutral one. But the subjective reasons we are now considering give each agent further reason to promote his *own* interests (whatever they may be) as distinct from the interests of others. Thus, for any given agent and any given state of affairs, whether that agent has one of these further reasons for promoting that state of affairs will depend on the interests of the particular agent. The obtaining of specific reasons of this sort will therefore vary from individual to individual; such reasons are, in short, agent-relative.

Note, finally, that these subjective, agent-relative reasons can easily *oppose* the pro tanto reason to promote the good. For these reasons support the agent's pursuit of his interests, while in a good many cases the promotion of the overall objective good will involve, in contrast, the agent's sacrifice of his interests. If, in cases involving such a conflict between the two kinds of reasons, the subjective reasons are weighty enough, then the pro tanto reason to promote the good may be unable to outweigh them. And since one condition necessary for moral decisiveness is that the given reason outweigh any opposing reasons, in such cases the pro tanto reason to promote the good will be unable to ground a requirement. In short, in cases where promotion of the good would involve a significant sacrifice of interests, this fact will generate counter-vailing reasons that prevent the pro tanto reason to promote the good from grounding such a requirement.

It may be worth repeating the point that there is nothing at all morally illegitimate about these subjective reasons. Despite their differences from the pro tanto reason to promote the good, they have genuine and legitimate weight, morally speaking. Or at least, this will have to be so if they are going to suit the moderate's purposes. For unless these subjective reasons are themselves morally acceptable, the pro tanto reason to promote the good will still outweigh any opposing reasons that are morally relevant, and so it may still be *morally* decisive—grounding a moral require-ment.[1] Since he wants to deny that there is any general moral requirement to promote the good, when the moderate argues that the subjective standpoint is of positive value in its own right the claim must be that it is of positive *moral* value. This is not to say, however, that the character of the subjective reasons we have been describing must be distinctively or especially moral, in some sense; it is only to say that these reasons must be morally acceptable ones, relevant in moral deliberation.

The suggestion, then, is that the appeal to cost works through the generation of such subjective reasons—morally acceptable counter-vailing reasons that can oppose the pro tanto reason to promote the good. Of course, the theoretical possibility of an account along these lines is something that we have noted more than once. Since

---

[1] Wouldn't it suffice if the subjective reasons were genuine reasons for action— even if they were morally unacceptable reasons? After all, this might suffice to make it *rationally* permissible not to promote the good (or perhaps: permissible all things considered). On such a position, however, although it might be rationally acceptable to pursue one's interests rather than the overall good—doing so would still be *morally forbidden*. Clearly, this is not the position of ordinary morality. Thus, if he is to defend options *within* morality, the moderate must claim that the subjective reasons are morally acceptable ones.

the appeal to cost—if it is to be successful—must yield counter-vailing considerations of some sort, one straightforward possibility has always been that it would work by creating such countervailing reasons. But what's more, some such account is likely to strike most moderates as extremely plausible in its own right. There is surely considerable intuitive support for the claim that a given agent's interests provide him with morally legitimate reasons (not provided to others) for promoting those particular interests, even at possible cost to the greater good overall. As usual, I do not take such intuitive support as an adequate defense of the view in question; but it reinforces the thought that the possibility of such an account is worth pursuing.

Of course, if the appeal to cost does generate such countervailing reasons, there is also a second way in which the pro tanto reason to promote the good will often fail to be morally decisive: it will frequently lack the motivational underpinning necessary for grounding a moral requirement. After all, the extremist's response to the negative argument was that, in the absence of reasons for endorsing the agent's natural bias in favor of his interests, the agent will in fact have motivation to (try to) overcome that bias. Yet if the agent's bias is no longer to be viewed as a mere hindrance, but rather as something genuinely supported by weighty, morally legitimate reasons, there is no longer any ground for assuming that—on balance—the agent will typically have motive even to *try* to overcome the bias. In this way, as we have seen, the positive argument allows the moderate to salvage the negative argument. But of course it also renders it superfluous, since the fact that the pro tanto reason to promote the good is unable to outweigh the countervailing reasons is by itself sufficient to prevent the gener-ation of a general requirement.

If, then, the appeal to cost can generate countervailing reasons of the kind we have been describing there will be no general requirement to promote the good. Of course the moderate does not believe that there are no requirements at all; in various cases some reason will manage to overcome (or escape) the countervailing considerations that may arise from the appeal to cost, and will ground a requirement. These exceptional cases are familiar: for example, agents are required to conform to constraints even though they may not want to; presumably the reasons grounding constraints are sufficient to outweigh the countervailing reasons grounded by the appeal to cost. Similarly, agents are required to make some few minor sacrifices in situations where a great deal depends on it (e.g., the drowning child); presumably, when a great deal of good is at stake, and the cost to the agent is slight, the pro tanto reason to promote the good will be able to outweigh the relatively weak countervailing reasons. But, on the other hand, when the cost to the agent is more significant, the countervailing reasons will presumably be sufficiently weighty so that the pro tanto reason to promote the good will be unable to outweigh them; and this will yield an option to allow harm. Thus the moderate still leaves the agent a tremendous amount of room in which he may favor his interests.

We still have not examined whether the moderate can actually defend the positive attitude toward the nature of persons upon which his entire argument depends. But I want to postpone this question for a bit longer, and assume for the time being that he can. For the most important difference between the negative argument and the positive argument has not yet been discussed. Indeed, up to this point it still seems that the differences between the two arguments are mainly matters of tone and detail. The two arguments concentrate on different particular conditions, but they seem to have the same upshot—i.e., that the pro tanto reason to promote the good frequently fails to meet some condition or the other necessary for moral decisiveness, and thus cannot ground a general requirement. I have claimed, of course, that the negative argument fails unless the moderate can indicate reasons for endorsing the subjective point of view. Yet if the moderate *can* indicate such reasons, then a refurbished 'negative' argument appears to be sufficient to ground options. It may seem, therefore, that the moderate gains nothing by moving beyond such an argument to the more ambitious positive argument we have been discussing.

I suggested earlier, however, that the positive argument has more far-reaching implications than the negative. As we have seen, if the positive argument is correct then an adequate moral system would fully reflect the nature of persons rather than merely minimally reflecting it. And this means that if the argument is successful it will support not only options, but constraints.

THE PATIENT'S POINT OF VIEW

Individuals assess the world with an eye not only to deciding how to react, but also to evaluating what *happens* to them. Even when they are passive recipients of benefits or harms countenanced by others, they make judgments about how they are affected, and typically these evaluations are made from the personal point of view. That is, as a recipient the individual generally does not assess what happens to him from the objective standpoint; rather, he assigns weights to his interests out of proportion to those they would receive from such an impersonal perspective. This means that his evaluations will typically reveal a presumption in favor of those interests: even though the considerations which favor his having been treated by another in a particular way may objectively outweigh the considerations which support an alternative treatment which better promotes his interests, the latter considerations will weigh more heavily for the recipient—creating a powerful presumption in their favor. Unless the recipient comes to recognize the existence of especially compelling reasons for his interests having been sacrificed, he will not *accept* the treatment which he has received as appropriate.

What this means is that the existence of the personal point of view has implications for the individual not only qua agent, but also qua patient. And if, as the positive argument suggests, it is appropriate to fully reflect the nature of persons in a moral system, then more than options are called for. Options are a response to the *agent's* point of view: they give the agent room to favor his interests, even when it may not be optimal to do so. A similar response to the *patient's* point of view is evidently in order: a feature is needed which will give the patient room to favor his interests, even when it may not be optimal to do so. That is, the patient must have the power to veto certain sorts of treatment at the hands of others, so as to protect his interests, even when such treatment is necessary to promote the good. In short, the patient must be protected by constraints. (Why does the agent recognize the veto of the patient? We shall see. It is worth bearing in mind, however, that not only must constraints—which favor the patient—be accepted by the agent, but options—which favor the agent—must themselves be accepted by the patient.)

Thus if a moral system is to fully reflect the nature of persons it not only must grant some sort of options, but must also grant some sort of constraints. It is for this reason that I suggested that the positive argument is more ambitious than the negative argument. With both arguments, of course, the moderate does in fact believe in the existence of constraints. But only in the positive argument is a motivation for constraints provided.

The negative argument asked what sorts of features are *forced* upon a moral theory by virtue of the nature of persons. Since morality is only effective if agents can be motivated to act in accord with it, it is necessary to make concessions to their motivational biases and grant options. But *constraints* are not forced upon a theory in the same way. As patients, individuals may desire room to favor their interests, but they are not in a similar position of power to force this concession from a moral system. As long as some agent is willing and able to impose some sacrifice upon another, that patient is in no position to prevent the sacrifice from being imposed. Therefore, a system which only minimally reflects the nature of persons will not need to grant constraints.

The positive argument, however, suggests that morality should *fully* reflect the nature of persons; if this is so, then it is inappropriate to stop with options. Both as agent and as patient, a person's evaluations favor his interests. If this is to be fully reflected a moral system must give the individual protected spheres in which he can guard his interests in both roles: the system must grant both options and constraints.

In its full-blown version, therefore, the positive argument comes to this. The fact that each individual is engaged in his subjective standpoint is a source of moral value in its own right; this generates reasons distinct from, and potentially in conflict with, the pro tanto reason to promote the good. As we have already seen, one such set of reasons has the effect of protecting the point of view of the agent. They give the agent reason to pursue his interests, even at the possible expense of the greater good, and they thereby yield options. However, given that individuals are engaged in their subjective standpoints not only as agents but also as patients, a further set of reasons will be generated as well. And these reasons will have the effect of protecting the point of view of the patient. When they are morally decisive, they will provide barriers to various ways of sacrificing the interests of patients.[2] Thus, such reasons will provide the foundations of constraints.

If a positive attitude toward the nature of persons is appropriate, therefore, there will actually be two kinds of subjective reasons— we might call them *agent-protecting* reasons and *patient-protecting* reasons—both of which will be capable of acting as countervailing reasons, and thus capable of preventing the pro tanto reason to promote the good from grounding a requirement. These reasons will form the basis of constraints and options. In this way, then, the positive argument seems to provide a general, unified account of constraints as well as of options. But the account is, indeed, only a general one so far. Can we say anything more specific about the particular options and constraints that might emerge from such an account?

One thing that we can say, obviously enough, is that the options and constraints must cohere. A moral system cannot offer agents an option to react in a particular way and at the same time offer patients protection through constraints against that same reaction: in such a case the agent would be both permitted and forbidden to react in the given way. So systems with incompatible options and constraints can be ruled out. Beyond this obvious restriction, however, the level of argument has been sufficiently general to leave it largely open what pattern of constraints and options is to be adopted.

Further argument would be necessary to motivate a particular system of options and constraints. And this would not be a trivial matter. To begin with, Chapters 3 and 4 showed how difficult it is merely to *describe* an acceptable constraint. But even if we leave this particular problem aside, it is not at all clear how the general argument just given is to be used to derive specific constraints and options. Although I do not want to consider the matter in great detail, two suggestions may be worth mentioning.

First, some particular systems may be preferable because of their formal properties. The positive argument supports granting individuals room to favor their interests in their capacities both as agent and as patient. But as I have just noted, a consistent system cannot

---

[2] These reasons will be agent-relative, giving each agent particular reason for concern that *he* not treat patients in certain specified ways; otherwise the claims of all patients would be equally demanding on all agents, that is, the special reasons would not actually give any patient at all protection against having his interests sacrificed for the greater good.

offer both an option to react in a given way and a constraint against being treated in that given way by others. Thus the particular combination of options and constraints will represent something of a compromise between the attempts to give protected spheres to the agent and to the patient. If reflecting the nature of persons is of great enough importance, however, we may expect, roughly, that options will expand to fill the space left by constraints, and constraints will expand to fill the spaces left by options. And the balancing process itself may get started when we recognize that certain constraints can be formally eliminated, leaving a gap where the appropriate option can be assigned instead.

For example, patients cannot be protected by a general constraint which rules out agents countenancing harm altogether. Such a constraint would be nondischargeable—for there are cases where an agent cannot avoid countenancing one harm or another. Indeed, for the same reason, there cannot be a general constraint against *allowing* harm. A constraint against harming, however, is not similarly ruled out. At best, then, patients can have general protection against being harmed. If patients are to have a significant protected sphere, therefore, something like the constraint against doing harm is to be expected. *Options* to harm will, accordingly, be ruled out. But the protected sphere for agents can expand to fill the space left unguarded by constraints; thus we may arrive at options to allow harm. In this way, it might be suggested, we reach a familiar result: options to allow harm coupled with constraints against doing harm.

But the argument just sketched would not be sufficient. For a similar argument could be developed using the intend/foresee distinction rather than the do/allow distinction. That is, one might argue (in parallel fashion) from the impossibility of a general constraint against foreseeing harm as a side-effect, to the conclusion that if there is to be a constraint it must be a constraint against intending harm, and thence to the conclusion that if there is still to be an option it can only be an option to foresee harm which is merely a side-effect. Thus it might be argued that the basic divide between constraints and options should be cast in terms of the distinction between intended and merely foreseen harm, rather than the do/allow distinction. Obviously, both the constraint against doing harm and the constraint against intending harm are formally acceptable; and less familiar constraints are available as well. So even when the need for balance between options and constraints is borne in mind, more would need to be said to justify the particular pattern adopted.

As a second possibility, it may seem plausible to suggest that the specific pattern of constraints and options should be informed by the nature of the subjective point of view. As I have already noted, any particular pattern will represent a compromise between the attempts to protect the individual's interests qua agent and qua patient. Granting a constraint protects the interests of the patient, often at the expense of the agent—and it must be reasonable to expect the agent to *accept* the particular limitations imposed by the constraint. Similarly, it must be reasonable to expect the patient to accept the particular losses which are the result of protecting the agent's interests through a given option. We might hope that more detailed examination of the subjective point of view will indicate which concessions it is reasonable to expect—thus determining an acceptable pattern of options and constraints.

For example, given that we are typically more concerned with what is near than with what is at some distance, it is normally easier to motivate agents to provide aid when they are in the presence of those in need. This suggests that agents may find it reasonable to be required by a constraint to provide aid to those nearby, recognizing also that patients would find it hardest to forgo such protection. And patients may recognize that it would be unreasonable to expect agents to provide aid to those who are distant, and may themselves find it relatively easy to grant options in such cases. We thus move toward a familiar-looking pattern.

But there are difficulties here too: given the impact of distance, we would expect not only an option to *avoid* providing aid to those who are distant, but also an option to *harm* them. Yet moderates want the constraint against harming to cover all distances. Perhaps further study of the subjective point of view will reveal why a constraint against harming is independent of distance, but an option not to aid is not. Such a study would also have to reveal whether the subjective point of view favors a constraint against intending harm, a constraint against doing harm—or some third possibility. Clearly, then, the line of argument is insufficient as it stands; but it may hold out promise for further investigation.

I do not intend to pursue the matter any further. It is obvious that it will not be easy to derive a specific system of constraints and options from the positive argument. But the implications of the argument are significant nonetheless. The moderate will have made considerable progress indeed toward justifying ordinary morality if he has succeeded in showing that the desirability of fully reflecting the nature of persons provides general grounds for both options and constraints.

GROUNDING CONSTRAINTS

Some may be sceptical, however, of whether constraints can actually be motivated in this way. If nothing else, we still have not examined whether a positive attitude toward the nature of persons is indeed appropriate. But scepticism may surface at any of several other points in the argument as well. To begin with, it might be doubted whether the value of the subjective standpoint is such as to generate reasons for protecting the patient's point of view. It seems logically possible, after all, for the sceptic to hold that although reasons are generated for protecting the agent's point of view, the complementary reasons—having to do with the patient—simply do not arise. Obviously, if the patient-protecting reasons are not even generated, they can hardly ground a constraint.

It will not do to dismiss such a sceptic with the response that if *full* reflection of the nature of persons is appropriate then the subjective standpoint must be reflected in its full impact upon the individual—i.e., with regard to its influence upon the individual both as agent and as patient. For the sceptic might retort that if *this* is what is involved in full reflection, then she sees no reason to believe that full reflection is appropriate. Endorsing a positive attitude toward the nature of persons does not logically commit one to the view that the nature of persons should be fully reflected.

The logical point should, I think, be conceded. Some sort of positive attitude toward the nature of persons might well be appropriate without it being the case that full reflection of the nature of persons is called for. More particularly, the belief that there are special reasons that support an agent's pursuit of his interests—agent-protecting reasons—does not entail that there are also special reasons that oppose treating patients in certain ways—patient-protecting reasons; the two kinds of countervailing reasons purportedly generated by the subjective standpoint are logically independent of one another. Nonetheless, it seems to me likely that if a positive attitude toward the nature of persons can indeed be defended, then *both* kinds of reasons will emerge. After all, it is not as though we only think it of value that we are engaged in our subjective standpoints as *agents*, considering it unfortunate that as *patients* we fail to adopt a more objective standpoint. Rather, it is the fact that *persons* are engaged in their subjective standpoints— both as agents and as patients—that we view as adding to the distinctive value and quality of our lives.[3]

In light of this, the sceptic might admit that full reflection is appropriate, in that the patient's point of view needs to be protected as well as that of the agent. But she might insist, nonetheless, that—contrary to what has been suggested— constraints do not actually provide such protection for the patient's bias in favor of his interests (or, at least, they are not the best way to provide such protection). In effect, patients will reject constraints, even from the subjective standpoint.

The sceptic might suggest that although the individual's desire to promote his interests does plausibly lead him to prefer a system with options, it does not give him reason to prefer a system with constraints. Indeed, she may object that it would be irrational for individuals to prefer the sort of protection of interests which constraints offer. For constraints stand in the way of promoting the good, thereby making it likely that a lower overall level of good will obtain. Thus, on the average, individuals are likely to find their interests further advanced under a system which lacks constraints than under a system which has them. This seems to suggest that far from it being the case that constraints reflect the disproportionate concern that people take in their own interests, the nature of persons would be better reflected by avoiding constraints as far as possible.

There are several things wrong with this argument, but the first thing to notice is this. If this objection were correct, it would apparently undermine not only constraints but options as well. For under a system of options agents are free to refrain from promoting the good, and this too makes it likely that a lower overall level of

---

[3] The same basic answer would be in order were the sceptic to suggest that although patient-protecting reasons are indeed generated these reasons are not morally acceptable ones (and so could not ground moral constraints): it is difficult to see why it should be of positive moral value that we are engaged in our subjective standpoints as agents but not of similar moral value that we are engaged as patients.

good will obtain. So here too individuals are likely to find, on the average, that their interests are advanced further under a system without options. Therefore options and constraints are still in the same boat, despite the sceptic's suggestion. But the question posed by the objection itself still remains: if a requirement to promote the good untempered by options or constraints will better advance the interests of individuals overall, why doesn't such a system better reflect the nature of persons?

Part of the answer, I think, lies in the fact that any given sacrifice of an individual's interests—even if it will lead to an overall increase in good—will obviously hurt that individual more than it will benefit him. Thus even though each of us has a reason to wish that on the whole people would sacrifice their interests or have them sacrificed when it would promote the good for this to happen, in any *particular* case in which *my* interests are at stake it would be better from my personal point of view if my interests were *not* sacrificed. When it is a matter of my interests being sacrificed, obviously enough, it will not be in my interests for the sacrifice to occur. And this will be reflected in my assessment of the potential sacrifice: as agent I will find it difficult to be motivated; as patient I will find it difficult to accept. Thus a system which is to fully reflect the disproportionate concern I take in my interests will have to reflect the fact that when a particular sacrifice of my interests is under consideration, from my point of view there will be a presumption against it. This presumption is reflected by a moral system incorporating options and constraints.[4]

Apparently the sceptic will have to admit that both options and constraints reflect the nature of persons. More precisely, the sceptic will have to admit that the value of the subjective standpoint will yield both kinds of countervailing reasons, that is, both agent-protecting reasons and patient-protecting reasons. But despite this admission, the sceptic may still maintain that it is only options and not constraints which can be derived from the positive argument.

---

[4] There is still a puzzle, however. Consider the possibility of voluntary mutual advancement societies. In such societies people would waive their options, and the protection of constraints, enforceably committing themselves to the promotion of the overall good of the members of the society. As long as the other members came in with similar resources and handicaps, it seems that it would be to everyone's advantage to be in such a society—at least if the enforcement were sufficiently effective. So the interesting question remains: why don't people join such societies? Some relevant considerations are to be found in Singer.

For the mere existence of reasons not to treat patients in certain ways is not in itself sufficient to ground a constraint: those reasons must also be morally decisive. And the sceptic may argue that the reasons in question actually fail to meet some condition necessary for moral decisiveness.[5]

For example, if they are to ground a constraint the given reasons must typically outweigh any opposing reasons. In particular, they must outweigh the pro tanto reason to promote the good. Therefore, the sceptic might be tempted to claim that the patient-protecting reasons are not in fact sufficiently weighty to do this. Such a claim, however, would endanger the argument for options as well. According to the positive argument, the pro tanto reason to promote the good frequently fails to be morally decisive for it often cannot outweigh the countervailing reasons that support an agent's pursuit of his interests. But these agent-protecting reasons—like the patient-protecting reasons—ultimately arise from the special value of the subjective point of view. Given their common basis, it is difficult to see why the one kind of reason should be able to outweigh the pro tanto reason to promote the good if the other kind cannot. Assuming that the sceptic wants to retain the defense of options along the lines we have been discussing, it appears that this particular objection to constraints must be withdrawn.

But there is a more refined version of the objection. The sceptic might claim that although the pro tanto reason to promote the good often cannot outweigh the various reasons arising from the subjective standpoint, nonetheless it can never be *outweighed* by them either. It seems that such a position would be sufficient to enable the countervailing reasons to ground options, but would leave them inadequate for grounding constraints. Of course it is not clear whether the sceptic could adequately defend such a position concerning the relative strengths of the various reasons. But since we still have not seen whether the countervailing reasons can be defended at all, perhaps the issue is best put aside.

There is, however, yet another version of the objection that the sceptic might raise. If a reason is to ground a constraint, it must be able to outweigh the relevant opposing reasons. But these include

[5] Such a position may be attractive to the neo-moderate. The patient-protecting reasons would be unable to ground a regular constraint, and yet still might be helpful in grounding the neo-moderate's zero threshold constraint. It should be noted, however, that the neo-moderate would have to reject some of the specific views to be suggested by the sceptic below.

more than the pro tanto reason to promote the good; often they will also include countervailing reasons arising from the appeal to cost. If the reasons that are to ground the constraint cannot override the appeal to cost, they will be unable to block unacceptably minimalist options (such as, say, an option to do harm). Now as we know, part of the moderate's very motivation for introducing constraints in the first place was to block such unacceptable options. So the moderate must claim that the reasons grounding constraints are able to override the countervailing reasons generated by the appeal to cost. But if both constraints and options are to be derived from the positive argument it is far from clear how such a claim could be maintained.

According to the positive argument, the reasons purportedly underlying constraints and the reasons generated by the appeal to cost are *both* ultimately derived from the same source: the value of the subjective standpoint. The sceptic may object, therefore, that there is no reason to believe that the former set of reasons—which protect the patient's point of view—will be able, in general, to outweigh the latter set of reasons—which protect the agent's point of view. Since there is no reason to believe that the patient's standpoint is more important than the agent's standpoint, the moderate is unable to explain why constraints should be able to override the appeal to cost. Thus, the sceptic may conclude, if the moderate is to defend sufficiently powerful constraints (so as to avoid unacceptably minimalist options), a different foundation for constraints is needed.

So far as I can see, the only way for the moderate to meet this objection—while defending anything like ordinary morality—is to embrace an asymmetrical treatment of the two kinds of reasons arising from the value of the subjective standpoint. He must either claim that the patient-protecting reasons are, in general, considerably stronger than the agent-protecting reasons, or claim that in cases involving conflicts between constraints and the appeal to cost, the agent-protecting reasons that *normally* arise simply are not generated. A defense of either of these positions might appeal to the following considerations: Unless such an asymmetry exists, the patient's point of view—unlike the agent's point of view—will receive no genuine protection. That is, although symmetry between the two kinds of reasons does not threaten the existence of options, it does threaten the existence of constraints. In contrast, an asymmetry (along one of the lines suggested) will preserve both options and constraints; it will thus effectively protect both the agent's and the patient's points of view. If, as the positive argument assumes, the distinctive value of the subjective standpoint is such as to make full reflection of the nature of persons appropriate, this will result in a properly asymmetrical generation of reasons.

This is, at best, the sketch of an argument. The sceptic might well challenge the moderate's ability to spell it out without begging the question. But rather than pursue this issue further, I want to turn to one final objection that the sceptic might urge against the derivation of constraints through the positive argument. So far, the sceptic has questioned whether the positive argument genuinely yields the alleged patient-protecting reasons and, if it does, whether those reasons are strong enough to outweigh the relevant opposing reasons. She might also question, however, whether the given reasons meet the various other conditions that may be necessary for moral decisiveness. More particularly, she may argue that the attempt to derive constraints, merely from the fact that they reflect the nature of persons, is undercut by some of the considerations offered in the course of the negative argument.

That argument observed that morality must be able to 'sell' itself to the agent—for it is the agent who will either react or fail to react as the moral system desires. That is, when it is claimed that a genuine moral requirement must possess the necessary motivational underpinning, what is meant, of course, is that it is the *agent* who must be capable of being motivated by the reasons that underlie the given requirement. Morality cannot require some particular re-action which runs counter to the interests of the agent, unless the agent recognizes the existence of sufficiently compelling consider-ations in support of that reaction. Failure to meet this condition would result in the rejection of the requirement to promote the good. But obviously the same condition must be met by constraints as well. That is, morality cannot require an agent to react in keeping with some constraint when this runs counter to his interests unless the agent recognizes the existence of sufficiently compelling considerations in support of the constraint. Here, too, the necessary motivational underpinning has to be provided.

After presenting the negative argument we simply allowed the moderate to assert bluntly that the considerations in favor of constraints *are* of a sufficiently compelling nature to be capable of motivating the agent to act in accordance with them; there was no attempt to state what those considerations are. But if the positive argument is to be used to *derive* constraints, a statement *is* being made as to what the considerations supporting constraints are. And the sceptic may doubt whether the considerations offered by the second argument are of a sufficiently compelling nature to meet the test suggested by the first. (She may have these doubts either because she believes a more adequate foundation for constraints is necessary, or because she does not believe in constraints at all.)

Note that the defense of options is not similarly threatened by the negative argument. For an option turns on the *absence* of a morally decisive reason. Thus, provided that the agent-protecting reasons are sufficiently weighty, the pro tanto reason to promote the good will be unable to outweigh them, and this will prevent the grounding of a general requirement to promote the good. In contrast, if a constraint is to be grounded, the patient-protecting reasons—which oppose certain ways of treating patients—must themselves be morally decisive. They must, therefore, meet all the conditions necessary for moral decisiveness, including the motivational condition. That is, if they are to ground a constraint, the patient-protecting reasons must themselves be capable of motivating the agent. But although it may be clear why the *patient* will be inclined to find such reasons compelling, it is not at all clear why the *agent* should find these reasons especially compelling.

The moderate who hopes to derive constraints from the positive argument may respond to the sceptic in this way: Individuals are engaged in their subjective points of view, and it is desirable that they are; it is a feature which is central to the value of the lives of persons. Now when agents favor their interests at the expense of the overall good, they do not consider this regrettable or shameful behavior—the result of some flaw in themselves. Rather, they feel that favoring their interests in this way is reasonable; and, in effect, they can justify their behavior by showing, first, that it is a natural outgrowth of the engagement of persons with their subjective points of view and, second, that it is appropriate to have a positive attitude toward the nature of persons. But the nature of persons also explains why *patients* desire room in which to protect their interests—and agents are capable of seeing this. Thus they are capable of appreciating that constraints are a reflection of the same facts about the nature of persons which they are seeking to endorse.

Therefore agents are capable of recognizing that both options and constraints are parts of an appropriate unified response to the fact the persons are engaged in their points of view. Both agent-protecting reasons and patient-protecting reasons are reflections of the distinctive value of the subjective standpoint. The ability to see this provides the motivational underpinning necessary for the requirement that agents react in accordance with constraints.

When an individual accepts a moral system, the moderate might continue, he is taking on a general theory of reasons for action—a package which the whole person can accept upon reflection, even if he is initially inclined to reject various elements. The individual can accept options, for he can see that it is less important to him as patient that he be the recipient of various forms of aid than it is important to him as agent that he be free to act in various nonoptimal ways. Similarly, the individual can accept constraints, for he can see that it is more important to him as patient that he be protected in various ways than it is important to him as agent that he be free of the restrictions which constraints impose.

As with the last several objections, I do not propose to settle here this final dispute between the moderate and the sceptic. Perhaps the considerations in support of constraints provided by the desirability of fully reflecting the nature of persons are not sufficiently compelling to underwrite the constraints by themselves. If so, then the moderate must continue his search for adequate foundations for constraints. But if the fact that persons are engaged in their subjective points of view is indeed as desirable as the positive argument suggests, then it does not seem implausible to hold that the moderate has actually succeeded in offering an account of (at least some) constraints. In one stroke, then, the moderate will have established both constraints and options. It would be a satisfying position for the moderate to have reached.

THE MORAL POINT OF VIEW

Up to this point we have simply assumed that the moderate will actually be able to indicate reasons for maintaining something of the subjective point of view. That is, we have assumed that the moderate will be able to defend his claim that the subjective standpoint is of distinctive value in its own right. This assumption was made so that we could examine the implications of the positive argument, and compare them to those of a refurbished negative argument. But the fruits of neither argument are available unless the moderate can indeed indicate considerations which support the subjective standpoint. If he fails at this then he will have no grounds for holding that a moral system should fully reflect the nature of persons—and so he will be unable to use the positive argument to ground both options and constraints. Indeed, if he fails to indicate reasons for endorsing the subjective standpoint, then the refurbished negative argument will be unavailable as well—and so the moderate will be unable to ground even options alone.

However, if the moderate *can* indicate reasons for endorsing the subjective standpoint then he may be able to provide a defense of both options and constraints. If the considerations are forceful enough, then it will be appropriate for the nature of persons to be centrally highlighted by a moral system—and this will result in a significant array of constraints and options. But even if the considerations are of a fairly modest sort, yielding only minor options and constraints—with limited ranges and low thresholds—this will still temper the pursuit of the good to *some* degree; the point of view which is supported all things considered will differ from the objective one.

Thus, if the positive argument is correct, the balance of reasons confronting an agent need not coincide with the verdict of the objective point of view. This observation is worth emphasizing: failure to react in the way supported by the objective standpoint is not necessarily a failure to act on the *overall* balance of reasons. This point was touched upon briefly in the previous chapter, when I noted that if there are constraints then an agent will sometimes find that the balance of reasons opposes reacting in the way that would lead to the best results from an objective standpoint. For the purely objective point of view takes into account only those reasons generated by something's objective value—i.e., only the agent-neutral, pro tanto reason to promote the good. But a constraint, in contrast, turns on the existence of further, agent-relative reasons for not reacting in the given way. Thus when *all* of the morally legitimate reasons confronting an agent are taken into account, the balance of those reasons may very well support a different reaction than the one supported by the objective reasons alone.

As we have seen, the positive argument suggests that at least some constraints are based on the patient-protecting reasons arising from the value of the subjective standpoint. But regardless of whether this account of constraints is correct, the fact remains that if there are constraints at all the overall balance of reasons will sometimes diverge from the objective standpoint.

This point is simply reinforced if—as the positive argument also suggests—there are also agent-relative reasons for pursuing one's own interests (i.e., agent-protecting reasons). All the more so does it become likely that when one takes into account all of the morally acceptable reasons confronting an agent the balance of reasons will diverge from the balance that would result from taking into account only the agent-neutral, objective reasons. At the very least, the point of view which encompasses all of these reasons—both agent-neutral and agent-relative—will be logically distinct from the purely objective point of view.

Let us call this more encompassing standpoint the *moral* point of view—since it takes into account all of the morally legitimate reasons, whatever they might be. According to the most straight-forward version of the extremist's position, which rejects both options and constraints, the moral point of view is identical to the objective point of view. This position may or may not be correct; but it is, at any rate, a substantive thesis, namely, the thesis that objective reasons are the only genuine morally acceptable reasons. In contrast, as we have seen, the moderate holds that the moral point of view diverges from the objective standpoint. This position may also be correct or incorrect; but it too is a substantive thesis: it claims not merely that the moral point of view is logically distinct from the objective standpoint, but that the former actually includes reasons not recognized by the latter.

If the positive argument is correct, the moral point of view goes beyond the objective standpoint in including subjective reasons as well—reasons protecting the subjective standpoint of the individual, both as agent and as patient. But of course this does not imply that the moral point of view is adequately captured by the subjective standpoint either.[6] On the one hand, since ordinary morality is committed to the existence of the pro tanto reason to

---

[6] Since the objective point of view is not necessarily the correct one (and subjective reasons may be just as real as objective ones), it may be worth distinguishing three ways that the subjective point of view can influence one's actions: On the one hand, (a) the subjective standpoint may generate nonobjective

promote the good, the moderate at least must hold that the moral point of view includes both subjective and objective reasons. And on the other hand, the mere fact that there are subjective reasons arising from the disproportionate weight that an individual gives to his interests does not entail that those reasons give as *much* weight to those interests as the individual himself gives them. The subjective reasons may have the effect of legitimizing some of the individual's natural bias, without justifying the *entire* bias; they may, for example, sanction its influence only in certain cases.

The question, then, is to what extent the moral point of view actually incorporates such subjective reasons. And since, as we know, it is the thrust of the positive argument that the existence of such reasons is a reflection of the importance and value of the subjective standpoint, the question becomes whether (and if so, to what extent) the subjective point of view has the requisite value. Even if it does not warrant blanket endorsement, the subjective standpoint may still be a genuine source of moral value in its own right, so that something of the subjective standpoint must be maintained from the moral point of view. If the moderate can indeed defend this position, he will have the basic premise of the positive argument. However, some care must be taken in understanding exactly what it is that the moderate must show.

The moderate wants to claim that the subjective standpoint has a place in the moral point of view. But on at least one straightforward way of understanding this claim it can hardly be denied by anyone who recognizes the existence of the pro tanto reason to promote the good. For it is not as though the objective standpoint gives little or no place to the subjective standpoint; on the contrary. Consequently, even if the moral point of view is identical to the objective standpoint, it will still be the case that the subjective standpoint has *some* place in the moral point of view. But this will, obviously, be inadequate to make the moderate's case.

After all, as I observed in Chapter 2, it is not as though the objective good is something utterly distinct from and opposed to the subjective good of individual persons. Subjective value and objective value are not, in this sense, alien kinds. Rather, on any

reasons, which, of course, it is appropriate to act on. But on the other hand, (b) the subjective standpoint may also mislead one as to the actual balance of reasons, or (c) make it difficult to be motivated to act on what one recognizes as the balance of reasons—and both of these are shortcomings.

plausible view, the objective good largely consists in the obtaining of the subjective good of individuals—i.e., in the satisfaction of the interests of persons. An adequate theory of objective value, I take it, can recognize that the ultimate source of value of many goods (and maybe even all of them) lies in the fact that people *care* about these things, that is, that it *matters* to people whether the various goods obtain or not (similarly for evils). And these things matter to people *from* the subjective standpoint; that is, the point of view from which they *take* an interest in one thing rather than another is the personal point of view.

I take it, then, that on any plausible view the objective standpoint gives weight to the satisfaction of the interests possessed from the subjective standpoint. It is not that the subjective has no place in the objective; rather it is just that, from the objective point of view, the subjective standpoints of all individuals have a place. Consequently, in any given case, meeting the interests of one individual may be more important objectively than meeting the interests of a second individual—despite the greater weight that the second individual may give to his own interests from his personal point of view.

What this means, of course, is that the moderate cannot defend his position simply by showing that the subjective standpoint has some legitimate—even central—place in the moral point of view. For example, the moderate cannot provide the necessary support for the subjective standpoint simply by noting that an agent who acts in keeping with the objective standpoint will frequently sacrifice her interests—and that there is *some* reason to avoid any given sacrifice. For the objective standpoint is perfectly capable of recognizing that a loss is involved when it requires an agent to sacrifice her interests. It is not *blind* to the existence of a consideration which supports avoiding the sacrifice; it simply holds that on balance greater considerations support *making* the sacrifice. What the moderate must do, rather, is to show that the objective standpoint does not give an *adequate* place to the subjective standpoint. Only a demonstration of this kind will provide the necessary support for the positive argument.

Now the moderate may well think that it is intuitively obvious that the subjective standpoint has a greater place in the moral point of view than that given to it by the objective standpoint. In particular, he may think it evident that an agent has special (agent-relative) reasons for pursuing her own interests. (The objective standpoint, in contrast, only gives the agent the same agent-neutral reason that everyone else has for promoting that agent's interests.) But the intuitive force of this conviction is not by itself an adequate defense. That I will typically be more *motivated* to promote my interests than will others can readily be conceded, given the nature of persons. But what exactly is the argument that shows that I will have greater *reason* to promote those interests than others do? It is, of course, a trivial truth that my interests are *mine*; but it is not a trivial truth (nor does it follow trivially) that my interests generate greater reasons for *me* to promote those interests than they generate for others. And it is not at all obvious how the moderate might argue directly for this claim. Accordingly, it is not clear how, or whether, the moderate can argue directly for the view that the subjective standpoint has a further and distinct role in the moral point of view.

This suggests a somewhat indirect strategy. The moderate might try to show that the subjective standpoint has an additional place in the moral point of view by focusing on the objective standpoint and establishing its *inadequacy*. But here too caution is in order. For it is important to see that there is a second sort of consideration which will not be relevant for the moderate's purposes. There may be cases in which there are good reasons from the objective standpoint for temporarily or tentatively adopting a nonobjective point of view. If the appropriateness of the nonobjective perspective is derivative in this way, the moderate is not presented with the case he needs.

For example, an agent who is forever trying to make all her beliefs as vivid as they possibly can be—so as to make her actual perspective as nearly objective as she can—will have little time or ability to do anything else. She will hardly be effective as far as actually promoting the good is concerned. But this poses no fundamental challenge to the objective perspective. Given the kind of being the agent is, with the sorts of limits she has, there may be good reasons objectively for adopting rough judgments about what sorts of behavior are apt to best promote the good. The agent should then guide herself by the light of these judgments—rather than perpetually seeking more vivid beliefs—keeping herself prepared to diverge from the guidelines in unusual circumstances and ready to revise them in the face of experience. Similarly, once a course of action has been justified from the objective perspective, an agent who vividly bears in mind the dangers or disadvantages may find her resolve weakened or her mind distracted. Objectively there may be reason to try to make some of these beliefs pale—but this too poses no threat for the extremist's claim that the objective standpoint adequately captures the moral point of view. In such cases, practical judgments are still being grounded (even if only indirectly) in the objective standpoint. To show the fundamental inadequacy of the objective point of view, therefore, the moderate needs to indicate considerations of a sort which *cannot* be appreciated—or at least cannot be sufficiently appreciated—from the objective standpoint.

Suppose, then, that the moderate could indicate a good or a value of some kind which, even after reflection, we are unwilling to deny, or dismiss as morally illegitimate. And imagine that this value could not be adequately appreciated from the objective standpoint: it might be that from the objective standpoint one cannot recognize the value in question, or explain it, or understand it; or perhaps one cannot actually have the value from the objective standpoint, or retain it, or possess instances of it; and so on. In any of these closely related ways, the objective standpoint might be unable to adequately incorporate the given value. What's more, let us suppose that it is the very impartiality of the objective standpoint that makes it incapable of incorporating the value in question. In contrast, then, the subjective point of view might well be capable of incorporating the value that cannot be adequately appreciated from the objective standpoint. If we imagine that the value can in fact be incorporated by the subjective point of view, then the moderate may have shown that the moral point of view must go beyond the objective standpoint in giving further and distinct place to the subjective standpoint.

If a disproportionate concern with one's interests is essential for the incorporation of the value—for embracing, generating, or maintaining it (or what have you)—then a place must be preserved in the moral point of view for such disproportionate concern. It will be of positive value that individuals are engaged in their subjective standpoints, and this will be reflected by the moral point of view. Yet, as I've already noted, such an endorsement of the subjective standpoint need not be tantamount to the claim that the moral point of view is itself adequately captured by the subjective point of view. That is, it may be that all that is necessary for the incorporation of the given value is that some disproportionate concern be maintained, but not necessarily so much as is typically to be found in the untempered subjective standpoint. The moral point of view can go beyond the objective standpoint by, in effect, giving the subjective standpoint a distinct impact, without itself collapsing into the subjective standpoint.

An argument along these lines seems the most promising way for the moderate to proceed. If the moderate can indeed point to a value of the sort we have been describing—one which can be incorporated by the subjective standpoint but not by the objective standpoint—then it seems that the basic premise of the positive argument can be defended. Of course, it will still be logically possible to resist this conclusion by rejecting the value in question. But if, in fact, the value is not one that we are willing to dismiss, then the moderate may have succeeded in showing that it is indeed appropriate to have a positive attitude toward the nature of persons.

MERITS OF THE SUBJECTIVE

The moderate's claim is that an endorsement of the bias in favor of one's interests is an essential component of any standpoint capable of adequately appreciating certain values. If there are indeed morally legitimate values, or other goods, to which the objective standpoint is incapable of giving adequate expression, and which can only be maintained given a disproportionate concern with one's interests, then—as I have sometimes put it—there is reason to maintain something of the subjective standpoint (i.e., beyond the role already given to it by the objective standpoint). And, as we have seen, given this basic premise of the positive argument, it seems that the moderate will at last have a plausible defense of options, and perhaps even constraints as well.

Can the moderate actually point to any considerations of the right sort? As I have suggested, we can bring the question into focus by asking whether—from the moral point of view—there are any inadequacies in the objective standpoint. The extremist, of course, denies that there are any such inadequacies (at least, on the most straightforward version of his view): one who adopts the objective standpoint will strive to promote the good; and this is as it should be. The moderate, however, insists that there are indeed morally legitimate values that such a point of view cannot adequately appreciate.

Such is the moderate's claim. But what exactly does the objective standpoint get wrong? Let us briefly examine several possibilities.

1. The moderate might start by offering a simple criticism of the objective standpoint: if its demands are to be met, a significant range of goods must be sacrificed; and it seems inappropriate to hold out an image of the world without these goods as the ideal to which we should aspire. Promoting the good would (largely) require one to forgo activities which are not maximally productive, and to abandon ends which are resource inefficient. Crudely, but forcefully put, the moderate's objection would be this: the extremist believes that no one should have any fun. We would, e.g., have to forgo flower-gazing; for an agent who whiles away the hours conferring with the flowers could probably do tremendously more good visiting the sick or doing volunteer work for some charity. But putting the criticism this way would not go far enough. It is not simply that 'squandering' valuable time and energy would be forbidden: one could not even promote various goods which happened to require a disproportionate amount of resources. Since the money spent producing a ballet, e.g., could save a staggering number of people if spent on famine relief, promoting the good would apparently require that we do without ballet.

We would have to do without ballet, opera, symphonies, and perhaps other forms of the arts; without gourmet cooking, elegant clothes, and more than adequate housing; without departments of philosophy, and programs in comparative literature; without stamp collecting, professional sports, and bowling teams. We would have to do without fun—and more: we would have to do without a vast range of goods which give our world color, diversity, and *value*. The world which would be created if we all adopted the objective standpoint would be a grey world—a far cry from the ideal. And this, the moderate might argue, is a consideration which supports maintaining something of the subjective standpoint—for from this perspective agents will continue favoring various ends, bestowing upon them an objectively disproportionate amount of resources, endowing the world with color.[7]

---

[7] Cf. Wolf, both with regard to this argument, and with regard to argument 2 below.

In response, the extremist might remind the moderate that the extremist does not value sacrifices for their own sake, but only insofar as they genuinely promote the overall good. And even when some sacrifice *is* required, the extremist can bemoan the necessary loss quite as much as the moderate. If some expensive good must be abandoned in pursuit of the *overall* good, that is an unfortunate toll of living in a world of scarce resources. Thus the extremist can *admit* that the effect of pursuing the good would not be an ideal world—in that we can imagine a world in which the sacrifices are not necessary. And the extremist may even hope that eventually a world of plenty will be produced in which there will be no need to forgo the expensive goods which we find so desirable. (Accordingly, it may make sense to preserve the basic knowledge of how to reproduce these desirable goods—so that, e.g., in such a world of plenty we can 'resurrect' ballet.) But the dream of such utopias should not blind us to the fact that *now* it is the case that greater good is done by forgoing various luxuries. We must consider not only which worlds are ideal in an absolute sense, but also which worlds are ideal relative to a given set of limited possibilities. Even if promoting the good should remove various elements of color, leaving the world grey, it is crucially important to recall that the reduction in overall good resulting from adopting a subjective standpoint reduces the overall color of the world even more: a small splash of color is only purchased at the cost of plunging far greater areas into dark black.

A more radical response must also be kept in mind. We must take seriously the possibility that some of the goods which are resource expensive nonetheless actually make a greater contribution to the overall good than a hasty appraisal might recognize. A world without ballet, e.g., might be able to save a large number of people from starvation. But it is at least possible that it is more valuable overall to have ballet and the extra suffering than it is to eliminate the latter at the cost of the former. It might be that a greater contribution to overall good would be made by promoting the arts than by diverting those resources to famine relief. (A pluralist theory of the good might give the existence of art considerable value in its own right; or it might be that art simply pays its way in terms of its overall contribution to human well-being.) Splashes of color *may* be worth their cost in extra black; the grey world may not be the most valuable accessible world overall. Such a claim is difficult to evaluate; there is, obviously, great risk of self-serving rationalization when such judgments are made by those who stand to benefit. (How many would agree that it is better that *they* should starve rather than endangering ballet?) But there is, I think, at least some intuitive support for claims of this sort. At any rate, it is a possibility that some such claims are correct; and the extremist is neutral as to their truth. Thus it may be that the requirement to promote the good does not support producing a grey world at all.

Either way, therefore, the moderate's defense of the subjective perspective is inadequate. As the second response notes, a general policy of promoting the good may not require the elimination of all luxuries, even in a world of scarce resources; and as the first response noted, those goods which must be given up are only sacrificed (and perhaps only temporarily, at that) because doing so purchases an even more valuable array of goods. There is no reason to think that the objective standpoint leads to an unacceptable image of the ideal world. Thus the moderate has offered no reason to retain any of the subjective perspective.

2. A somewhat more plausible cousin of the moderate's first objection would be the claim that adopting the objective standpoint would lead to an unacceptable picture, not of the ideal world, but of the ideal *life*. The moderate might suggest that one comes to morality in order to discover the good life—i.e., to learn what would be involved in a person's life going best for her or, to put it another way, what sort of life is most worth having. And it seems clear, the moderate might continue, that, in this sense, an individual who lives in conformity with the objective standpoint will come nowhere near to possessing the good life.

Given the parameters of the actual world, there is no question that promoting the good would require a life of hardship, self-denial, and austerity. Even if the radical response mentioned above is correct, and the world is better off with a splash of color and a good deal more black, it is still most likely that any *given* agent can make a greater contribution overall by *personally* forgoing luxuries. A life spent promoting the good would be a severe one indeed. But it is obvious, the moderate might argue, that this falls far short of capturing an adequate image of the good life. After all, we value the luxuries which an agent would have to sacrifice in the pursuit of the overall good; they tremendously enrich an individual's life. Thus, total adoption of the objective standpoint is a faulty human ideal. And this is a consideration which supports maintaining something of the subjective standpoint—for from that perspective agents will continue to favor their own interests somewhat, retaining for themselves some of the luxuries which are essential to the good life.

Now the extremist will certainly concede that luxuries might enrich an individual's life, so that the best sort of life of all would be one which included them. But this is only to consider what the good life would be in a utopian fantasy world with unlimited resources for all. It is quite another matter to ask whether this is the best sort of life to have in a world in which others are suffering and one can do something about it. As before, we must contrast the good life in an absolute sense, with the good life given a world of limited resources. In such a world, purchasing luxuries for oneself when one could have used the resources to help meet the essential needs of others may well form part of an ignoble sort of life. At the very least, the moderate has given us no reason to think that our own world is *not* such a case. Thus the extremist need not deny that luxuries are worth having, considered in themselves. He need only deny that the moderate has shown that they are worth having, all things considered, in a world where having them involves countenancing the suffering of others.

The extremist can go further. Even if the extremist were to concede that there is an important sense in which living in accord with the objective standpoint can fall short of the good life, the moderate would still have failed to make his point. For we do not simply ask morality to describe the good life: we ask to what extent it is *appropriate* to live the good life. There may well be reasons to act in various ways which involve living a life which falls short of the imaginary standard; if there are, then the mere fact that a moral system enjoins a life which departs from that standard does not necessarily reveal a flaw in the system.

Clearly, the moderate himself believes that there are such reasons. If the moderate is to fend off the minimalist, he must admit that the appropriate life to lead in a world of limited resources is one in which an individual will undertake sacrifices—at least on *some* occasions—for the sake of others. The life which the extremist feels is appropriate departs even further from the imaginary yardstick—but the moderate has given no reason to think that this must be a flaw. The extremist can certainly recognize the loss involved when an individual fails to attain the good life; but he will suggest that it is the very fact that people generally fall so appallingly short of this ideal that makes it inappropriate for an agent to pursue the good life when she could make a greater contribution to others.

Perhaps the two points could be combined. It may be plausible to suggest that the good life must include acting on the balance of reasons. (To think otherwise, apparently, is to think that the ideal human life might involve being irrational.) If this is so, then the good life may actually coincide with the appropriate life:[8] both of course may fall short of the utopian ideal; and they may fall short of the approximation to that ideal in *material terms* which an agent can attain if she is willing to make this her goal. In effect—given this view of the good life—the moderate has only noted that a life in accord with the objective standpoint will fall short in one or another of these unproblematic ways: he has not shown that it will fall short of the good life. Since the truly good life might well involve the sacrifice of luxuries in a world in which the essential needs of others go unmet, the moderate has given no reason for sustaining the subjective perspective.

Finally, the extremist will note that even in material terms the cost to the individual agent of promoting the good might not be especially significant if all or most agents did their part in promoting the good as well. It is, in large part, because most people make such minimal contributions to the overall good, that any given individual who *did* try to promote the good would probably have to make substantial material sacrifices. That is, it is largely because most of us fail so completely to act in accord with the objective standpoint that action in accord with that standpoint by any given individual may involve significant sacrifices. But it hardly seems surprising—or objectionable—that individual agents who strive to act in keeping with a given moral theory against a social background of general *noncompliance* with that theory may have to sacrifice various goods or values that might well be available to all if only there were greater conformity with that moral theory. (After all, the same thing would hold true for ordinary morality: in a society of minimalists, e.g., an individual agent's decision to

---

[8] I only say 'may' coincide, since they might *not* coincide if there are morally unacceptable but nonetheless genuine reasons for action. (Although they might still coincide for all that, if the morally legitimate reasons are always overriding.) I do not believe there are such reasons; but I won't directly argue the point here.

conform to ordinary morality might well involve her sacrificing much of the good life.) Seen in this light, the claim that the objective standpoint cannot give adequate place to the good life seems even less compelling.

3. In the first two objections, the moderate claimed that an unacceptable or inadequate stance toward various goods emerges from adopting the totally objective standpoint. The extremist replied that it was not that the objective standpoint failed to recognize the value of certain goods—but only that given the character of the actual world, at least as it is now, the objective standpoint required that those goods be sacrificed in the pursuit of the greater good overall. In response, the moderate might want to argue that this very willingness to sacrifice anything at all in the pursuit of the greater overall good betrays a deep inadequacy in the objective standpoint. Truly valuing some object (or project, or end, etc.), the moderate might suggest, is incompatible with a willingness to sacrifice the object simply because the overall good would be promoted by doing so. If one is fundamentally committed to some end—say, doing philosophy—then one will be unwilling or unable to abandon that end at the mere beck and call of the good. Thus an agent who *was* prepared to act in accordance with the objective standpoint would lack something that we consider of great value: the ability to be committed to an end, to value an object directly and deeply. Limited to what can be defended from the objective perspective, the extremist is unable to provide an adequate account of this central way of valuing an object. Therefore, insofar as the ability to value in this way is something that we consider desirable about persons, it is a consideration which supports maintaining at least a partially subjective standpoint. For if an agent retains some bias in favor of his own interests, his projects and his commitments, then he will be prepared to promote those ends which he values most deeply even at the possible expense of the overall good.[9]

As it stands, however, the moderate's argument is inadequate. The extremist can certainly admit that an agent might value some

---

[9] This argument is suggested (at the very least) by certain of Williams' remarks (see, e.g., 'Persons', pp. 13–14, 18; and 'Critique', pp. 115–17), although it is somewhat obscure exactly what Williams intends to be asserting in these passages. Arguments 4 and 5 below, which are progressive refinements of this line of thought, are similarly indebted to Williams.

end so highly that he would be quite unwilling to sacrifice it for the greater good. But the moderate has given no reason to think that such devotion is reasonable or desirable. For the moderate to insist that this is the level of commitment appropriate to the 'true', 'fundamental', or 'deep' valuing of an object, is simply to beg the question; there is no reason why the extremist—in a similarly high-handed way—should not label such devotion as 'fanatic' or 'obsessive'. Thus the moderate has failed to support his claim that the extremist cannot provide an adequate account of valuing.

Indeed, were the objection sound, it seems that the moderate himself would fall prey to it as well. We can easily imagine an agent with so deep a level of commitment to some end that he would simply be unwilling to undertake any sacrifice of that end whatsoever, whatever the circumstances. The moderate of course would not find such a commitment reasonable; only the minimalist would welcome it. Apparently, therefore, the moderate would have to insist that valuing an object too deeply may not be desirable. But if such a response is available to the moderate, it is available to the extremist as well.

To support his claim that the moral point of view must remain at least partially subjective, the moderate must argue that there is some value which cannot be adequately appreciated from the objective standpoint. Now the moderate can, of course, properly insist upon the value of intense levels of commitment, but it seems that he himself must admit that such commitments can be too deep, all things considered. This being the case, however, the moderate has given no reason to think that the value cannot be properly appreciated from the objective point of view. For the objective standpoint can certainly recognize the *intrinsic* value of an agent's being able to satisfy a commitment so deep that he would not sacrifice it for the sake of the overall good. It is simply that on balance the value of satisfying such commitments may on occasion be outweighed by the overall losses. Overly deep commitments are not desirable all things considered; but the objective standpoint can recognize the loss involved in being unable to satisfy them.[10]

4. Perhaps, however, it is not the depth of the commitment per se with which the moderate is concerned, but rather the *nature* of the

[10] Given certain empirical assumptions, it might be argued that the possession of certain commitments so deep that one would not sacrifice them for the greater good is *itself* conducive to the greater good. If so, then even though it will sometimes lead

commitment. When the moderate disparages the objective stand-point, and the willingness of the individual who adopts that perspective to sacrifice any object for the greater good, he may do so not because such a willingness indicates that the individual's valuing of the object is relatively *shallow*, but rather because such a willingness indicates that the individual does not value the object *directly*.

Not all valued objects are valued directly. The moderate might admit that typically one would be willing to exchange a valued object of a given kind for more objects of that kind. Certainly one might do this in order to get more of the objects for oneself—and no doubt one might do this in order to provide the valued objects for others. Yet the moderate might insist that it is different when one *directly* values an object: one can value a *particular* object—perhaps because of some incident in its history, or one's own—so that one would be unwilling to exchange the object even for more of the same kind. With this kind of attachment, one would be unwilling to exchange even in order to provide more objects for *oneself*. Indeed, one might be unwilling to exchange even in order to acquire a greater number of valuable objects to which one has this same sort of direct attachment. One might form this sort of attachment to a rose, although perhaps it would be easier to value an original Rembrandt in this way; and attachments to friends and loved ones are no doubt the most important cases.

When one directly values an object one is unwilling to exchange it (except, perhaps, in cases of unusual need). Thus the willingness of an individual who has adopted the objective standpoint to sacrifice any given object in the pursuit of the greater good shows that he values *no* object directly. But, the moderate argues, the ability to form such direct attachments is one that we value highly; we need only think how impoverished life would be with neither love nor friendship, to see this. This then provides a consideration in support of retaining something of the subjective standpoint—for it is only from the nonobjective perspective that the agent could favor the objects he directly values, retaining them even when their sacrifice would promote the greater good.

one to fail to promote the good, *possession* of such commitments will nonetheless be justified by the objective standpoint. I'm unconvinced of the relevant empirical assumptions; but since such arguments don't claim that the subjective standpoint merits a greater role than that given to it by the objective standpoint, I won't pursue the matter here. See Parfit, Chapter 1; and Railton.

The nature and significance of such direct attachments is an important topic for moral philosophy—concerning which much needs to be said. But for the purposes of meeting the moderate's argument, I think it may suffice if the extremist challenges the moderate's claim that if one directly values a particular object one will be unwilling to consider sacrificing it. Two examples may call the moderate's claim into question. First, if an agent cannot save all three of his children, he might be willing to choose between saving only one or saving two—although he will obviously be greatly distressed at the need to choose at all. Second, a painter with direct attachments to several of her own works might agree to part with a directly valued painting still in her studio if this is the only way to regain a previously sold painting (sold, no doubt, while she was in the throes of poverty) that she values even more.[11]

What these examples suggest is that when an agent cannot retain all of the objects that he values directly, he may be willing to consider exchanges. He may be distressed at his inability to avoid sacrificing any at all—but his willingness to sacrifice need not indicate that the sacrificed object was not valued directly after all. And if this is correct, then the extremist can plausibly suggest that an agent might be willing to sacrifice the objects that he values directly so that *others* may gain. This agent too will be distressed that any sacrifice at all must take place—but his willingness to sacrifice will not indicate that he did not actually value the sacrificed object directly.

Thus the extremist can concede the importance of direct attachment to particular objects—and yet deny that the moderate has given any reason to retain the subjective perspective. The objective standpoint is not blind to the magnitude of the loss involved when an agent must sacrifice an object he values directly. Nor is it simply that the objective standpoint recognizes the loss—but nonetheless always *will* require agents to sacrifice the objects

[11] Interestingly, although I am fairly confident intuitively that an agent might sacrifice a directly valued object in order to obtain another object to which he is already attached, it is not clear to me that an agent could normally sacrifice a directly valued object in order to obtain an object to which he is *not* yet attached (barring great need, and so on)—even though he expects to *become* attached to the newly gained object. On the other hand, I *do* think that the agent could sacrifice the directly valued object so that some *other* individual could gain an object to which she was not yet, but would become, attached. The intuitions here need sorting out; but I think that what is said in the text should be sufficient to challenge the moderate's argument.

they directly value. For possession of such objects need not always stand in the way of the pursuit of the good. Sacrifices of directly valued objects may occasionally be required; but there is no reason to think it would be a matter of course. And a willingness to make the sacrifice when it *is* necessary will not reveal that the object was not valued directly after all.

5. Yet doubts may remain. The moderate might suggest that even if a willingness to sacrifice an object in the pursuit of the good needn't always show that the object is not directly valued, nonetheless there *are* cases in which commitment to promoting the good is incompatible with the existence of certain sorts of direct attachments. Love and friendship may be such relations: to love an individual one must be willing to favor that individual in various ways, even when doing so fails to promote the greater good; if one is not willing to show such favor then this indicates that the given individual is not loved after all.

To treat all persons equally, never bestowing any favors, never departing from the indifference implicit in the pursuit of the good— this is to love no one at all. An individual who adopts the objective perspective would not give a rose to anyone if greater good could be done by giving the rose to someone else; he would not spend time with someone if visiting someone else could do more good; he would not choose to save a person if greater good could be done by leaving her to die. But all of these reactions, unavailable to such an individual, are the very ways in which someone reveals and acts out his love for another. To love someone is to desire to favor them, and to be willing to do so—and this is a consideration which supports maintaining something of the subjective perspective, for it is only from this perspective that an agent is able to favor those in whom he takes an interest.

Once again, however, the moderate's support for his claim is inadequate. The extremist will readily admit that we frequently favor those whom we love. But this is only to admit the uncontroversial; given that an agent *does* favor his interests, it is not surprising that one form of this is favoring those persons to whom he feels direct attachment. The question, however, is whether such willingness to favor is an essential part of love or friendship; and I do not think that it is obvious that this is so. The moderate suggests that favoring is an essential expression of love. But if we recognize the existence of other possible expressions of

love—and see therefore that favoring is not the only possibility—
then the plausibility of the moderate's claim will be greatly reduced.
It will remain *possible*, of course, that favoring is essential to love—
but the moderate will not have given adequate reason to think so.

Love and friendship are, of course, rich and varied phenomena,
each involving a complex of more specific attitudes and relations:
both typically involve an openness toward the friend or loved one, a
desire to make efforts to correct misunderstandings and to deepen
the level of intimacy; one usually takes pleasure in the happiness of
the other person, and the recognition of the mutuality of the
relationship is itself a source of pleasure; furthermore, since one
typically finds some traits of the friend or loved one particularly
attractive, the esteem of the other person is often especially central
to one's feelings of self-worth, and one may derive special pleasure
from being in the company of the other, or in the sharing of
experiences. Obviously, these are only a few of the factors that can
be involved in friendship or love. But that's just the point. For when
this multifaceted character is borne in mind, I think, it becomes less
plausible for the moderate to insist that these relationships *must*
involve a willingness to favor some at the expense of the greater
good.

Let us ask, therefore, whether there are ways that an agent's
feelings of love or friendship can fit into his life without requiring
that he sacrifice the overall good. Once the question is asked
explicitly, I think it is fairly clear that the answer is 'yes'. If we are
tempted to answer in the negative, it may be that we mistakenly
think of the agent who is in pursuit of the good as frantically
running around, pushing himself in every direction, until he drops
from exhaustion. Such a person would have no time to establish
genuine relationships, and no room in his life for love or friendship.
But most likely such a person would not actually be making his
greatest possible contribution to the good either. In contrast, an
individual who shapes and carries out a life plan with an eye to
promoting the good is likely to make a greater contribution in the
long run. And such a person may well have room, and perhaps the
need, for partners in his undertakings. But 'partnership' may be too
weak a term to describe the relationships that can develop: they
may be friendships; and they may be more. Obviously, these brief
comments cannot do justice to the complexities of love and
friendship, but it is at least not implausible for the extremist to

suggest that an individual committed to promoting the good can nonetheless form such direct attachments to others, and that such attachments needn't require that he be willing to sacrifice the overall good. If this is correct, then the moderate has still failed to offer a reason to think that the subjective perspective must be retained.

As before, the extremist will certainly concede that there may be cases in which the commitment to the other is so deep that the agent would be unwilling to refrain from favoring the loved one at the expense of the overall good. And the extremist can even recognize the intrinsic value of such relationships. The moderate too will have to admit the possibility of attachments so deep that the agent would be willing to act immorally for the sake of the loved one. Presumably the moderate believes that attachments of too strong a nature are not desirable all things considered; the extremist makes a similar claim. Were all cases of love and friendship ruled out by the objective standpoint, that might show the importance of retaining something of the subjective point of view after all. But if the extremist is correct, and love and friendship can have a legitimate place in the life of an agent who adopts the objective perspective, then the moderate has failed to offer the necessary support for the subjective standpoint.

AVOIDING MORAL DECISIVENESS

There are, perhaps, other considerations that the moderate might adduce in an attempt to support the subjective point of view. But the five arguments we have just considered are unsuccessful; and I am unaware of any which do better. In discussing the five, something of a common pattern has emerged, and we might hazard the guess that other considerations which might be mentioned by the moderate would elicit a similar response from the extremist.

In each case the moderate has indicated something of value (e.g., the obtaining or possession of some good or relation). He has claimed, in effect, that the objective standpoint is unable to offer an account of these values, and so it is inappropriate for an agent to attempt to act in accordance with a totally objective point of view. Since it is only a (partially) subjective point of view which can adequately incorporate the values, there is reason to maintain something of the natural bias which is involved in the subjective standpoint.

In response, the extremist has noted that the objective standpoint is perfectly capable of recognizing the intrinsic value of the various goods, relations, and so on. But recognition of intrinsic value does not necessarily involve endorsement all things considered. In a world of limited resources, some things of intrinsic value are to be avoided. The extremist can admit the loss involved when agents act so as to promote the overall good; but he will stress the overall gains which would not otherwise be procured. Thus the extremist denies the moderate's claim to have indicated values which cannot be given an adequate account from the objective standpoint.

Furthermore, the extremist suggests, he is not limited to mere *recognition* of the values in question. He is not doomed to be constantly advising that the objects of value should never obtain; for not all of their instances will need to be sacrificed in the pursuit of the good. In many cases, although certainly not in all, agents acting in accordance with the objective standpoint will be able to find a place for the values in question in their own lives.

In at least a limited fashion, then, the extremist can incorporate the values to which the moderate has referred. At the same time, the extremist can recognize that frequently agents have attitudes toward many of these values which preclude promotion of the good. The extremist need only note that the moderate has not shown that such attitudes are reasonable. And so the moderate has not shown that there are considerations which, on balance, support maintaining something of the subjective standpoint.

Obviously, it is controversial whether the extremist's treatment of the various values is adequate. I do think, on the one hand, that it has *not* been shown by the moderate that there are, on balance, reasons for endorsing the subjective standpoint. That is, it has not been shown that the moral point of view gives the subjective standpoint a further and distinct place beyond that given to it by the objective standpoint. But on the other hand, I do not think it *has* been shown that the moderate could not develop one of the arguments offered in the previous section more fully. The objection to be made to some of the moderate's arguments is not so much that they are dealing with considerations which could not conceivably offer support for the subjective point of view, as that they simply fail to make their case: as matters stand, the moderate simply has not mustered sufficient evidence to show that the objective standpoint is inadequate.

For some moderates, perhaps, such a situation may still seem encouraging: it seems *possible*, at least, that a defense of the subjective standpoint might yet be produced. But surely moderates should find the situation *discouraging* as well: the extremist appears to be capable of countering the moderate's initial moves, and it is far from clear how the moderate might strengthen his arguments.

Yet if the arguments could in fact be strengthened, there would be a further difficulty facing the moderate. If successful, the moderate's arguments would have given some ground for the claim that the objective standpoint does not adequately capture the moral point of view. If certain morally legitimate values could only be properly accounted for from a somewhat subjective standpoint—a point of view from which individuals could continue (at least in part) to favor their own interests—then there would be reason to believe that the moral point of view includes subjective reasons, and not only objective ones. But if there were such subjective reasons, the question would arise as to whether these reasons could themselves be morally decisive.

Answering this question poses something of a dilemma for the moderate. For he wants to claim of at least some of the subjective reasons—the patient-protecting ones—that they can indeed be morally decisive, and typically are. According to the positive argument, such patient-protecting reasons form the basis of (many) constraints; obviously, however, if they are to ground constraints, they must generally be morally decisive. But at the same time, it seems that the moderate must also hold that the other kind of subjective reason—the agent-protecting ones—are not, in general, capable of being morally decisive. For it is the agent-protecting reasons, according to the positive argument, that provide the basis of options. Yet if these reasons are similarly capable of being morally decisive, and typically are, then this will actually undermine the defense of options.

This last point is one that we have noted previously. An option permits the agent to pursue his interests rather than sacrifice them for the greater good. But it does not *require* him to pursue his interests; he may, if he chooses, make the sacrifice. So if the moderate is genuinely to defend an *option* it must not be the case that promotion of the good is opposed by a morally decisive reason. Of course, it is not that there can be no reason whatsoever for the agent to pursue his interests; but if it is to suit the moderate's purposes, this reason cannot be a morally decisive one.

This, then, is the moderate's dilemma. If he claims that subjective reasons can typically be morally decisive, then he preserves the suggested defense of constraints, but undermines the defense of options. Yet if he claims instead that subjective reasons cannot generally be morally decisive, then he preserves the defense of options, but abandons the suggested defense of constraints.

Of course the moderate might simply insist that patient-protecting reasons are indeed typically morally decisive, but agent-protecting reasons are not. And it must be admitted that there is nothing logically inconsistent about such a claim. But this is not to say that it is easy to see why such a claim should be thought to be correct. In a moment, I will be considering the various potential defenses of the claim that agent-protecting reasons fail to be morally decisive. Although I will not pause to establish the point explicitly, I think it fair to say that these accounts—whatever their plausibility—seem just as well suited to serve as explanations of why patient-protecting reasons would fail to be morally decisive as well.

Still, if pressed, the moderate might be willing to abandon the suggestion that the basic defense of constraints is provided by the positive argument. He might be willing (or possibly even eager) to look elsewhere for the basis of constraints, insisting only that the basis of options is indeed to be found in the existence of agent-protecting reasons, which are capable of opposing the pro tanto reason to promote the good. As we have seen, such a defense of options requires that the moderate hold that these countervailing reasons cannot (typically) be morally decisive. So let us focus our attention on the question of whether the moderate can adequately defend this claim.

Since the moderate is hardly in the position to claim that the agent-protecting reasons do not exist (the suggested defense of options depends upon their existence), he must maintain either that they (typically) fail to outweigh the opposing reasons, or that they (typically) fail to meet some further condition necessary for moral decisiveness. Let us consider both possibilities.

No doubt an agent's pursuit of his interests could, in particular cases, be opposed by a variety of reasons (for example, the reasons that ground constraints, whatever they are). But in many cases, the only relevant opposing reason will be the pro tanto reason to promote the good. And if he is to defend a genuine option, the moderate must claim that the agent-protecting reasons fail to be morally decisive even in cases of this kind. So, for simplicity, let us restrict our attention to cases where the only reasons involved are the agent-protecting reasons and the pro tanto reason to promote the good.

Now the most straightforward way for the agent-protecting reasons to fail to outweigh the pro tanto reason to promote the good is for the former to be simply *outweighed* by the latter. This is just what we would expect, of course, when the promotion of the good would not involve a significant sacrifice of the agent's interests; but the moderate might suggest that the same is true even when it is actually a fairly significant sacrifice of interests that would be involved. On this suggestion, then, in conflicts between agent-protecting reasons and the pro tanto reason to promote the good, the overall balance of reasons always favors promotion of the good (that is, given our assumption that no other reasons are involved). If the agent-protecting reason is always outweighed, there is clearly no danger that it will be morally decisive. What's more, this approach also has the advantage of explaining the judgment—one that moderates typically want to make—that sacrificing one's interests for the greater good is morally meritorious. For an agent who makes such a sacrifice, although not required to do so, is freely choosing to act in accordance with the balance of reasons. (Note that such an account is unavailable if the overall balance of reasons does not support promotion of the good—and especially if it *opposes* it. If subjective reasons, e.g., outweigh the objective reasons, why in the world should it be meritorious to go *against* the balance of morally legitimate reasons, and promote the good?)

The obvious difficulty with this suggestion, however, is that the moderate no longer has an explanation of why there is no general requirement to promote the good. Since, on this hypothesis, the pro tanto reason to promote the good outweighs the countervailing reasons—even when the cost to the agent will be high—what is it that prevents it from being morally decisive?

The negative argument, as we know, suggested that the pro tanto reason to promote the good failed to meet the motivational condition on moral decisiveness; but the extremist seemed able to dismiss this claim provided that the agent's natural bias in favor of his interests could be properly viewed, on balance, as a hindrance. Now even if there are agent-protecting reasons—and the fact that agent's have such a bias is not totally devoid of value—if those reasons are always outweighed by the pro tanto reason to promote the good, as the moderate is suggesting, then it still seems as though the agent will properly view his bias as, on balance, a hindrance. The agent will, therefore, have a motive to (at least try to) overcome his bias. Thus the motivational condition can be indeed be met, and the pro tanto reason to promote the good can ground a general requirement.

I take it, therefore, that the moderate should not hold that the agent-protecting reasons are always (or even typically) outweighed by the pro tanto reason to promote the good. So the moderate might suggest instead that the two reasons are exactly balanced in weight, neither able to outweigh the other. Since neither reason will outweigh the given opposing reason, neither will be morally decisive, and so the agent will be permitted either to pursue his interests or to promote the greater good, as he sees fit.

Such exactly balanced reasons are, of course, possible. So if there were subjective reasons, capable of opposing the objective reasons, an agent's having an option in a particular case might occasionally be explained in this way. But such cases would be extremely rare, and could not provide the moderate with anything like a general account of options. For if in any given case the subjective reasons and the objective reasons were exactly balanced in weight, such a tie would be broken as soon as one or the other of the two reasons grew stronger (or weaker).

Suppose, for example, that by making a certain sacrifice—say, $500—I could save an innocent stranger from undergoing a great deal of physical pain. And let us assume, in accordance with the moderate's suggestion, that the subjective reason which opposes my thus sacrificing my interests is of exactly the same weight as the objective reason which supports my helping the stranger. Here neither reason outweighs the other, and so there is an option. But now consider a slight variation of this case, in which the cost of helping the stranger will be $750 rather than $500, and the pain to the stranger will be somewhat less than in the original case. Here, presumably, the subjective reason will be somewhat stronger, and the objective reason somewhat weaker. So if the original two reasons were of exactly the same weight, in this new case the subjective reason must outweigh the objective reason. Yet here too, obviously, the moderate thinks that I have an option—to help the stranger or refrain, as I choose—and so it is clear that the possibility of exact ties won't do as a general account of options. Indeed, when one considers how widely the strengths of the objective and subjective reasons might vary, it seems likely that exact ties could be nothing more than extremely rare accidents.

The moderate might propose, therefore, that the subjective reasons and objective reasons simply cannot be *compared* in terms of strength. That is, *no* agent-protecting reason is stronger than, or weaker than, or exactly the same strength as any instance of the pro tanto reason to promote the good; the one kind of reason never outweighs, weighs the same as, or is outweighed by the other kind of reason. (Note that such a view is perfectly compatible with the claim that agent-protecting reasons can be compared among *themselves* in terms of strength, as can instances of the pro tanto reason to promote the good.) Since, on this suggestion, neither the agent-protecting reason nor the pro tanto reason to promote the good will ever outweigh the other, neither will be morally decisive. Thus if subjective reasons and objective reasons are incomparable in this way, the moderate has a perfectly general account of options.

It is far from obvious how the moderate might defend this claim of incomparability; but we can put this difficulty aside. For the simple fact of the matter is that the moderate is committed to the view that subjective reasons and objective reasons often *can* be compared in terms of strength, and so the latest suggestion is not genuinely available to him. After all, only the minimalist holds that options are unlimited. At the very least, the moderate insists that when enough good is at stake, and the cost to the agent is sufficiently low (although not necessarily negligible), the agent is indeed required to promote the good. In such cases the pro tanto reason to promote the good is morally decisive; that is, in those cases it is able to *outweigh* the relevant agent-protecting reason; so the two kinds of reasons can, at least sometimes, be compared.

If he is going to avoid the minimalist, the moderate must, accordingly, admit that subjective reasons and objective reasons often can be compared. But he might suggest, nonetheless, that subjective and objective reasons are only partially or *roughly* comparable. On this proposal, for any particular subjective reason and any particular objective reason, it might indeed be the case that one of these reasons will outweigh, or be outweighed by (or, perhaps even, weigh exactly as much as) the other reason; but often none of these relations will hold, and all that one can say is that the two reasons are 'roughly comparable'.[12] In those cases where the subjective reason and the objective reason are only roughly comparable, neither will outweigh the other, and so neither will be morally decisive; they will, therefore, form an option. What's more, in such cases of rough comparability, we may expect that even if one or both reasons are varied in strength within a reasonable range, the resulting pair of reasons will remain only roughly comparable; the option will, therefore, appropriately extend over a range of cases. However, if the reasons are varied sufficiently, one of them may indeed come to outweigh the other; and so the possibility of grounding requirements remains.

This seems an attractive suggestion for the moderate to pursue. If subjective and objective reasons are only partially comparable, this allows the moderate to maintain a broad range of options, while still recognizing that sometimes agents are required to promote the good. There is, of course, still the need to explain the origins of this merely partial comparability; but let us put this difficulty aside once again, for there is a more pressing problem facing the moderate. As noted, occasional requirements to promote the good are possible, because partial comparability leaves open the possibility that in some cases the objective reasons outweigh the subjective reasons. We might expect, then, that subjective reasons could, similarly, occasionally outweigh the objective ones. In such cases, however, we are back to our original question as to what prevents the subjective reason from being morally decisive. If it is decisive, then there will be no option: agents will be *required* to pursue their own interests in such cases; even though greater good could be done by making the sacrifice, this would simply be forbidden. I think it unlikely that many moderates would be content with such a possibility; but I do not see how partial comparability suffices to rule it out.

[12] See Parfit, p. 431, for a brief discussion of rough comparability.

The moderate could, I suppose, insist that despite the logical possibility, the fact is that no possible agent-protecting reason can outweigh any instance of the pro tanto reason to promote the good. I find this implausible—why should it be possible to break the rough comparability only in the other direction?—but presumably any apparent counterexample could be denied by the moderate. Luckily, however, we can sidestep this question, by considering instead a case in which the agent-protecting reason is, in effect, *unopposed*.

Suppose that by making some personal sacrifice, I can save a stranger from having to undergo a similar loss; for example, I can give up my life to save hers. Let us assume that all other things are equal, so that in terms of the overall good there is no more reason to save her life than to save my own. The pro tanto reason to promote the good provides some reason, of course, to save her life, but it also provides an equally strong reason not to sacrifice my own—so that, on balance, it is indifferent. Here, I think, the moderate would have to admit that the agent-protecting reason outweighs the relevant countervailing reasons, for the pro tanto reason to promote the good, in effect, offers no opposition at all.

Most moderates, I take it, would want to claim that such sacrifices are meritorious; they are, at least, permissible. (Such cases should not be confused with gratuitous sacrifice, which the moderate may well want to forbid; and lest the moderate be tempted to say that in cases like this, where the agent-protecting reasons are extremely strong, it is indeed forbidden to make such sacrifices, it should be borne in mind that similar cases could be described where the sacrifices involved are far less significant.) Surely ordinary morality permits me to give up my life to save that of another. But how can the moderate preserve this judgment? What prevents the agent-protecting reason from being morally decisive, thus grounding a prohibition against sacrificing my interests in this way?

Apparently the moderate must hold that the agent-protecting reason fails to meet some *other* condition necessary for moral decisiveness. So even in those cases (whether rare or common) where it outweighs any relevant opposing reasons, the agent-protecting reason will still fail to ground the undesired requirement for the agent to pursue his interests. Only in this way can the general defense of options be preserved without undermining the very existence of certain other options. Thus the moderate has still not found an account of the structure of options adequate to his particular needs.

NONINSISTENT REASONS

Let's review the argument. If the moderate is to adopt the general defense of options offered by the positive argument, he needs a general account of what prevents the agent-protecting reasons from being morally decisive. We have, so far, been considering variations on the first basic possibility, namely, that agent-protecting reasons cannot outweigh the pro tanto reason to promote the good. However, it seems that no such account will be adequate on its own. Indeed, even the most promising will be inconsistent with the defense of certain options—unless, that is, the moderate can indicate some further condition necessary for moral decisiveness which the agent-protecting reason may fail to meet.

Note, however, that to appeal to such a condition is simply to resort to the second basic possibility: agent-protecting reasons do not undermine options, for they fail to meet some further condition of moral decisiveness. Thus if the moderate is indeed able to point to such a condition, it may no longer be necessary for the moderate to hold that the agent-protecting reasons cannot outweigh the pro tanto reason to promote the good. An adequate account of the second type should suffice on its own.

The moderate, therefore, might do well to claim that when the cost to the agent would be significant, the agent-protecting reasons simply outweigh the pro tanto reason to promote the good. This would offer a straightforward explanation of why there is no general requirement to promote the good. (Of course in extreme cases, the objective reason could still outweigh the subjective reasons, grounding a particular requirement to promote the good.) At the same time, it would still be permissible to sacrifice one's interests, for the agent-protecting reasons would fail to be morally decisive. Thus a genuine option would be generated.

One drawback of such an approach, as I have already noted, is that it leaves it somewhat mysterious why it should be considered morally meritorious for an agent to sacrifice his interests for the greater good—given that, on this approach, the balance of reasons actually opposes making such a sacrifice. But it may be that some account is available to the moderate that would eliminate, or at least reduce, this mystery. At any rate, it is obvious that the entire approach is not available to the moderate at all, unless he can defend the claim that there is indeed some further condition necessary for moral decisiveness that the agent-protecting reasons fail to meet. Unfortunately for the moderate, however, it is difficult to see how the claim can be defended.

Now the extra condition that we have devoted the most attention to is, of course, the motivational condition. But it seems clear that this won't do for the moderate's purposes. The moderate can hardly claim that an agent typically cannot be motivated by the prospect of pursuing his interests. Whatever it is that prevents the generation of the unwanted requirement to pursue one's interests, it is certainly not the lack of the necessary motivational underpinning.

Is there a more plausible suggestion? In Chapter 7 we considered the possibility that only reasons with other-regarding content can be morally decisive. Since agent-protecting reasons have self-regarding content—indeed, this is true by definition—this would certainly do the trick. But I saw no reason to accept the claim that other-regarding content is indeed a condition for moral decisiveness. We can, of course, simply *stipulate* that moral decisiveness is to be understood in such a way that agent-protecting reasons cannot be morally decisive; but in the present context it is clear that this does nothing more than beg the question.

I can only think of one other possibility worth considering. Could there be reasons which are intrinsically incapable of being morally decisive? Such reasons would have genuine weight, and might well be able to outweigh various other reasons. But they themselves would not be *insistent*, in that from the rational perspective it would be perfectly acceptable to neglect them. Presumably, by the very nature of the case, such noninsistent reasons could never ground a *requirement*. But, in contrast to the previous suggestion, this would be due to the intrinsic nature of the *reasons*, rather than merely verbal gerrymandering with the notion of 'moral requirement'. If such noninsistent reasons are possible, then the moderate might go on to try to defend the substantive claim that agent-protecting reasons are noninsistent.

However, I do not know what reasons of this kind would be like. The sort of considerations which are familiar from typical practical deliberation do not seem to me to be of this noninsistent nature. More than this: it is hard to imagine how reasons for acting *could* be of this kind.

This may not seem correct. It might be objected that the considerations of typical practical deliberation are precisely of this noninsistent sort. (Indeed, that's why this possibility is worth considering in the first place.) After all, if typical reasons were insistent, as I have just suggested, then there would be few cases in which agents would have any significant room for choice if they were going to act in keeping with the balance of reasons. But we do not typically think that rational choices are so thoroughly constrained.

Consider the case of choosing between two meals in a restaurant. We generally consider it rational for the person to pick either of the two dishes. Yet this would be fairly unlikely if reasons were insistent—for it would mean that the reasons in favor of each dish would have to be in exact balance: otherwise, to pick one or the other of the dishes would be irrational. And even if they were in exact balance, a slight alteration in the weight of one of the reasons—e.g., a minimal change in price—would have to *shift* the balance, settling the matter. If reasons are noninsistent, however, the problem disappears: either choice would be rationally justified; neither choice irrational.

I think, however, that the objection misdescribes the case. If the choice of either dish would be rational, this is because we normally assume that there is overriding reason to eat what one *wants* to eat. Choosing between the two dishes is not so much a matter of evaluating the weight of reasons as determining which dish is more appealing at the moment. Given one's preference, it *would* be irrational to pick the other dish. Thus reasons appear to be insistent after all. Furthermore, consider a situation in which taste, cost, diet, nutritional value, and so on, all strongly support one dish, while the second dish is only supported by a slightly more attractive appearance. In at least some cases of this sort it would be obviously irrational to pick the second dish. Yet if reasons are noninsistent, it is not clear why this should be.

The insistent nature of reasons comes out even more clearly when they are considered in isolation. Imagine that my acting in a particular way has the support of only one reason—but that there is absolutely *no* reason *not* to act in that way. In such a case it seems fairly clear that it *would* be irrational not to act. There would be no rational justification for neglecting the sole reason: the reason is insistent. Yet why should the reason be any *less* insistent when it is opposed by countervailing reasons? It may be outweighed, to be sure, but it is difficult to see what could suddenly make it noninsistent.

Indeed, I simply do not understand how a reason *could* be noninsistent. To be a reason is to support a particular course of action. For a reason to be noninsistent, however, it would have to be rationally justifiable for the agent to neglect that support. But if the support is genuine, I cannot see how such neglect could be justified.

It would not be implausible, then, to suspect that we cannot give a coherent account of noninsistent reasons. And even if such an account could be given, I see no reason to believe the further, substantive claim that agent-protecting reasons would be of this kind. I claimed, of course, that the arguments for the inadequacy of the objective standpoint were unsuccessful. But even if they had succeeded, and had justified the adoption of a partially subjective standpoint, I see no reason at all to think that the subjective reasons recognized from such a standpoint would be any less insistent than the objective reasons. Noninsistence seems an unpromising line of argument for the moderate.

I am unable to think of any other, more promising candidates for the moderate. If there really were agent-protecting reasons, I cannot see how the moderate would defend the claim that they could not be morally decisive. Such moral decisiveness would undermine the existence of options, but I do not see how it could be adequately avoided.

THE DEFENSE OF OPTIONS

The moderate's problems come in two layers. First, I have suggested that it may not be possible for the moderate to offer a coherent model of options which is at the same time compatible with the various features of ordinary morality. It is not that there is anything conceptually confused or incoherent about the notion of an option per se. On the contrary, the basic structure of an option is relatively simple: there will be an option with regard to a given reaction provided that there is neither a morally decisive reason which supports that reaction nor a morally decisive reason which opposes that reaction. The moderate's difficulties arise by virtue of the fact that he is a defender of ordinary morality, and so is committed to the existence of certain options and not others, as well as to various other specific judgments, requirements, and so on.

If the moderate—like the minimalist—could deny the existence of the pro tanto reason to promote the good, the defense of options might be made easier. But I have argued that the existence of such a reason is part of the best explanation of various judgments that the moderate wants to make: it seems that the moderate is committed to the claim that there is always *some* reason to promote the good, even if it is not required; and without such a reason it is hard to see how promotion of the good could ever be required at all, even when the cost to the agent is slight. Yet once the moderate has admitted the existence of the pro tanto reason to promote the good, the challenge from the extremist arises, and the moderate needs to point to countervailing considerations that prevent that reason from grounding a general requirement to promote the good.

As we have seen, the most plausible attempt to specify such countervailing considerations ultimately turns on the claim that there are subjective, agent-relative reasons for an agent to pursue his interests. Presumably such agent-protecting reasons could oppose the pro tanto reason to promote the good and keep it from being morally decisive. But granting the existence of such reasons creates a new problem for the moderate. For these reasons will themselves suffice to undermine the existence of options—saddling the moderate with an undesired requirement that agents pursue their interests—unless it can be shown that they too somehow fail to be morally decisive. Unfortunately for the moderate, however, a survey of possible approaches to defending the claim that agent-protecting reasons will indeed lack moral decisiveness produced none that would fully suit the moderate's purposes: all were either incompatible with some requirements or options of ordinary morality, or were implausible in their own right.

Forced to defend options within the parameters of ordinary morality, the moderate is driven to the positive argument. But once he has gone this far it is no longer clear that the moderate is in fact able to state and defend a coherent model of options.

Whatever the merits of this first objection, there is a second layer to the moderate's problems. For it seems that the moderate has not even succeeded in showing that there *are* any countervailing reasons that oppose the pro tanto reason to promote the good. The positive argument, whatever its drawbacks, relies upon the claim that the objective standpoint fails to give adequate place to the subjective standpoint; if this could be shown, there would be reason to believe that the moral point of view recognizes subjective reasons, and not only objective ones. But the moderate was unable to show that the objective standpoint is indeed inadequate in this way. None of the considerations he presented sufficiently supported maintaining a partially subjective (i.e., nonobjective) point of view; they did not show that on balance some of the agent's natural bias should be retained.

Thus the positive argument fails. Even the second point alone is sufficient to show this. The argument hoped to ground both options and constraints by demonstrating that an adequate moral system would fully reflect the nature of persons. The success of the positive argument depended upon the moderate's being able to present considerations which supported the subjective point of view— considerations which made it inappropriate for a moral system to endorse a totally objective standpoint. But the moderate has not been able to defend his claim that there are considerations of this sort; and so the positive argument is unsuccessful.

Nor is it only the positive argument which is thus undercut by the moderate's failure: attempts to refurbish the negative argument also collapse. As I argued at the end of the last chapter, the only way to resurrect the moderate's claim that a requirement to promote the good would lack the necessary motivational under-pinning would be to show that there are positive considerations which support the subjective point of view. Since the moderate has been unable to indicate such considerations, the negative argument too must be laid to rest.[13]

The negative and positive arguments, it will be recalled, were the moderate's two most plausible attempts to offer a defense of

---

[13] Strictly speaking, a refurbished negative argument might still be possible, despite the failure of the positive argument as I have developed it—if there were morally unacceptable but nonetheless genuine subjective reasons: despite being irrelevant from the *moral* point of view, such reasons would still support the subjective standpoint, so that—on balance—the agent might lack motivation to try to overcome the bias. (At the same time, however, since the subjective reasons would

options in terms of the principle that an acceptable moral system must adequately reflect the nature of persons. And this principle in turn seemed the most plausible way of basing a defense of options on an appeal to cost. For it seemed likely that, if the appeal to cost genuinely yielded countervailing considerations capable of blocking a general requirement to promote the good, this was because of the special importance an individual's interests can have for that individual, given the nature of persons. The conclusion, then, seems to be that the moderate cannot turn the appeal to cost into an adequate defense of options. And this suggests that options cannot be defended.

It is possible, of course, that the moderate might be able to offer a defense of options which was not based on the appeal to cost. (Let us leave to the side the general objection that the very attempt to preserve options within the confines of ordinary morality may be incoherent.) But in Chapter 6 we considered a few attempts to do just this; and they too were unsuccessful.

Furthermore, it seems unlikely that a defense which was not ultimately based on the appeal to cost would be acceptable to the moderate. For at some point the moderate is going to have to fend off the minimalist's claim that agents are *never* required to promote the good—even when it takes no sacrifice to do so. The moderate may not believe that I am required to devote myself to famine relief; but he does believe that I am required to save the drowning child. Thus he must point to some relevant difference which allows options to be grounded in the former case but not the latter. And it is difficult to see how anything other than the difference in cost to the agent could be plausibly suggested.

What this means is that a defense of options must be based on the appeal to cost if it is to yield options limited in the way that the moderate desires. In this light, the moderate's inability to develop an adequate defense out of the appeal to cost is all the more telling. The moderate himself recognizes the existence of the pro tanto reason to promote the good to which the extremist appeals in

be morally *unacceptable*, there would be no danger that they themselves would ground a moral requirement, undermining options.) I suspect, however, that on reflection most moderates will actually find this possibility unsatisfactory (ordinary morality does not in fact regard agent-protecting reasons as unacceptable, or illegitimate, from the moral point of view); at any rate, I know of no adequate argument for the existence of such reasons.

support of a *requirement* to promote the good. Faced with his own inability to defend the claim that the pursuit of the good is tempered by the existence of options, the moderate has reason to suspect that the pursuit of the good may not be tempered at all. If the moderate cannot establish the existence of options, perhaps this is because there aren't any.

10

Extraordinary Morality

The intuitive grip of ordinary morality generally makes it difficult for us to take the claims of the extremist seriously. But intuitive support is not sufficient: the promissory notes of intuition must eventually be redeemed with a more adequate defense; when this cannot be done, we have reason to be sceptical of the counsels of intuition.

Ordinary morality, I have admitted, is supported by our intuitions. But as I have argued throughout this book, the moderate can actually defend neither of ordinary morality's two major features. Both the attempted defense of constraints and the attempted defense of options ended in failure. We must take these failures seriously: they give us reason to move beyond ordinary morality.

As we revise our views in the hope of acquiring a more adequate moral theory, there seem to be two directions in which we can move: toward the extremist or toward the minimalist. That the extremist's alternative remains open despite the moderate's failures is obvious—for as I have noted, the most straightforward extremist position recognizes neither constraints nor options. It is less obvious, however, whether the minimalist alternative remains as well—for minimalists seem to want to claim options of some sort, and the moderate was unable to offer a defense of options.

This question deserves careful consideration; but here I want to limit myself to two brief comments. First, *some* of the moderate's difficulties arose from his need to defend options which were *limited* in various ways. More generally, the moderate was restricted to a defense of options compatible with the views of ordinary morality. It might be that the minimalist—eager to embrace more powerful options, and thus free of those difficulties— would be more successful than the moderate. Second, some minimalists, strictly speaking, may not believe in *options* at all. For options imply that it is justified for an agent to promote the good at his own expense if he chooses; and some minimalists may believe that it is simply unreasonable—or perhaps even *wrong*—to sacrifice one's interests, even for the greater good. Thus such minimalists too will escape some of the problems which face the moderate. It is not clear that all the difficulties which confronted the moderate would be avoided by the minimalist; but rather than pursuing these matters further, let us assume that despite the moderate's failures the possibility of maintaining the minimalist's position remains.

Given the choice between the minimalist and the extremist, I would like to think that most of us—even if only somewhat grudgingly—would find the extremist's position more plausible. Perhaps I am wrong about this; but at any rate it is obvious that such grudging support would hardly constitute a satisfactory defense of the extremist. Nor, it goes without saying, would a mass defection to the minimalist—accompanied, perhaps, by feelings of liberation—be a vindication of that position either. Both the extremist and the minimalist must offer defenses of their respective positions—and it is the adequacy of those accounts which should settle the dispute.

It has been clear that my sympathies lie with the extremist. But, as I stated in the first chapter, my intention in this book has been to present and criticize the moderate's position; I have not tried to adjudicate between minimalist and extremist. Nonetheless, it may be in order to indicate, quite briefly, along what lines I think the defense of the extremist might proceed.

Ultimately, the dispute between the minimalist and the extremist comes down to the existence and moral decisiveness of the pro tanto reason to promote the good. In this work, of course, the existence of the pro tanto reason to promote the good has simply been assumed, for it is common ground between the moderate and extremist. But the minimalist recognizes no such reason, and legitimately demands an argument for its existence. So what the extremist must do, roughly, is establish the existence and power of a particular reason. Now claims about reasons, I think, are connected to claims about motivation, in that the latter can provide *evidence* for the former. That is, the claim that there is a reason to do such and such can be supported by knowledge of what an agent could be motivated to do. The relevant evidence, however, does not necessarily concern what an agent *will* in fact do: for a variety of factors can prevent an agent from acting on a reason. Rather, the relevant evidence has to do with what an agent *would* do under certain ideal conditions. Roughly, then, the fact that under various ideal conditions agents *would* promote the good provides grounds for accepting the claim that there is indeed a *reason* to promote the good.

A full defense of the extremist would have to include a specification of those ideal conditions, and I do not propose to offer that here. But the discussion of vividness has already revealed what I take to be *one* of the relevant conditions. An agent will not necessarily be motivated by a reason of which he has only pale appreciation. If an agent acts on a consideration when his beliefs are vivid, however, that is some support for the claim that there is a reason to react as he does. Of course, as I also noted in Chapter 8, a more complete account would identify other relevant conditions as well: beyond vividness, and the addition of various relevant beliefs (as well as the correction of erroneous beliefs), these might include attentiveness to the relevant facts, elimination of various distorting influences, prejudices, and so on. We considered at some length the extremist's original counterfactual thesis that agents with vivid beliefs would tend to act in keeping with the objective standpoint; but, as I have previously observed, given the relevance of these various other ideal conditions, ultimately it is an 'expanded' version of the counterfactual with which we should be concerned, one which takes these other factors into account as well.

If this appropriately expanded counterfactual hypothesis is correct—and agents attentive to their suitably supplemented vivid beliefs, freed from distorting prejudices, and so on, would tend to act in accordance with the objective standpoint—then the extremist has the core of a defense for the claim that there is a strong pro tanto reason to promote the good. To block the conclusion that there is such a reason, or at least a reason of such strength, the minimalist would have to either challenge the list of ideal conditions (e.g., challenge the inclusion of vividness), challenge the substantial truth of the counterfactual (i.e., deny that vividness in combination with the other ideal conditions would move agents to act largely in accord with the objective standpoint), or challenge the adequacy of the evidential connection (e.g., deny that the truth of such counterfactuals supports claims about the existence of the corresponding reasons); I think it would be difficult, however, to sustain any of these challenges.

Now the minimalist, as I've noted, would be troubled by this conclusion—i.e., that there is even so much as a pro tanto reason to promote the good. But he would still be able to ward off the extremist's position, at least, if he could show that the pro tanto reason to promote the good somehow fails to be morally decisive. Thus the minimalist must point to some countervailing consideration sufficient to prevent the grounding of a requirement to promote the good. Of course we have already examined in considerable detail the unsuccessful attempts of the moderate to establish the existence of such countervailing considerations, but it must be admitted that the minimalist would be free of some of the restrictions that hampered the moderate. Nonetheless I believe that the minimalist would meet with no greater success.

Assuming, then, that the extremist would indeed be able to defend the existence of the pro tanto reason to promote the good— and in the absence of a parallel demonstration, on the part of the minimalist, of the existence of powerful countervailing considerations in support of the subjective standpoint—we would have grounds for accepting the extremist's position. Obviously this is only the sketch of an argument; but it is, at any rate, the direction that I find most promising.

Even if it can eventually be rejected, the intuitive pull of the minimalist's position should not be denied. On a theoretical level, the existence of reasons for favoring one's own interests is as much in need of demonstration as is the existence of any other purported reasons. Reasons for favoring one's interests have no privileged theoretical status; and it is exceedingly difficult—if not simply impossible—to come up with an adequate demonstration of their existence. But on the intuitive level, such reasons do indeed have a special claim on our belief. It often strikes us as unquestionable that agents have strong reason to favor their own interests, while reasons for aiding others seem uncertain, weak, and in need of demonstration. Because of this, the demand has often been made that it be shown that reasons of the latter sort do not conflict with reasons of the former sort—i.e., that it be shown that morality can never demand an overall sacrifice of the agent's various interests. Sometimes the demand is even bolder: morality must not only be consistent with the agent's interests, but must ultimately be grounded—find its *foundation*—in the agent's interests. And sometimes the demand is bolder still: morality must find its foundation in the agent's *self-interest*; it must be shown to promote the agent's own personal well-being. The demand is, I believe, theoretically dubious—even in its most modest form. Prior to argument, there are no grounds for granting any sort of reason a priviledged status. But intuitively the demand is pressing; and it is one that we can rarely comfortably leave behind.

It is an ancient demand. It is a demand as old as moral philosophy itself, as old as our reflections on our interactions with others. The minimalist is one who makes the demand in its unalloyed form: he challenges us to show how being moral is in his interests (i.e., either promotes his self-interest, or at least promotes his various aims, projects, and concerns). The moderate is one who tries to make the demand without allowing it to drown out all other voices: he offers the appeal to cost, but tries to avoid its more unacceptable implications. The extremist alone gives the demand no role in the fundamental shaping of morality: we may be morally required to sacrifice our interests, and that is that. But even the extremist will feel the intuitive pull of the demand, and wonder in what ways, if any, acting morally can be in an agent's interests. An agent who promotes the good may lose much: but does she gain anything?

There is, I believe, something which can be gained by an agent who lives in pursuit of the good. We might begin by noting that there is a harmony in an agent's life when she acts in accordance with the moral system she espouses—a congruence of thought and action. The life of such an agent coheres in a way we value. Now such coherence is absent when the agent fails to act on her moral standards. In such cases there is a fragmentation within the agent herself—for she must, in a sense, disavow herself: the life she leads is unjustified in her own eyes; she cannot approve of herself. In contrast, an agent who acts in keeping with her moral views can be at one with herself. Such unity, I think, is part of what we mean when we say that an an individual's life has *integrity*.

It will be observed, of course, that this aspect of integrity is possessed by any agent at all who follows her moral code— *whatever* that might be. So it is not a quality uniquely possessed by extremists: moderates and minimalists too may display such unity of belief and action. But the congruence of thought and action to which I have referred is not all that we mean by integrity. It is not sufficient to act on one's code of action; the code itself must not be unjustifiable—at the very least, it must not be unjustifiable by the agent's own lights.

Now I have suggested that it may be the extremist alone who can offer an adequate defense of his moral system. If this is right, then it is only the extremist who can defend his moral outlook against the challenge of critical self-examination. So it is only extremists who can lead lives that they are able to justify fully to themselves. If no one other than an extremist can offer a coherent explanation of his own moral system, then only extremists can offer adequate accounts of their own lives.

The tensions inherent in the views of non-extremists are, perhaps, rarely made explicit. Few individuals take the trouble to reflect very long about their ability to justify their own moral beliefs. But the tensions are there nonetheless, and the failure to recognize them would hardly satisfy us as an adequate substitute for eliminating them. If the extremist can indeed justify his moral view, however, then such tensions will be absent in his case. Thus the depth of coherence which is available to the extremist goes beyond that which can be possessed by others. Although he may sacrifice much in the pursuit of the good, the extremist at least has integrity.

How important is such integrity to us? I am not sure. I think that it would be easy either to overstate or to understate the value we place on it. Consider the ease with which most people can walk away from paradoxes and philosophical puzzles. Such behavior is, perhaps, an indication that many people would not attach significant disvalue to the possession of views which could not form part of a coherent whole. And the very fact that so few people actively engage in investigating the justifiability of their moral views suggests that, in general, people are not greatly concerned with the possibility that their lives may lack this sort of integrity. Yet at the same time it seems to me that even fewer people could rest content in the knowledge that the moral code on which they act could *not* be justified. The regularity with which people attempt to justify their actions—even when the justifications offered are poor— suggests that most of us do attach significant value to the possession of a coherently justifiable moral code. It is simply that many people assume—incorrectly, I believe—that such coherence is easily come by. Integrity has a central place in the moral character to which we aspire.

Nonetheless, integrity is, I think, only one value among many—and it can be outweighed. An agent might have interests in any number of things that might conflict with the protection of his integrity. It is important to be clear about this. The promotion of the good may well require sacrifices of such a sort that the agent's interests will be damaged overall. If my comments about integrity are correct, of course, then *failure* to make the sacrifice will *also* involve harm to one of the agent's interests—i.e., his interest in his integrity. But for all that, the value that the agent places in his integrity might be outweighed by the value he assigns to other of his interests—so that, on balance, the agent would be better off (at least by his own lights) were he not to make the sacrifice. In such cases, of course, the extremist retains the position he has maintained throughout: even if pursuit of the good would involve taking on an overall sacrifice of his interests, this is what the agent is morally required to do. Morality can indeed conflict with the agent's promotion of his own interests.

But this raises a further point. As I have suggested, although an agent who promotes the good may sacrifice much, his life possesses a coherence which it would otherwise lack. This means that even if an agent were to choose to promote his interests at the expense of the overall good, by failing to promote the good he would damage his own integrity and thus fail to promote one of his own interests. This suggests the bleak possibility that it may be impossible to avoid sacrificing either one's integrity or one's other interests. If the good life involves promoting all one's interests, then this would mean that the good life could not even be attained.

The extremist, however, has a possible way out of the difficulty. For the conflict only arises when an agent has interests which are (at least potentially) opposed to the promotion of the good. Only in such cases would an agent's interests be best served overall by failure to promote the good, with the ensuing loss of integrity. However, an agent *might* have the pursuit of the good as his fundamental project—and in such a case promotion of the good would never require an overall sacrifice of his interests. And thus promotion of his own interests would never involve loss of integrity. If the good life for any given individual is in large part a function of his particular interests, then it seems plausible to suggest that an agent whose fundamental interest was in the promotion of the overall good might be able to live the good life while abiding by the demands of morality. All other individuals who valued their integrity would generally find unavoidable conflict between that value and their other interests.

There is thus a satisfying form of the good life which is available to the extremist alone—although it is certainly not possessed by all extremists. For not all extremists have the promotion of the good as their fundamental interest—even if out of conviction they live their lives in pursuit of the good. Such individuals may well be called upon to sacrifice their own interests. But the extremist whose fundamental project is promotion of the good need never sacrifice his interests overall.

Some individuals, perhaps, are raised to take such fundamental interest in the overall good. But what about the rest of us—those whose interests might well conflict with the pursuit of the good? If we value the coherence of our lives sufficiently, then the alternative open to us is clear: we must change. Such change is not easy; but neither is it impossible. An individual may be converted by an increase in the vividness of his appreciation of the needs of others; or he may find himself convinced of the truth of the extremist's position through examination of arguments such as those we have considered; and there are, no doubt, other possibilities as well. Whatever the source of the strength and will to change, an individual's interests are not fixed—and he may be able to alter them so as to eliminate or reduce the conflict between his own interests and the overall good. Ultimately, then, morality asks us to change.

POLITICAL AND SOCIAL STRUCTURES

The simple fact remains that for almost all of us, our overall interests can conflict with the promotion of the good. And given our natural tendency to favor our own interests, this means that we will generally find it difficult to promote the good and will frequently fail to do so. Even were we all intellectually convinced of the requirement to promote the good it would still be important for the extremist to take account of the fact that it would be difficult for us to motivate ourselves to make the sacrifices pursuit of the good may require.

One implication of the extremist's position is that we should, perhaps, make greater efforts to make ourselves vividly aware of the needs of others. We have already discussed at some length the impact of vividness on motivation: frequently, e.g., an agent will find it easier to take on some sacrifice if he is able to increase the vividness of his recognition of the suffering of the persons whom he is in a position to aid. In a general way, then, we should perhaps expose ourselves more frequently to information about the misery and pain which fill the lives of many of our fellows. And in particular cases it may help to focus our attention on the good we are about to perform.

But as I have noted, there are limits to how far vividness can take us, in that a policy of trying to make all one's beliefs as vivid as possible would probably be counterproductive—wasting energy, causing psychological strain, and reducing the efficiency with which we can promote the good. (And, of course, totally vivid beliefs may well be beyond our psychological capacity.) I suggested that the proper approach is probably to guide ourselves by general rules— being prepared, first, to depart from these rules in unusual cases, and second, to increase our motivation through vividness in those cases where this would be helpful.

If, however, we are not to try to make all our beliefs as vivid as possible, then of course the problem of motivation remains. Our general rules may tell us to make some sacrifice which we nonetheless will find it difficult to undertake. This is one point at which moral philosophy opens into social and political philosophy. For one way to make it more likely that we will do our part in promoting the good is to alter the social and political structures.

Let us start with the political arena—more particularly, the state. People design the state to serve various ends; if the extremist is correct then an over-arching purpose of the state should be to promote the overall good. That is, the political economy should be so structured as to bring about the greatest good. Were there constraints, there might be limits to what sorts of sacrifices the state could impose upon particular citizens for the greater good. But as we have seen no reason to believe that there are constraints—and the most straightforward extremist's position denies their existence— in designing the state the extremist is guided instead by empirical considerations of how the good can best be promoted.

Now it should go without saying that genuine promotion of the overall good will involve the proper distribution of a variety of more specific goods, such as education, opportunity, and political power. But let me here restrict myself to a few comments about the distribution of wealth. Presumably promotion of the good will involve taxing the well-to-do so as to provide for the essential needs of the poor and handicapped; and so on. At the very least, then, it seems that the requirement to promote the good supports something like the liberal welfare state. However, it may be that a more radical political economic structure is called for: it may be that greater good still could be brought about through widespread redistribution of resources, the abolition of private property as we know it, and the institution of one or another form of socialism. On the other hand, it might be that the good could be most effectively promoted by shying away from such radical alternatives. I noted in the first chapter the possibility that if imposed sacrifices are too great—e.g., if taxes are too high—the decline in motivation to produce might be so significant that there would be an overall decrease in the good which could be achieved. Thus even within the liberal welfare state there might be limits to how much the state could claim for the public good without actually bringing about a decline in its ability to promote that good.

There are, of course, a host of other, similar problems that would ultimately need to be considered as well. But I want to mention only one other central issue involving the distribution of wealth—the problem of world poverty. In designing the state it is crucial to recall that the requirement to promote the good does not stop at the borders of our own country. Indeed, in terms of potential contribution to the greater good, much of the most pressing work to be done involves redressing some of the staggering inequality that presently exists between nations: on any plausible account, promoting the good involves using the vast resources of the wealthy nations to facilitate meeting the needs of the poor and disadvantaged in other countries. Unfortunately, it is often far from clear what sort of political economic institutions might most effectively promote the good on this appropriately global scale.

These issues are all of fundamental importance, but I will not try to settle any of them here. They depend upon what are in a broad sense empirical judgments beyond the scope of this book, and from the extremist's perspective the point is simply to institute that government and those institutions—whatever they may be—which will best promote the overall good. Nonetheless it seems fairly evident that even if there are limits to how much the state can take from the well-off so as to help the needy (whether here, or abroad), such limits are well beyond current levels of taxation. And it is equally clear that the government's use of its resources should reflect priorities quite different from those which are espoused today. That is, on the one hand, more could be taken than is currently taken; and on the other hand, what is taken could be used to make a more effective contribution to the good.

We might think of the government as taking from an individual (at least some of) the resources which he is required to devote to the good—and then distributing this for him. What are the advantages of having such a process? Part of the reason for having the government do this is that—at least in theory—it may be able to distribute the resources more effectively. And part of the reason, no doubt, is that such a procedure ensures contributions from individuals who would not otherwise make sizable sacrifices at all. Furthermore, having the government tax us and distribute the resources for us frees us from the need to distribute those resources ourselves: we are left with more time to follow our own life plans; and this in turn contributes to an increase in the overall good.

Yet another important consideration is that the existence of a government committed to the promotion of the good can alleviate some of the difficulties of motivating individual sacrifices. Even for those individuals who would be somewhat motivated to undertake the sacrifice, it is simply easier motivationally to do it through the government. First of all, the mandatory nature of the sacrifice when it is backed by political sanctions brings self-interest more in line with the public interest: one is more ready to give up one's resources if one faces jail otherwise. Second, it is easier for most of us to give one lump sum—in the form of taxes—than it is to give an equivalent total amount spread over a number of occasions, as we might be required to do if we had to direct the resources to worthy causes personally: it would be harder to motivate several acts of giving. Third, we find it easier to give knowing that others too are doing their part: the existence of government taxation guarantees that we are not the only individuals sacrificing so that others may have.

Having the proper political structure, therefore, can contribute to the promotion of the good. On the one hand it makes it more likely that others will make their contribution; and on the other hand it makes it easier for me to make mine. The same is true of having the proper social structure. Since people respond to social sanctions as well as to political sanctions, it is important that public expectations of individual behavior be sufficiently demanding. Currently any individual who acts in keeping with ordinary morality—and its minimal demands—is thought to be leading a morally acceptable life. In such a climate of social opinion there is little or no social pressure for an individual to take upon himself significant sacrifices for the sake of the greater good. In a society in which expectations were higher, it seems likely that individuals would produce a greater amount of good overall.

As with the political realm, it is something of an empirical question just what the social norms should be. It might be plausibly suggested that if the standards that society held out were too high— so that, e.g., all who failed to make their maximal contribution to the good were subject to public moral condemnation—the net effect would be counterproductive: since few people would meet the standards, public criticism would be hypocritical and lose its motivating influence as a result of overexposure. It may be that more good overall would be produced if blame were not levelled against all those who fall short of doing all that they could, and if praise were given to all those who surpassed some particular level of contribution. This issue too is of fundamental importance, but once more I shall not try to settle it. I will only note that it seems likely that the appropriate level of social expectation is far higher than that which obtains in our own society. People would do much more than they currently do if we lived in a society which expected it of us.

As in the political realm, the proper social atmosphere would, first, apply pressure on those who would not otherwise make contributions to the overall good, and second, aid those individuals who would be somewhat motivated to make such sacrifices but would find it difficult to do so without support. Furthermore, it seems likely that the sphere of social influence is appropriately broader than that of legitimate political force. For the most part, politically imposed sacrifices should probably be limited to contributions of material resources (although there may be room for greater Good Samaritan legislation and perhaps even limited mandatory public service). Social expectations about the contributions of individuals do not seem as sharply limited in their legitimate range: it does not seem inappropriate for social norms to demand contributions of time and effort as well as mere sacrifices of material resources.

Another important aspect of the social arena is the moral education of children. If people were raised to understand the existence of a moral requirement to promote the overall good, and if they were taught to be more attentive to the needs of others, then they would find it easier to lead lives in accord with the pursuit of the good. The bias in favor of their own interests would be more easily overcome in those cases where pursuit of the good was in conflict with promotion of their interests; but more importantly, people would be more likely to have developed interests whose pursuit would be to the advantage of the overall good.

This last point is worth expanding. Children should be taught the importance of developing a life plan whose pursuit would result in their making their greatest contribution to the good. The shape of such a plan will of course have to reflect the external state of the world; but it will also be a function of the specific talents and handicaps of the particular individual. A nation of agents collecting charity would hardly produce the greatest amount of good overall. There is obviously a need for scientists, educators, farmers, artists, and so on. Pursuit of the good involves developing and utilizing one's talents in a way that will frequently be satisfying to the individual as well as beneficial to others. This is not to lose sight of the fact that promoting the good will also involve contributions of time and effort—and more, on occasion—beyond what is already devoted to one's career. But if individuals are taught to keep the needs of others in sight as their interests develop, the split between those personal interests and what is in the overall interest will be lessened, and so the actions required by the pursuit of the good will less often be perceived as *sacrifices*.

This provides an answer to an objection which moderates frequently urge against extremists—i.e., that agents must be free to lead their own lives. Moderates may suggest that human well-being should be construed not in terms of the amount of this or that mental state, but rather in terms of the degree to which individuals are able to carry out the plans they have made for their lives. To a large extent people want not only that certain interests should be satisfied, but that they themselves should be the agents; people not only want things to happen—they want to *act*. Thus, unless people are free to lead the lives they have chosen for themselves, human well-being, a central element of the good, will be absent. Extremists— it is objected—chain individuals to the pursuit of the good, and thus deny them the freedom to live their own lives.

These observations about the nature of human well-being are indeed significant. But as objections to the extremist they misfire. First of all, extremists are obviously capable of recognizing that the good should largely be measured by the extent to which people are able to carry out the plans they have made for their lives. But of course this requires their having the resources as well as the freedom to promote their projects, and satisfy their interests. The extremist insists that we recognize the appalling degree to which people currently lack even a chance at carrying out satisfying lives. To a large degree promoting the good is simply trying to bring it about that the greatest number of individuals overall are in a position to lead the lives they envision.

Second, even if we redirect our attention from the recipients to the agent himself, the extremist is still capable of recognizing the importance of being able to live a life in accordance with the plan one has formed for it. The extremist certainly recognizes the loss involved when an agent has to abandon his life plan in order to promote the good: this is one of the central reasons that he stresses so the importance of developing a life plan whose *pursuit* would involve the agent's greatest possible contribution to the good. If, as I suggested, the appropriate life plan would be a reflection of the particular characteristics of the individual, then there would be no question of extremists trying to deny agents freedom to live their own lives. This brings us back to the importance of moral education: it is only in a society which expects and teaches individuals to live lives through which the overall good can be promoted that the need to abandon inappropriate life plans can be minimized.

FREEDOM

There is a tradition in moral philosophy which attempts to locate the foundations of morality in the nature of persons as free beings. Our worth as persons arises (at least in part) from this freedom;

and moral behavior, it is suggested, is best viewed as an expression of that freedom. I want to conclude by connecting this position to the extremist's position, although my interpretation of the importance of our metaphysical freedom is not the traditional one.

An individual whose fundamental project is the pursuit of the good will find no conflict between the promotion of his own interests and the promotion of the overall good. The rest of us, however, are not so lucky. For us, the conflict between our interests and the promotion of the good is sharp. Our natural inclination is to favor those interests at the expense of the overall good; but to do so is to fail to meet the requirements of morality. Therefore what we must do is change: we must either overcome our natural biases, or alter our very interests. We are able to change in both of these ways; that we are able to do either is a sign of our freedom.

Consider, first, our ability to overcome our natural bias in favor of our interests. I have suggested that one of the reasons for having the proper political and social structures is that they apply external pressures upon the individual, making it more likely that he will make a significant contribution to the overall good. Even if successful, however—so that individuals subject to these pressures do indeed promote the good—such a situation is hardly ideal. It would be preferable, after all, if agents pursued the good simply because this is the right thing to do.

The extremist believes that there is a moral requirement to promote the good: but to say that there is such a requirement is simply to say that the promotion of the good is supported by morally decisive reasons. Now ideally, at least, agents should be able to recognize the existence of these reasons and to *act* on them; that is, agents should promote the good because they see that there is decisive reason to do this. Generally, however, this is not an easy thing to do: given the natural bias of our subjective standpoint we find it much easier to favor our own interests even when the balance of reasons opposes this. Nonetheless, we are not chained to the subjective point of view—but are, instead, able to disengage ourselves from it and to act in accordance with the objective standpoint. We are able to recognize the course of action indicated by our best theory of reasons; and we are free to do what there is reason to do.

A further comment about motivation may be in order here. One might wonder whether it is better to be motivated by the recognition of the existence of reasons or by direct concern for the well-being of others. For example, if I may perform some act which will alleviate the suffering of another, does the extremist find it preferable for me to be acting in response to that other's need—to which I am sensitive—or to be acting in response to the fact that my moral theory tells me that there is a reason to act—i.e., to my recognition of a reason? There is, I think, a difference between these two alternatives, at least in some cases. But I will not pause here to examine the issue or to take sides except to suggest that much of the difference is just a matter of description. For recognition of a reason is largely a matter of recognition of the existence of an aspect of the situation the proper appreciation of which has the power to motivate. Ideally agents should act on their recognition of reasons; but this just is a matter of seeing, e.g., that the suffering of another is more significant than the inconvenience to me of alleviating it. The subjective standpoint pressures me to act as though my own interests were more important simply because they are mine; but morality asks that I take advantage of my ability to disengage myself from the subjective standpoint and to promote the overall good rather than my own.

The first aspect of our freedom is our ability to act on the balance of reasons, even though this involves overcoming our natural tendency to favor our own interests. The second aspect of our freedom lies in our ability to alter those interests themselves. Just as we are not chained to acting in accord with the subjective standpoint, neither are the contents of that standpoint fixed: our interests can alter; we are free to change them. Such change can come gradually, or suddenly; it may come unheralded, or, I think, one can set out to produce it.

From the extremist's perspective, of course, the relevant sorts of changes are those in which the individual develops a greater interest in seeing that the needs of others are met. Although not inevitable, the growth of such an interest may be one effect of coming to appreciate that the needs of others should count as heavily as one's own. Ideally, perhaps, one should have the promotion of the overall good as one's fundamental interest. More specific interests would then be monitored with an eye to whether they are in harmony with this fundamental project. Probably few of our present interests completely meet this standard; but we are able to change ourselves. Doing so increases our likely contribution to the good; and it decreases the cost to ourselves of acting morally. For to the extent that one acquires interests whose pursuit is in accord with the promotion of the good, one eliminates the need to *sacrifice* those interests and to overcome the bias in favor of them.

I believe, then, that the sorts of changes urged by the extremist are connected in interesting ways with our nature as free beings: our ability to change ourselves is grounded in that freedom. It is worth speculating whether that connection goes deeper. As I have noted, it is sometimes suggested that our worth as persons arises (partially, at least) from this freedom. It would be quite satisfying if the following related claims could be supported: we have a deep interest in being valuable beings; such value arises not through the mere possession of the freedom to change, but through the exercise of that freedom; and the freedom is genuinely exercised only when we change so as to act in *greater* accord with the objective standpoint. If all three of these claims were correct we would have a second answer to the question—raised at the beginning of this chapter—of what, if anything, we gain by acting morally: acting morally would enhance our value. It would be satisfying, as I say, if all three claims could be supported. But I do not see how this is to be done; and so the matter must be left as mere speculation.

THE DEMANDS OF MORALITY

I began this book with the claim that few of us believe that we are morally required to promote the good, and that none of us live in accordance with such a requirement. If I have been at all successful, the reader may now be willing to take the possibility of such a requirement more seriously; perhaps he or she may even have come closer to accepting it. However, although intellectual conversions may be satisfying philosophically, they are hardly satisfactory morally. What is called for is not just the recognition of the requirement to promote the good, but greater *effort* in the pursuit of the good. And such efforts are hard.

There may be limits to what we can accomplish. Are we able to alter our own interests thoroughly, so that promotion of the overall good becomes a project of such fundamental importance that it grounds all other interests? I am not sure. Are we capable of disengaging the subjective standpoint completely—so that we give the interests of all equal weight? I do not know. It may be that the full pursuit of the good is a limit which few if any of us can attain, and to which we can only aspire. But it is a direction in which we can move, and we may try to go as far as we are able. And this, I believe, we are morally required to do.

Ordinary morality judges our lives morally acceptable as long as we meet its fairly modest demands. It is not surprising that this view should be so widely—and uncritically—held: it is not pleasant to admit to our failure to live up to the demands of morality. But the truth remains that we are morally required to promote the good and yet we do not. Faced with this realization what we must do is change: change our beliefs, our actions, and our interests. What we must not do—is deny our failure.

REFERENCES

Aristotle. *Nicomachean Ethics*. Translated by Terence Irwin. Hackett, 1985.

Brandt, Richard B. *A Theory of the Good and the Right*. Oxford University Press, 1979.

Bricker, Phillip. 'Prudence', *The Journal of Philosophy* 77 (1980), 381–401.

Davis, Nancy. 'The Doctrine of Double Effect: Problems of Interpretation', *Pacific Philosophical Quarterly* 65 (1984), 107–23.

——'The Priority of Avoiding Harm', pp. 172–214 in *Killing and Letting Die*, edited by Bonnie Steinbock. Prentice-Hall, 1980.

DiIanni, Albert R. 'The Direct/Indirect Distinction in Morals', *Thomist* 41 (1977), 350–80.

Donagan, Alan. *The Theory of Morality*. The University of Chicago Press, 1977.

Duff, R. A. 'Absolute Principles and Double Effect', *Analysis* 36 (1975–6), 68–80.

Dworkin, Ronald. *Taking Rights Seriously*. Harvard University Press, 1978.

Foot, Philippa. 'The Problem of Abortion and the Doctrine of the Double Effect', pp. 19–32 in *Virtues and Vices*. University of California Press, 1978.

Frankena, William K. 'Obligation and Motivation in Recent Moral Philosophy', pp. 40–81 in *Essays In Moral Philosophy*, edited by A. I. Melden. Washington University Press, 1958.

Fried, Charles. *Right and Wrong*. Harvard University Press, 1978.

Gauthier, David. *Morals By Agreement*. Oxford University Press, 1986.

Godwin, William. *Enquiry Concerning Political Justice*. Oxford University Press, 1971.

Harris, John. 'The Marxist Conception of Violence', *Philosophy & Public Affairs* 3 (1973–4), 192–220.

Heyd, David. *Supererogation*. Cambridge University Press, 1982.

Kagan, Shelly. 'Does Consequentialism Demand Too Much?', *Philosophy & Public Affairs* 13 (1984), 239–54.

——'Donagan on the Sins of Consequentialism', *Canadian Journal of Philosophy* 17 (1987), 643–54.

—— 'The Present-Aim Theory of Rationality', *Ethics* 96 (1986), 746–59.

Kamm, Frances Myrna. 'Killing and Letting Die: Methodological and Substantive Issues', *Pacific Philosophical Quarterly* 64 (1983), 297–312.

Kleinig, John. 'Good Samaritanism', *Philosophy & Public Affairs* 5 (1975–6), 382–407.

Mack, Eric. 'Bad Samaritanism and the Causation of Harm', *Philosophy & Public Affairs* 9 (1979–80), 230–59.

——'Causing and Failing to Prevent', *Southwestern Journal of Philosophy* 7 (1976), 83–90.

Mackie, J. L. 'Can There Be a Right-Based Moral Theory?' *Midwest Studies in Philosophy* 3 (1978), 350–59.

Mangan, Joseph T. 'An Historical Analysis of the Principle of Double Effect', *Theological Studies* 10 (1949), 41–61.

Melden, A. I. *Rights and Persons*. University of California Press, 1977.

Mill, John Stuart. *Utilitarianism*. The Liberal Arts Press, 1957.

Nagel, Thomas. 'Libertarianism Without Foundations', *Yale Law Journal* 85 (1975), 136–49.

——*The Possibility of Altruism*. Oxford University Press, 1970.

——*The View from Nowhere*. Oxford University Press, 1986.

——'War and Massacre', pp. 53–74 in *Mortal Questions*. Cambridge University Press, 1979.

Nisbett, Richard, and Ross, Lee. *Human Inference: Strategies and Shortcomings of Social Judgment*. Prentice-Hall, 1980.

Nozick, Robert. *Anarchy, State, and Utopia*. Basic Books, 1974.

Parfit, Derek. *Reasons and Persons*. Oxford University Press, 1984.

Plato. *Protagoras*, pp. 308–52 in *The Collected Dialogues of Plato*, edited by Edith Hamilton and Huntington Cairns. Princeton University Press, 1963.

Railton, Peter. 'Alienation, Consequentialism, and the Demands of Morality', *Philosophy & Public Affairs* 13 (1984), 134–71.

Rawls, John. *A Theory of Justice*. Harvard University Press, 1971.

Richards, David. *A Theory of Reasons for Action*. Oxford University Press, 1971.

Ross, W. D. *The Right and the Good*. Oxford University Press, 1930.

Scanlon, T. M. 'Contractualism and Utilitarianism', pp. 103–28 in *Utilitarianism and Beyond*, edited by Amartya Sen and Bernard Williams. Cambridge University Press, 1982.

Scheffler, Samuel. *The Rejection of Consequentialism*. Oxford University Press, 1982.

Sidgwick, Henry. *The Methods of Ethics*. Macmillan, 7th edition, 1907.

Singer, Peter. 'Utility and the Survival Lottery', *Philosophy* 52 (1977), 218–22.

Slote, Michael. *Common-Sense Morality and Consequentialism*. Routledge & Kegan Paul, 1985.

Thomson, Judith Jarvis. 'A Defense of Abortion', *Philosophy & Public Affairs* 1 (1971–2), 47–66.

——'Killing, Letting Die, and the Trolley Problem', *Monist* 59 (1975–6), 204–17.

Urmson, J. O. 'Saints and Heroes', pp. 198–216 in *Essays in Moral Philosophy*, edited by A. I. Melden. Washington University Press, 1958.

Wachsberg, Milton. *Identity, Concern, and Ethics*. Forthcoming.

Williams, Bernard. 'A Critique of Utilitarianism', in J. J. C. Smart and Bernard Williams, *Utilitarianism: For and Against*. Cambridge University Press, 1973.

——'Persons, Character and Morality', pp. 1–19 in *Moral Luck*. Cambridge University Press, 1981.

Wolf, Susan. 'Moral Saints', *The Journal of Philosophy* 79 (1982), 419–39.

INDEX